FLIGHT SURGEON

FLIGHT SURGEON

A War Diary, 1941–1945

Colonel Thurman Shuller
US Army Medical Corps

Edited by Vernon L. Williams

[signature]
7-20-2021

TCU
Press

Fort Worth, Texas

Library of Congress Cataloging-in-Publication Data

Names: Shuller, Thurman, author. | Williams, Vernon L., editor.
Title: Flight surgeon : a war diary 1941-1945 / Colonel Thurman Shuller, US
   Army Medical Corps ; edited by Vernon L. Williams.
Description: Fort Worth, Texas : TCU Press, [2021] | Includes
   bibliographical references and index. | Summary: "Colonel Thurman
   Shuller's war diary traces his story from Las Vegas Army Airfield in the
   summer of 1941 to the desperate days of the air war in Europe. The group
   surgeon character in the motion picture *Twelve O'clock High* was based on
   Shuller during his time as Group Surgeon of the famed 306th Bomb Group
   at Thurleigh, England, where he struggled with finding medical solutions
   for high altitude frostbite, oxygen deprivation, combat fatigue, and a
   growing crisis of hopelessness among the air crews. Shuller campaigned
   for setting the maximum number of missions for air crews to fly in a
   combat tour and argued for the elimination of "Maximum Effort" missions
   that forced them back to base from furloughs and passes. Shuller's diary
   brings his wartime experience back to life. His descriptions of the
   journey across the North Atlantic in the nose of a B-17 Flying Fortress
   are vivid and personal. His accounts about life among the British during
   the war bring a fresh look at the air war as it emerged from the
   pleasant meadowlands of East Anglia"-- Provided by publisher.
Identifiers: LCCN 2021005733 | ISBN 9780875657790 (paperback) | ISBN
   9780875657844 (ebook)
Subjects: LCSH: Shuller, Thurman--Diaries. | United States. Army. Medical
   Corps--Surgeons--Diaries. | United States. Army Air Forces. Bombardment
   Group, 306th--History. | World War, 1939-1945--Personal narratives,
   American. | World War, 1939-1945--Medical care--United States. | LCGFT:
   Diaries. | Personal narratives.
Classification: LCC D807.U6 S537 2021 | DDC 940.54/7573092 [B]--dc23
LC record available at https://lccn.loc.gov/2021005733

Unless otherwise noted, all photographs are from the
Shuller Historical Collection, EAAWA.

TCU Box 298300
Fort Worth, Texas 76129
To order books: 1.800.826.8911

Design by David Timmons

Contents

Acknowledgments

I would first like to thank Dr. Thurman Shuller for the time that he spent with me in the oral history interview one evening in San Antonio in 2005 and later, in conversations on the telephone and at 306th Bomb Group reunions. Dr. Shuller was kind enough to provide me with a copy of his diary at a time when he kept the manuscript closed. He encouraged me as I wrote a conference paper on military aviation medicine in World War II and allowed me to use his diary as an important primary source in that study. He once explained to me that the diary was a frank and private discussion with himself, and that sometimes his candid and forthright notations about specific people and events could be hurtful to those individuals or their families. He wanted to wait to release the diary to full circulation until all the principals were no longer living. His careful and deliberate protection of them was a reflection of his character and the kindness that dominated his life.

I also want to thank William "Bill" Houlihan, a 306th Bomb Group medic, who served with Dr. Shuller at Wendover, Utah, and in wartime England until the end of the war. I am grateful for the time that he spent with me during his oral history interview in San Antonio in 2005, and the telephone conversations and the written memories that he sent to me about Thurman Shuller and their service together during World War II.

Special thanks go to Mary Beth Shuller Carney for her commitment to this project, and for her indefatigable efforts in answering the multitudes of questions posed by me during my work to bring Dr. Shuller's war diary to print. Our many telephone conversations and email traffic were an enjoyable part of researching, writing, and editing the diary. I appreciate the confidence shown by Mary Beth Carney, her sister Margaret Davis, and her two brothers, Henry and Frank Shuller, in asking me to edit the diary.

For producing hard copies of Thurman Shuller's original handwritten diaries, I want to thank Jennifer Carney Adams, Dr. Shuller's granddaughter, and her son, Nathaniel Shuller Adams, Dr. Shuller's great-grandson. I

am grateful to have third and fourth generation family members participating in the preservation of the Shuller war diary. These handwritten copies provided by Jennifer and Nathaniel were essential when corroborating
the digital scans of the original typescript during my work on Dr. Shuller's
actual diary entries. Sometimes, the computer scans were not clear or part
of the text was missing or broken up, and the entries needed to be matched
up with the original handwritten volumes still held by the family.

Special thanks go to Raymond Blasingame, a businessman and special
friend who has the gift of editing and proofing, which he eagerly applied
to this large and extraordinary project. Raymond offered many suggestions for making the manuscript clearer and more precise. His obvious
love of history and his reading of this manuscript contributed much to
my finished work on Dr. Shuller's personal story of World War II. I am so
grateful for Raymond's dedication to the craft of writing, and to his continued contributions and interest in my work as a historian.

Others along the way made significant and important contributions
to my research and the Shuller story. I appreciate the efforts of several
generations of my Abilene Christian University students and interns who
worked tirelessly during the seven years (2007–2014) that it took to digitize
the enormous 306th Bomb Group Historical Collection.

I especially want to thank four people who joined me in Abilene, Texas, in May 2014 to organize and finalize the digital scans and copies of
the 306th Bomb Group Historical Collection, an enormous collection of
documents, photographs, and records collected by Russell Strong over
many years. Our digital project in Abilene proved to be an intense "boot
camp" of long hours and diligent work to bring the final digital collection
to finished form. These archival assistants included Barbara Neal, Charles
Neal, Clifford Deets, and Brandy Deets. Over three weeks during that May
"surge," as Charles called it, the five of us handled tens of thousands of
digital files as we compared files, deleted duplicates, and organized the
digital collection onto several hard drives. These hard drives held copies of the entire collection, and a set was deposited in the archives of the
National Museum of the Mighty Eighth Air Force in Pooler, Georgia, the
East Anglia Air War Archives (EAAWA) in Abilene, the 306th Museum
at Thurleigh, England, and two copies placed with the leadership of the
306th Bomb Group Association. The EAAWP's set of files produced by
this archival effort supported much of the editorial research and writing
that I have done on Dr. Thurman Shuller and his wartime diary.

I am grateful for answers to some research questions about the Bedford society during World War II. My friend and colleague, Stuart Antrobus, a longtime historian on the British Land Army and local Bedford history, has been a valuable resource for many years. His colleagues, Trevor Stewart and Linda Ayres, also contributed to important questions on the Camden and McCorquodale families, whom Dr. Shuller encountered many times during the war.

Historian Jim Flook, with the Ninety-Ninth Air Base Wing at Nellis Air Force Base (formerly the Las Vegas Gunnery School), provided valuable details on the Gunnery School and the early days when Shuller arrived to begin his military career. Jim also provided some photographs of the World War II base as it began to take shape in the early days of the war.

Dr. Tracy Shilcutt, first a graduate student of mine and later a colleague who became, for a time, the head of the History Department and my boss, has done seminal work on combat medics in the European Theater of Operations. Her study of medic training in the United States during the war gave me important background material on the medical administrative officers and enlisted medics who arrived in England during Dr. Shuller's tenure at Thurleigh and later, when he supervised medical services in the First Air Division commands across East Anglia. It is so rewarding for a teacher to watch a graduate student develop and become a contributing historian and colleague in our field of military history.

Jim Szpajcher has long been interested in bomber doctrine and aircrew survival rates and has been active in research and writing on the Ninety-First Bomb Group and its history in World War II. Special thanks go to Jim for sending me important documents on a Ninety-First BG air crash in England during the war. Other members of the Ninety-First BG Facebook community who have contributed include Gary Hall, Terry Flemming, and Clive Stevens. Thank you all.

I want especially to thank my family, my wife Kay Williams, my daughters Mary Elizabeth Purcell and Minda Jane Ciardi, my son James Andrew Williams, and our five grandchildren. My family has made it possible for me to pursue my career as a historian, a career that has led me to the far reaches of the globe. I am so grateful for each of them and the journey that we have traveled together.

Finally, I want to thank the TCU Press editorial staff led by Dr. Dan Williams, for the work and effort that they have made to turn the Shuller diary into a finished book.

Abbreviations and Code Words Used in the Shuller Diary
(Entries are listed in alphabetical order.)

10/10	Amount of ground area obscured by clouds, expressed in "tenths." Thus 1/10 coverage means only one-tenth of the ground area is obscured by clouds, while 10/10 coverage means a solid layer of cloud completely obscuring the ground.
AAFRS #1	Army Air Force Recruiting Station #1 in Newark, New Jersey
ACGS	Air Corps Gunnery School
ack-ack	Anti-aircraft fire
AF	Air Force
ATC	Air Transport Command
B-10	The first all-metal monoplane bomber to be regularly used by the United States Army Air Corps, dating from June 1934.
B-18	The twin-engine B-18 Bolo was the first Douglas medium bomber. It was a combat version of the DC-2 commercial transport, absorbed punishment well, and was especially useful during the early days of World War II.
BC	Before Christ, dating used in calendars
BOQ	Bachelor Officers Quarters
C-64	A Canadian single-engine bush plane designed to operate from unimproved surface.
CO	Commanding Officer
EM	Enlisted Men
ETO	European Theater of Operations
FO	Flight Officer
GI	Literally translated "Government Issue," but term refers to an enlisted man in the army or anything related to him or his world in the army, such as GI chow or GI shoes.
Gp	Group
Hqs	Headquarters
IP	Initial Point. This is the location where a bomber begins its bomb run on a mission.
Jerry	Nickname used by the Allies to refer to the Germans; plural is Jerries

JP	Justice of the Peace
MAC	Medical Administration Corps
MD	Doctor of Medicine
MP	Military Police
OD	Officer of the Day
OAF	Occupational Air Force. This term applied to those air units in the ETO that were transferred to Germany and other locations for duty in the occupation of Germany and Italy.
Pinetree	Eighth Air Force Headquarters at High Wycombe
PRO	Provost
PW	Prisoner of War
R&R	Rest and Relaxation passes and furloughs
Red X	Red Cross
Sta.	Station
USAFE	US Air Forces Europe
USSTAF	The United States Strategic Air Forces became the overall command and control authority of the United States Army Air Forces in Europe during World War II.
WAAF	Women's Army Air Force
WAC	Women's Army Corps
WC	Wing Commander
WVS	Women's Voluntary Services in the United Kingdom
ZI	Zone of the Interior (the United States)

Editor's Note

Thurman Shuller's wartime diary appears in the following pages, essentially as he penned the entries during the war. I have been careful not to interfere with his style or the format that appears in the original handwritten diary. I have corrected some grammar and punctuation, and removed a few sensitive comments, but the manuscript is largely presented as he wrote it and left it for his family.

There are many last-name references to fellow officers and enlisted men throughout the diary. I have identified many of these persons with first name and middle initials in brackets. The late Russell Strong facilitated this process with his comprehensive records created on the 306th Bomb Group and First Air Division leadership.

I have added chapter introductions and other occasional narrative observations (italicized entries) in the diary to provide context to Colonel Shuller's entries. However, the greater part of my explanatory and clarifying information can be found in the endnotes, organized by chapter at the end of the diary. Colonel Thurman Shuller's wartime journey was a unique and significant one, filled with great accomplishment, drama, joy, and sadness. I hope that you will find his story compelling and significant, one that adds to our knowledge of the citizen soldier and the struggle for victory in World War II.

Vernon L. Williams
Abilene, Texas

Introduction

I first met Thurman Shuller in San Antonio, Texas, in October 2005. I was there to interview veterans for my East Anglia Air War Project,[1] then only about five years old. I had already spent several years traveling across England, interviewing British family members who had lived among the Yanks in countless villages and towns scattered across the rural landscape that had once been Eighth Bomber Command. I followed up those many interviews with more oral history work at bomb group reunions held in the United States. Over the years, I have observed or participated in many interviews that were compelling and important to the story of the air war in World War II: talks with air crews, ordnance men, crew chiefs, supply and administrative personnel, officers, and men and women of every description who contributed in countless ways to the victory secured in Europe during World War II. In 2005 I encountered two such people in San Antonio when I interviewed Thurman Shuller and William Houlihan at the 306th Bomb Reunion. Dr. Shuller, first a squadron surgeon, quickly rose to Group Surgeon, and eventually Division Surgeon in the First Air Division.[2] Bill Houlihan, a medic and non-commissioned officer, was one of the mainstays in the 306th's medical services who provided routine care at Thurleigh at the same time that he dealt with the catastrophic casualties from modern combat at high altitude. Returning planes brought the wounded and the dead home to Thurleigh. Flak, oxygen deprivation, high impact weapons, chronic combat fatigue—all consequences of the new tools of war that played out in the skies over Europe. These two men painted vivid portraits of what military aviation medicine had come to be in the new age, and their accounts suggest that there was more to the story of military aviation history than has been told. It was during these interviews that these two quiet-spoken men revealed glimpses of wartime Thurleigh and the drama that played out there.

I am most grateful for the assignment to bring Dr. Shuller's war diary to a new and larger audience, where new generations can feel the fear, suffer the losses, and revel in the human spirit displayed in the air and on the ground at Thurleigh.

Very few of the air crews who flew missions in the ETO and survived to go home knew the debt that they owed to Dr. Thurman Shuller, 306th Bomb Group Surgeon. At every bomb group base stretching across East Anglia, air crews benefitted from the sustained campaign by Shuller to counter the hopelessness and desperation experienced by air crews early in the air war. When the 306th Bomb Group arrived at Station 111 in 1942, air crews flew their missions until one of three things occurred: 1) they were killed in action, 2) they were shot down, captured, and became POWs, or 3) the war ended. This stark reality sank in early on as the 306th crews faced a grim certainty—there was little chance that they would survive the war. But that would soon change when Group Surgeon Shuller acted decisively to meet the growing morale crisis.

This story begins long before World War II, on a small farm near Ozark, Arkansas, in late spring 1914 when Thurman Shuller was born in a modest farm house on the land where he would grow up.

Young Thurman Shuller attended New Hope School, a two-room rural elementary school, and later went on to achieve his dream to be a physician,

Thurman Shuller feeding turkeys on the farm. Mt. Nebo is in the background, circa 1917. Courtesy of the Thurman Shuller Family Collection.

Thurman and mother Sarah taking water to the field where older boys are plowing. Edgar, Elbert, and Herbert. Older brothers Frank and Albert were in service during WWI, circa 1918. Courtesy of the Thurman Shuller Family Collection.

Thurman Shuller with Model A Ford at home, 1930. Courtesy of the Thurman Shuller Family Collection.

Thurman Shuller on horseback headed for high school in Ozark five miles away, circa 1930. Courtesy of the Thurman Shuller Family Collection.

graduating from the University of Arkansas School of Medicine at Little Rock in 1939.

In 1939 Shuller was commissioned a first lieutenant in the US Medical Corps Reserve and served a two-year medical internship at Charity Hospital in New Orleans. Shuller's journey to wartime England was about to begin, a journey that would impact countless bomb groups in the Eighth Air Force.

In July 1941 he signed up for active duty and received assignment as a general physician at the Air Corps Gunnery School in Las Vegas, Nevada. Many years later Shuller explained that "with war raging in Europe, it seemed the practical thing to do was to spend one year of service in the Army." Just six months later, the attack on Pearl Harbor changed his one-year stint in the army to an extended enlistment that lasted for the duration of the war, "nearly five years."[3]

At Las Vegas he received his first glimpse of the fundamentals of military medicine and worked under his hospital commander, Major Paul R. Holtz, who tutored and mentored the young Shuller. He would draw upon this experience in England as he dealt with the demands of military medicine in combat against the Axis powers in Europe.

Major Holtz advised Shuller to apply to the School of Aviation Medicine, where he could qualify as a flight surgeon. Holtz also advised Lt. Shuller "to pay attention to the promptness, accuracy and appearance of all his reports"—a characteristic that became a part of his service and a contribution to his rapid rise from first lieutenant to colonel during the war. Shuller's application was approved, and he attended the twelve-week course at the School of Aviation Medicine at Randolph Field in San Antonio, Texas, where he qualified as a flight surgeon. In April 1942 Shuller was promoted to captain and assigned to the 306th Bombardment Group as the 369th Bomb Squadron Flight Surgeon. Leaving the pleasant confines of San Antonio, Shuller traveled to Wendover, Utah, where the 306th was engaged in activation and training on the salt flats in the desert country of Utah.[4]

At Wendover, living and training conditions were very "primitive," and the enlisted medical personnel who assembled there with the 306th had only a minimum level of training. The Group Flight Surgeon, Captain Ralph C. Teall, along with Captain Shuller and the other flight surgeons in the four bomb squadrons, faced a difficult mission as they struggled to maintain day-to-day tasking initiatives that were designed to prepare the 306th, "in a medical sense, for combat."[5]

In July 1942 Group Surgeon Teall was transferred, and Dr. Shuller was named to take his place. He did not have long to get adjusted to his new duties and make final preparations for assignment overseas. One month later, in early August 1942, the group's ground and air echelons departed Wendover for the East Coast and within just a few weeks, the 306th began the journey to the European Theater of Operations. For Shuller and his medical command, the war was about to begin.[6]

A Note from the Diary's Author

To put this diary in perspective, think back to July 1941. I was a twenty-seven-year-old single man who had been born and raised on a working farm near Ozark, Arkansas, and received primary education in a two-room rural school before high school in Ozark. It was in my freshman year in college that I made the decision to follow an older brother into the medical profession. I was graduated from the University of Arkansas School of Medicine in 1939, and with twelve of my classmates, took a commission as First Lieutenant in the US Army Medical Corps Reserve. In July 1941 I had just completed a two-year general internship at Charity Hospital in New Orleans, with the intention of becoming a family physician. I was professionally inexperienced in that I had not yet treated even one patient on my own except under the supervision of a senior hospital resident or staff physician.

At that point in time, the war in Europe had been going on a couple of years, and the US Army began calling up some of the Medical Reserve . . . [I needed] to serve my required one year of active duty at that time before setting up my private practice. It didn't work out that way because Pearl Harbor was attacked five months later, and my one year was stretched into five.

I had had no prior military experience except for one year as a private in the Arkansas National Guard while in college, and had taken two or three correspondence courses. Neither did I have any significant experience in leadership, had never been president of anything more important than president of my 4-H club in the eighth grade, had never been a team captain, not even an athlete. My greatest virtue was a work ethic acquired on the farm, and a determination to fulfill my parents' admonition to do right and work hard.

Nothing in my background could have predicted that I would go through the series of promotions from first lieutenant to captain to major to lieutenant colonel, as chief flight surgeon of the First Air Division of the Eighth Air Force in the space of twenty-eight months, and at the age of twenty-nine—with the rank of full colonel conferred on me upon

Family gathers in front of the home place at the farm near Ozark, 1916. Left to right: Albert, Edgar, E. W. holding Thurman, Sarah, Frank, Elbert, and Herbert. Courtesy of the Thurman Shuller Family Collection.

New Hope School, built on land donated by the McWhorter and the Shuller families. Grades 1-9 were taught in two rooms, circa 1920s. Courtesy of the Thurman Shuller Family Collection.

Family portrait at family farm. Front row, left to right: Frank, E. W. [father], Sarah [mother], Thurman (just before medical school). Back row, left to right: Albert, Edgar, Elbert, and Herbert, circa 1935. Courtesy of the Thurman Shuller Family Collection.

my relief from active duty in 1946 at the age of thirty-two—unheard of for a medical officer. That could only have occurred during the explosive expansion of the Army Air Corps during the years 1942–1944, and having had the extraordinarily good luck of being at the right place at the right time.

Mine is the story of countless young officers who, because of the demands of rapid expansion of the military force during World War II, were placed into positions of responsibility far above their previous training and experience, and were therefore forced to quickly grow into their jobs. It was a treasured opportunity for me and a life-changing experience to have served.

ABOUT THE DIARY

This diary was handwritten on six bound Government Issue notebooks, which have been lovingly transcribed by my daughter, Mary Beth Carney. The division into chapters is strictly arbitrary and denotes simply the end of one book and the beginning of another.

The first book, called Prologue [Chapter 1], covers the period of service from soon after induction into active duty through the preparation, training, and organization of the 306th Bombardment Group prior to going overseas. That period covers three specific assignments. It begins abruptly on September 5, 1941, twenty-seven days into my first assignment as a general medical officer at the small station hospital at the developing Army Air Force Gunnery School on the desert near Las Vegas, Nevada, a small town of eight thousand at the time. Next was my application and assignment to the School of Aviation Medicine at Randolph Field in San Antonio to train for becoming a flight surgeon. Then permanent assignment to the 306th Bomb Group, as it was being organized on the salt flats of Utah at Wendover, on the line between Utah and Nevada.

That book ended with the completion of organization and training of the 306th Bomb Group at Wendover Field. It [the Prologue] did not make it to the war zone, as it was left behind among my personal effects that were mailed home before the group went overseas. It did not become a part of the War Diary until it was retrieved several years after the war, made a part of the diary, and called Prologue to War. That is the explanation for the unusual numbering of the volumes.

The actual War Diary begins with Volume I [Chapter 2] on August 1, 1942, as the flying echelon of the 306th Bombardment Group lifted off from Wendover Field, headed for the staging area at Westover Field, Massachusetts, then on to England. The five volumes of the War Diary cover a period of thirty-nine months, and end as I boarded the train at St. Louis on December 9, 1945, headed for home at Ozark, Arkansas. I did arrive in time to help celebrate my parents' Golden Wedding Anniversary, along with my five brothers and their families.

T.S.

Chapter 1

Prologue to War

Induction and Training
September 5, 1941–July 31, 1942

In December 1940 the War Department issued orders to establish an Air Corps gunnery school at Las Vegas, Nevada. The site had a long history of aviation activity, first as Western Air Express Field and later as McCarran Field in the 1930s, located just northeast of Las Vegas. In early 1941 the army signed a lease for McCarran Field with the city of Las Vegas. Construction began on Las Vegas Army Air Field immediately.[1]

The construction of the base included plans for "an infirmary and a 111-bed hospital." The Medical Corps submitted a plan for medical operations at Las Vegas to headquarters, and the War Department incorporated the plan into the base development. Unfortunately, the hospital was not operational when the base opened, so the medical staff commandeered a two-story barracks building and installed a makeshift plan for temporary medical services for the growing number of base personnel. One room on ground level "was used for general medication, one for sexually transmitted diseases, and an upstairs room was used for semi-contagious cases."[2]

Meanwhile, Major Paul R. Holtz, the first surgeon, arrived in June 1941 and took command of the meager medical staff, such as it was. At the time of his arrival, Holtz had no other surgeons or nurses on staff, with only a few enlisted medics and very few supplies to treat anyone for any malady. Serious cases had to be sent into Las Vegas to the civilian hospital. Over the next few months, the staff would grow and equipment and supplies began to improve.

A month later in July, First Lieutenant Thurman Shuller arrived and took up his station as Holtz's assistant, and Shuller's military education began in earnest. Holtz became a mentor to the young Shuller and to the other surgeons who would arrive in the coming months. During that time Holtz embarked on a survey "of the base and the surrounding Las Vegas area." He was convinced that he needed to know more about the soldiers who served at Las Vegas, and the environment in which they worked and where they spent

Entrance to McCarran Airport, later Army Air Corps Gunnery School, circa 1941. Courtesy of the Nellis Air Force Base Collection.

Station Hospital, Army Air Corps Gunnery School, circa 1941. Courtesy of the Nellis Air Force Base Collection.

Patients and nurse, Station Hospital, Army Air Corps Gunnery School, circa 1941. Courtesy of the Nellis Air Force Base Collection.

Thurman Shuller, First Lieutenant, 1941. Courtesy of the Thurman Shuller Family Collection.

their off-duty hours. Shuller would learn much during his five months under Holtz at Las Vegas.[3]

Holtz and Shuller, and later the other doctors as they arrived at Las Vegas, investigated "the possible effects of the local environment on the troops," specifically the "climate, weather, and the lack of a sufficient water supply." But the more dominant factor discovered in the study proved to be "the Las Vegas social mores of prostitution and gambling." Legalized under Nevada law, these activities provided the potential for significant morale and health difficulties that led to "many variant behaviors including AWOL, drunkenness, high levels of debt, and the ever-present sexually transmitted diseases (STDs)." As seen later in his diary, Group Surgeon Shuller would face many of the same issues at Thurleigh and in the British communities where the same behaviors threatened combat operations on every level. Drawing on his experiences at Las Vegas, Shuller focused on solutions that he learned under Holtz during his first assignment in the army.[4]

Thurman Shuller's diary begins two months after his arrival at Las Vegas Field. The diary entries reveal the routine of army life that Thurman Shuller faced, and his attitudes and concerns during his maturation and evolution as an army combat surgeon during training, and later in the combat theater of operations from his base at Thurleigh in Bedfordshire, England. The first diary, organized here as Chapter 1 (described by Shuller as the Prologue), covers his training at Las Vegas under Holtz, his transfer to the Aviation School of Medicine in San Antonio, and his assignment as squadron surgeon in the 369th Bomb Squadron in the 306th Bomb Group during activation and organization at Wendover, Utah. He would soon be elevated to Group Surgeon.[5]

*

To him who may chance to scan these pages.

You will bear in mind that this is strictly a private diary written for my own record and not for general comment or discussion. There may be many errors in spelling or grammar; most of this I have not read myself, and I have no intention of doing so for a long time to come. No apologies are offered for repetition, for many seemingly unimportant details, for opinions or emotions expressed. It is a record of events and ideas of the moment, many of which change from time to time. If it suggests a note of vanity on occasion, it is because those are occasional expressions of personal feelings that one would never speak verbally. If the idea is conveyed that some of the reactions expressed are abnormal, just remember that these were abnormal times.

T.S.

*

Sept 5, 1941 - Today, I did something that I thought I'd never do—was party to the notorious Nevada marriage racket. While down at the J.P's [Justice of the Peace's] at Las Vegas to a Coroner's inquest, a young couple dashed in with a marriage license, and before I knew what was happening, I was standing to the groom's right and holding the ring. It was over in a jiffy, I signed my name as witness, and they were off in a flash before I realized I didn't even know their names—only that they were from Chicago.

*

In early September within just a few days, more of the medical staff began to arrive. Three new doctors and the first two nurses, Barbara McLaughlin and Hazel D. Sutton, reported in. Hazel Sutton became the head nurse, and within days, the nurse complement had risen to seven. While these nurses in the Army Nurse Corps held the "relative rank" of second lieutenants, they "held the title, wore the insignia, were admitted to officers' clubs, and had the privilege of the salute," but their authority remained "limited in the line of duty and initially received less pay than men of similar rank." It was not until December 1942 that "Congress authorized military nurses to receive pay equivalent to a man of the same rank." It would be June 1944 before "Congress authorized temporary commissions with full pay and privileges to military nurses."[6]

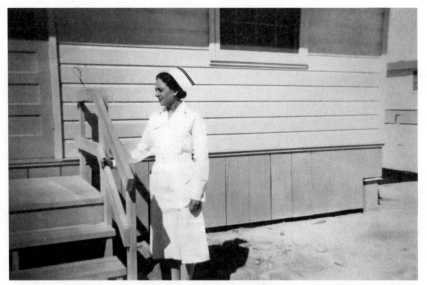

Chief nurse Hazel Sutton, Station Hospital, Army Air Corps Gunnery School, 1941.
Courtesy of the Thurman Shuller Family Collection.

Visit to Boulder Dam. Left to right: Barbara McLaughlin, Hazel Sutton, David D. Fried,
and Thurman Shuller, 1941. Courtesy of the Thurman Shuller Family Collection.

Hospital ward hallway, Station Hospital, Army Air Corps Gunnery School, 1941. Courtesy of the Thurman Shuller Family Collection.

*

Sept 7 - Sunday and a long lonesome day. Lt. [Theodore R.] Stepman is in Los Angeles for the weekend, and I have been O.D. for 3 days. Two new M.D.s came in yesterday and another tonight, but they don't start work until tomorrow. Lt. Owens seems exceptionally nice, and I know I'll like him—as for the other two, I'll reserve my opinion for a few days.

Sept 8 - My first ride in an Army plane this afternoon—a B-10 with Lt. [John C.] Kelso as pilot. It was a rattletrap old crate, but the ride was swell. I think I rather like flying. Had only a very faint sensation of sickness at one time—but I'll never admit it.

Sept 9 - Tonight four of us medical officers went over to pay a social call on the nurses—there are seven of them now. Took over a dozen bottles of beer, and they had some cokes in the ice box. We danced some and had a very nice time in general. They all are unusually nice for Army nurses, apparently. Stayed till midnight before we realized it.

Sept 12 - Stepman and I bought four records for the nurses' phonograph today, and Owens did the same. So we all went over there after supper to try them out. Had a lot of fun dancing. In fact, it was almost midnight before we realized it. The nurses are one more swell bunch of girls, and Miss [Hazel] Sutton, the head nurse, is really a queen. She has a wonderful personality and is a most unusual head nurse.

Sept 13 – Saturday - went on another of those Squadron picnics up on Charleston Mountain.[7] This is my third. Was given by Lt. Woods' outfit, the 352nd Sch. Sq. There was the usual 5 kegs of beer and a world of eats. Several of us went mountain climbing immediately after dinner and almost to the top, I got sick and lost my dinner. Thurman, you didn't drink too much beer, did you? No, I'll blame it on mountain climbing too soon after eating.

Sept 14 - I was O.D. this Sunday again, but [David D.] Fried (he's from Mena, Ark) relieved me in the afternoon so Owens, Gutekunst and I drove over to Boulder Dam. It was a sight worth seeing. That sure is one more big pile of concrete.

Guess I have about seen most of the interesting sights around here now, so that should leave me about ready to move on.

Sept 15 - Speaking of being ready to move on, it looks like I might actually do just that in a couple of weeks. This morning at Staff meeting, the Major started talking Randolph Field [and Shuller's application to the Aviation School of Medicine].

Sept 29- Was O.D. today but surprisingly little work. The nurses had us over to help them sandpaper the living room floor. They served a meal buffet style. Dancing is so much easier. I am appreciating this opportunity to dance more. It goes without saying that I have plenty to learn about it, and some of these girls are swell dancers.

My orders to Randolph Field did not come today either, so I guess that about eliminates my chances of leaving here.

Oct 1, 1941- Four of us doctors and four of the nurses went horseback riding across the desert at sunset. It was a lovely sight, lovely weather and afterwards, a most enjoyable picnic supper of roast wieners and buns. The congeniality of this bunch here makes life worth living. Miss Sutton rented a piano yesterday. She and I play about alike. We are going to learn some duets. Had the privilege of touching the keys of the new Hammond organ down at the Chapel today. Wish I could play that thing.

Oct 2 - One of the big buildings went up in smoke here today. Furnished plenty of excitement for a while. Pvt. Miller almost fell over himself with excitement with the ambulance. Only one slight burn admitted, thank goodness. I hate to treat burns.

Received that long awaited check today, $554.79. Boy, Oh Boy, how long do you suppose it'll be before I see that big pay check again? But almost $450 is going to Dad, and another $100 for uniforms today. Hard come, easy go—that's me.

Oct 6 - Went over to Glendora for the week end with Layden and Gutekunst. Had a most enjoyable time visiting Myrtle, Joe, Robert Ray, Harvey and Ralph and many others. Went over to L.A. [Los Angeles] twice. Picked some oranges and English walnuts. Everybody seemed glad to see me, and I was glad to see all them.[8] It was my first week-end out of town and believe me, I was plenty ready for one. We got back to camp at 5:30 a.m. today.

Nov 11, 1941 - Got home at 6:30 a.m. today after delivering my first baby in the Army, wife of Sgt. Folsom. Gee, it was fun to be doing that sort of thing again. Wish we could get to do more of it. There's some certain comfort to be gotten from executing a successful delivery. I was elated that the first baby, a 7-pounder was delivered without a tear - a very small mother too.

Nov 13 - Spent a couple hours tonight over at the nurses quarters playing while the nurses sang. They sent for me because Miss Sutton wanted to sing herself. I enjoyed that.

Did a circumcision on Cadet Anthony today. Very small surgery, but it was good to get to do a little cutting once more.

Nov 14 - The major threw a big feed for the medical personnel and nurses tonight, and it was my luck to be O.D. Isn't that a hell of a note. Miss McLaughlin was the nurse who was left out. We were both disappointed but, of course, someone had to hold down the fort.

Gave the first lecture of my life today. A lecture on bones and joints to the Detachment. Most of the men seemed interested except Corporal Jones, who pulled a chair out from under Pvt. McAllister - that is just about his speed.

Nov 16 - Miss Sutton, Miss McLaughlin and I went to Death Valley today. It was a most delightful trip. Were gone 12 hours and must have traveled 400–450 miles. Scotty's Castle was well worth the $1.10 it cost. Scotty himself was there. He sure must be a screw-ball. Why that magnificent structure was built there is beyond me. I'm sure he doesn't care for it now that he has it.

Nov 20 - Was I disappointed today! Lt. Kelso went to Dallas a couple of days ago, and they haven't even heard from him. We were to have hopped over to Oklahoma City today, you know. The day wasn't a failure though. Thanksgiving, and all the medics and their families dined here, and we went over to the nurses' quarters for a while afterwards. It was very nice. A grand feed, and the Major and his wife the center of attraction. Hated to send that telegram to Albert that I wouldn't be there though.

Nov 21- Lt. Kelso got in sometime last night. I was surprised that he had practically forgotten about our trip and really didn't seem much concerned.

Nov 23 - Miss McLaughlin and I went shooting this Sunday afternoon. She had a 22 pistol, so we used her gun, her shells, and her car. Shame on you Thurman! Neither of us would qualify as sharp shooters.

Nov 26 - Back from a show at the Post Theatre—"The Married Bachelor," I believe it was. A very delightful comedy it was. But there was one line that was particularly significant. It went, "Don't set a girl up on a pedestal—Someday she will look down from her pedestal and say, 'How nice you are! You are just like a brother to me." How true! How true! How true!

Dec 4, 1941 - Gave the boys an exam in Anatomy 3 days ago. The answers were most amusing. Sat up till 2 a.m. last night copying off some of the most amusing answers. Showed that copy to the Major this morning, and he got a real belly laugh out of it. They got a little out of the course, evidently.

Dec 5 - The major was on a tear today. Really ate poor Stepman out for not signing a memo—random slip for some towels that he had not seen. Also he put out an order that no supplies can be drawn without the officer going over to sign for it. Often we have to go over to sign for toilet paper, soap, etc. I used to think I came into this army to be a doctor, but it looks like less doctoring and more property responsibility is the thing they want. I'm expecting to get caught for a lot of property anyway. It's a hell of a damn organization this army is.

Dec 6 - Gave my first lecture on Sex Hygiene to the 351st Sch. Sq. One of those routine 6 months things that the men get tired of. I talked for about 20 minutes. Guess I learned more than they did because I was nervous, talked too fast, and walked back and forth across the stage so much. My public speaking is terrible. Maybe I'll do better next time.

Dec 7 - PEARL HARBOR

Japan attacked Pearl Harbor and Manila as well as British possessions today—the lid is now off!! All soldiers were ordered back to the post and everybody is to be in uniform at all times. There is a slight wave of enthusiasm throughout the camp, boys are looking for and wanting action. Don't believe the situation will affect our camp markedly yet. Tomorrow will be Dec. 8. That's going to be a day to remember!

Dec 8 - War is declared against Japan! Only one vote against it in both houses. There is a wave of enthusiasm apparent here. Stepman and I were downtown tonight and were approached by several young men who wanted to know where they could enlist. The nation is united at last, even [Senator Burton] Wheeler and [Charles] Lindbergh are for it. It took a Japanese attack to do it. In that respect, it is a blessing.

We are into uniform now for the duration of the war. The uniform is to be worn at all times. The clothing store is no longer inviting. All leaves, passes and furloughs are canceled until further notice.

Dec 9 - The Navy, by admission of the President, has suffered a glaring defeat at Pearl Harbor. We're getting off to a bad start. Had our first taste of black-out tonight, trial for only 15 minutes.

Dec 10 - Went to the show tonight and in the middle of the picture, the show was ordered closed. We were already in the midst of a black-out which lasted for some time, two to three hours. We didn't know why the show was closed. Boulder Dam is a most vital spot, and that explains why this field may become a source of protection.

Dec 11 - We found out this morning why the show was closed last night. It was in tribute to Lieutenants John C. Kelso and [George E.] Turner who were instantly killed in a crash near Boulder City during the black-out. That was quite a shock to everybody, but I suppose we might as well get accustomed to it, because we'll be seeing plenty of that sort of thing. But it certainly is hard to see young fellows you know and like snuffed out like that. Lt. Kelso took me up on my only Army plane ride thus far, and it was with him that I was going to fly over to Oklahoma City.

Dec 12 - Little excitement today—no black-outs for a couple of nights. It does look like our men in the Pacific are holding their own a little better now. Congress declared war on Germany and Italy yesterday. But that was just routine because we were already actually at war with them ever since last Sunday when Japan struck.

Dec 14 - What a night was last night! Miss Sutton threw one of those formal parties where the Colonel and all the bigwigs were invited. It started at 6 p.m. and ended at—well it was almost 3 a.m. when I got to bed. I expected it to be so stuffy—but honestly, it was one of the most enjoyable parties I have ever seen.

Miss Sutton was a marvelous hostess. She's just a pretty swell person anyway. It was the first real social function right here on the post. They'll be coming more often now that the Officers' Club is opening in another week—more expense! But that has cost me very little up until now so I should not complain, have gotten off much easier than I expected. Am glad too because ordinarily, I don't care so much for the social graces. But the one last night was exceptional.

Dec 18 - Stepman and I went out to the "Meadows"[9] last night on an "inspection" tour. That is the city's most glorified whore house. Lt. Wier went out with us. It was the first time I had seen the real inner workings of a whore house, since I was in Pensacola with the guards in 1934. It was amusing the way the manager and the house lady leaned over backwards to be nice to us. They thought we were on an official inspection tour since we were in uniform, but in reality we were only sightseeing. It was an elaborate layout, but to me it was rather revolting. It clashed so strongly with my upbringing that honestly, diary, I don't believe one of those girls could even arouse any lust in me. It is conducted in the best possible manner, however, and I suppose is, in the long run, beneficial to the morale of soldiers who feel they need to keep their appetite satisfied. Sex life in the Army certainly is a problem. I wish I knew the answer. That sort of thing is such an awfully poor substitute for a girlfriend back home.

There was also an interesting riot downtown. Pickets at the Market Spot crowded Lt. Smith and his wife off the sidewalk, and the soldiers retaliated by dispersing the pickets—no violence—but it could have been.

Dec 19 - Oh, the experiences of a doctor. Lt. Bonnett came over to my room tonight with the news that he is to be married in eight days. He was coming to me for advice and recommendations on sex hygiene, birth control and technique. It is the first time I had occasion to carry on such a discussion with a prospective groom. A bachelor probably is not as good counsel as a married man, but I hope I helped him out. He is 23 years old and is a nice fellow. He goes out with Stepman some and is more a pal of his than mine, yet he chose me to discuss his intimate problems. I really believe the young officers here respect me a great deal. That makes me very proud.

Dec 21- What a delightful day! This Sunday afternoon Stepman and I were hosts to Misses Sutton, Day, and McLaughlin at the Charleston Lodge. We played in the snow for a while, it was about knee deep. Then about 6 p.m. we had dinner at the lodge. It was a marvelous dinner and then we sat around the open fire, danced, etc. It was 11 p.m. before we knew it. Mr. and Mrs. Travis are wonderful hosts. And in addition Mrs. Travis invited the nurses to come up during Christmas week for a party on the house and asked each one to bring a date. Hope I get in on it. They were skiing up there a little. Would like to try that sometime.

Dec 22 - Another new experience today. The firing range has been opened at Indian Springs 60 miles away. The ambulance up there turned over and three were injured. So I was flown to the rescue by Lt. Cairns. Boy Oh Boy! I have read of doctors doing such things, but had no idea I would ever fly with a medicine bag. But I shall not deny that I got quite a thrill out of it. I'll probably be doing that more, however, before the war is over. We flew up there in about 15 minutes, but it took 3 hours to return by ambulance. One of the fellows had a severe fracture of the femur and another, a fractured wrist.

Dec 23 - Major Holtz told me this morning that my orders had come through for Randolph Field. I am very happy about it. The orders say that I'll come back here after 3 months. Of course those orders could be easily changed. But I wouldn't much mind being sent back here.

Dec 24 - I was a father confessor again today to one of the soldiers who was recently a patient in the hospital. It seems I have run into an epidemic of sexual problems lately. The sexual problem is certainly a big one among the lads in the Army. I suppose it's because they are uprooted from normal associations and thrown into strange surroundings and lack of feminine associations. Boys who never before considered it a problem nor worried about it at all find themselves submitting to sexual relationships that they really had no intention of doing. This one today was. He was Pvt. Wilhelm, a boy from the middle west, twenty-two years old, two years in college, unusually clean cut and intelligent, Catholic, devoutly religious, but not at all fanatic. In a weak moment, he had gone down to the "Meadows" and indulged for the first time in illicit sexual intercourse. This is three days later, and I have never before seen a fellow suffering the mental anguish that he was going through. He was a little worried about the possibility of venereal disease, but much more than that, he hated himself because he had destroyed his own self-respect in the cheap thing that he had done. Diary, that boy actually cried like a baby for several minutes. He had a sweet girl back home whom he adored, and he felt that he could not bear to ever look her straight in the face again. His home training had been strict, and he loved and respected it, and had prided himself upon the fact that he was keeping himself absolutely clean these 12 months he had been in the Army. In one brief moment he had thrown away all the ideals he had cultivated for years, and he was so profoundly disgusted with himself that he could no longer tolerate himself, so he chose me to unburden to. I think he would have liked to talk it over with his dad, but since he couldn't, he, for some reason came to me. I don't know if I comforted him any, but it did him good to get it off his chest anyway. I had always considered him a particularly nice fellow, and in my opinion, this experience has made him finer. It has impressed upon him even more than ever the importance of maintaining one's self-respect, and he is stronger for it. I don't know whether I am getting more than my share of such confidential problems, but seems like I get a lot of them lately. I think the public thinks that preachers hear most of such troubles, but the doctor has occasion to hear plenty of it. Diary, I wonder if a good doctor couldn't be of even more benefit in such cases, because patients feel much more free to be perfectly frank to a sympathetic doctor. Even some preachers might have to leave town, if we told all we know. Diary, just between you and me, I am proud that the fellows take me into their confidence. There sure is alot to this practice of medicine besides dishing out pills.

Dec 25 - Christmas Day! To me it is just another day. I think the Major is going to give me three extra days and maybe I can go home. So I spend the whole day checking property getting ready to turn it over to my successors. If my work today helps in getting me home, then I'd say that it is a very fine Christmas.

Dec 26 - Just back from the party at Charleston Lodge on the house. Given in honor of the nurses. The snow was two or three ft. deep. Had to push the car part of the way. Boy, it was fun. Wish I could be here during the sports season.

House rented by Shuller and Lt. Oliver in San Antonio while they were attending the Aviation School of Medicine, January-March 1942. Courtesy of the Thurman Shuller Family Collection.

Dec 27 – Capt. Wallace this morning gave me permission to leave in the morning. It was unexpected but much appreciated. Will be home Tuesday morning.

Dec 30 - Missed train connections in Kansas City last night and had to stay until this morning. Ran out and had breakfast with Fred McWhorter for about 45 minutes. Will be home tonight.

Jan 1, 1942 - This is the first time I have written the date 1942. God only knows where I'll write the first date 1943. Have been home for about 48 hours. Am leaving early in the morning so I can stop off to see Herbert and Mary. No New Year's celebration last night. Went to bed at 9:00 p.m. Boy, I'll bet I wouldn't have done that if I had been in Las Vegas. Mother and Dad are fine, and they seem so glad to see me. Have played several games of dominoes with Dad—that always pleases him. Went to Clarksville yesterday afternoon to see Shrigley. He's the only one of my classmates I've seen in a long time. It sure was good to talk over old times.

Jan 3 - Arrived at Herbert's at 7 this a.m. Expected to get here last night but missed train in Little Rock. But it was enjoyable anyway because I saw so many friends there. Ann Boch had me for dinner. It was all very enjoyable.

Herbert did not have to work this p.m., so I got to visit with him more.

Mary is up now after the arrival of little Walter Warren, who occupies most of her time now. He is a little over 2 weeks old. Donald is as cute as he can be, talks a blue streak.

Jan 4 - Arrived in San Antonio this a.m. Went out and registered at the field. There I met up with one Lt. Oliver from Camp Shelby. We teamed up and have taken an apartment near town. It's a little stiff in price but very comfortable, in fact, compared to barracks, it is luxury. I'm hoping this will be an enjoyable 3 months.

*

The Aviation School of Medicine had long been a part of the army's training for aviation medicine. In 1918, the school was known as the School for Flight Surgeons and thereafter, the name changed and the base it was assigned to changed a number of times over the years. By the time Thurman Shuller arrived in San Antonio to begin the Flight Surgeon's course, the Army Air Corps had experimented with the curriculum and the length of the course in the face of the growing demands from the rapidly expanding Air Corps.

Earlier General Hap Arnold, chief of the Air Corps, decided that the need for large numbers of flight surgeons and medical examiners in the coming months was critical and ordered that the course "be shortened from four to three months, effective with the current class." By the summer of 1940, the flight surgeon course was further reduced from three months to six weeks. The outcome of the schedule cuts proved to be detrimental to the program's mission. The faculty and medical commanders at other stations reported that aviation medical examiners from the six-week program "were not as well trained as their predecessors, particularly in connection with the examination for the selection of flying cadets for training." The program was redesigned back to a three-month course, and with the arrival of Shuller and his classmates in January 1942, the adjusted curriculum would last twelve weeks. This change was fortunate for Shuller and others who would be assigned to tactical units where expertise beyond Form 64 testing[10] at induction centers would be needed during times of intense combat operations.[11]

*

Jan 7 - Classes are not actually under way yet—will start in earnest tomorrow. The Commandant gave his welcome address this a.m., and he talked like he didn't want any foolishness. Think they plan to make us study a little. He said that we might be given about 3 hours flying instruction—that's an unexpected opportunity.

School of Aviation Medicine, Randolph Air Field, San Antonio, Texas, circa 1941.
Courtesy of the Thurman Shuller Family Collection.

Identification card mugshot, First Lieutenant, 1941. Courtesy of the Thurman Shuller
Family Collection.

There is only one fellow in this class that I have ever seen before—that's Lt. Layden, the skunk. He's the one who made himself so obnoxious at A.C.G.S., and who did so notoriously little work.

Jan 11 - Arrived here in San Antonio one week ago this morning but honestly, it seems a month. Guess I just haven't gotten acquainted here yet, but somehow I get awfully lonesome. Lt. Oliver is excellent company, but I'm missing something or other. Diary, I miss the fun around A.C.G.S: more than I thought. Everything was so personal there, and it can never be so here, living off the post. With such a big post, nobody cares whether you go or come, except to mark you present or absent on the roster. That nurses' quarters was a big asset, and I'm going to miss it more than I thought. Diary, much as I hate to admit it, I believe I am beginning to need feminine companionship. God only knows when I will have it, if ever.

Called up Hudson a couple of nights ago, and they came after me and took me out to their place. It was good to see them. Sullenberger is here in town too.

Received word the other day that Capt. [Harry B.] Jewell and wife [Mary Louise] were killed by a gas heater. That's a tragic thing. Sort of makes me ashamed of the many times I have cussed that man.

Jan 12 - Got in touch with Sullenberger tonight. Gosh, it was good to see him. We drove around all over town, he, his girl Pat and I. Had a Mexican dinner in the Mexican quarter. I think he is going to liven up my stay in San Antonio a little.

Jan 13 - The idea of our flying is to give us some idea of what a pilot must go through, and I found out today. I got as sick as a dog as we were coming in, and vomited after we reached the ground. Messed the plane up enough to cost me that carton of cigarettes. That's the first time I ever got to the stage of vomiting. This was my first lesson. All I did was a few turns and a stall, but I did fly the plane. At the last he took me through a couple of slow rolls. It was fun. If only I hadn't gotten sick. I'm awfully ashamed of myself.

Jan 15 - Well, I redeemed myself today. Went through quite a few acrobatics and didn't get at all sick. I handled the plane a little more myself. Gosh, there's a lot of things to watch and think about at the same time. I think eventually though it might become automatic. I enjoyed it thoroughly.

Jan 17 - Completed our allotted flying instruction at Randolph today.

Thurman Shuller in flight gear during training at San Antonio, spring 1942. Courtesy of the Thurman Shuller Family Collection.

I didn't have the excellent instructor that I had the two days before and didn't learn so much but it was an enjoyable ride. Wish we could have some more of it.

Jan 19 - Went out with Sullenberger and Pat last night. It was a poop out almost. Sully and Pat had been drinking rather heavily before I got there, and Pat got sick and had to be taken home. Cecil Dickerson had gotten me a date with a nurse out at Santa Rosa, who from all appearances must have been a "woman of the Air Corps." At least I enjoyed dancing with her for a while out at the "Tower." But while we were there, Sully passed out, and we had a hard time getting him out of there. What a spectacle it must have been. Sully was still running true to form.

Then, too, I found out something else about Sully. You know, Diary, he is married to that little girl up at Little Rock, but they haven't lived together in ages, but she won't give him a divorce, even though he has begged for it. So upon direct point blank questioning, Sully admitted that he and Pat were living together as though they were married. He has moved into her apartment. Pat seems awfully sweet, and I have always been crazy about Sully. This thing is against every principle that I was brought up to value dearly, but Diary, in this particular case—well, somehow I wasn't shocked by it. Somehow, I don't even seem to blame them much. They are apparently most devoted to each other. Let it not be said that there is not a variety of personalities among those I call my friends.

At school today we began our regular planned physical education. We're going to have some sore muscles, but boy, we need it plenty.

Jan 24 - This ends my third week here. Time is beginning to fly once more. Randolph has a peculiar glamor to it that is beginning to get under my skin. There is something thrilling about the Air Corps, and it is a treasured opportunity to be here at this, the West Point of the Air—the pride of the U.S. Air Corps. You know, Diary, my hat is off to those boys. Oh God, it almost makes me sick in the pit of my stomach to think of what is behind this all. Those cadets—they are such fine looking, physically perfect young men, many of them from America's best families and are truly the flower of young America. You can just see the determination in their faces. And the thing that makes me sick is the realization that a couple of years from now few of those boys we see saluting us with that grace and snap will be alive. I wonder if they realize what they are in for. Perhaps so—or maybe it's just the adventure they are seeking. At any rate the result will be the same. God, we pray that America may become worthy of the sacrifice of the lives of these, her finest.

Jan 28 - Yesterday noon they turned us out to attend the International Post-Graduate Medical Assembly in San Antonio. As far as yesterday afternoon, it was a waste of time. Those doctors talked only of how they would be willing to come into the Army if they gave them a Captain's or Major's rank. They may put it over too. I suppose in reality, it would be correct to do so, but it is going to make it harder on us fellows who have been in longer. We will be keeping our present rank I'm afraid. The stag party last night was typical of a medical convention. You know what I mean.

Jan 31 - Another new experience today. They placed us in the low pressure chamber simulating altitude of 30,000 feet. That gave us an idea what pilots in that altitude have to endure. It was a strange feeling to remove the oxygen mask at that pressure. I don't envy the high altitude pilot his job. There were changes in vision, one could not talk in the lower frequencies, the gas in one's stomach expanded and one could not whistle—along with other things.

Feb 1, 1942 – Just another Sunday. Oliver and I went to church the first time since we have been in San Antonio. We just struck out and went to the first church we came to. After we were in, we discovered it was Presbyterian. It's the first time I ever went to church like that. Then, we had a real Mexican dinner at the Original Mexican Restaurant. That will satisfy my taste for Mexican foods for a while. But we tried a new delicacy this afternoon. Over at the reptile garden, they kill and fry a rattlesnake each Sunday afternoon, and I sampled it. It really was good. Tasted a great deal like fish. You could never have convinced me I'd ever eat rattlesnake.

Feb 12 - Went out to Sully and Pat's house for waffles last night. Played hearts until I had to come home to study a while. They are swell company.

Feb 13 - We went out to Ft. Sam Houston tonight to hear and see Bing Crosby and Bob Hope in person. Gosh, what a crowd. Bob was in a hurry to leave and was only fair, but Bing gave out with several nice songs. He led off with "San Antonio Rose," and Oh Boy, can he sing it! He really brought down the house. Bing really has something in that voice. He was surprisingly thin and bald headed. But it was worth the time to go out there to see that show. We went with the Russell's and came back to their house for a little party afterwards.

Feb 18 - Had a long letter from [James W.] Headstream[11] today. He has been transferred to Keesler Field, Miss. I am so glad he is out of the field at last. Jimmie is one more swell kid. He's one friend I have who is worth one in a million. They are expecting a baby in July. I know they are happy. It will be good for Janie Lee.

Feb 20-Had the new experience of paying my first income tax today, $20. One hates to pay taxes but I hope I shall have to pay income taxes every year as long as I live.

Had a class over at the Station hospital at Ft. Sam Houston today. The hospital is nice.

Had a sweet letter from Roy Webb today. He was the second patient of my medical experience and the very favorite of all my patients at the

Children's Hospital in Little Rock. He must be 14 now. He enclosed one of his pictures, he's as freckled as a turkey egg but that makes him all the more attractive. Diary, I'll let you in on a little secret why that child will forever have a warm spot in my memory. He was eleven years old then, and he had a huge contracted scar on the back of his leg from an old burn. Dr. Newman operated on him and the next day Roy was in terrific pain, but he took it like a man. That night we (the hospital staff) were all going out on a picnic, and on the way out, I went by to see how he was resting. In the midst of his soft groaning he smiled and took my hand between both his and said, "Dr. Shuller, be sure to come back to see me when you come in from the picnic." I could have hugged him. That was the first time that I had experienced the confidence of a patient, and it is a thrill that I shall never forget. You may be sure that I did go see him when I returned, and ever afterwards. In fact, I fear I was almost jealous when anybody else did anything for him during his long weeks there. He was such an appreciative youngster, and although I was just a green senior medical student, he thought I was the finest doctor in the world, and apparently still does. He could repay me with nothing but his respect and admiration and profound appreciation, but of those he gave so generously. Diary, that is something that money could never buy. It is so good to be a doctor. He taught me the first fine thing about the profession.

Feb 23 - Went to the Auditorium to hear Marian Anderson. I'll never hear a sweeter voice because they just don't come any sweeter. She was very generous with her encores and her final number was Ave Maria, and I swear I think I almost noticed a tear in my eye. Her group of spirituals were classic too. She is a negress, but a voice like hers has no race. Mrs. [Eleanor] Roosevelt did a good job when she condemned the DAR for their stand against her. I got my $2.20 worth.

Feb 24 - Was sent out to the Kelley Field Replacement Center to examine cadets today. There were over 150 of them. It was a regular mill. I sure would hate awfully bad to get assigned to a place like that permanently. As sure as I do, I'm going to volunteer for foreign duty. I can think of nothing more monotonous than looking at that assembly line day after day.

Feb 28 - As we came out of the show tonight we heard the news boy yelling, "Two Randolph pilots killed in crash." That is such an awfully frequent occurrence. There must have been a dozen killed since I have been here these two months. Those instructors are giving a lot more than they are given credit for. The combat pilot gets all the glory, but no one ever thinks about the sacrifice to his country when an instructor climbs in behind a student and risks his life every time he goes off the ground to try to turn out another pilot for Uncle Sam. If a combat pilot is killed in action his name is plastered across all the newspapers and maybe be recommended for a medal. But an instructor who loses his life—well, it is considered unfortunate and that is about all there is to it. We owe a tremendous debt to these instructors. Some begrudge these pilots their flight pay, but as far as I am concerned they deserve it and more. I consider it a privilege that I am going to be so closely associated with these fellows in these months or years to come.

March 1, 1942 - Went with Sully and Pat up to College Station today to visit with Dwight Andres, but he was not at home. It was a lovely trip though. We drove a total of about 450 miles. It sure was good to get out of town.

March 2 - They took us in the low pressure chamber up to 35,000 feet today and left us up there for 4 whole hours. They gave us a series of tests to test our cerebration during the interval. It was no fun, but I am glad to know that I do not react adversely to high flying conditions for long intervals.

March 3 - Oliver and I remained out at Randolph Field tonight to see "Sergeant York." It was an inspiring show and most timely. They should make it training film #1 and require every soldier to see it. I only hope I can achieve just a portion of the courage and principles that were his. God being with me, I am going to do my best to deliver the goods when the time comes.

March 7 - Wayne King is appearing at one of the theatres downtown. Oliver and I went this afternoon, and we really got our money's worth. When he struck out on "Josephine," I could hardly keep my feet still. I must get that recording for the girls at A.C.G.S. Las Vegas.[12]

We made a sort of tour of some of the old missions about the city this afternoon. They are over 200 years old, two of them being built in 1720. We had a lucky break this afternoon in that there were no examinees so we got out at noon. Everybody is getting tired and are practically counting days—three weeks now.

March 12 - Sent in an application for a 10-day leave today. Don't much expect to get it, but they can't do anything but say no.

March 14 - Well, Blow me down! Fried really got married the first of this week as I learn today in a letter from Miss Sutton. The last thing he told me when I left was that he might be married when I got back, but I didn't believe it. It gave me a sinking feeling when I read it. Guess it's just that I envy him. He is such a grand fellow.

I probably think more of him than anybody else at Las Vegas. It's going to make things different there now. I do hope she is worthy of him. He's that sort of old common country boy who deserves the very best.

March 17 - The 10-day leave is denied. But I have a scheme to get two or three days extra by claiming to go by private conveyance. Am hoping to be able to go home. Albert and Paul have insisted on my coming to Oklahoma City.

Paul is deferred from the draft again on the basis of migraine. Unless I miss my guess, Paul is a classic case of psychasthenia.[13]

March 18 - They took us to 40,000 feet in the low pressure chamber today and left us there 1 hour. No ill effects whatever. That is one "fer piece" up. The barometric pressure at that level is only 140 mm Hg. This is enough of that stuff. It gets tiresome just sitting in that thing.

March 23 - The unexpected happened today. The new list of orders came out today, and my name was on it. There was no reason to be surprised, though, because anything can happen in this man's Army. It's to Geiger Field, Spokane, Washington. Was disappointed at first, but after the initial shock, I am beginning to be quite thrilled about it because I have always wanted to see the great northwest. Guess it's to be a tactical unit. Hope that it is a bomber squadron. I hadn't anticipated that sort of thing, but now that it is shoved in my face, I am looking forward to it.

The reason I was disappointed at first is because I had anticipated going back to my friends in Las Vegas. They are such a wonderful bunch, almost all of them. Guess it's just natural to want to be where one knows that he is genuinely liked. But I'll be making new friends, I'm sure. Anyway, I relish the chance to practice some of the things that we have learned here at this school in the way of the care of pilots under stress. Am anxious to see if I can really gain their confidence. I believe I can unless I try too hard. It's going to be fun.

March 26 - Our last lectures today. Hooray! Are we all glad. Only have to clear the post tomorrow and "practice graduation."

I have been writing my farewell letters to the folks back at Las Vegas, and I even shed a tear or two over it before I was finished. Silly, yes, but much as I am looking forward to my new post, there is a sharp pang every

Graduating class at School of Aviation Medicine, San Antonio, 1942. Shuller is in top row, second from the left. Courtesy of the Thurman Shuller Family Collection.

time I think about not getting to see those friends again back in Las Vegas. Some of them are pure gold. I'm glad I can feel this about them.

March 28 - Graduation this morning, lasted almost 10 minutes. I now have a diploma that says that I am a qualified medical examiner (aviation). Everybody was in a hurry to leave, and I'll be leaving at 1:30 p.m. for McAlester. It's a let-down to be all through like this, but happy it's all over.

Sully and Pat helped me celebrate graduation last night. I had a date with a Brooks nurse and we had a most enjoyable time at the Tower after first gathering over at our apartment [Shuller and classmate Lt. Oliver shared an apartment during the flight surgeon course at San Antonio]. The Russell's were there too.

*

Thurman Shuller departed San Antonio by train for McAlester, Oklahoma, where his brother, Elbert, who practiced medicine at the McAlester Clinic, had offered to drive him home to Arkansas. In the days that followed, Shuller details in his diary, the short two-day visit at home before going back to Oklahoma to meet Lieutenant Harold D. Munal for the long cross-country motor trip to their next assignment in Washington State. The trip was eventful for both doctors and, at the end of their journey, held a typical army surprise for both men when they finally reached their destination.[14]

*

March 29 - Arrived at Ell's [Elbert] at 5:00 this morning, and he drove me down home to arrive about noon. It was nice of him to ask to do this. It's so good to be home and visit with Ell's family too. Mother and Dad look well.

March 30 - Left Ozark early this morning. Was at home a total of only about 20 hours. Such a short visit but I wouldn't take anything in the world for having gotten to go home even for such a short time. I could tell that Mother and Dad hated to see me go so awful badly this time, although they didn't say anything much. I wonder if they fear I won't be coming back - But I will be coming back.

Arrived at Albert's[15] in Oklahoma City almost night. Paul came over and stayed a long time. It was nice to see and talk with him after almost 12 years. He is so thin. He probably deserved a physical deferment. He apparently is a bright youngster, and I wish I could be around him more often.

March 31 - Am on my way to Washington state, traveling with Lt. Munal who picked me up in Oklahoma City, and tonight we are at Raton, New Mexico. We drove 480 miles in 8 hours which is averaging 60 miles an hour. Some driving! Am looking forward to this trip.

April 1, 1942 - Denver, Colorado: Hotel Shirley Savoy. Have actually approached our destination by only a little over 200 miles, but we have been driving all day. This morning we attempted to drive up Pike's Peak, but at just above 10,000 feet the road was too slippery. We then drove on past Denver to Estes Park and Rocky Mountain National Park. They were far more beautiful than Pike's Peak. The snow was several feet deep, and the road was open only part of the way. Lovely weather and a most enjoyable sight-seeing day.

April 2 - Salt Lake City: Hotel Utah. We had a most wonderful trip today. The beauty of the mountains west of Denver is indescribable. The roads had been cleared with snow plows for scores of miles. I wouldn't take anything for having seen those mountains with their full coat of snow. I could have stayed up there for days. The innumerable ski tracks made me want to try my hand at that sport.

Tonight we went to see "Fantasia." It is absolutely crazy, but the music, which is the important thing, is superb. Was really too tired to enjoy it though. The only unhappy thing about the whole day is the utterly exorbitant price of $6.00 we are paying for a room. It's shameful the way Army officers are taken advantage of.

April 4 - Arrived in Spokane about sundown. We were pretty tired and only went to a show. We'll be looking around tomorrow.

April 6 - Surprises again. Reported in to Geiger and found out that the headquarters had been moved over to Fort George Wright. We reported in over there and were told that we'd probably be tactically assigned to a group located at Wendover, Utah. From all reports, it is a hell-hole of a place right on the salt flats of the Utah – Nevada border with no town for 50 miles or so. That is the penalty for being single. This is a repeat on the situation of being sent to Moffett Field and landing down at Las Vegas. But I learned to like Las Vegas, and I probably will this one too.

April 7 - We just wandered around making ourselves as scarce as possible today, trying to stay out of work. Waiting on definite orders. Did draw a nice little lump of travel money today, $172.04 - wasn't hard to accept.

April 10 - At last we got our orders to move on to Wendover, and am I glad! This loafing about town doing nothing is getting awfully boresome. We did have a swell time today though. We made a several hundred mile trip around the shores of Lake Coeur D'Alene and down to Moscow. I spent the evening with one of Munal's friends. They showed us a swell time and the scenery along the typical northwestern lake was magnificent. We'll be shoving off tomorrow.

April 11 - Walla Walla, Wash., Marcus Whitman Hotel—We started out to drive way down through Oregon today but had two blowouts just outside Walla Walla and had to come back here. Were able to get a new tire, fortunately. The first real car trouble since we started. Have now abandoned the idea of the longer trip through Oregon.

April 12 - Gowan Field, Boise Idaho. As we drove in here this afternoon we ran into Lt. Newell, one of the Randolph Field boys, on the street. He had us out to the post, and we are quartered in the visiting officers' quarters for the night. The 50 cents is better than the $2.50 hotel bill. This is a nice, well-organized post. The officers' club is swell. Hope it is as good at Wendover, but we'll not be expecting much. They called a practice "alert" here tonight and started up the motors of the planes. There are 36 B-17's here. Some aircraft!

*

At Fort George Wright, Washington, Shuller and Munal were two of four Medical Corps physicians ordered to the 306th Bomb Group at Wendover. Captain Ralph C. Teall was assigned as the Group Surgeon, 1st Lt. John J. Manning to the 367th Bomb Squadron, 1st Lt. Harold D. Munal Jr. to the 368th Bomb Squadron, and 1st Lt. Thurman Shuller to the 369th Bomb Squadron. Of all of the squadron surgeons, Shuller was senior due to his early entry into the reserves in 1939, following medical school graduation. The two extra years of service in rank placed Shuller as the senior surgeon in the squadrons. Later in July, Captain Teall received orders out of the 306th to become the base surgeon at Wendover. Shuller moved up to Group Surgeon. He was uneasy about the sudden promotion, but he was soon organizing and managing the new medical staff and tackling the massive operation of getting the bomb group medical organization ready for overseas shipment.[16] In the entries below, Shuller refers to a "64," which is a medical examination for eligibility to serve in army aviation.[17]

*

April 13 - So this is Wendover! What a post. They haven't even gotten to first base yet with construction. The hospital isn't even started, there is only one B-17, our medical detachment isn't even here, and there are no rooms for quarters in the B.O.Q., so we are holed up in the dispensary. And what a town! A small series of squatter houses, one small store, some tourist cabins, filling stations, and a gambling house (Stateline Hotel). We have really hit the bottom. If one needs to get acclimated for the African desert, I guess that is what we are getting. But I'm determined to make the best of it.

April 14 - The second day at Wendover. Maybe it won't be so bad. I was O.D. this very first day, although that doesn't mean much. I did see several patients though. The first ones since last December—3 ½ whole months. Gosh, it is good to be a doctor again, even if it is only treating the usual Army complaints. Went to the show tonight. Really the day didn't seem so long.

April 17 - We got our assignments a day or two ago. I am now the Surgeon of the 369th squadron of the 306th Bombardment Group (H). There sure is going to be a lot of work to this. My present headache is the so-called sanitary inspector. I am also assigned to lecture on first aid. I still say this is a hell of a place.

April 20 - We've really been busy the last few days. There is enough to

Aerial view of Wendover Air Base, circa 1942. Courtesy of the East Anglia Air War Collection.

Wendover, looking toward the west, circa 1942. Courtesy of the East Anglia Air War Collection.

Wendover, looking west towards the Utah-Nevada state line, circa 1942. Courtesy of the East Anglia Air War Collection.

Wendover barracks area, circa 1942. Courtesy of the East Anglia Air War Collection.

keep us humping all the time. Am having a hard time getting the sanitary area started. We're doing 64's every day now. Even yesterday (Sunday) we worked all day on them. There is a swell bunch of fellows here though—thank God for that. There are now five living in this small room. Our veterinarian came in yesterday.

April 22 - There was a stage show tonight sponsored by the U.S.O., and it was really swell. If this is a good example of what the U.S.O. is doing then I'm for them. Was expecting to see a more or less sexy leg show, but they were good clean acts, expertly executed. The fellows really received them well too, a most appreciative audience. Maybe the so-called morale builders have at last discovered that soldiers like this sort of thing much more than vulgar stuff. The camp's morale went up 100% after this show.

April 26 - Had my first ride in a B-17 today. We flew over the salt flats for a couple hours. Lt. [John L.] Ryan was pilot and three of the younger pilots took turns as co-pilot. It was a grand ride. I had been looking forward to this first flight for a long time, and now that I have made my maiden flight in a fortress I am not disappointed. When one looks out over those wings from the air it looks like a city block flying around. The fellows halfway expected me to get sick I think. Every five minutes or so someone would ask me how I felt. Am glad I didn't disgrace myself. I have to stand up to those fellows and maintain their respect.

May 3, 1942 - One week later—gosh, this has been a busy week. We are still doing "64" examinations. Friday, I started in on my series of lectures on First Aid to the officers. Was a little apprehensive about those lectures, and worried a little over their preparation. It is the first time that I have attempted to talk to a class of educated men, and I wondered how I would do as a lecturer. But the fellows were very attentive and apparently got something out of the first two lectures. I trust that my next two lectures will come off as well.

We're still sweating this sanitation problem down at the sanitary area in tent city. Capt. Teall really blew up yesterday about it.

May 5 - Finished my course of lectures today to the pilots. I actually think they enjoyed them. My first experience at teaching but apparently successful. At least I have learned by the "grapevine" from higher up that the fellows feel they have really benefitted from them. I am glad I did try to make my first venture a successful one. I'll be doing it so often though that it will eventually get pretty old later on.

May 6 - This is a happy day. Received a sweet remembrance from home.

My big birthday surprise, however, was when the telephone rang immediately after lunch, and the voice at the other end said, "Come over to headquarters right away, and we will make you a Captain." I almost dropped the receiver, but I sure did make tracks toward headquarters. It was a complete surprise. I certainly hadn't asked for it. It must have been a recommendation from Maj. Holtz at Las Vegas. Maybe that letter I wrote him did bear fruit. I lost no time getting the bars on. Capt. Wise, who got his captaincy yesterday, helped me get some and put them on me. It cost me a box of cigars and a round of drinks for some of the boys, but it is worth it. Captain Shuller - sounds a little strange.

May 9 - In addition to my other duties today, I supervised the moving of the squadron aid stations. Building moving, that's a new field for me. I didn't realize that would ever come into a doctor's profession.

May 14 - We moved out of our crowded quarters into the big temporary barracks. Boy, they look like they will be plenty cold, but there is lots of room. It is rumored that we will move again in a couple days. We had been sleeping six to a room. We figured up the other day that our room was drawing $280 for the government per month. I would be drawing a quarter's allowance of $80 per month that I am not receiving now if I were married.

May 16 - Last night there was a crash of a B-17 about 10 or 15 miles over the mountains from Wendover. Two of the men wandered in last night and the co-pilot was picked up this morning, suffering from exposure. They sent out a searching party last night, but they didn't find the plane until this a.m. All the group doctors were out on the searching party except me this a.m., while I was doing sick call and 10 - 64 examinations. They came in at noon and Capt. Wise and I went out this afternoon. That plane is a million pieces. We still haven't found the pilot. This is my first experience in looking for crash victims, but I'm sure it is only the beginning. Fortunately, this was not one of our planes. They were from Seattle, I believe. But if I stay at this long enough, I suppose I'll be picking up some of my buddies. That's not a pleasant thought, but after all, one might as well look at it realistically.

May 17 - Have just seen a most excellent movie tonight—"Kings Row." It's so rare that a purely dramatic show can hold one's interest so. The movies are the Army's best entertainment.

This afternoon again went out with the ambulance at the scene of the plane crash. They had found something in the buried part of the wreckage that looked as if it might be a charred body. The pilot is still missing and it is a strong possibility that this may be he.

I wrote a letter home tonight, but I did not mention the crash, and I made a resolution that I will not write anything home about crashes. There is no need of stimulating any anxiety in Mother and Dad about my flying. I got a sweet letter from Mother a couple days ago after she learned of my promotion. Gosh, I wish I could be the man my parents think I am.

May 21 - Colonel [Curtis] LeMay said today that we weren't flying with the boys enough. So this afternoon, I flew over two hours with Capt. [Ralph L.] Oliver and Lt. [Jack A.] Spaulding. Spaulding was shooting landings with the B-18. He didn't do so well at first, but he'll straighten out O.K. Capt. Oliver certainly has remarkable control of the ship. He apparently has a good head and has a knack for flying. He let me take the controls for a turn around the field. After it was in the air, I controlled it very well but my approach and attempted landing was one for the book. I think I am a better doctor than flier. But it was a most enjoyable afternoon.

May 23 - I picked up a little of the American fighting spirit today in one of my physical examinations for combat crew. This particular lad is from Boston, is 26 years old, played football for Duke three years. He was one of those fellows whom you just know are going to pass without much difficulty. It was easy to recognize at first glance that he is far above the general run of soldier. I inquired why he didn't take cadet training, and he replied that he had considered it but had decided that he would rather be a gunner. That struck me as being most peculiar. With coaxing, he said that he volunteered the day war was declared to try to avenge the death of his best pal at Pearl Harbor. And he still has the spirit. He doesn't want one Jap, he wants at least a dozen. And he was just on edge all the way through the exam for fear he might not pass and get to go on with his desire. He's a fine clean lad, apparently, the kind that is really America. His name is White. I'm going to keep my eye on him and see how he turns out.

May 26 - Several of the B-17's left out yesterday and today on secret orders. All of the experienced pilots, except the squadron commanders, are gone. They left out loaded to the gills with ammunition. They were all excited about it. This is their first mission, but it is only the beginning. No one has any idea where they are going. I wonder if they'll all get back. Guess I'll be wondering that every time they start out on a mission.

May 27 - We moved our quarters again today. Hope we are settled for a while. We spent most of the afternoon building shelves and a table. The fellows made fun of my carpentering, but it wasn't so bad after it was finished.

June 2, 1942 - Our flying status came through yesterday. Whoopee—That means $60 more a month. That's not hard to accept. Today my pay is $93.33 a month more than it was a month ago.

I am just recovering from the worst attack of sinusitis since leaving Little Rock. Felt absolutely rotten and was in bed for a couple of days. Beginning to feel almost normal again now, except a very rotten nose.

The ground school for combat crews started with a bang. I gave three lectures, an hour each, today. Had the experience of lecturing to a packed theatre—about 500 men this afternoon and was amazed that I held their attention so well. Lecturing isn't at all bad when one has something to say and knows more or less how he is going to say it. My new detachment men came in today. Another training program. Hope we have some smart boys.

June 7 - Guess I missed the boat on this guy named White that I mentioned I was going to keep my eye on a couple weeks ago. His service record came through yesterday, and it showed that of the six months he has been in the Army, he has been A.W.O.L. almost half the time. Does that put me in my place as a character picker!

June 12 - Received a telegram from Doyle Pierson today that he has a new son and has named him William Thurman for his dad and me. That was unexpected of Doyle, and I am quite flattered. That is the first baby ever named for me, as far as I know. Guess I'll send him a War Bond or something.

June 14 - Have just gotten back from a weekend in Salt Lake City. It was a very quiet weekend as far as any celebration was concerned, but it was a good rest. One almost gets stir crazy after staying around this post too long. Had a hotel room just over the Mormon temple court, and it was really beautiful. Went with Lt. Munal Saturday night, we went to the Starlite Garden at the Hotel Utah; but we went alone. Things were quiet, and we saw very few we knew, but the relaxation and quiet of a hotel room and good bed were worth it for a change.

June 21 - Captain Oliver, my commanding officer, is Major Oliver this morning. There is going to be an awful lot of quick promotions some of these days. A number of the second lieutenants are slated to become Captains. The Air Corps offers unlimited opportunities for a good pilot. Semi-official telephone communication from Hqs., Second Air Force warns to be prepared to move August 1. That's not too soon for me. But I've got to get out and start buying some more clothes. I have already started doing all my re-vaccinations in preparation for moving. Some of these poor boys are going to get a dozen punctures in the next three weeks.

June 25 - The new T/BA [TO&E—table of organization and equipment] came out yesterday, and we are going to have 12 planes in the squadron. That will bring the strength up to 402. More work getting the immunizations done. There is a slight change in the medical detachment too. Am getting a new sergeant from the 368th. Hope he turns out O.K.

*

With three of the four surgeon positions filled in the squadrons, it became apparent that Thurman Shuller was the senior squadron surgeon, based on his date of rank (commission) and his promotion to captain in May. Charles P. McKim, the last of the surgeons to be assigned to the 306th, was senior to Shuller in date of service, but by the time McKim arrived in July, Shuller was already a captain and serving as Group Surgeon.

Since Shuller received his commission as first lieutenant in 1939 following graduation from medical school, his service number reflected a date of rank in 1939. Only McKim had a lower service number than Shuller. The other two surgeons, Manning and Munal, were commissioned after Shuller. In June 1942, the only medical officer in the group senior to Shuller was Group Surgeon Teall. Shuller's seniority followed him throughout the war and opened significant opportunities for him, some of which he only reluctantly accepted. His first opportunity presented itself on the evening of June 27, 1942.[18]

*

June 27 - Capt. Teall just informed me tonight that Col. Corliss has informed him that he will be leaving here as group surgeon. That will automatically make me group surgeon, and I ain't happy about it. I really fear the job. I just don't believe that I have the "staff" and the experience to be that much of an executive. I'll bust a gut trying though if it is put on me. Gosh I do hope he stays on here until the training program has been completed.

July 2, 1942 - Whew!!! That was a close one! There were nine of us from the Medical Dept. who flew to Salt Lake City today in an old B-18 to inspect the Cudahy packing plant. Everything was lovely until we were within about 10 miles of the field on the way home. Both motors suddenly began cutting up and finally went out. Lt. Ryan was the pilot (thank God for that), and he really worked pumping that plane in. He brought it in about 100 feet short of the runway on the salt flat. This is one time when I have tremendous appreciation for that hard flat stretch of waste land. I dread to think what would have happened if the field had been surrounded by trees or high lines like most of them are. Lt. [William E.] McKell took us over, and I'm glad that a more experienced pilot was at the controls when this emergency arose. Guess it's lucky there are not thirteen of us strewn over the salt flat. When I heard the motors go out I lost no time checking to see that my chute was O.K.

It was my first time through a big packing plant and it was an interesting experience for me. They certainly can dispose of big bones in a hurry. They served us a nice lunch too. Went shopping afterwards, getting ready for foreign duty, but bought very little.

P.S. 9:30 p.m. Boy, this is my unlucky day! I have just learned that Captain Teall has received his orders to go to Pendleton, Oregon. That makes me group surgeon. I am so sorry that it happened so quick. It would be much more fun going over as a squadron surgeon.

July 5 - Well, I am now Group Surgeon. Capt. Teall left yesterday afternoon and left me with the headache. And what a headache it may be. I have plunged right into it, however, and if will power will help any, I'm going to do O.K with it. I can't even sleep well the last couple of nights for worrying about it. Maybe it won't be as big a job as I think.

July 6 - I got out early this morning and drilled the boys for a while. I didn't do so bad as I might have. They at least didn't trip me up on anything. A doctor out drilling soldiers! Some Army!

July 8 - Had my first experience today of picking up bodies out of a plane crash, our first fatal accident since the Group was organized. Seven men (three officers and four enlisted men) were literally blown to bits. Lt. [Van] Vander Bie was the only one that I knew well, although they were in the 369th Squadron. I took out four of my enlisted men to help me pick up the bodies, and they proved to be real soldiers. Not one of them got sick, and they all pitched in like old hands at the job. Probably 25 pounds was the most any one piece weighed, and it was really a job trying to match up the pieces. Five of the bodies we were able to identify by laundry marks, but two of them were not accounted for. That was not at all a pleasant job, but I don't believe it was as bad as it would have been had I been able actually to identify an individual. As it was, it seemed very impersonal because it was like just so many pieces of meat. The bodies were that mangled. Think I'll not do any flying on dark nights.

July 10 - Major [John R.] McGraw was down from the Second Air Force today to look over the medical situation. Apparently he was well satisfied with the group set-up. All the organization, however, was due to Capt. Teall's work, and I deserved none of the credit. He said that I'd be in line for Majority Aug. 1. That is just getting too far ahead of my experience and capabilities. The pressure on me is really getting pretty great.

July 11 - Sgt. [Francis J.] Tropeano and I went out looking for a place to hold our field day on first aid. Went way out on the Montello highway and actually found a place with trees. The real experience, however, was that we ran across a wash-out in the road too rapidly and badly bent the engine brace. We really did some tall mechanical repair. After about a couple of hours it was in running order again. I thought for a while we'd have to walk that 30 miles back to Wendover. It was really good to get out. This place was rapidly getting on my nerves.

July 12 – Took my first altitude hop today with Lt. [Paul D.] Cunningham as pilot. Dropped bombs at 20,000 feet. The fifth bomb stuck, and we had to come in. I want to go higher on the next one. We would have gone to 30,000 today if we had had time.

July 14 - Lt. Munal and I took the enlisted men out on a field day. We went out to the place we picked out last Saturday. We took our lunch and the men really seemed to enjoy it. We took the ambulances way up on the mountain and had the men evacuate 5 men from an "airplane crash" in each ambulance. Some of the men showed up pretty well, but there were some pretty bad errors, which was to be expected, of course. Hope they learned a little from it. They enjoyed lying in the shade under the trees and got into a water-fight in the irrigation ditch. There was once a time when I didn't appreciate shade and water so much.

July 15 - Drove into Salt Lake City today to see about getting glasses for the men in the group. Chaplain Macleod went with me. It was a good shopping tour as well as a business trip. This thing of getting ready to "go-across" is becoming quite a big job! I think I am going to get the glasses situation worked out satisfactorily though.

July 18 - The other medical officer reported in last night. His name is Lt. [Charles P.] McKim. He seems very nice. I have all the officers now, but lack a couple of enlisted men. Col. [Charles P.] Overacker[19] said today that we will probably pull out of here two weeks from today. I sorted out a bunch of my stuff that I want to send home. Time is getting short now, and I am anxious.

July 20 - I had occasion to buck the boys today. A number of the men are developing considerable flying fatigue because of the increasing flying since the planes came in last week. Two or three of the boys are really getting to the end of the rope. I think that they took it all right though when I asked for less flying time and more rest for the pilots. Even took the matter to Col. Overacker.

This has been a busy day. It was like pulling teeth to get the fellows up to get their glasses checked. I chased the fellows all over the field several times.

July 22 - The big drive to pack and get ready to move is underway. Official warning orders are here, and the ground echelon is supposed to be packed and ready to move in five more days. That is going to be a job and a headache. The squadron surgeons have been going on a pilfering campaign to collect enough supplies to last us a while. We have done pretty good too if only we can get by with them without having them lifted off of us. It's the port of embarkation that is going to be the rub.

July 24 - Packing is proceeding at a rapid pace, and we will soon be finished. It is quite definite now that I will be in the flying echelon. That is good. Flying schedules will come to a close tomorrow or the next day.

Lt. Cunningham had a taxiing accident yesterday and destroyed his plane and the one he ran into. Over half a million dollars' worth of planes destroyed in a split second.

July 28 - Moving orders have now been officially received. That means that the ground echelon will be leaving in two or three days, and we should be leaving in the flying echelon a day or two later.

Manning and Munal got their promotions to Captain today. It has been a happy day for them. We were going to have a little celebration up at the State Line Hotel, but it was closed to officers tonight. Capt. Teall got his promotion to Major yesterday. That really makes me happy to have him get it before Capt. Crago here at the base hospital.

Well, this ends the first volume of this book. I started eleven months ago principally for my own amusement, but it will be continued as a War record at Dad's request.

I have diverted all my energies into my work in the Army, and thus far, it has paid dividends. I have become a Captain after nine months, and

Medics practice casualty field work in the desert near Wendover, July 14, 1942. Courtesy of the East Anglia Air War Collection.

Medics practice casualty field work in the desert near Wendover, July 14, 1942. Courtesy of the East Anglia Air War Collection.

Medics practice casualty field work in the desert near Wendover, July 14, 1942. Courtesy of the East Anglia Air War Collection.

already after only a year, I have been recommended for Major by the Commanding Officer. I have made a lot of friends in this year, much more easily than I ever have before. I have always been slow to make friends, but for some reason in the Army it has been fairly easy. In that way, this year has been worth most to me. And last but not least, in the one year I have decreased by $1150.00 my personal debt. This has been a fairly good year, everything considered, but I hope that next year will be even better. I have seen every western state except Montana now, and prior to last July, I had seen none at all.

I am choosing this as the point to close the first volume because we are on the verge of entering upon our first troop movement as a unit. Our training is nearing completion now, and after a short stay in a staging area on the east coast, we will actually enter the combat area.

I am anxious to be off to the battle area. There is a lot of advantage in being single at a time like this, but somehow I envy the fellows who have someone back here waiting for them. Is that selfishness on my part? No, diary, I think it is a perfectly normal reaction. I do have the grandest family in the world who are most anxious about me, but somehow it is different. It isn't quite like having someone all your own. Well, I'll just put those thoughts aside and think about it after the war is over. One can get lonesome among a multitude even among friends. One fine day, some day, things will be different.

Chapter 2

A Doctor Goes to War

August 1, 1942–May 12, 1943

During July, the group sent a number of officers and enlisted men with B-17E aircraft to Westover Field to pre-position a part of the aircraft inventory there in advance of the group's departure from Wendover on August 1, 1942. At Westover, the group would be issued new B-17Fs. By the time of departure, the bomb group reported an inventory of forty B-17E aircraft, all of which would be replaced with the new model F at Westover.

On August 1, 1942, the four squadrons departed Wendover with the 368th and 369th Bomb Squadrons flying to Scott Field, Illinois, and the 367th and 423rd Squadrons flying to Chanute Field, Illinois. Group Commander Charles B. Overacker, piloting "Group Airplane Number 1," flew with the Chanute Field group with Thurman Shuller and his medical sergeant, S/Sgt. Francis J. Tropeano, on board. The next day the two squadrons took off from Scott Field and made it to Westover easily. At Chanute Field, Overacker and his aircraft took off at 8:45, delayed forty-five minutes by weather clearance. However, the 367th and 423rd takeoff was delayed even more by weather and later forced to fly a more southerly route to avoid "a reported storm," landing at Bolling Field, Virginia, that evening. Overacker had flown the designated route and landed at Westover as planned. The next day the two squadrons at Bolling flew to Westover, joining Overacker and the 368th and 369th squadrons already at Westover Field.[1]

As the air echelon began to depart Wendover, the ground echelon with the bulk of the group's officers and enlisted men, under the command of Lt. Col. Delmar E. Wilson, entrained for the journey to the Richmond Army Air Base in Virginia.

The journey took four days. At Richmond the men who received "passes and leaves" during the next ten days spent their time "in drilling and receiving equipment." On August 14 the ground echelon boarded trains "for its staging area at Fort Dix, New Jersey."[2]

Meanwhile Col. Overacker with the air echelon at Westover decided that the "fortresses could not carry the load 'across the pond' that they had car-

Wendover Railroad Station, circa 1942. Courtesy of the East Anglia Air War Collection.

ried east, approximately one-quarter of the air echelon were ordered" to leave Westover on August 14 by train, and "join the ground echelon at Fort Dix." Shuller remained with the air echelon, but Sgt. Tropeano departed for Fort Dix with the group transferring to the ground echelon that would board the Queen Mary *for the voyage to Glasgow, Scotland.[3]*

Thurman Shuller's observations on the movement overseas gives us more details than previously available from the official documents and other writings by members of the 306th Bomb Group. Positioned in the nose of the B-17, Shuller had a first class seat and view of the journey, and he took advantage of the opportunity. In this second group of diary entries, Shuller gives the reader a running commentary of that view and his experiences and observations along the way.

*

Aug 1, 1942 - Wendover Field, Utah - This is it, we are off to the east coast at last. Our wheels left the runway at 5:00 a.m. with Col. Overacker in the cockpit. It is now an hour and a half later, and we have already completely crossed the state of Utah and are now flying at 13,500 feet over the snow-capped mountain peaks of Colorado. It was a real thrill sitting up here in the very tip of the nose of this ship and watch the gorgeous sunrise over the mountains with our faces directly into it at 188 miles per hour ground speed. One can scarcely realize the power of man until he sits out here and looks back on those four powerful engines, humming in perfect synchronization, pulling us up and over the mountains. Most of the pilots are excellent pilots, but right now I rest easier because the boss himself is at the controls. He has had over 6000 pilot hours.

It doesn't at all seem like I am changing stations. I have never before gotten up so early to leave and I have never before left by this means. There were few farewells because most of the people I worked with are coming along too.

8:00 a.m. Three hours after take-off and now over Nebraska. We passed over Cheyenne a few moments ago. It is a nice looking city from a mile up, but I was surprised to discover that it is flat country, not mountainous as I had suspected. The change in the type of country since take off has been remarkable; formerly rough mountain peaks, some barren, now flat fertile land evenly plotted out into good looking farms. It has just occurred to me that I may sort of miss those rugged mountains a little after all. Perhaps I have just said goodbye to the west for many years to come.

I am helping the navigator navigate and am having a whale of a lot of fun. My navigation however consists mainly of studying the regional maps and recognizing the landmarks as we pass over them.

9:30 a.m. We are directly over Omaha. It looks very, very pretty from the air. Has a lot of trees and is located right on the banks of the Missouri River. Two of the other fellows here in the nose are sound asleep, but I am too afraid of missing something to sleep.

12:00 noon. Have just landed at Chanute Field, Ill. Approximately 1,300 air miles in 7 hours. We came in an hour ahead of schedule. The other ships are landing now. Seventeen of our ships are coming to this field and nineteen are going to Scott Field near St. Louis. The Colonel has just told us that our destination is Westover Field, Mass. We all suspected it anyway, but it is nice to know for sure. Chanute Field is an old air field, and specializes in training mechanics.

The time here is 2 hours ahead of Wendover time so our watches are changed. They took us over for our dinner, and they gave us a huge steak, potatoes and gravy, a nice salad, asparagus, canned pineapple, milk, raisin bread and blackberry pie a la mode. That for 25¢. But golly! It is hot here. We complained a little about Wendover, but this is the first time this summer that my clothes have stuck to me. We're to take off at 8:00 tomorrow.

This kind of heat here makes me realize for the first time just why there are so many heat strokes in Chicago.

Aug 2 - We took off from Chanute Field at 8:45 a.m. We were 45 minutes late waiting on weather clearance. Now only 45 minutes after take-off we are over Indianapolis.

9:45 a.m. One hour after take-off, and we are over Dayton, Ohio. In this short time, we have crossed most of Illinois, completely crossed Indiana, and are well into Ohio. This is quite a big city and very pretty. The only bad feature about this trip is that it is too hazy to make good pictures, and it was almost as bad yesterday. These Ohio farmers certainly look prosperous - have beautiful homes and barns. I hadn't even imagined such a network of paved roads. It seems that even the private roads are paved.

Just out of Dayton and the haze is closing in and it is getting so rough I can hardly write. We have been flying at 1000 feet this morning under the overcast, but now we are going over it to 5,000 feet. This is shame. Can't see anything below but clouds.

10:05 a.m. I can just get a glimpse of Columbus now and then through a hole in the clouds.

10:45 a.m. Wheeling, West Virginia

10:50 a.m. Washington, D.C. is just to our right, but it is so hazy I can't identify anything.

10:53 a.m. Pittsburgh is faintly visible to the left. It hadn't occurred to me that these big cities were so close together.

The mountains of central Penn. are interesting. They resemble huge long terraces thrown up to a sharp ridge by a huge turning plow. But they are thickly covered by vegetation and don't appear to be very rough. They are very pretty. I'll bet the Ozarks look something like this from the air.

12:00 noon. Passing over so many industrial cities here in eastern Penn. that it is difficult to identify them.

12:15 p.m. Elizabeth, Newark, Jersey City, and New York City all at once. I can't tell from a mile up where one ends and the other begins, but there sure are a lot of buildings down there. A big cloud prevents me from seeing the tall buildings of Manhattan. I do wish it were a clear day, the trip this morning would have been priceless. Can see quite a bit though as it is.

12:45 p.m. Hartford, Conn. Boy, it doesn't take long to get places nowadays.. I never saw so many white buildings before. We have come under the overcast again and visibility is better. The houses are all built about alike, 2 and 3 stories, New England architecture, I suppose. I see innumerable fields of tobacco, acre upon acre, covered with cheese cloth. A New Englander told me about the covered tobacco fields here before we left Wendover, but I thought he was blowing. It hadn't occurred to me that tobacco was grown in New England.

12:50 p.m. Five minutes later, and we are over Springfield, Mass. The airport at Westover Field is visible.

1:10 p.m. We have landed at Westover. Had to circle the field a few times before it was clear. Two of the other squadrons from Scott Field were already here. As we landed we learned that the rest of the bunch didn't even take off from Chanute Field. The weather officer canceled their clearance immediately after we took off. They could have made it easily though.

8:00 p.m. We have had supper and are moved into our barracks. They are quite a distance from the hangars, and there is almost no transportation on the post. Here is one of the first real evidences of a war that I have seen. Even the post Army vehicles are allowed only one gallon of gas per day. This post is only about a year old, but it has huge runways and is already pretty well developed. These pretty trees and grass really do look good after 3 ½ months at Wendover. It is anticipated that we will be here 3 or 4 weeks. I met the surgeon of the 301st Bombardment Group today, the Group that preceded us here. Their planes have gone out, and he is just waiting transport by ferry command. He should be able to give me a few pointers about things.

Aug 3 – On my first day here I have met Col. Schwichtenberg,[4] the post surgeon, laid out plans for our first aid station, and started a troop dental inspection. Everybody at the hospital seems awfully cooperative. The fellows are all griping about having to walk, but it will do them good. I don't mind it a bit.

Aug 6 - I like it better and better here all the time. I like everything about it. It is pleasant, cool (am sitting around the room after supper with my sweater on), the food is superb for only - $1.25 a day, the hospital personnel are cooperative in every way with anything that I undertake, and everything is so pretty around here. I have setup a small aid station right in the hangar, and we have been giving immunizations by the score down there the last two days. We are getting it pretty well stocked too. One more thing that makes this seem more like home is the wooded hill between here and the hospital is covered with dead ripe huckleberries. I stop there most every day.

I went to one of the briefing sessions for the North Atlantic patrol last night. It was most interesting to learn something about the recognition, approach and attack of submarines by airplane. The fellows all came back enthusiastic about the prospects of finding and sinking a sub. I also came back wanting to make one of those trips, and I will as soon as I get things organized here. Am scheduled to fly with the Colonel down to the ground echelon tomorrow. I am particularly interested in getting this business of supply and immunizations straightened out.

Aug 7 - This was a swell day. Flew with the Colonel down to Richmond where the ground echelon is. In the 2 ½ hours we flew over Hartford, New York City, Philadelphia, Washington, Baltimore, and Richmond. We flew at 2000 feet down the Hudson River right by the tall buildings of Manhattan. My eyes stood out on stems. I recall seeing pictures of all the harbor traffic with a big transport plane flying overhead. Little did I ever realize I'd ever be in that spot in an even bigger plane. We saw the overturned Normandie[5] and then out over the Statue of Liberty. Central Park looks funny right in the middle of all those tremendously tall buildings. It's too bad I didn't have my camera.

Capt. Manning seemed to have everything under control as far as immunizations were concerned. I sure am glad that he is down there. That camp sure is scattered all over everywhere. We are fortunate to be up here.

Wonder why I remembered that this is Ruby's birthday. Just about one year ago I started all this foolish worrying. Someday I'll forget.

Aug 11 - Got back early this morning from New York City. Major Oliver and I and Lt. Kirkpatrick took the train down Sunday afternoon. We got in there about 8:00 p.m. and set out to go to a good show, but being Sunday night, everything was closed except Irving Berlin's "This Is the Army" and it was full up. We were plenty disappointed on that score. Grand Central Station amazed me to begin with. I knew it must be big, but I had no idea just how big. It was just as crowded as a New Year's Celebration somewhere. We wandered around awhile and ended up going to a picture show that had a good vaudeville act. We then visited the La Conga. That is supposed to be a high class joint, but there was nothing there that interested me much. Their floor show was just ordinary. About 2 a.m. we took a room at the Astor on Times Square. Broadway was fairly well blacked out and it no longer has the glittering lights.

Monday morning we took a three-hour tour of the city for $1.50 and saw a great deal of interest. It took us downtown to Wall Street, a dinky little street with tall buildings, down to the waterfront on East End. Then to

Chinatown and back through the slums. The slum districts evidently have been cleaned up. We then visited Radio City, then a subway ride out to Coney Island. That is a cheap joint place, more like an overgrown Carnival. Back then to Radio City to hear a broadcast and time to start back about 9:00 p.m. It was a hurried trip and there was so awfully much I wanted to see that I didn't. But am a little better acquainted with the place now and can find my way around a little better. It sure is a big place and lots to do.

*

While at Westover Field waiting for the journey across the North Atlantic to Thurleigh, Shuller was hard-pressed to finish his work on the group's records, complete the inoculations and dental work still needed by the men in the air echelon, and be ready for takeoff. Time was getting short and soon Captain Munal, the only other doctor with the air echelon, and the four enlisted medics left to join the ground echelon. Their departure for Fort Dix, New Jersey, left Shuller as the lone medical officer with the 350 men who would make up the modified air echelon during the movement to England. Shuller once described the difference between being a squadron surgeon and his role as group surgeon was less doctoring, but with the increased administrative work that came with the top job. The next two weeks were busy for Shuller and the 306th. September would bring the long-awaited takeoffs as each squadron followed their scheduled departure. For Shuller, there was still much to do.[6]

*

Aug 14 - 192 officers and men left here today to join the ground echelon; supposedly at Fort Dix. Things looked awfully vacant around here with them gone. They composed all our duty crews. Capt. Munal and my four enlisted men left too, so that leaves only me to look out after the Air Echelon of 350 officers and men. That is going to turn into quite a job. A lot of the immunizations are not yet completed, and I am starting to run them in for dental treatment.

Aug 16 - I made out and mailed my first reports today. I rather miss Tropeano even though he was a worthless sort of cuss. It has been rainy for several days and that has helped me get off the necessary immunizations and dental treatments while the boys are not working much. A couple of the new B-17F's came in today. Maybe it won't be long now before there is some action.

Aug 20 - Have just gotten back from a trip to Springfield. Went in this afternoon to buy some surgical instruments and a pair of shoes. I got the instruments but not the shoes because government priorities has caused the shoe I wanted to go out of business. Had dinner in town and then went to a show. Was good to get out and away. Left an hour before I was officially off duty, but there was nothing to do and I am sort of my own boss now anyway. Most all my time has been taken up lately issuing out those vitamin pills. I have counted out 25,000 of them in the last week and there will be at least 10,000 more to go. Believe me that is some job.

Had a sweet letter from Mary Opal today in response to the carbon letter I sent out to all the boys' families last week concerning my trip out here and to New York. She raved about it, also Mother seemed to appreciate it a lot. So it must have been an all-right idea.

I was made officer in charge of this barracks a couple of days ago. For my first official act, I thoroughly chewed on Joe, the orderly, for not scrubbing our latrines, but it was just like water falling off a duck's back. We sure are not getting our money's worth in orderly service. What our room service lacks, the food compensates for, though.

Aug 21 - There are about 21 new B-17F's now. They will soon all be here, I guess. It is amusing to see the pilots and crews out working on the planes since the mechanics left. They are pitching in and really trying to learn something it seems. We all have to do odd jobs now. They even had Tech sergeants cleaning latrines the other day.

These pilots sure are proud of their new planes. They call them their "baby." It's a rather huge baby though to the tune of $300,000 worth plus. They swell up with pride because they know that these are the ships they will be with from here on—the ones that will carry them into enemy territory to victory or defeat. Morale seems to be high. Each man is anxious to be getting into the thick of things with but few exceptions

Aug 24 - Major Oliver and I took another little trip into New York over the weekend. We were flown down to Mitchell Field where we did some shopping at the PX then rode on over to New York. Had to stand to see "Star and Garter" but it was worth it. Gypsy Rose Lee unrobes most gracefully—and I mean just that. She's really an artist. After the show we went to a dance at the Hotel Commodore, but I was so tired, I came back soon and let the Major play on. The next morning we took a ferry trip across the river and got a good look at the docks. The Normandie has every bit of her superstructure removed now in preparation to attempt to raise her. The Queen Mary and Queen Elizabeth are now in dock, and it is suspected that our own troops may be preparing to embark on them. In the afternoon we went to Yankee Stadium. An hour before the game we had difficulty finding seats. The Senators beat the Yanks 7 to 6. But the big attraction was Walter Johnson pitching to Babe Ruth between games and Babe clouting a couple of his homers, one going high into the third deck in right field. He received a tremendous ovation as was expected, and when he hit his last homer, he tipped his hat to the crowd as he rounded the bases toward home. There were lots of soldiers there, and it was funny how everything military seemed to disappear for the afternoon. It was good to see the good old American sport carried on just as in peacetime. We took the train back to Springfield and got back to camp just after midnight Sunday. It was another pleasant weekend.

Aug 25 - The weather is now cool and clear after 2 weeks of cloudy rainy weather. Yesterday I saw the first signs of restlessness among the high command and today in a confidential session the Colonel announced that the first squadron is expected to pull out Sunday and the one I go in is to leave Tuesday, a week from today. There are several fellows in the hospital and the pressure was put on me at staff meeting to say yes or no whether or not such and such person would be ready to leave. That was pretty hard, but I think it can be worked out to everybody's satisfaction. There are two officers in the hospital who show every sign of neurasthenia[7] brought on by arrival at post of embarkation. That is a shameful situation, and some disciplinary means should be devised for handling that sort of thing. But certainly we can't use men like that and they will be left behind.

I ran into Lt. [Carl Bemis] Hall, a man I interned with at Charity Hospital. He has been in the Army 5 days. He's the first Charity Hospital doctor I have met in the Army.

The mass carbon copy letter I wrote to all the boys has certainly paid dividends. Have received a long letter from every brother or his wife, except Frank, and also a big box of cookies from Mrs. Alton King, a friend of Mary Opal's. That letter must have been O.K.

Aug 26 - We had another taxi accident today, tearing up a couple of those valuable new planes. The flying pieces of metal struck Sgt. [John M.] Loftus,[8] causing a compound fracture of the left leg. That was our first casualty on this field. It was luck that I was on the spot at the time of the accident. It leaves a good taste in the minds of the fellows to find medical aid available when they need it like that. There are a dozen other places that I could have been at the moment when they started hollering for me.

Being the only medical aid in the group has its disadvantages. He's a good gunner, but he's lost to the Group now. He'll be out of action for several months.

Aug 27 - This is the third night in succession that I have worked rather late trying to get the records in shape for movement. Also made a small raid on medical supply to outfit my new emergency bag.

Aug 28 - Flew down to the Ground Echelon at Ft. Dix today. They were getting ready to move on up to the port of embarkation.[9] The 423rd squadron (ground echelon) is quarantined because of mumps and are going to be left behind. It's too bad they couldn't have waited until they got on the boat before they got the mumps.[10]

Sept 1, 1942 - The 423rd [air echelon] was scheduled to hop off today, but some of their equipment did not arrive and it had to be postponed until tomorrow. Three shipments out of Wright Field were mis-sent. Smells like sabotage to me. Maybe they'll get out soon though. This is ideal weather here and would like to see them get on out.

Last night Major [Watts S.] Humphrey[11] had Major and Mrs. Oliver and me out to dinner. We drove to South Hadley to see Mt. Holyoke College then over to Northampton to see Smith College. It was a lovely drive, low mountains covered by heavy vegetation, looked remarkably like the Ozarks. We had dinner at Wiggins Tavern in Northampton. It was a very rustic sort of place cluttered up with junk from former days, and the meal was simply delicious. It was a real treat. Major Humphrey is a grand person. Saw John Kieran[12] there.

Sept 2 - Well, this was the day of the beginning. At 9:00 a.m. I stood out on the ramp and watched the planes of the 423rd take off and disappear into the north. It was a lovely sight. They, of course, didn't look any different than usual, but the realization that they were heading out over the Atlantic and would be in Scotland in a couple of days gave it an added meaning. My turn is coming up next. Am leaving with Lt. [Ralph J.] Gaston[13] of the 367th, and we are scheduled to take off day after tomorrow morning.

Tonight I started packing, but it is now midnight and I am sitting up putting hot packs on a big boil on Lt. [Joseph N.] Gates' head. He is a co-pilot in the 367th, and I have just 36 hours to get him ready to fly. It seems like old times to be sitting up nursing a patient. I'm not sure that many Army doctors would do this sort of thing, but somebody has got to see that he gets well in time to go, and that means me. (Lt. Gates went down with his ship over the target at Lille, France, Oct. 9, 1942.)

Sept 3 - Tomorrow we are scheduled to pull out. It is raining tonight, but it may be clear tomorrow. It's funny, but so much as I have been looking forward to it, I am not a bit excited about the whole thing. It seems like just an ordinary trip. This is perhaps the most adventurous and dangerous thing that I have ever done, but I am not a bit apprehensive about the outcome. I have scarcely considered the possibility of an unsuccessful journey.

Sept 4 - At 11:45 a.m. we took off into the north, the second ship off the field. I am flying with Lt. Gaston and my position is again in the nose. Lt. Gaston is one of the younger pilots, but he is very good. It is a coincidence that I took my first ride in a B-17 the day he went up for the first time in a B-17 for his first instruction in that ship. Lt. Ryan was the instructor that day. Little did I realize that Sunday back in April in Wendover that it would be Gaston who would fly me across the Atlantic.

We were nearly three hours late on the take-off, some of the ships were not ready. It is raining, but the weather man has assured that it will not be raining near our destination. At this moment it is one hour after take-off and I am beginning to wonder if he knew what he was talking about. There is a ceiling of only 500 or 600 feet and we started out flying at about 500 feet, but after only about 15 minutes in the air we lost our flight leader completely and have been unable to contact him since. We were flying so low trying to stay under the ceiling that we seemed to be awfully close to the tree tops, and I confess that it wasn't too comfortable a feeling sailing along at 155 miles per hour. But we have now gone up to 6,000 feet and no sight of the top. The "soup" is so thick we can barely see the wingtips. Even so I feel safer with a little altitude. We have given up the idea of following the planned course and have headed out to sea directly to Newfoundland. Here's where I'm hoping the navigator is worth his keep because we're sure depending on him now. This calls for total instrument flying too, but Gaston can handle that O.K.

3:30 p.m. At last we have broken out of the soup. The navigator said he knew our position, nevertheless I was gratified to be able to confirm his assertation that we were over New Breton Island, off the northeast tip of Nova Scotia. It has just occurred to me that we are in foreign territory now and I didn't know when we left the U.S. That was three hours of blind flying and everything is exactly as desired, so I'm regaining confidence in this crew and this old battle wagon—and the weatherman, by the way.

4:15 p.m. We have just touched the southwest tip of Newfoundland and made a turn to the east. It's only 200–300 miles overland to Gander Lake, our stop-over point.

5:30 p.m. Broke out of the overcast directly over Gander Lake. We're having to circle the field because a Group of B-24's are taking off (The 93rd Bomb Group).

6:30 p.m. Landed after a full hour of circling. We learn that the 24's are off to England tonight. They say that, weather permitting, we will take off this time tomorrow night. The 423rd Squadron is still here and all of us are to take off together.

Sept 5 - Gander Lake, Newfoundland—This is some place. Nothing here at all except an Army post, partly U.S. and partly Canadian. Newfoundland is one of the roughest most desolate places I have ever seen. The ground is extremely rocky and rough with little vegetation other than fir trees. Lakes are innumerable and they say that they swarm with fish. It was rather cold and windy last night and the steam heated barracks felt awfully good. They say it is 250 miles to the nearest town.

It was amusing to see the fellows buy things at the Post Exchange this morning. We all bought candy by the box and it was really funny when one fellow stepped up and bought a single bar. We all act as if there won't be anything to eat in Britain, but it is certain there won't be much candy. One of the fellows was considerably upset when, after buying a whole case of cigarettes at Westover for $1.30 per carton he discovered he could have bought them here for 75¢. The ships are loaded down with a peculiar assortment of things—cases of cigarettes, cases of candy, cases of liquor and cases of soap.

The Officers' Club here is quite a big affair and an interesting place. Hordes of interesting people pass through there all the time—generals, ambassadors, royalty—in fact everybody who is doing Trans-Atlantic traveling by air at this time. Their photograph album over there looks like a collection of Who's Who.

Sept 6 - Prestwick, Scotland - This is 2,100 miles from where I wrote yesterday's edition, but I have lived a long time in that short period. We took off from Gander Lake at 10:00 p.m. Greenwich Time, but it was dusk at Newfoundland. The ship was awfully heavy because we were carrying 800 gallons gasoline extra, but a short way out, I began to wonder if that would be enough. We were in the soup before we had gone up 200 feet, and we didn't see a thing, not even a star for five whole hours. Guess that now qualifies Gaston as a good instrument pilot. I enjoyed the trip thoroughly, all except about the first two hours. We were so heavy, and it was so difficult to get the weight distributed properly up in the nose, that we just "mushed" along, and it was most difficult to maintain air speed and altitude. We flew at 9,500 feet most of the way and a lot of the time, it was raining in torrents, snowed a little. But the air was fairly smooth. It was long after daylight before I first saw the ocean under me. Maybe that was good, because all night I had scarcely realized that it was many hundred miles to land of any kind. About 6 a.m. we saw two other ships sailing along above the clouds. They were the first visual contact with any of the other planes we had had since take off, with the exception of one who "blinkered" us about midnight. However, we were in radio contact with someone all the time. That was a comfort to know you weren't out over the North Atlantic all alone. There is so much radio equipment on these planes that it is almost impossible to get lost. After daylight the boys loaded all their guns and fired two or three rounds to be sure they were in working order. We had to be ready to meet Jerry if he should have shown up. It would have been an ideal time for him because the last few hundred miles were quite clear. Touched the northern tip of Ireland about 7:15 a.m., must confess it was nice to know that land was near.

The first part of Ireland was very poor, swampy and unpopulated, but over the northeastern section it was perfectly beautiful. We could see why

Control tower and hangar area at Gander Field, Newfoundland. Courtesy of the East Anglia Air War Collection.

they called it the Emerald Isle. Across the channel to Scotland, it clouded up again, and we ran into the roughest weather on the trip, once it threw us all over the ship. Arrived at Prestwick after 8 a.m. and were able to land about 9 a.m., a tired bunch of boys. We had been in the air just a little less than 11 hours. That made the total air time across the Atlantic from Westover about 17 hours. Upon landing, we discovered that one of the planes from the 423rd piloted by Lt. Leahy is long overdue. All the other planes are now in without mishap; except one ran out of gas and had to land down the coast a ways, but [the plane] is here now.

We got here just as they were getting out of church. The R.A.F. boys were being marched back in step with a Scotch bagpipe band. Frankly, I couldn't see how they knew whether or not they were in step.

Sept 7 - Prestwick, Scotland - This must be the British weather they speak of. Clouds are very low and raining at intervals. We were scheduled to pull out of here for our home Aerodrome in England today, but weather prevented. So after eating lunch, we (four of us) seized the opportunity of catching a bus into Glasgow about 30 miles away. It was one of those big 2-decker affairs that looks like it would turn over at every corner. Glasgow is a city of over a million people, but it doesn't look much like an American city of a million would look. Big buildings are conspicuous by their absence. We found the food terrible, but the limitation of 5 shillings for a dinner did prevent an exorbitant price charge we found on some things. The rain was so hard and persistent that we went to a movie we had seen to get out of it. We didn't see anything particularly interesting. Just before we started home we ran into a couple of amiable young women from the W.V.S. [Women's Voluntary Services], who were willing to chat with us for an hour or so. We got back about 11:30 p.m.

Sept 8 - Checked out of Prestwick and took to the air for the last leg of the journey just before noon. Was the weather bad! I thought they must surely be crazy to send us out in such low cloudy weather. That was perhaps the most apprehensive part of the trip. The ceiling was from 400 feet on down. Once we just barely missed a hilltop, but before we had reached our destination again, it was perfectly clear again, so the weather man scored once more. The field was not quite ready at our home station, so we had to land about 30 miles away and ride by truck tonight over to Thurleigh, arriving here about midnight. That finally completes this overseas journey we have looked forward to so long.

*

Hangars and motor pool at Gander Field in Newfoundland. Courtesy of the East Anglia Air War Collection.

Overview of runways at Prestwick, Scotland, located three miles northeast of the town of Ayr on the coast. Courtesy of the East Anglia Air War Collection.

Hangar area at Prestwick, Scotland. Courtesy of the East Anglia Air War Collection.

Operations building at Prestwick, Scotland. Courtesy of the East Anglia Air War Collection.

This sign greeted the 306th air echelon when they touched down at Prestwick, Scotland. Courtesy of the East Anglia Air War Collection.

While Shuller and the air echelon moved across the North Atlantic, the ground echelon, minus the 423rd under quarantine for the mumps, boarded trains at Fort Dix on Sunday, August 30, and departed for the short trip to New York. Later that day the train arrived at the Port of Embarkation and boarded the Queen Elizabeth at 3:45 that afternoon. The next morning, tugs maneuvered the ship from the pier, and the Queen Elizabeth sailed through the harbor, passing the Statue of Liberty and leaving New York behind.

Joe Albertson remembered that "there was 20 something thousand of us on board. We were assigned a deck for 12 hours and a cabin for 12 hours. We were supposed to rotate." The overcrowding was oppressive. Albertson said he "pulled a trick on the group who was supposed to rotate with us in the cabin." When the time came to rotate, the other group arrived at the cabin, but Albertson told them that "we had just got there, and that they couldn't come in. Eventually they just gave up, and we had the cabin for the whole trip."

"You had your [meal] ticket, and you stood in line in the hallway, leading into the dining room. And it was really crowded." Albertson and his buddies went up on deck to buy their snacks, and *"used to buy boxes of Hershey bars to last us for the day. So half the time, we wouldn't go to the dining hall for meals. It was hard to put up with."*[14]

It took the Queen Elizabeth *six days to make the crossing, arriving in Scotland on September 5. The ground echelon boarded trains for the journey to Sharnbrook, not far from Thurleigh. The ground echelon arrived*

Walter H. "Joe" Albertson, a mechanic in the 369th Bomb Squadron and one of the original ground personnel to join the 306th Bomb Group at Wendover, Utah, in 1942. Courtesy of the East Anglia Air War Collection.

at Thurleigh on Sunday, September 6, a week after leaving Ft. Dix. In a few days, the air echelon airplanes began to arrive, and later in the week, on Saturday morning, September 12, the 423rd ground echelon passed through the Thurleigh gates, having sailed across the Atlantic on the Queen Mary. *The 306th Bomb Group was reunited, and preparations for combat operations began in earnest.*

The 306th ground echelon arrived at Sharnbrook Railway Station from Scotland and were hauled to Thurleigh Air Field by truck. Courtesy of the East Anglia Air War Collection.

Major Thurman Shuller in front of the dispensary at Thurleigh, circa early 1943. Courtesy of the Thurman Shuller Family Collection.

*

Sept 9 - This is a new day in a new station. It was good to see all the fellows again from the ground echelon. Was I surprised at the hospital set-up! There is quite a large building, well built, has three wards with 18 beds, fully equipped (except tonsil instruments) for surgery, and last but not least, an elaborate bomb proof gas decontamination setup. It's better than anybody has any right to expect. We are taking over this post lock, stock, and barrel, I understand, so that makes me station surgeon. Boy, how do you like that! If you had told me when I came into the Army less than 14 months ago that I'd be a station surgeon, ever, I'd have thought you crazy. Met Lt. Col. [Arthur L.] Streeter, the Wing Surgeon. Guess I'll be having a lot of questions to be asking him. There is one English Medical Officer here, Squadron Leader Trethowan (our equivalent of Major). He seems like a nice fellow.

Sept 14 - Have been neglecting you, diary, the last few days. Been awfully busy. This job is going to be a hell of a big one. The first two or three nights, I couldn't even sleep for worrying about it, but I'm getting over that now. Reports, reports, reports! I thought we'd get away from a lot of that in the combat zone, but it is even worse. It'll be a month before we get all that straight. Then I have been ordered to submit a detailed plan of defense and medical aid to be put into effect during an air raid, bombing or gas attack. My biggest headache is in finding something for all my enlisted men to do. The whole post is being centralized and acting as a Group organization, so as Group Surgeon, I am practically Medical Detachment Commander, a job I dislike very much. Lt. [Edmund F.] Longworth came in a couple of days ago, and already he is a thorn in the side of everybody. The climaxing thing was when he booted a Second Lieutenant out of his room by "pulling his rank on him." I fear action is going to have to be taken.

Sanitation certainly is a headache. McKim has been placed in charge of that, and he is trying hard but getting nowhere much. There are only open bucket latrines, and the emptying of the buckets is a source of much trouble. It's a tough nut to crack here in England where their requirements along those lines have never been as great as ours. Housing is another trouble. I slept in a different area every night for the first 5 nights, but have now moved into the hospital. It's plenty comfortable there. The squadron officers wanted to move in too, but their place rightly is with the squadrons.

Sept 15 - One of the pilots broke his leg in a jeep accident last night, and I took him into Oxford today, about 65 miles from Thurleigh. It was fun getting there. The English have done a marvelous job of removing all road signs, so it was quite a task maneuvering over these crooked and crossed roads without losing one's way, but we had some good maps, fortunately. I didn't see any of the University. That's strange isn't it? If I had been touring England, I certainly would have wanted a look at Oxford University, yet when I went there on business, I just went there and came back - that is, most of the way. About 3 miles short of camp, we ran out of gas. We should have had enough, but we got lost on the way back and went a little over our quota. One cannot buy from civilian stations without coupons. The walk did us good. At Oxford, I ran into [Hartwig M.] Adler, a boy I interned with at New Orleans. I suppose in Madagascar, there would be somebody I knew.

Sept 17 - More bicycles came in today, and I was issued mine. I am not a very graceful rider, but it will be a lot of help if it doesn't buck me off.

Those poor boys who live at the far end of the post really have two or three miles to go to their planes. Casualty rates will now be going up. Threw one of my boys in the jug last night for leaving duty without pass and breaking confinement to post.

Sept 21 - Took some supplies over to Cardington[15] to have them sterilized today. Flight Commander Smith was a very likable person. He is an old time R A.F. doctor, and he was willing to give me a few helpful pointers. I'm still trying to work out how I'm going to run a successful prophylactic station downtown.

Sept 22 - Went up to Thrapston today to medical supply. I was agreeably surprised just how much stuff was available up there. These winding, crossed roads are most confusing to me. Don't know if I'll ever learn how to get around here. There are innumerable little villages along the way, all with houses crowded right up against each other, not scattered like ours. This is truly a foreign country.

Ran into Captains Henry, Brazelton, and Gans, all in my class at Randolph, while up at Thrapston. About all my class is now in England.

Sept 24 - The boys flew a perfectly beautiful formation today. The improvement in their formation flying since coming here has been amazing. There were 24 ships in the formation this morning and there was scarcely a flaw. It is the first time I have ever seen a complete squadron of six planes come in in one straight line one behind the other. One of the ball turret gunners had a hair-raising escape this morning. The trap door flew open and he fell out through the hatch, catching only with his feet. He pulled back in only after several minutes of effort. Some of these days they are going to take off on a mission, and we'll learn later that they had been into combat. Things look to me like they are about ready. I got the first wind yesterday that our position here may not be permanent for the winter. The possibilities of movement toward North Africa don't look too unfavorable.

Sept 27 - This was one of the nicest Sundays that I have spent in a long time. I did little or nothing at the hospital, put everything off till tomorrow for a change. This morning I went to church, the first time in quite long time. I went last Sunday, but the time was moved up on me and I missed it. It was a nice service, and the Chaplain was a little better than usual.

This afternoon Capt. Manning and I rode our bicycles over the Sharnbrook and beyond, it was such lovely afternoon. We were just wandering about over the countryside when we ran into an old English estate be-

Bar area in the Officer's Key Club in Bedford. Courtesy of the Steve Snyder Collection.

longing to Lord somebody whose name I can't remember. We were wandering about on his grounds when ran into the big boy himself. He was very gracious and most willing to show us about the place. It was one of those huge affairs built in 1750 or thereabouts with extensive landscaping, stables, dog kennels, and everything that goes with such an estate. It must really take a rich man to keep a thing like that going. I was particularly interested in the row of apple trees with the branches trained to run along a wire fence such as we do our grapes. We came back by the Falcon Inn and had tea. It also is a historic place of some centuries old. Time is really old in this country. We must have cycled at least 10 or 12 miles this afternoon, but I'm surprised that I do not feel particularly tired. Cycling on Sunday afternoon in England and having tea (and enjoying it). If you had told me two years: ago I'd do that today, I'd have snapped, "You're nuts."

Oct 1, 1942 - Last night I just felt like taking off, so Munal and I went into Bedford. It was my first night in town during the three weeks I have been here, and that's a long time. We went to a very good movie then went to the Key Club, an officers' bar in town.[16] It's so awfully difficult to get in and out of town that it is hardly worth the trouble, but last night, we went with Major [James W.] Wilson. When we get our ambulances, we will operate one for our men.

A couple of days ago, I got my very first mail, a letter from Dad. It was certainly welcome, more than a month without word from home. It took ten days.

Today I went up for the first time since coming here. We were going to do a bombing mission (practice) at 25,000 feet, but weather interfered before we got up very far. We had better get in our flying time before operational missions begin. As of yesterday, headquarters has been notified that we are ready for combat duty. (This ride was with Capt. [John W.] Olson)

Today we heard rumor, which was fairly reliable, that all the Bombardment Groups are going to be sent out of England to Africa, except ours. If that is true, then I guess we are settled here for the duration. That is not good, if true.

Oct 2 - We had another disaster today. They sent up a 24 plane practice bombing mission, and one of the planes crashed, cause undetermined as yet. It was piloted by Lt. [William W.] Ely, Lt. [Edwin F.] Patterson as co-pilot. Don't know yet who the others in the crew were. It is known that the tail gunner and the engineer parachuted safely. Capt. Manning has gone out with the investigating party. That is a real tragedy. It wouldn't have been quite so bad had those boys lost their lives for some good reason, but this was just a routine training flight. Ely and Patterson were really swell fellows too. That makes four ships we have lost since leaving Westover Field, and we haven't seen combat yet. The first was Lt. [John T.] Leahy and crew who went down into the Atlantic soon after leaving Newfoundland. The second was Capt. [William C.] Melton's plane whose motors gave way on him and crashed into the Atlantic just off the coast of Ireland on the way over, all the crew were safe after some of them swam for a while. The third ship to go out was Lt. Gaston's ship, the one I rode over in. It was up at 25,000 feet about a week ago when a supercharger[17] blew up and literally riddled the plane. Gaston landed it safely, but the plane is being dismantled for the parts. This one today is the fourth. We left Westover Field one month ago with 35 planes. Now we have 31.

The medical crew had a little work-out today with some simulated casualties. We got the ambulances out there O.K., but we're going to have to work out some sort of system better than we have.

Oct 3 - The investigating committee is back, and the facts of the crash are known. They had a new waist gunner who apparently was unfamiliar with oxygen. He had some sort of difficulty with it and became unconscious. The ball turret gunner noticed him on the floor and came up to revive him. Lt. Ely put the plane into a dive (from 25,000 feet) which apparently was too steep and the plane disintegrated on the pull-out. The tail broke off and the tail gunner found himself floating around in the air in a tail without a plane. He finally kicked himself out in time just to break his fall and landed about 1 yard from the tail. The ball turret gunner was sucked out through the broken belly, receiving a slight scalp laceration and abrasion on the ankle. The others were unable to get out and were instantly killed, six of them. This is a terrible thing. Six men killed and a valuable plane lost because of one green kid.

Oct 5 – Paid a visit to Chelveston today (301st Bomb Sq.). Had nice chat with Major Speaker, the Gp. Surg., Major Hall, the Service Gp. Surgeon, and Major Ferris the 12th Bomber Command Surgeon. I found them intently checking "field" equipment for shortages. This fact more or less confirms the rumor noted on Oct 1.

The pilots really put us medics on the spot today. The crash three days ago has stimulated an intensive study of oxygen, and it is demanded of us how long at 25,000 feet can a man live after he has become unconscious. I wish I could give them a satisfactory answer.

Oct 6 - Have just gotten back from a Variety show featuring Bebe Daniels. It was a top notch show full of professional talent. Bebe Daniels has been in the show business for at least 20 years, but she still is a beautiful woman and looks no more than 30. She is quite a fine singer and is a wonderful personality on the stage.

I was witness in court today for the first time in my life, a court martial. I was the accuser in this case. One of my medical men was placed on restriction for leaving his post, and then he broke the restriction. He was found guilty and given a light sentence.

Tonight after the show, I opened a peritonsillar abscess [in the throat near one of the tonsils] on one of the officers and successfully evacuated a great deal of pus. That's more real surgery than I have done in quite some time. I enjoyed getting to do even that little bit. The squadron surgeons take care of most of the jobs around here. The records are my chief responsibility.

Oct 9 - This is the day - the one we have been waiting for. It was in April that three of us doctors, Manning, Munal and I, became members of the 306th Bomb Gp, saw it spring from its very beginning, grew up with it, have lived and flown with these boys, and today, exactly six months later, they made their first combat mission. They have been just "itching" to get going for weeks on end, and last night few of them slept a wink. I have been sick for two days with the flu and temperature to 102° yesterday, but this morning I would have gone out to see these boys come in, if it gives me pneumonia and lays me up for a month. We just got wind of this raid last night when everybody was restricted to the post. They began taking off soon after daybreak and were headed toward the target by 8:30. They had been told the first would be an easy mission, but as it turned out they were a part of a force of 108 bombers raiding a big railroad and steel works center at Lille, 60 miles inside occupied France. Our Group furnished 24 bombers.

Tonight they are a weary bunch, some of them stunned a little, but most of them plenty game. In their baptism of fire, they took a pretty bad beating. They hit and apparently devastated the target, but once across the target they encountered Goering's pet yellow-nosed FW-190's in droves. Almost all our planes came back looking like sieves. The greatest tragedy of the raid was the loss of Capt. Olson's ship. Remember I went up with him only 8 days ago. They were directly over the target when for some reason or other, he got just a little out of formation and was pounced upon by a whole flock of German fighters. One of the motors began to smoke so that drew them like flies in for the kill. He went down with two motors aflame and fighters on him all the way. It is thought that one or two of them may have bailed out, but the war may be over before we know who or how many. The other officers aboard were Lt. [Joseph N.] Gates, [KIA] co-pilot; Lt. [William J.] Gise,[18] navigator; and Lt. [Albert W.] LaChasse,[19] bombardier. It's hard to realize that "Olie" should be the first to go down in enemy territory. He was one of the very finest, most level-headed pilots we had. He was a rugged, unpolished sort of individual, but a grand fellow and a grand pilot. But proficiency as a pilot does not guarantee against a lucky hit by the enemy.

As they came back at eleven this morning, I stood in the watch-tower and acted as ambulance dispatcher. Only one ship came in and signaled that casualties were aboard. Lt. [Robert W.] Seelos' waist gunner got a 30 calibre bullet through the chest and is here in the dispensary in pretty bad condition. It was a dramatic thing to see those planes come in and land so terribly shot up. Lt. Seelos had one motor out and the propeller feathered. Major Wilson had one motor out and as he landed, the propeller flew off halfway down the runway. He had taken a full burst of 20 mm. cannon right in the belly of the ship and not a soul was hurt. Lt. [William H.]

Warner landed on one tire that was shot up, also had a huge tear in his gas tank, but the thing didn't catch fire. Lt. [John R.] Barnett landed without a tail wheel. Others landed with tails, wings, fuselage and motors shot up. Any one of these ships landing in ordinary circumstances would have been a show, but today was a circus. The amazing thing is that only the one man received bullet wounds. The only other casualty (except Capt. Olson and crew) is a case of frozen hands received when the man foolishly removed his gloves to fix his oxygen mask and was unable to get them back on.

It's too bad the fellows ran into such a tough mission on their first, but they made a remarkable showing. They shot down a number of German fighters, but the number is not yet known. Tonight every little group of fellows has fought that battle over and over again. Last night they didn't sleep because of the anticipation, tonight they'll fight it over till morning. Man must be nothing but a fool to face a hell of fire like that, but that's what we came here for and we'll have to see it through. Frankly I'm glad my job doesn't call for combat duty, but if it did, I'm sure I could face it just as well as the next one.

Oct 10 - The whole attention of the hospital has been focused on S/Sgt. [Arthur E.] Chapman, the lad who got the bullet through his chest. He was awfully bad yesterday afternoon, we filled him full of serum, and last night we called in a blood transfusion unit to give him blood. It is gratifying to see how these boys of ours here take hold in a real emergency and work. It is the first time they have seen a seriously injured patient. Three or four of them have practically fought for the opportunity to sit right by his side and watch his every movement. They are a pretty fine bunch, most of them. Late this afternoon, we had a cargo plane come in to evacuate him to the General Hospital at Oxford. That was quite a super-dramatic stunt, the first time it has been done in the English theatre of operations. Capt. Munal and three enlisted men took him down there, along with three other patients.

Oct 11 - A nice peaceful Sunday. Munal is back from Oxford, and says the patient is fine and is being made quite a fuss over because he is one of their first real battle casualties, the first to be flown there in a plane and also because he was injured in a fortress. It's a strange thing that they haven't had some fortress casualties there before, but it seems that battle injuries in the flying fortress have in the past been either fatal or relatively minor. Inside I am proud of our bunch here for the treatment that boy was given. I feel that, though we have nothing fancy to work with, he got as good treatment all the way round as he could have had anywhere. Some of the other fellows think so too. Munal ran into a big dance at the hospital at Oxford and had a whale of a big time last night. He was quite the hero for having brought in the "flying fortress casualty."

Today Col. Overacker said that our Group on its first raid made the journey into French territory farther than has ever before been done by Americans, that of the 108 planes in the raid, we got more planes over the target and more bombs on the target, and that all the English fighters somehow missed our Group and went in with other Groups, leaving us absolutely without fighter protection for 60 miles return journey from the target. Nevertheless besides hitting the target squarely, our Group definitely destroyed ten of Goering's pet fighter planes, perhaps four or five more, to our loss of one ship and crew, and with only the two casualties previously mentioned. Our Group did itself proud on its first mission.

Oct 20 - Diary, I have almost forgotten you. Quite a lot has happened since my last note. The gritty lad with the chest injury we sent to Oxford died five days after he got there. Yesterday morning we admitted Sgt. [Edward J.] Mulvihill with an almost identical injury, a bullet through his chest, but this one self-inflicted and intentional. The boy is sorry he tried to kill himself now, but he doesn't have a very good chance of pulling through. I have just finished giving him a blood transfusion tonight, and he might be a little better tomorrow.

A raid was scheduled today but was postponed on account of weather. We'll be having a lot of that, I guess. We had plenty of medical rank around here today. Lt. Col. Streeter was here from Wing, and Col. [Edward J.] Tracy was here from Bomber Command. Col. Tracy seems particularly nice.

I received orders yesterday to report to Bomber Command this weekend for a two-week schooling for Flight Surgeons. I'm not particularly excited about it, but maybe it won't be too bad.

We had two promotions in the medical department over the week-end. McKim and [Rex D.] Stutznegger both became Captains. That makes us all Captains together. Lt. Longworth was transferred out of the outfit last week. It was most sudden. For a long time, I have been rather wanting to get rid of him simply because he did not fit in with the rest of the medical crew, nor with the personnel of his squadron, but he was definitely improving in his general attitude I think. The thing that instigated the suddenness of the transfer was suspicion along subversive lines, which I think are unfounded. But nevertheless, I'm glad he's gone, simply for sake of harmony here, and also because I'd like to see him get a chance to pull himself out of his hole.

Oct 21 - The boys went out on a mission this morning and were gone 4 ½ hours, but after they got over the channel the clouds were so thick they couldn't see anything, so they came back and dropped their bombs in the Wash. The Battle of the Wash is getting to be quite a joke. It is a shame. About $400,000 worth of bombs dumped into the sea. Poor taxpayer! Bomber Command sure made a mess out of this weather forecast today. The fellows were awfully disappointed that they couldn't complete their mission. The target today was to have been the submarine base at Lorient.

My day was made unhappy by a visit from the inspector corps of the Eighth Air Force. There has been more medical rank around here the last couple of days than I have ever seen. Personally I could get along just as well without them.

Oct 22 – Have just returned from Oxford. Took Sgt. Mulvihill, the chest injury case to the General hospital in a B-17, Lt. [Earl C.] Tunnell as pilot. A fortress is not the best ambulance plane in the world, but it was quick and more comfortable than a car. This is the second case within 10 days that we have evacuated by air. It is the second time I have been to Oxford and haven't had a chance to see the city yet.

Oct 24 - Here I am at High Wycombe for that two weeks of school. It is Saturday night and no time to be staying in when one has no work to do, but I know no place to go and didn't get here in time to go with anybody who did. I left Bedford at eleven this morning and got here about three. Came through London, but didn't stop. If I had known then that classes do not start until Monday, I'd have stayed there tonight. I haven't seen any of the other "students" yet. Capt. Jackson, one of the chief moguls of the school was at Randolph when I was. Col. Harry Armstrong, the Commandant, was an instructor there at that time. We live and go to school in a big house up on the hill over High Wycombe. Am sleeping next to Capt. Smith, the instructor of physiology. He seems nice.

Yesterday and this morning before I left, there was an undercurrent rumor that we would be moving out of the English theatre before long. The failure of the last mission, I suppose, is responsible. It really does look foolish to keep a bunch of big planes like this around all winter when so much depends on good weather. There are other places where they would be more useful it seems. The morale is getting rapidly bad. There is nothing quite so bad as starting a mission you can't finish. There is an indefinite rumor of an organization of pilots to do hedge-hopping over enemy territory individually. Too many of the boys are interested in volunteering for such an organization. I hope to find the morale better when I get back.

Oct 26 - This completes the first day of school here. The first day was rather dull and unimaginative, but there is promise that the next days will be better. There are several fellows here that I know and am getting acquainted with more. There are more colonels than a few around here. We may stay here only a week, instead of two as planned.

Oct 29 - This completes the fourth day of school and it will be officially over Saturday noon. Today we had a very good lecture by Col. Brown, plastic surgeon from St. Louis. Yesterday Col. Middleton, former Dean and Prof of Med. at Wisconsin, gave an extremely interesting lecture along medical lines. Tuesday the highlight was a 2-hour lecture by an Eagle Squadron Spitfire pilot, Capt. [Harold H.] Strickland. It was very informative to have a pilot of over a year's experience lecture about his experiences and the sensation a fighter pilot has over enemy territory.

This certainly isn't a very lively place. A headquarters station is a far cry from the vim and vigor of combat unit station. A bunch of young flying second lieutenants can find plenty to do where there was no life at all. I sort of miss it already. Saw a show night before last, visited a pub last night. Sgt [Morris] Cohen of the 369th Sq. was through here today collecting 15 days per diem for an unknown [purpose] that he and Capt. McKim are ordered on [TDY or temporary duty allowed the two men extra pay per day for expenses incurred]. I don't like the tenor of this thing. They are mysteriously secret orders to a "two weeks" duty to a south England town. We're all curious. It could be to accompany a task force of some kind, you know. There is also the possibility we might not get him back. I'll just not think about that now.

Nov 1, 1942 - Early morning (10:30 a.m.) - London - School was over at noon yesterday, and we left as soon as possible after lunch. Capt. Ross and I were lucky to catch a command car coming into London. It was better than riding one of those crowded English trains. I don't think I'll ever like those trains with the multiple compartments and a side door to each compartment.

We got in too late to do any sight-seeing. Had tea at the Piccadilly, then to a most excellent play, Noel Coward's "Blythe Spirit." It was a very able cast, some say that it is better than the New York version. We then tried to find a place to eat, but it was very difficult in the black-out. We wandered into the Regent Palace and finally wound up in the Cabaret Club. They really took us for a rooking last night. They charged us an exorbitant price for admission, overcharged for the things we ordered, made a 10 shilling ($2.00) error in addition of the itemized bill, and to top it all off, the waiter griped because our liberal tip wasn't more liberal. They say we live and learn. Well, we learned fast last night. My London visits hereafter are going to be confined mainly to sightseeing. The Londoners are taking Americans for a bunch of saps (which we probably are), but as far as I am concerned it is going to become less evident.

Sunday night—back at my home station. Was disappointed that I didn't get to take any pictures in London, it rained all the time. We took a taxi and made a tour of the bombed east London. It is one more pitiful sight. The Londoners have had to take a lot. The most impressive sight I saw was St. Paul's Cathedral. We were shown through the crypts and saw a lot of interesting things. A lot of famous people are buried there, including the Duke of Wellington. The most fascinating thing as far as I was concerned was his funeral carriage, a huge affair made of cast iron from old cannons that he captured in his battles. We later went to a movie to see "In This We Serve," a most gripping dramatic movie of a British destroyer. It was really good. Got home about ten tonight. Everything seems to have run along very smoothly. Even the sanitary situation at the mess has improved.

Nov 4 - We had another raid scheduled for today, but it was again postponed on account of weather. Was to have been Lille again to finish the job that didn't turn out so well on the last mission there. Sorry the boys didn't get to carry it out. Their morale is getting bad because so many missions have been cancelled.

I am becoming greatly alarmed over the venereal rate in our command during the last few days. It is exceedingly high among the combat crews, the rate being at the present time 183 per 1000 per airman as compared to the usual rate of 20–30. The thing came to a head this afternoon when Lt. Warner, one of the very finest and most conscientious pilots in the group showed up with the gonorrhea today. It just makes me sick. Something is going to have to be done, and done quick. As in the last war, we are beginning to run more casualties due to venereal disease than due to enemy action.

Nov 6 - The gonorrhea cases are still pouring in, nine in the last 2 weeks. There was an officer who came in yesterday who is 38 years old, married with children, and has taught school all his life. How awfully true is the old saying, "There's no fool like an old fool." We started an education campaign again today. It's a sorry situation when fellows that old and with that much experience need educating along such lines. Colonel Overacker was in on all those lectures today, and I think the fellows were finally impressed by the figures we quoted them. I do hope it does some good. A certain amount of this is expected among the younger fellows, but it is the first time I have ever seen it get out of hand. I am just sick over it. As of today, we have 12 under active treatment.

*

From the beginning of Shuller's service at Las Vegas and during his work under Major Holt, he learned much about the negative impact of venereal disease on military operations and the difficulty doing anything to decrease rates. Holt's survey of conditions in the surrounding area, where prostitution was legal and public houses were available to soldiers from Las Vegas Field, illustrated the difficulty of the problem facing the army medical establishment on base. Thurleigh and the wartime communities around the base and in other places like London brought an escalating VD rate that threatened combat operations at every level. Group Surgeon Shuller was determined to do something about it. He embarked on an aggressive education program that had the full backing of the group commander, and he did much more.

Medic Sgt. Bill Houlihan remembered that Dr. Shuller "arranged very early to get us into town [Bedford], by having an ambulance go into town every night at 6:00 o'clock" and the medics would park "down by the theater, down by the river, and we set up a prophylactic station." The town officials did not like having the ambulance there, visible to everyone in the community, revealing the significant problem of prostitution. It was a problem that the town wanted to keep in the background and pretend it did not exist. Houlihan explained that Shuller "was an innovator." Over time, Shuller's programs reduced the VD rates and brought them under control.[20]

*

Nov 7 - The Group went on a raid today to the submarine base at Brest. But it was a little cloudy over the target and a couple of the squadrons did not drop any bombs. The other two squadrons think they hit somewhere in the "neighborhood" of the target. All the planes came back safely. One blew a tire on landing, one had a feathered motor, and only one or two had any gunfire holes in them. Lt. [Clay E.] Isbell had a wing shot up pretty bad by 20 mm. cannon. But this time they met very little opposition. Lt. Pollock remarked, "It was the sorriest excuse for a raid he ever saw. There was no opposition at all." It is a blood-thirsty bunch we have. Most of them really would prefer to run into a few fighters. We'll know in two or three days if they hit the target when the pictures come through. Two other groups are in on this raid. It is likely that there will be another tomorrow.

Nov 8 - Another big raid today, again on the steel and railroad works at Lille. The bombardiers say they really hit the target this time. Twenty ships took off, but only fourteen got across the channel. The radio report tonight went, "A force of American fortresses accompanied by RAF spit-fires bombed Lille today. It is reported that great damage was done. One bomber and six fighters are missing." One bomber missing! That sounds so impersonal. But to us, that means Captain [Richard D.] Adams. There are few pilots in the group that I am closer to than Adams. He is one of the older pilots, joined us very soon after I joined the group, and he has always been friendly with me. It started perhaps when he discovered that Ell [Shuller's brother, Elbert Shuller] had delivered his sister's baby, and she thought he was about the finest thing going. Adams is from Tulsa. I have flown with him when he was checking out younger pilots and humored him along with his various little neurasthenic complaints. With him went his crew including Sgt. [James T.] McCloy, a lad from McGee, Arkansas, an awfully friendly kid whom I have always liked. They were last seen in a spin with an engine afire, and nobody saw whether anybody got out or not. This is the kind of war we are fighting. We send them out and then sit with our fingers in our mouths, wondering who will fail to come back. Thus far it has been hard on our Captains.

The 369th took a terrible beating. They turned around and made a second run on the target. They plastered the target but met unmerciful resistance from the German fighters. Lt. Riordan did a superhuman job of bringing back a hopelessly crippled ship and landing it without a bounce in a strong cross wind. His tail gunner, Sgt. [John T.] DeJohn was badly injured in the left arm and leg by a 20 mm cannon burst right in the tail. A huge hole was blown in the belly, the left wing was badly torn, the right horizontal stabilizer was torn, and the controls were practically jammed. We flew DeJohn down to Oxford about an hour later. We have two other lesser casualties, one with frozen cheeks, and one with a perforating wound above the left ankle from flak, probably. That was Sgt. [Harry N.] Meyers from Lt. [Charles W.] Cranmer's ship. He is all excited and is ready to go out again. He shot down a F.W.190, saw it burst in mid-air, and got a real thrill out of it. These gunners are real men, almost all of them. We certainly owe them a lot of credit. The other two squadrons who went out were not severely attacked. The 369th is credited with 9 confirmed fighters destroyed and 14 probables.

Another raid is scheduled for tomorrow. Today seemed less like a Sunday than any day I have ever seen in my life.

Nov 9 - The Group caught Hell today. They were sent to St. Nazaire, on the southwest coast of France to bomb a submarine pen. They did something fancy this time - an experiment. And the experiment ended up at the expense of the lives of a lot of our fellows. Bomber command sent them in over the target at only 8,000 feet, and they were just simply smothered with flak. It was a long mission, and they landed at Portreath [Land's End], on the very southwest tip of England on the way back. A plane full of us went down to meet them today, getting here about an hour before the planes returned. Sgt. [Francis J.] Tropeano and I represented the medical department. We didn't know just what the situation would be as to medical care, but we found it very good.

*

Lt. Col. Delmar E. Wilson, the group's deputy group commander and later a major general, declared that the St. Nazaire mission "has to be one of the worst planned bomber attacks in [the] 8th Air Force European operations." Wilson wrote after the war that problems with the Eighth Air Force mission planning rested with the fact that "the operations staff was totally unprepared to direct a bomber offensive. This includes [General Ira] Eaker." Eaker's staff included successful businessmen and others who were fighter pilots and had no bomber experience. "As a result, operations orders that initially came out of 8th Bomber Command were flawed in many respects." The consequences were devastating to the inexperienced crews flying their first missions in combat. "Bomb runs in strong cross winds, into the sun, and IPs [point at beginning of the bomb run] that were hard to identify. The distance between IP and target was far too short for inexperienced bombardiers to synchronize and aim properly." Wilson concluded that "a shop clerk could have properly written ops orders as well as the initial orders coming out of 8th Bomber Command."[21]

The St. Nazaire raid on November 9 proved to be a disaster for the group, so Wilson gathered support personnel and prepared to go to Land's End to meet the returning planes. He "flew Dr. Shuller, intelligence interrogators and maintenance personnel to Land's End to meet the 306th returning from St. Nazaire." Wilson reported on what he saw when the aircraft landed: "We had several airplanes crack up landing on a 3,500-foot runway. Some without brakes, [and] some with dead aboard." The air crews "were highly emotional and under great stress. One drink and they seemed to go berserk." The officer's club on the RAF base "probably had few glasses left since hundreds were used to toast those left behind in the target area." Wilson wrote that the debacle at St. Nazaire and the ensuing spectacle at Land's End convinced him "that this had to be Chip's Waterloo." His premonition proved correct. Two months later, Overacker was relieved.[22]

٭

They got back at 5:00 p.m. [November 9th], after 7 hours in the air. They had been whipped to a frazzle. Three ships did not return. Lt. [Loyal M.] Felts was hit just before he reached the target, the whole nose was blown off. Three or four chutes were seen to open before the plane crashed to the ground. Lt. [James M.] Stewart and Lt. [John R.] Barnett each were set afire and fell into the sea just after crossing the target. Some of them bailed out but not nearly all of them. Others were badly shot up. Major [Harry J.] Holt over-ran the runway on landing and went over a high dirt ledge and crashed onto the field on the other side, throwing Lt. [William L.] Eubank out right through the plastic nose onto the ground, but he was scarcely scratched. The bombardier, Lt. [William P.] Erickson, was already dead from a flak wound in the neck just as he was approaching the target. There were no other major casualties.

The boys were much more tired and harried than they had ever been before. All of them were just literally scared to death and admitted it. The anti-aircraft fire was much more severe than they could imagine. They don't fear fighter planes so much because they have a way of fighting back. But there is no possible way of fighting flak. One just has to wade right through and hope for the best. It seems that actually not one expected to get out of there alive, once he was in. They are sure they destroyed their target, but four planes and three crews is a terrible price to pay for it. It showed up in their reactions tonight. They got started drinking and singing and before 10 o'clock, they were almost all uproariously drunk. They overdid the thing and almost wrecked the Officers' Club, but I'm not sure they didn't do the right thing. It got them over those first few hours after returning without so many of their fellows. I sincerely hope they'll never be called on to face an ordeal like that again.

Nov 10 – We arrived at our home station about noon today. All of them came in safely, in spite of the very bad fog. Two planes were left at Portreath for repair before return and the one that crashed makes three. Everybody is tired and glad to be home.

My promotion came through today, and I will henceforth be known as Major Shuller. Gosh! That's quite a title. I have been recommended for it for a long time. I'm certainly not a big enough man to be a Major. However, I have been holding down a Major's job for four months. It was just luck on my part that I happened to be in the right spot when the vacancy occurred, and it certainly is no mark of brilliance on my part. This will make the folks happy though. There is one thing that I am very proud of and that is that both my promotions came without having asked for either of them or pulling strings from anybody in any way. That makes me feel good, especially when I think just how disgusting some fellows are about their wire pulling for promotions. I hope I can do everything that can be expected of a Major. I'll write Mother and Dad about it in a day or two.

Nov 11 - This is Armistice Day, but who would know it. Incidentally, it is Mother's birthday. This is the first time in some time I haven't sent a remembrance of some kind.

Today I took some more patients to the hospital at Oxford. For the first time, we experienced real English fog almost all the way there, and all the way back. I've heard of fog so thick one could cut it with a knife, but actually this was so thick you could see it scatter when the car ahead went through it. It was dark before we got back. I hope we don't have to do that anymore. Corp. [Louis W.] Brookins did an exceptional job of finding our way back. Yesterday we had difficulty landing by plane because of the fog. I don't like it.

The most extraordinary thing happened today. I was promoted yesterday by the Commanding General of the European Theatre of Operations. Today I receive notice of promotion from Washington dated Sept. 21. So I have been a Major for 6 weeks and didn't know it.

Nov 13 - The king and three generals visited the post today but I didn't see them. There wasn't much fanfare. They visited the enlisted men's mess and one of the sites.

Nov 16 - The boys just got back off another raid this morning. They went out a couple of days ago to bomb the submarine base at LaPallice, France but there was an overcast so they blasted St. Nazaire again. They had no difficulties this time and apparently they hit the target again. They landed at David Stow Moor, on the south coast and spent a miserable couple of days there before the weather cleared for them to get home.

Lt. Col. Streeter called us up to wing headquarters for a surgeons' meeting today. The main subject of the meeting today was to tell us that General Longfellow desired that officers "not have venereal disease." In other words he wants them sort of treated on the sly and diagnosed something else so as not to be a reflection upon their reputation and not stop any allotments they may have made. Of course, I will have to follow their instructions, but I did not like it. It is showing a partiality to officers that is not given enlisted men. Officers are declared by Congress to be gentlemen, and they should be expected to conduct themselves as such. We have had six officers with gonorrhea thus far and not one of them thinks any less of me for not particularly trying to keep it quiet, but on the other hand considers himself a sort of lesson to the other fellows. Every single one thus far has volunteered that it was all due to his own carelessness, and he blames nobody but himself. I think the "big-dogs" are barking up the wrong tree when they adapt the "ostrich" attitude to it. The rate continues to increase.

Nov 17 - They did another raid today. Hit St. Nazaire for the third time in succession. All the ships got back to England, but Capt. [Robert] Williams, 423rd just did make it to the coast with three badly injured men aboard. One, T/Sgt. [Kenneth R.] Aulenbach, top turret gunner died soon after reaching the hospital. One of the others is critically ill. They are down at Exeter on the south coast. We'll have to go down there tomorrow to see about it. With those injured and one more ship washed out, it is really an expensive raid. The Group has now been given three brand new ships. We're going to need a lot more.

This war game is beginning to get very nerve-racking on everybody. It is beginning to show up in a number of the fellows. One can't just keep on going over and staring death in the face without getting suddenly a little older or something. I even go through a little anxiety myself as these boys are coming in. Today I was at my usual station in the watch tower watching the planes return and watching the names being checked off the board as they landed. We went through some anxious minutes for a while when all the ships were accounted for except those of Lt. [John M.] Regan and Capt. [John B.] Brady. My heart was in my throat particularly for Capt. Brady, not that he is such a close friend of mine, but I have always admired his tall, slender, youthful handsomeness. He is a perfect gentleman in every sense of the word, a real fellow, a wonderful character, intelligent, and a grand pilot. He is more my idea of a grown-up boy scout, a perfect example of the finest of American young manhood. It was a great feeling of relief to see Brady finally come in and to learn that Regan was down somewhere else in England. We go over this sort of thing again and again. I have Brady in the hospital tonight, simply to see that he gets a good night's sleep for his mission tomorrow. He showed a few signs of weakening under the strain this afternoon.

Maj. General [Ira] Eaker is here tonight to present medals. This is the first presentation of medals that our men have had. A decoration is awfully little reward for the things some of these fellows are doing though.

Nov 19 - A nice USO show here tonight by Kay Francis, Martha Raye, Carole Landis, and Mitzi Mayfair. They came over to the club afterwards. I liked Martha best.[23]

The boys went out on another raid on LaPallice yesterday. They took a terrible beating again. Gaston, the boy I rode across with is "missing in action." He was forced down somewhere near France, it is reported, and is probably a Prisoner of War. At least I hope he made a landing safely. He had just gotten his new ship, and it was her maiden flight. Lt. [Kenneth H.] Jones, his bombardier, was just cleared for flying that morning after being grounded for several days. (Jones was killed. The others are safe.)

The heaviest blow to the whole group was that Lt. [Charles G.] Grimes, a 368th navigator, was killed by flak. The other fellows practically worshiped him, and his death is having a tremendous effect on the group. He was older than most of them and was a wonderful navigator. Lt. [John R.] King and Lt. [Robert] Dresp, co-pilots were also injured. All the fellows are beginning to feel now that they don't have long to live. I hate to see them getting into this frame of mind, but there is nothing else to be expected. Our losses have been terrific thus far.

This raid apparently was a failure, too, as far as hitting the target was concerned. If only they had bombed the target successfully, the cost might not have seemed so great. But apparently the lead navigator got off his course a little and took them right over the excellent gun installation at St. Nazaire by mistake. It was just messed up in general. We'll know more about it when all the fellows get back. All the planes landed in south England last night, and only one came back today on account of weather.

Nov 20 - The boys are still grieving over Grimes. I hate to see some of them taking it so hard. At the moment they are looking upon the group navigator as practically a murderer. On the other hand some of the boys are beginning to get mad at the Germans now. If we worked up a little fighting enthusiasm, maybe we'd do better. However, I'm afraid some of the fellows are beginning to break. We'll be running into all sorts of complaints and ailments in order to stay on the ground, I'm afraid. It is most interesting to observe their reactions at this time and at the same time feel a sort of heart pain every time one thinks about it. All the fellows now will frankly admit that they are just scared stiff every time they go up. They can't eat nor sleep the night before. This terrible tension is never relieved until after they have gone over the target and are out of enemy territory on the way back. Yet they go back again and again. They are a grand bunch.

Nov 22 - The mission today was a failure. They took off with 2,000 lb bombs for the submarine base at Lorient, but there was a solid overcast over the target and they came home with their bombs. They came home all in one piece this time, but they met no opposition. The greatest opposition today was the ground fog on landing. They could scarcely see the field and had to be "talked in" by the control tower. They all made it safe though.

Nov 23 - Today another raid on St. Nazaire. Nine planes were scheduled to go. Seven ships actually got off and three of those turned back, leaving only four that got over the target. There were supposed to be representatives from five groups on this one. Lt. Isbell's ship got a wing knocked off it before it reached the target and went down. At least three chutes were seen to open. Isbell was another of the original bunch of young pilots at Wendover and was in the 369th squadron. A bunch of good men, and friends of mine went down with him. Peter Fryer especially will be missed sitting around the fire over at the club and drinking his double Scotches. Lt. [William J.] Casey's ship was hard hit and several of his crew were injured, but he got back O.K. Lt. A[lbert] G. Smith, bombardier was hardest hit with a deep thigh and elbow wound. If only these boys could make a couple of raids without losing a plane or injuring anybody. Fortunately, nobody was brought back dead. It isn't nearly so hard on the fellows to see a whole ship and crew go down as it is to see one of their buddies brought back dead. When a ship goes down, they always hope that their friend got out safely. We just can't keep up this pace much longer. Our losses are too high, much higher than any other group, and more expensive than the results we are getting. Since leaving Westover Field, we have lost nine complete crews out of the original 35, and in addition, have lost at least five other ships. We can't continue long at this pace. I think I feel sorrier for Isbell's wife than anybody else over this trip today. She is a frail little thing anyway. She was about four months pregnant and lost her baby about a month ago. She wanted that baby so awfully bad. And now he's gone.

Nov 24 - Took Smith and [Walter C.] Leeker to Oxford today. This time I took off enough time to go through Madelin College, part of Oxford University. It was quite an experience. The chapel is very, very old. The mess hall was built in 1458 and has a lot of the original woodwork and furnishings. The kitchen is a twelfth century model. The furniture was perfectly beautiful, extremely highly polished. They showed us all sorts of mugs and cups of solid silver with the remark that Henry VIII used this one or someone else owned this one. I was particularly interested in some unbreakable glass tumblers. All their silverware was sterling and none of it newer than 50 years old. By chance we bumped into a "fellow" (professor) in chemistry. He was kind enough to show us through the living quarters, two hundred years old. Everything looked awfully cold and drab though. No central heating or plumbing.

Oxford University we found is a sort of federation of colleges of which Madelin is one of the largest and oldest. It has a broad range of subjects all the way from languages to medicine, law and the sciences in general. They teach very little by the lecture system, but use the tutor system instead. The standards for entry appear to be extremely high. The corridors and halls look just like I had pictured them. I still don't have any desire to go to school there, though.

Nov 25 - Our group has been taken off operational duty for an indefinite period—two weeks or more—until we have time to lick our wounds and get organized again. We need a lot of new planes, need a lot of repairs on the ones we have, and need a lot of new men. The boys are really needing a rest. Maybe I'll even get a chance to get our medical records straight once more.

Nov 28 - I'm right in the middle of a big fight with Col. Tracy, the 8th Bomber Command Surgeon. We had transferred Lt. [Samuel D.] Simpson into the 423rd Sq. from the service group to fill the vacancy created by [Lt. Edmund F.] Longworth's leaving. Later Col. Tracy ordered one Lt. [George C.] Schumacher into that position so that gives us two doctors in that outfit. I particularly want to keep Simpson so I am bucking sending anyone else in here with all I have. This is the first time I have ever used my official position to buck the big shots in anything of any great importance, but I want to keep Simpson so badly, I'm going to fight it to the last ditch.

Schumacher showed up this afternoon. He seems O.K. but I've entered the fight now and I'm going to see it through. I wrote a rather hot letter yesterday to the Commanding General up at Wing for Col. Overacker's signature. We'll just sit back and see what happens.

We got our rating as Flight Surgeon today. That entitles us to wear our wings, but most of all it means a substantial increase in pay.

Nov 30 - Yesterday I went up with Brady just for the ride. It was a low altitude practice bombing mission, but the ceiling got so low we couldn't see the target. We then went toward the Wash to that target, but it was closed in too. So Brady stopped at the R.A.F. Station Duxford to see one of his classmates. While we were there, the weather closed in there, and we couldn't take off. So we spent the night. We were all interested in the German planes they had on display there. The most amusing thing happened last night. The British are dead set on dressing for dinner, but there we were in our flying clothes. After dinner we sat down in front of a nice fire, and the warmth after being chilled made us awfully sleepy. Churchill was making a most important address on the radio, and all the English were huddled around the radio to catch every phrase, while we snored away in our chairs. They must have been disgusted with us. We came back this morning. Brady was feeling good, and he buzzed the field at about ten feet, almost taking the wind sock off at the other side of the field. That's a thrill, but I don't care for it.

Dec 2, 1942 - I have just returned off another ride. Started out in a plane again yesterday morning and for the second straight time, the weather closed in behind us. Sgt. [Chester W.] Aarts was run over by a truck the day before, and Lt. Warner flew us down to Oxford. Since the weather had already closed in up here at Thurleigh, we decided we might as well go on down to Exeter to spend the night and see how our patients there are getting along. We spent the night in a lovely old hotel across the street from a magnificent cathedral 800 years old, or rather the walls of it. The inside is burned out as result of bombing. Great sections of the city are just leveled. Exeter is almost in the southwest corner of England, it is where Sir Francis Drake planned some of his voyages. All the patients were well, except Lt. Dresp (the co-pilot on Ferguson's ship, injured Nov. 18). That poor boy is just going through hell. He has one whole buttock shot off, a fracture of the hip, a complete section of the sciatic nerve and a ruptured urethra. He has been suffering terrifically. The poor lad doesn't know yet how poor his prospects are for a happy life if he lives. As badly injured as he was that day, he kept right on in the co-pilot's position and not once did he lose consciousness in the three-hour trip back to the landing field. My sentiments in this war have not been touched quite so much as when I stepped into his room. He grabbed me by the hand and started sobbing and saying over and over, "I thought you'd never come." They have done a grand job for him there, but he wants so awfully bad to get up to Oxford with his own people. British hospitals aren't the best. He, in spite of the condition he's in, wants to get back in shape to repay some Jerry for what he did to him. He has the spirit that is winning this war. The United States cannot ever repay that boy for the sacrifice he has and will make. I'm going to get that boy moved up to Oxford and made as happy as possible if it is the last thing I do. He was so awfully appreciative of my coming, and insisted he felt better. How can a guy help being touched a little?

'Casey at Bat' Means Certain Grief to Nazis

Fort Which Got Seven FWs In 12 Minutes Helps Flaming Bomber

" Casey's been at bat again."
This was the story going around Eighth Air Force yesterday as it was learned how 1st Lt. William J. Casey, San Francisco, whose Fortress recently knocked off seven German fighters in 12 minutes, broke formation in a raid over St. Nazaire last week to help another ship that was in flames.

Breaking formation is not required—nor recommended—in a Fortress raid. In fact, it's almost certain destruction.

However, with all his own bombs dropped over the Hun submarine pen, Casey turned back to escort Capt. Robert C Williams, Flint, Mich., through a swarm of enemy fighters that had set Williams' Fortress afire.

" I wouldn't be here if it weren't for that Casey," Capt. Williams told an intelligence interviewer, according to Air Force headquarters. " He seems to have a knack for getting into hot spots."

Capt. Williams also spoke of S/Sgt. Colon E. Neely, Columbia, S.C. Neely, a waist gunner, was hit early in the fight by a piece of shell. Despite his wounds, the sergeant administered first aid to another injured gunner, continued to fire his own gun, helped put out the fire, and finally went aft to help the tail gunner, who also was wounded.

The men, Capt. Williams said, beat out flames with their bare hands. Among them also were 2nd Lt. Emmet V. Ford, Siloam Springs, Ark., bombardier, and T/Sgt. Eddie F. Espitallier, radio operator, of Clovis, Cal.

"'Casey at Bat' Means Certain Grief to Nazis." *Stars & Stripes*, December 2, 1942. Courtesy of the East Anglia Air War Collection.

COMMENTARY

My boy Casey has made the headlines in a big way. He has been here in the hospital for several days with a severe cold, and the publicity isn't phasing him in the slightest. That's Casey! He's going to London tomorrow for some sort of broadcast.[24]

But these newspaper articles don't tell near all that lies behind the scene. In the first article [Figure 2], no mention is made of the fact that nine ships started out on this raid; that five of those ships turned back for some reason or other (some suspected of little cause); that only four ships were left to go over the target when 12–18 is generally considered a minimum; that Lt. Isbell's ship was hit and lost a wing and went down with most of the crew before it ever reached the target; that Lt. Leeker and Lt. Smith in the nose of Casey's ship were injured, Smith very badly, yet carried on and dropped his bombs; that the three remaining ships came on back to the field after sundown and with a thick ground fog so that they had to actually be "talked in" by the control tower.

The stunt written up in the second article actually happened the day before the other one. [See Shuller's remarks on the second article on pages 112–13 on the day it was published.] He actually did break all rules in breaking away to help Capt. Williams out. Williams and his co-pilot did a marvelous job of getting that ship back to English soil. Aulenbach, his top turret gunner was killed; Shively, the navigator was badly shot in the arm; [Hubert] Houston, the waist gunner was shot in the leg badly; and [Colin E.] Neeley the other waist gunner slightly wounded. The entire radio room caught fire, but they managed to put it out and fight on.

As for Casey, the publicity he's receiving will probably bring him a high ranking medal, and it should, though after all is said and done we have others just as deserving. Casey is a rare character. He is always in some sort of trouble. He's always in bad with his C.O., he drinks too much, he talks too often when he should be listening, is typically Irish. He's been that way all his life, got kicked out of college, etc. But from the first day I saw that boy I've liked him and been fascinated by him. I've probably spent more hours just sitting and talking to him than any other pilot we have, unless it's Mack McKay. I've tried to negotiate between him and his C.O., have given him sleeping pills when he got a "crying jag" one night when Major Oliver took his plane away from him and grounded him for disciplinary reasons, and have helped him home when he got too drunk. Why have I stood up for him? I don't really know. But it seems my patience and confidence in his flying ability is bearing fruit. It is always the "crazy" fellows who do the glamorous things.

Casey has joined a lot of the others in adopting a fatalistic attitude about these missions. He is firmly convinced he will be killed. Less than a week ago he used as an excuse for his heavy drinking the fact that he expected to be dead "week after next." It was interesting to get his reaction to the situation where his men shot down seven planes. He stated that when he knew his bombardier and navigator were hurt, his top turret gunner was hurt, his co-pilot slightly injured, a lot of his controls shot away and the ship out of control, and the German planes pounding him with everything they had, his impulse was just to throw up his hands and quit and say "What the hell's the use" and let the plane dive into the ground. I actually believe he'd have done it if it hadn't been for the rest of the crew. But he's brought them back.

This is a lot of writing about Casey. We owe him and his crew a lot. Actually this Group is full of Caseys though, it just so happened that he had the opportunity and is now getting the publicity. America need have no fear for her security with this kind of young manhood. God Bless Them— It's a treasured privilege to know, live with and be one of them. (note— Casey was shot down over northwest Germany April 11, 1943 and was taken prisoner.)

Dec 4 - Manning and I have just returned from a two day trip to London. This is actually the first time that I have officially taken any leave since I have been in the Army. We had a very quiet time of it, but enjoyable. Went to a couple of stage shows, a movie, went sight-seeing to Parliament, Westminster Abbey, Buckingham Palace and the city in general. We got hungry so we came home. It was nice getting away from everything here for a while.

Dec 5 - Tonight we were told that we were back on combat status now and were scheduled to be briefed for a mission tomorrow morning early, but it was canceled, probably on account of weather. We have a lot of new planes now and the fellows are rested up now and ready to go. It is remarkable what a few days of complete relaxation, knowing for certain they would not be going out next day, could do for their morale.

Some of the best of them were on the verge of breaking up. Even Major Holt was pretty badly upset on the last mission at the loss of Isbell, but worst of all he saw a ship in the formation ahead of him spin down enveloped in flames with a man hanging out of the bomb bay entangled in his shroud lines. Capt. Ryan also has developed a very moody attitude. Let's hope for some good luck on the next raids and we will be all set.

Major Oliver was relieved of his command of the 369th Bomb Sq. today. He had become unpopular with his men for some time. He is an awfully conscientious man, perhaps he tried too hard, but he never seemed to click as a C.O. as he should have. I hate to see him relieved the worst way. I personally like him very much, but am also sure it's better for the organization to replace him. Capt. [Henry W.] Terry assumes command. He'll make a good C.O.

This health situation is getting out of hand. Almost everybody has colds, some of them really bad. Every single bed in the hospital is occupied tonight. There isn't enough fuel to keep the fellows comfortable at all and there is little chance of its getting any better. I don't see how we are going to keep the lads in physical shape to do any flying at all this winter.

Dec 7 - Manning and I have just returned from the first Inter-Allied Medical Meeting (monthly) in London. We went down this morning and back tonight. We learned very little that we can apply, but their intentions were good, I suppose. We didn't stay for anything else. There is a possibility of a mission tomorrow. On the other hand there are rumors about the flying echelon going to Africa on short notice. It looks like we may be on the verge of something hot.

Dec 10 - It doesn't look as much now like we are going to Africa as it did three or four days ago. To make it look even more like we have settled down for the duration is the fact that we officially took over the post. The U.S. flag is flying over in front of headquarters. It is said that this is the very first time a foreign flag has flown on English soil since William the Conqueror.

Dec 11 - Had a little trouble among my enlisted men yesterday. Sgt. Tropeano got tired of trying to get the boys to make up their beds so he turned a bunch of them upside down. Somebody then retaliated by tearing his up. We compromised by my clamping down on all of them and the barracks looked dandy today. Those boys are just like a bunch of kids. One has to be on his guard all the time to be absolutely fair. They're an extremely jealous bunch.

Some of the escapades of these fellows are rare specimens and are well worth recording, though some of them would not be passed by the Hayes office. The experiences of frivolous youth are well illustrated by one of my own men. Corporal [Louis W.] Brookins, who is one of my very most dependable fellows, is quite a demon with women. The payoff was some time ago when he went to bed with a married women in Bedford whose husband was supposed to be working that night. As luck would have it, the husband came in unexpectedly, and Corporal Brookins went out through the window taking the blackout curtains with him and ran down the street in his underwear, carrying his clothes on his arm. He lost his hat somewhere along the line and hasn't found it yet. It was several days later before we learned why he had such a terrible cold for three or four days.

Another episode that illustrates to what ends some of these fellows go is that of Sgt. [William E.] Kellum. Sgt. Kellum is the lad who bailed out of Lt. Ely's ship in the crash over at the Wash before we went into operational status. He is only 19, but is a regular little toughie. He was in London with one of his buddies. They picked up one girl between them, and then tried every means possible to get her up to their room. The final try met with extraordinary success. Kellum pulled off his uniform and put it on the girl. Thus she had little difficulty getting in. He then stood outside the second story window in his underwear expecting to catch the clothes when she threw them out, but in the meantime the house officer happened along, and Kellum was standing there in his underwear trying to explain when the window upstairs opened and his clothes came tumbling out the window and lodged on a ledge just out of reach. It cost him about £2 to smooth it out with the house officer. These are the boys who are running up our venereal rate.

Speaking of venereal rate reminds me of a lad we started treatment for syphilis a little while ago. He picked up a girl in Piccadilly Circus (London). He paid £4 ($16) to spend the night with her, was "rolled" for another £10 ($40) and got syphilis to boot. I am happy to note that the rate has fallen markedly since our determined effort a month ago to bring them face to face with the facts of the situation.

Dec 12 - Another mission today. It was a sorry state of affairs from the beginning. They sent out 18 planes from this Group to bomb an important aerodrome southeast of Paris, a very dangerous mission. Three other groups went. Seven out of 18 of our ships turned back before they reached France. Even at that there were fewer abortions in our Group than in any other, there was 47% for the Wing. That is awful. Even Col. Overacker turned back today when he had to feather an engine. Major [William A.] Lanford then was left leading the flight, and he had an absolutely green navigator. There was a solid overcast all over France, and they wandered aimlessly around down almost to Switzerland. All the time with German fighters attacking them relentlessly. They didn't even see their target. As they came out, six planes dropped their bombs on the last resort target, or rather at it. For the first time in quite a long time, all our planes came home, although a couple of them were pretty badly injured, and three or four minor injuries. Another Group lost two planes. Our Group shot down 14 German fighters with 5 other probable victories. So, running true to form, we are still more of a fighter Group than a bomber Group. Apparently none of the other Groups shot down any planes. All of which further proves that this climate is no place for high altitude bombing. The two more serious injuries, Lt. [Max H.] Bergen and Sgt. [Clifford R.] Langley were flown to Oxford late yesterday afternoon. It was a peculiar coincidence that Langley was the tail gunner for Riordan, who had a previous tail gunner injured, the bullet going directly through the patch of the previous bullet hole, and the gunner sustained almost identical injuries.

Dec 13 - Well, General Longfellow has had his session with the Colonel, and it seems that contrary to all expectations he was commended for yesterday's raid rather than criticized for shooting down 14 German fighters without loss to ourselves. That all sounds good, but wonder if he actually knows what really happened. Perhaps Major Lanford may even get decorated, who knows? These are the fortunes of war.

Dec 18 - Well, I have just gotten out of my own hospital after having had a severe attack of sore throat and bronchitis for four days. Feel much better now.

Dec 20 – Another big raid today! They did over that job they attempted eight days ago. Went to that huge German repair depot at Romilley-sur-Seine, 80 miles southeast of Paris. This time they apparently plastered it to the ground, but what a price to pay! Couldn't our group ever just once make one successful raid and come back all in one piece? This time we lost three planes in France, all of them 367th – [Lt. Lewis R.] McKesson, [Lt. John R.] McKee; and [Lt. Danton J.] Nygaard. My God! That's awful. It is thought McKesson made a forced landing. They saw nine chutes open out of McKee's ship, but Nygaard's ship exploded in the air, and it is believed all of them were killed. There are only three crews left now in the 367th out of the original nine that came across. That is a terrible toll. They are [John L.] Ryan, [William W.] Dickey, and [Earl C.] Tunnell. It's having a terrible effect on those fellows too.

In addition Capt. [John M.] Howard caught hell (369th). His bombardier, Lt. [Conrad J.] Farr, was killed and several other members of his crew injured. Lt. Seelos brought home another injured navigator. And of all things, Lt. Riordan had to fight his ship home again. For the fourth straight trip, he had his ship shot to pieces and had to decide if he would order the crew to bailout or not. This time he and his co-pilot were slightly injured by shrapnel themselves. When he landed his elevators stuck on him and had to take off again on two motors. It was quite a feat. That boy deserves every medal in the book. He is about the hardest working, most conscientious, most unassuming man I have ever seen. They made plenty of work for us today. About eleven casualties of various degrees, our hardest day thus far.

McKee is going to be missed awfully in this Group. He is a real Irishman and the life of any party, probably has amused the fellows more than any one man. His Irish songs and dirty jokes are not going to be easily forgotten. McKesson was such a grand pilot. One just doesn't think about the better fellows going down, but they all catch it alike. Nygaard is a replacement and hasn't been with us long, but he adds up the total and makes the fellows consider more and more how little their chances are. The 367th squadron is in a terrible state now. Capt Ryan's crew is particularly broken, because both his wing men were shot down and left him flying out there all by himself. He had a narrow escape too. All his crew saw the other two planes go. Tonight little Kellum, his tough little ball turret gunner is just sitting and staring into space. Ryan is so drunk, he can't hit the ground with his hat, something I have never seen before. But that is good. He'll feel better tomorrow. The Group is back into the psychological state we were in before we were taken off Operational status November 25. Even Riordan, as steady as he is, is shaky tonight. God help us if we have anything like this again.

Dec 25 - Christmas Day in England. Gosh! It is quiet around here. Nobody is working today except just a skeleton office force, and no planes are in the air. We had a very fine dinner even though the turkey had to be spread pretty thin to make it go around. It is such a beautiful day out, a wonderful day to pull a raid, but all the fellows are resting and a considerable portion of them recuperating from a riotous evening last night. Everybody is appreciating this rest too. This is a quieter and more pleasant Christmas than I saw last year.

Dec 28 - For once since I have been in England I have been glad to see bad weather—There has not been an airplane off the ground since the day before Christmas, and it has had a remarkable effect on the boys. Just a few days rest was all they needed. In spite of the trouble they had last raid, they are about ready to be on their way again. It is really remarkable what a few days rest can do.

The new hospital is open up at Diddington now so we shouldn't be going to Oxford quite so often. Already we have four patients there. Went up there this afternoon with Capt. Wright to see the place, and also to look over the nurse situation for our New Year's Eve party. Most of the nurses are hideous looking, but beggars cannot be choosers they say, so I guess we shall invite some of them down.[25]

Dec 30 - A mission today directed at the submarine base at Lorient, and another tragedy connected with it. This one has hit closer to me person- ally than any yet unless perhaps it was Dick Adams on Nov. 8. Today, of all people, they shot down Capt. Brady. I recall my anxiety about that boy on previous raids, particularly Nov. 17, perhaps a sort of premonition. Since then I have flown with him several times and have thought a world of him. He was one of the cleanest most highly respected pilots in the Group. The story is this. Brady got off the ground this morning several minutes be- hind the others but expected to catch them. The rest of the Group turned back at the coast of France because of bad weather, but Brady, who had never found our Group; attached himself to the tail of another Group and went on over the target. One man out of our Group over the target and one man shot down. How's that for luck! We're "snake-bit." Fighters knocked his plane out. Ten parachutes were seen to open as they bailed out near Brest, but one was seen to fall out of his opened parachute. At least we have hopes they are all alive except this unknown man. This is another case where the cost would not have seemed so great had the Group been able to complete a successful mission and hit the target. Always before Brady's ship had been scarcely scratched except for the one just before this one. These are the fortunes of war, but he has created a vacancy in the organization that is going to be hard to fill.

Jan 1, 1943 - The first entry of the new year. There was a big party for the officers at the club last night to see the New Year in, and practically ev- erybody was nursing a headache today. It was a nice dance, and everybody had a lot of fun. Munal brought out a couple of X-ray technicians from Bedford. It lasted until very, very far into the morning. In fact it was four thirty before I got back into my room. Then it was even later before I got to bed, because Capt. [James A.] Johnston had tried to open a can with his hunting knife and cut his hand badly, requiring several stitches. However, amazing as it may seem, he was the only casualty of the New Year's Eve celebration on this post.

The only heart pangs of the evening was the remembrance of Brady— something he said last Sunday—in fact the last thing I remember him say- ing. He was one of the few pilots who ever went to church here—he went occasionally. At breakfast last Sunday, he volunteered the information that he was going to church. Someone asked him what he'd done that he was repenting for. He replied, "It's not what I've done, it's what I might do New Year's Eve." I just couldn't keep from thinking about his not being here to carry out his plans. I wonder if he is in a German prisoner camp or perhaps not alive. We have just received information from the Group with whom he went over that they bailed out at 5,000 feet and German fighters strafed them as they went down. If only I knew that Brady was killed by German machine guns as he was hanging helpless from his parachute, I'll be damned if I wouldn't take up gunnery and go over there to get a shot at the bastards myself.

Jan 2 - There is another mission scheduled for tomorrow. There were few at the club, except Casey was over there drinking himself silly as usual. Wish I could do something about that, but guess it wouldn't be normal for him if he didn't. Doubt if he could fly straight if sober.

Lt. Al Smith came back from Oxford today. His leg isn't entirely healed yet, but he begged so hard to get back on flying status that I consented to let him go on the mission tomorrow. How do you like a guy like that? He had his leg almost blown off less than six weeks ago, and now he says he's got a few things to settle with those Germans. I'd much rather have a lame guy who was eager than a perfect one who didn't want to go. He got his way, as he usually does.

Jan 4 - The raid went off as scheduled yesterday, but they landed in south England again, and they haven't returned yet because it was bad weather there today. Manning and Simpson went down there to look after their medical needs. It was another raid on St. Nazaire submarine base. We still haven't gotten all the details, but it is known that we lost two ships again. Lt. Ferguson went down off the coast of St. Nazaire, and Lt. Cranmer went down somewhere in the channel. It still isn't known whether or not Lt. Cranmer's crew was picked up. Apparently they really caught hell again. I just heard that Capt. McKay went down too, but it was a tremendous relief to learn it was not true. I keep thinking about Lt. Levy on Ferguson's crew, the bombardier. He is a Jew and a very distinctive personality. At first nobody liked him, but later everybody began to think a world of him. He gave the impression all the time of being scared to fly and after each mission would invariably get himself grounded for something or other, but just as sure as another mission turned up, he tore his hair and everybody else's until he got to go. He was afraid of mice to such an extent that he put his bed posts in buckets of water to keep them from getting on his bed. It was utterly impossible to offend him, perhaps that is why everybody began to like him so much. But his greatest horror was the thought of capture by the Nazis. If he is captured, I hope he is treated as any American and not as a Jew. We'll have to wait until the fellows come back here to get any details of their difficulties.

Jan 6 - Because of bad weather, the boys have still not returned here from their last raid. So we do not yet know the extent of our damage. It is rumored that Lt. Spaulding crash landed down there, and that he had several injured aboard. We do have word that Lt. Cranmer's crew were machine gunned in the water by German fighters after they crashed into the sea, and that no trace could be found of them by the rescue parties. It is a terrible thing to think about those poor boys floundering around out there in the channel being mowed down by bullets, though that is far more legitimate than their strafing Brady's crew as they fell in parachutes over German territory. It is said that Sgt. A.T. Harris, the top turret gunner, kept his guns blazing even as the plane hit the water. How can sufficient tribute be paid to guys like that?

Cranmer was one of our "problem children," a running mate of Casey's, but a very, very fine pilot. But I can never forget him the night before he went out on this raid. He was sitting over at the club drinking himself into a stupor and trying to get all the rest of the fellows around him to drink with him. Lt. [Albert] Brunsting his co-pilot was begging him to quit drinking and go home and told him he wouldn't fly his best next morning. Yet Brunsting that night said that anytime Cranmer went on a mission, he wanted to fly with him. Sgt. [Arizona T.] Harris had been heard to say he'd never leave the ship as long as Cranmer was at the controls, and evidently he didn't. It is remarkable what devotion and respect these pilots command from their crews. I hope his drinking the night before had nothing to do with their tragedy - I'm sure it didn't.

I went up to Cambridge this afternoon to a medical meeting to see a demonstration of how the British handle their orthopedic service cases. It was a good demonstration and a nice trip. It was raining a little though and we saw very little of the University. It snowed quite a bit last night— our second snow of the season. The rain is making the ground sloshy again. We enjoyed a couple of days of dry ground before this by virtue of the fact only that the ground was frozen. That is the only time that one doesn't sink to his ankles in mud.

Jan 8 - The planes finally returned today. They made an attempt to come back yesterday but the field was closed in here, and they couldn't land so they were ordered back to their taking off point, which was also closed in when they got back there. They got lost and came out under the overcast on the coast of France near Brest and were attacked by Fock-Wolfe's. They high-tailed it back to England and had difficulty getting down. All of them finally got down except Lt. Brandon who got lost and circled around until his gas ran out, and he and his crew bailed out, but unfortunately they were over the channel. They have not been heard from since. That was another 367th ship, which makes eight planes that one squadron has lost since flying the Atlantic. Brandon had been a co-pilot and had just taken over his own ship with a new replacement crew, but he had one of our older co-pilots with him, Lt. J.O. Jones, and also our little Englishman Lemuel Smith, the navigator. That misfortune was so uncalled for. There was no excuse for their having taken off in such bad weather and expecting a relatively unexperienced man to be able to make it. By just the barest stroke of fate Capt. Manning was not on that ship. The final report on casualties is three minor injuries, but three complete crews missing. This is the third raid in which we have lost three crews. We are not winning the war at this rate. Another raid is scheduled for tomorrow.

Jan 10 - Col. Overacker was relieved of his command a few days ago and has been sent to the staff of Bomber Command. I hate to see him go. He has certainly been O.K. by me. Col. [Frank A.] Armstrong, the former commander of the 97th Bomb Gp, has assumed command of this Group. He seems nice and is quite impressive as a commander. He made a pep talk to the combat crews yesterday and he elevated their spirits a little. Their spirits were so low, however, that anything offered them would sound good.[26]

Jan 13 - The lads pulled another raid on our old friend Lille again today. This time they had excellent fighter protection, and they had very little opposition. They would have come home for once without a bullet hole anywhere, all safe and sound after having hit the target—but alas! The hand of fate presses heavy on this Group. Something happened today that has not happened before in this outfit. Two planes crashed together at 24,000 feet and went down just off the target. Lt. [Jack A.] Spaulding ran into Capt. Johnston in a steep turn and knocked off his tail and a part of his own wing. It is not known just how many of them got out, perhaps not many. These boys were in the 369th, a part of my old gang and barracks-mates back at Wendover. Capt. [Doyle L.] Dugger and Lt. [Russel G.] Kahl were also with them. This tragedy today really cut into our older personnel. Capt. Johnston was one of our most experienced pilots, a really fine person. He's going to be awfully badly missed in his squadron. Spaulding was my very first roommate at Wendover and always a good friend of mine. He had a million questions to ask me before he got married last June. He was a fair pilot too, though a little nervous. Sixteen of our original crews are now gone. That is almost half. What is this thing getting us?

I hold myself partly to blame for this crash this afternoon. Spaulding was hit on his last mission out over St. Nazaire and was pretty badly shaken and nervous. He expressed himself immediately after he got back that he did not want to fly again, but several days had elapsed before he went out this time and I thought he'd probably make it. If only I had grounded him things would probably be different now. If only I had been a little quicker to act. My responsibility is great when it comes to determining who is fit to fly and who isn't. One can only do his best.

Jan 16 - There has been a raid scheduled the last three mornings, but each canceled because of weather. The weather is bad tomorrow, and they are not even trying to run a mission. It will be the first Sunday in a long time that a hard day has not been planned.

Jan 20 - There have been further changes in the Group. Major [Claude E.] Putnam has now joined us from the 91st Group which probably means that Lt. Col. [Delmar E.] Wilson is leaving us. I certainly hate that, though everybody is impressed with Maj. Putnam. The big shake-up is that Maj. [William A.] Lanford is being relieved of his command. This is a repercussion from the raid he led over St. Nazaire Jan 3. There are several things he did wrong, but the glaring mistake was when he ordered the planes to take off from St. Eval to return back to the base when he knew the weather was closed in. He is being sent to the replacement center, which is the worst spanking they could give him. It is a tough break. He was an excellent squadron commander, but he has made two bad mistakes on raids. He is being replaced by Capt. [Mack] McKay. Mack will make a good commander, and I am glad to see him get a break.

Morale is hitting a new low. Night before last Lt. [Oliver E.] Tilli, co-pilot for Casey, came to me and confessed that he has lost his nerve. He is one of the last men I would ever have suspected of cracking. It just seems that you can't tell who this thing is going to hit. It has reached the stage on him where he says he wishes the bullet that came so close to him a few weeks ago had killed him, and thus got him out of his suspense because he feels that he will be killed within the next couple of raids anyway. This is a terrible thing for a young man to experience. He fears the censorship of his fellow crewmen, however, to the extent that he would rather just go ahead and be killed rather than be considered yellow. I was the first one he had spoken to about this thing, and it took him three days to get up nerve enough to spill it. These fellows are real men, and it is a shame that they have to be affected this way. We expect it though, and I do not want another Spaulding incident on my hands.

Jan 22 - Just got back from a couple of days in London. Manning, Munal and I went down. Ordinarily the three of us would not all leave at the same time, but they were running no missions so Simpson and [Alfred W.] Erb held down the fort O.K. It was a quiet but enjoyable time. We went to see "Let's Face It" and "Best Bib and Tucker," a couple of good musical shows, especially the latter. It was the most wonderful staging and producing that I have ever seen, some really fine talent in it. Saw the movie "Casablanca" but didn't care so much for it. Did a little shopping and the rest of the time, we just sat around and relaxed. I got my stay out and am now ready to settle down and work a little again.

Jan 24 - A mission to Lorient submarine base again yesterday. All of the planes came back O.K. Not a single casualty except for a few frost-bites. This is the first time in over two months that a mission has been run without casualties. Spirits are high now, the boys are really feeling good. Their high spirits can be attributed partly to the news that Lt. McKee, who was shot down in France, has escaped into Allied hands. He is just about our most popular pilot, and it was a wonderful tonic for the fellows. The mission called for today was scrubbed at the last minute.

Jan 27 - This was a wonderful day! It is the greatest day since the very first raid. The occasion was the attack on Wilhelmshaven, the very first time Germany has been attacked by American planes. All the planes returned with not one single casualty, the second time in a row. They met very little opposition. They are not so sure what they did to the target which was the big naval base there, but they are happy just for the fact of having actually bombed Germany itself. Here's hoping there can be many more like it. It is known that there will be no mission tomorrow, so the boys are really cutting loose tonight.

Lt. McKee and Lt. Hardin are already in London. This is a remarkable feat. Lt. McKee went down in France Dec. 20 and was back in London Jan 26, only 37 days later. That is an all-time record for rapid escape. He will be back here in a few days. We can depend on a real celebration then.

There were more press agents here for the raid today than there were fliers. Since it is the first German raid, there will be plenty of publicity back home I guess. Capt. Gene Raymond[27] is here on the post. He is just an ordinary fellow it seems.

Jan 29 - Today is another memorable day for this organization. McKee came back to visit us a few hours this afternoon. The sight of him has done this outfit more good than any amount of hearing about it, and morale has taken a decided change for the better. It's a strange feeling to see a fellow like this whom you weren't sure whether or not he was killed, and even if he wasn't, chances were not good that we would see him again. He has a lot of tall stories to tell, but of course he can't tell any details of his escape for obvious reasons. He bailed out and landed at a little French cross-roads of about a dozen houses. It seems that almost before he got to his feet, there were 10 or 15 French women gathered in a reception committee to kiss his cheeks. He got away from there as quickly as possible and he hadn't gone many days before he was in the hands of the underground. One of the most gratifying stories he brought back was that one of the bombs on the Romille raid (the one he went down on) hit a Nazi mess hall directly and killed 200 Germans.

Went to a very dull medical meeting at Diddington tonight, but got to see a lot of the doctors up there. It was successful from that point of view.

Feb 2, 1943 - There has been little activity lately - activity that has brought results, I mean. Today we sent 18 planes out to bomb the railroad yards and repair shops at Hamm, Germany, but the clouds became so thick near the Dutch coast that they turned back. This was quite a long trip over land, but S-2 had assured them that it was not a particularly hard one. This raid was scheduled three or four days ago but called off because of weather. There is so very little time that weather is fit for operation that it seems a shame to keep us here.

Feb 3 - This was about the quietest day one could imagine. No mission scheduled, few patients. Manning and I went with Capt. McKay to Bedford to see a show in the afternoon, then a haircut. There are days like that, even in a combat unit.

Feb 4 - The fellows completed a raid over northwestern Germany today and hit a town which they think is Emden. They started out for Hamm again but it was too cloudy there. They're not sure what they hit, but unlike France, anything they hit in Germany is O.K. Fortunately for us not a plane was lost, and no one was hurt at all. The only casualties were about a dozen frost bite cases, some severe. It was about −40° F at altitude today, and that's cold in any man's language. There were 3 fortresses and 2 B-24's lost from other Groups. This is the fourth raid now without losses or casualties, which makes us feel much better.

We have learned today that some of the fellows who went down Jan.13 in the collision are dead. Capt. [James A.] Johnston, Capt. [Doyle] Dugger, Lt. [Gordon R.] Grant, Lt. [Jack A.] Spaulding and Lt. [Frank J.] Jacknik were all killed. Lt. [Russel G.] Kahl, Lt. [Shedrick E.] Jones and Lt. [Wallace B.] Kirkpatrick are prisoners of war. This is the one that I could have prevented by simply grounding Spaulding. And to think that I put Capt. Johnston on flying status just so he could make this raid after having had him off for two weeks because of injury to his hand. He had cut it with a hunting knife on New Year's Eve night. I put some sutures in it at 4:30 a.m. Why did I have to send Johnston out on that raid? If we could only know. They just don't come any finer than Johnston.

They had a presentation of medals here a couple of days ago—mostly Purple Hearts. Capt. [Robert] Riordan and his co-pilot [Edward M.] Maliszewski were given the Distinguished Flying Cross. Riordan deserves that award far above anybody else in this Group, and he is just about the proudest man I have ever seen. I'm happy for him.

Feb 6 - The unheard of happened today. The whole wing was given a holiday today for no obvious reason other than the generousness of heart of the Wing Commanding General. It was decreed there would be no flying or ground school today so everybody really cut loose last night. This afternoon we went into Bedford to see a show, but since all of us had seen all of them, we wound up in Rushden. They should have holidays like this more often, it would be a tremendous morale factor for the fliers. It's the first holiday since Christmas.

Capt. Howard received a card and photograph from Lt. [Peter J.] Fryer in a German prison camp. Several of our officers were in that photograph, and it did our fellows an awful lot of good to see it. The following were in it:

Lt. Barnett, 423rd, pilot, Nov. 9
Lt. Gaston, 367th, pilot, Nov. 19
Lt. [Don H.] Eldredge, 367th, Gaston's co-pilot, Nov. 19
Lt. LaChase, 367th, Olson's bombardier, Oct. 9
Lt. [Julius C.] Landrum, 369th, Adams' bombardier, Nov. 8
Lt. [John A.] Latchford 369th, Adams' navigator Nov.8

Lt. [Abraham L.] Burden 369th, Isbell's bombardier Nov. 23
Lt. Fryer 369th, Isbell's navigator Nov. 23

It has been rumored that Capt. Adams and Lt. Gise, Olson's navigator, are in the underground on the way out. These reports help wonderfully in relieving the hopelessness of the situation in the minds of these combat crews. I certainly hope it is true about Adams. There is nobody I'd rather see get out.

Feb 11 - A couple of briefings this week but no missions. A very quiet week altogether. Munal, Simpson and I went to the R.A.F. Hospital at Ely today to a medical lecture on burns by Flight Commander Morley. It was very good but the trip itself was better. Simpson got his promotion to Captain a day or so ago. He was about the happiest man that I have ever seen. Simpson is an awfully good man, and I am more than pleased with myself for winning the scrap to keep him here. Col. Tracy, Bomber Command Surgeon, hasn't spoken to me since.

Five new medical enlisted men reported to me today from the Casual Pool. Don't know what I will do with them. There are overages now.

Capt. McKim reported back here for duty a few days ago after being gone 3 months. Am glad to have him back. He's gone to London tonight though, and he's going to Pinetree to school a couple of weeks next Sunday, so he isn't worth much to us yet.

Feb 12 - Simpson, Erb and I went to Diddington to their staff meeting tonight—Subject—orthopedics. I like the fellows up there much better than their meetings.

Feb 14 - The 423rd Squadron had their party last night. It was a good dance, a good orchestra, better than average girls, and everybody had a big time. A lot of nurses came from Oxford and Diddington which tended to make it more of an American affair. Liquor flowed a little too freely though, and a lot of the officers were in a sad state to start off on the mission this morning. They headed out for Hamm, Germany again, but turned around just about the Dutch coast because of weather. Another screwed-up detail. They got shot at though and received credit for a mission.

Feb 15 - Col. Armstrong is now a Brig. General. Maj. Putnam was made a Lt. Colonel two or three days ago. Col. Falk (Col. Flak as he is called here) was booted out of here on his ear today along with his [flak] suit. He has gone to Bassingborne. His suit is a good idea perhaps, but the boys don't like it, and they particularly don't like him.

Feb 17 - There was another big raid on St. Nazaire yesterday. We had been told that St. Nazaire was already devastated and evacuated, but I guess we had been misinformed. This time they really blasted the target, as shown us by photographs this morning. The fellows don't mind an expensive raid so badly when they can see some results of their efforts. And it was expensive. We lost two ships. One of them was Lt. [Joseph A.] Downing, 367th, a replacement crew which did not hurt so bad, but the big loss was Lt. Warner, 423rd. Warner was undoubtedly the most eager, most respected pilot we had and was the sort of individual who made a team out of his crewmen. He is 6 ft. 4 in., tall and lean as an animal but weighed over 200 lbs, very good looking and a perfect physical specimen as well as a perfect gentlemen and a fine fellow. It is not known exactly what happened, but it is thought that Warner himself was hit by flak. If that is the case there is every reason to believe that he went down with his ship because it would be almost impossible for a big man like him who was injured to get out. If he is dead, I am glad he didn't get back here. As long as the fellows are not sure he's dead, they will hope. It's remarkable how little they grieve over the loss of a whole crew reported missing in action as compared to one man who they know is lying in the morgue. Warner was one of my favorites, and one with whom I have flown quite a bit.

Word has been received that Lt. [James M.] Ferguson who went down Jan. 3 is a prisoner of war along with his co pilot, but Lt. [Robert T.] Levy was killed. All the fellows had learned to like him. I suppose it is just as well that he was killed because the Nazis would have led him a miserable life.

Feb 19 - They briefed for the raid on Amiens again today but scrubbed the mission as usual. This is the fourth time that I have heard that briefing myself, and there have been others I'm sure. The fellows are getting awfully disgusted with that.

Went to Diddington to the weekly meeting—was on meningitis this time. Was very fine for a change. A Major May and Lt. Col. Middleton were guest speakers.

A Lt. Gluck is here from Pinetree to get "atmosphere" on how a bomber station works, problems, etc. He's a psychiatrist.

There are some more changes in our organization today. Major [Delmar E.] Wilson becomes Executive Officer, and Capt. [John L.] Lambert takes over his squadron. Capt. [Henry W.] Terry became a Major today. Lts. [Robert J.] Salternik and [Frank D.] Yaussi, the Gp. navigator and bombardier became Captains. They deserve it plenty, especially Lt. Salternik. The fliers trust his navigation to the nth degree.

Feb 21 - Sunday - Cool and a thick ground haze. No flying at all today. A P-47 pilot spent the night here, but he can't even get out today. There is very little work going on and everybody is enjoying the rest.

The chapel was almost full this morning. I asked one of the tail gunners who was here at the hospital on sick call if he wanted to go with me, and he said, "Sure." I think some of these fellows who meet death so nearly so often do a lot more thinking than they once did. The Catholics have just completed a "mission," and they had excellent attendance every night. Even Mack McKay says he catches himself praying when he gets in a tight spot, though I don't suppose he does much praying any other time.

In the nearly six months we have been over here, it is very striking that some of the young officers have aged 10 years or so. When they first came, they stayed out as late as possible as often as possible, but earlier in the week I went to a movie in Bedford and to my amazement about eight of the most notorious playboys caught the 10:15 bus back to the field.

They are enlarging the hospital here a little. That doesn't make me a bit mad. Some of the plans I am getting modified a little. True to form the British made everything backwards to what we would have done. It'll probably be completed in about three months.

Several nights ago Corp. [Robert C.] Spry bought a dog at the dog pound and the medical enlisted men operated on him here at the hospital. They got the biggest kick out of that of anything we have ever done. They started out to do an appendectomy but couldn't find an appendix. We opened up the chest and one of the boys was almost overwhelmed by the fact that he had seen and felt the heartbeat. It was a good experience for them. We'll try to do it again—provided it is kept under cover. I'm not quite sure what the British attitude is toward – vivisection.

Capt. Ryan and Major Oliver seem to be the heroes of the last mission Feb. 16. A shell burst in the cockpit set off one of the flares. It bounced around the cockpit a few times and set Major Oliver's cap on fire. The burst had knocked out Capt. Ryan's controls, and Maj. Oliver had to keep on flying the ship even though his head was on fire. His forehead was badly burned. The ship was awfully badly shot up, but they landed it O.K. In addition Lt. Hamilton and Lt. [Stanley N.] Kisseberth in other ships received flak wounds, but all of them are getting along O.K.

Feb 24 - Went flying this afternoon with Capt. Regan. He gave us several thrills when he buzzed our own airdrome and the Twinwood airdrome at about 10 feet. I don't mind doing those daring things with a pilot in whom I have plenty of confidence.

A Mr. Grant is here yesterday and today getting a story about Flight Surgeons for Look Magazine. He has taken several pictures. Don't know what he can make out of us, but he is trying, strictly at his own risk.

Feb 26 - A big raid again today. The target was the F-W [Foch-Wolf] airplane factory at Bremen, but it was cloudy and they settled for dropping their bombs on Wilhelmshaven again. Once again all our planes returned without casualties other than frost bites and minor burns. They are feeling very good about it. The other Groups lost several ships, but running true to form, it doesn't affect this group any since none of them were hurt. These fellows are funny that way.

Feb 27 - Seventeen planes raided Brest today. No one aborted and all planes returned safely. That is the first 100% raid we have had in a long time. But it was the same old story—too cloudy to see the target well, so they don't know whether they hit it or not—the better guess is that they didn't. Casey distinguished himself again by having a motor go out on him just before he reached the target. However he didn't feather the prop because that is a dead give-a-way that a man is in trouble, and the fighters concentrate on him. He lagged behind his own group and tagged onto a second. He lagged behind that group and tagged onto a third and got safely home. That boy is an individualist if there ever was one.

March 1, 1943 - They were doing a practice formation flight today and had a mid-air collision. Lt. [Ralph W.] Jones, 423rd, ran into Capt. Regan, 368th. Regan's ship had the top turret knocked off, the whole propeller of the no. 1 engine knocked off, and the propeller of no. 2 engine bent like a cork screw, also he had the under turret of Jones' plane lodged in his left wing. Both planes landed at other fields. Jones made a belly landing. Nobody was hurt, just a couple of cases of minor glass cuts. Miracles never cease. We could have had two crashes with twenty deaths in the space of a split second. $700,000 worth of aircraft totally washed out. That sort of thing makes one wonder if flying is here to stay.

Let it not be said that we don't have some resourceful lads. The 367th squadron officers had a party last night. There is no such thing as ice in this vicinity, so Capt. Ryan took a ship to 33,000 feet where the temperature was −50° C with some buckets of water in the belly of the ship. The result was ice for the drinks last night. I'll bet those were about the most expensive drinks in England or anywhere else. They had to take the ship up for a high altitude test anyway, but even if it hadn't been necessary, I don't think it would have made any difference.

March 3 - They attempted to run a mission to Rennes, France yesterday. They got all the ships up off the ground and then called it off because of weather. It has been cloudy all day today and nothing happened at all exciting.

I am actually getting bored with this place. I have felt that way for a couple of weeks or so. When one gets that way, it is time to move on to something else. Everything runs smoothly except for an occasional squabble between the men, there really isn't work enough for all of us, little ever really happens, and one just sort of gets in a rut. Somehow I feel like we are in for something big in the next few weeks.

March 4 - Was up at 4:00 a.m. to attend briefing at 4:45. They get earlier and earlier as the days get longer. I go to almost all the briefings, not that I can actually be of any use there, but it is well to be in all that goes on if possible. Anything I can pick up might help in handling problems that might arise.

The weather is fine today. The first plane left the ground at 7:45. Twenty-one planes had left the runway in 10 ½ minutes or 30 seconds each. That's the smoothest they have ever done. Here's hoping for a smooth mission all the way through. It's a long and dangerous one to the marshalling yards at Hamm, Germany. They'll be back over the field at l p.m. We are safe in expecting trouble today.

Afternoon - The planes arrived back over the field a little after 11 this morning. The weather man had slipped up badly, and they ran into terrible clouds and haze just as they reached enemy territory, so they turned around and came home without dropping their bombs. Nevertheless a couple of enemy fighters picked off Capt. [William E.] Friend's ship just off the Dutch coast. That is such a tragic thing, a useless and wasteful loss. To lose a plane and nine men when absolutely nothing is accomplished is an awful dose of medicine for our crews to swallow. They have absolutely nothing, but contempt for Bomber Command for ordering them out when the weather is like that, and I think perhaps they are right. Besides Capt. Friend, there were Lt. [Aaron E.] Cuddleback, Lt. [George W.] Owens and Lt. [George W.] Frederick, all of them awfully nice fellows. Seven chutes were seen. It is hoped that they didn't fall into the North Sea. The

91st Group went on in to the target and dropped their bombs, but lost four ships over the target and another by crash landing back in England. Our suspicions were right in that it would be a bad day.

March 5 - I was nothing but flattered today. Lt. Col. Putnam came into my office today, and then started out by saying that he was relieving Major Holt as C.O. of the 367th Squadron (which I knew already). But then he said he was undecided definitely which of two Captains in the 367th he was going to elevate to that job and actually asked what was my opinion. That was unexpected, and I must say I was more than pleased because it indicates I have his confidence. But for the Group Surgeon to be able to put in his two-bits worth—well, in so many military organizations the medical department is just a necessary evil. The choice was between Ryan and [William S.] Raper. He probably had his mind fairly well made up and simply wanted just someone else to assure him he was right, but he did follow along the lines I was thinking. Ryan had been slated to go back to the States in an instructor's capacity and there was some question whether he would willingly accept. The Colonel said he was going to call Ryan in and give him the choice of going back to the States or of taking the squadron. I told him Ryan would choose the squadron. He did. The squadron is very happy about it and so am I.

That is the last of the original squadron commanders. The four new ones are all young pilots who have come up from our own squadrons, all are conscientious and most enthusiastic. I think our Group is now a better organization than it has ever been. I like our new C.O. more and more.

Major Jackson and Capt. Hastings were here from Bomber Command today to get some ideas about handling the cases we send them for disposition for flying fatigue, etc. Col. Putnam is very, very sore about the way previous cases were held, and he let them have it with all four feet. He minces no words, but I think they liked it, and I hope found out something they were wanting to know.

Five of us doctors went to the staff meeting at Diddington tonight, lecture on dermatology, and an excellent one at that.

March 6 - This is one of the hardest entries I have had to make. Yesterday I wrote about Ryan's promotion to Squadron Commander and his pride and happiness about getting it. Tonight, 24 hours later, I write about his going down over enemy territory. We sent out 21 ships this morning to that damnable place, Lorient. Next to St. Nazaire the boys hate it worse. As usual the ships were shot up badly by flak and Ryan and [Earl C.] Tunnell did not return. They landed down in south England and we don't know the details yet, but it seems nobody was hurt of those who returned. On the telephone it was reported that Ryan was taking his ship back into France under control after being hit by flak.

Ryan took me on my first ride in a Fortress one Sunday afternoon about 10 months ago. That seems so short a time ago, but we've done an awful lot of living since then. He is one of my closest friends among the fliers here, in fact none I value more closely unless perhaps McKay and Williams. He is even closer to Manning. Manning is going to take it hard. Ryan is such a grand flier and a popular fellow. It was he who checked out most of our original commanders on the B-17. He is an extremely intelligent fellow, speaks and writes several languages, an excellent pianist, and is quite in a class all by himself. I pray he's still alive. He'll take care of himself if he is. Tunnell is an awfully swell fellow too, but he has never been what was classed a strong pilot. We have all felt that he was more or less living on borrowed time. Today's raid leaves only one of the original crews of the 367th squadron, Capt. [George R.] Buckey. I hope they send him back to the States. I can imagine what the psychological effect would be on me if I realized I were a last man. (The fellows are now calling Buckey, the Last of the Mohicans)

A kid I feel awfully sorry for tonight is Sgt. [Robert T.] Schaming, one of Ryan's gunners. He is in the hospital for a minor ailment, and he is just about mad. I am snowing him under with Sodium Amytol. He swears he'll never set foot in another airplane. Time and time again, we have had to handle isolated crew members who have been left behind. It is hard on those. Most often they would prefer to have gone down with the rest of the crew. A combat crew develops a powerful bond of fellowship after several months of flying together through the hell of combat.

Capt. McKay today became Major McKay. I'm happy as I can be about it, but none of us are feeling much like celebrating tonight.

March 7 - Went flying with McKay today. As long as I have known and liked McKay, I don't believe I have ever flown with him before. He is without a doubt the smoothest pilot I have ever flown with. We "beat-up" all the airdromes in the country, flew formation with everything in sight, made tight turns on the wingtips and everything that a B-17 shouldn't do. But McKay can do it and not scare me a bit. It was a pleasant but wild afternoon.

March 8 - We have been on this field six months tonight. The anniversary was celebrated by raiding the marshalling yards at Rennes, France. Apparently it was a successful mission as far as bombing was concerned, but we lost another ship, and again it was one of our original crews, Lt. [Otto] Buddenbaum. He had a fine crew, and the one that will perhaps be missed most is Lt. [Joseph C.] Wilkins, commonly known as "the Gremlin." A few of the fellows in the 368th are taking it a little hard. The enlisted crews are showing the stress of combat a little again. There is another mission scheduled tomorrow, and if we have bad luck again, I think we may have trouble.

It was brought to my attention today that of the approximately 44 flying officers who flew the Atlantic as members of the 367th Squadron last September, and who arrived here on this field exactly 6 months ago, tonight, there are only five left. Think of it, five lonesome souls out of 44, yet they are called upon to keep on keeping on, going over the target again and again, knowing they can't last much longer. If only these fellows could be assured that their efforts are worth it. They are not at all convinced of it. Our visible results do not at all justify our loss of life.

March 10 - They briefed for Amiens yesterday and for Wilhelmshaven today, but both were canceled. There is no mission for tomorrow so everybody is relaxed tonight.

Went to a Group Surgeon's meeting at Wing today. They were trying to reach an agreement on the matter of leaves, prevention of flying fatigue, etc. It was fizzle as usual. It is my opinion that one thing would absolutely relieve the situation, and that is that a man should be promised that after a certain number of missions, he will revert to non-combatant service for a while. As it is, none of these fellows have any hope for the future, no hope but to keep on fighting until they are finally shot down. Some of the fellows have about reached the state where they are going to quit, and I don't blame them.

I paste in this clipping from "Stars and Stripes." March 10, 1943 [Figure 3], today because I couldn't have written it nearly as good myself. Unlike most newspaper stories, there is nothing in it that is not absolute fact. Mack is a great flier and was the idol of his crew before he became Squadron Commander.[28]

March 12 - Maj. Terry led a 100% raid on Rouen, France today. All planes got off the ground on schedule, all bombed the target and all returned without a casualty. That is the second time Terry has been lucky that way within a couple of weeks. Furthermore, the pictures reveal that

No Thriller Stuff—Just Blasts Target

By B. W. Crandell
Stars and Stripes Special Writer

A U.S. BOMBER STATION, England, Mar. 9—This is the story of a 23-year-old pilot who never brought his 'lying Fortress home on two engines, whose crew never has been shot up and bout whom there are no sensational arns of battling flames in a flak-holed hip.

This is the story of a guy who has aken off on 23 raids against Nazi targets 1 Europe, dumped a total of 65,000 pounds of HE on the arget and returned home. It is the story f Capt. Mack McKay, of Compton, Col.

The story is best told on the operations hart of McKay's group Operations; it hows how many bombers start on any iven mission and how many actually nake their bombing runs. Mack and his ite haven't drawn a blank yet, and he's the only pilot in the group with that record, possibly in the entire command. There's a reason for the record.

The ugly word " abortive " is attached to every ship that returns home without bombing the target. And there are a hundred reasons why a Fortress becomes " abortive," without any reflection upon the pilot or the crew. There may be mechanical trouble—turrets, engines, guns, oxygen or battle damage.

But to McKay, the only reason is a complete failure of two engines, without which you can't coax 48,000 pounds of aluminum, guns, ammunition and bombs into the air.

Mack almost had to go up on three engines one morning. The fourth refused to start, but that didn't stop him. He was taxiing out for the take-off, confident that the fourth would catch. It did, and Mack got off okay. He bombed the target.

Mack has an unusual understanding with his gunners, any of whom might find something wrong with his guns once they were headed East.

" If you just want to go along as spectators, you can let your guns go to Hell," Mack tells them politely. " But guns or no guns, if the ship can fly, we're going to reach the target."

The policy of " bomb or bust " also has paid dividends to McKay's crew. So far, there hasn't been an injury, although the first Fortress he had went through nine raids and was struck by flak or bullets more than 400 times.

After nine raids, Mack was made a squadron commander. His determination to get his bombs on the target, come Hell or high fighters, had already affected the group.

His former squadron commander, Maj. James W. Wilson, of Bowling Green, Ohio, says McKay, " is an inspiration to the whole group."

" In the first place," Maj. Wilson ex-
(Continued on page 4)

"No Thriller Stuff—Just Blasts Target." *Stars & Stripes*, March 10, 1943. Courtesy of the East Anglia Air War Collection.

Fort Pilot - -

(Continued from page 1)

plained, " Mack knows his airplane from A to Z. And he's a natural flier. He's a hell of a lot scareder to stay at home and have others say he's an ' abortion artist ' than he is to go up on a raid."

" On one of the Lille raids two of his uperchargers went out before he reached he target. In spite of the big loss in power he managed to stay at the head of tie squadron and get his bombs on the arget.

" You can always count on Mack. If 1e takes off, he's going across."

Now a squadron commander, McKay s " benched " occasionally by the Group ommander. Brig. Gen. (then Col.) Frank A. Armstrong, of Nashville, N.C., kept .im out of the second raid on Germany, ʻeb. 4, figuring that Mack had had ʻnough for a while. At the last moment Mack tried to go as a tail gunner; but 3rig. Gen. Armstrong discovered the plot and took his pilot-gunner into the control ower with him until all planes were off.

McKay was graduated from flying chool July 11, 1941, and had some experience in medium bombardment before getting into the heavy stuff. He went hrough Compton Junior College and erved a year in the Naval Reserve enisted ranks before entering flying school.

they plastered the target right on the nose. A good raid like this certainly makes the fellows feel better.

March 13 - Maj. McKay led a raid on Amiens today. It was another 100% raid, but they bombed everything but the target it seems. Bad weather again, two raids within two days without loss or without casualty. Say, us medics are going to get out of practice at that rate.

March 14 - Am in London tonight to attend a five-day school of surgery at the Hammersmith Hospital. Hope it's good, but I shall not worry too much about it, yes or no, because five days in London is five days in London. Went to a movie tonight and am turning in at a reasonable hour. Haven't seen any of the other fellows yet.

March 19 - The school was over here in London this afternoon, and I'll be going home tomorrow. It has been a good week.

Nothing new was advanced, but it has been a good review on a lot of subjects. Today one of our most interesting lectures was by a young doctor in the paratroops. A Mr. Franklin was our best lecturer, and Prof. Grey-Turner the best known.

I have gone to a show of some kind every night in London including two plays, which were most enjoyable. One, Shaw's "Doctor's Dilemma" with Vivien Leigh was particularly good. Vivien Leigh was not so good, but the doctors were magnificent. Maybe I'm prejudiced. Shaw gives the doctors a stiff "raking over the coals," but one has to admit that most of what he said was true. The other play was "Watch on the Rhine" with Dianna Wyngard and Anton Walbrook. It was a very dramatic thing, but humorous enough to be entertaining. It was a very powerful story, really propaganda, but well done—the sort of play one will long remember. If our combat crews could see that play it would be quite an inspiration to keep on fighting, I think. The whole theme is about the strength of will and determination of anti-Nazi Germans.

March 20 - Back at my home station. Everything has run along awfully smooth in my absence. All the big shots in the country came along on an inspection tour while I was gone, and thanks to Manning he had everything in good shape.

They ran one mission while I was gone day before yesterday, and it was perhaps their most successful one run thus far. It is the very first raid out of about thirty that our Group has run that I have not been on hand to "sweat them in." They raided Vegesack, Germany, a big submarine plant near Bremen. According to all reports, they did extraordinary fine bombing, and what's more, it was another 100% raid for our group. No casualties at all except for some very minor ones. All the papers have carried some nice accounts of it. It is the first time that they have really plastered a German target right on the nose, and with the loss of only two bombers for the whole show. Even Churchill has extended his congratulations. Maybe this will show the boys that Fortresses can stand up on their own feet without fighter escort. These four fortress groups over here in England are really crackerjack organizations now. They are meeting the stiffest opposition in the world and are holding their own most of the time now.

March 22 - Another raid on the docks at Wilhelmshaven. For the fourth straight time now, every scheduled ship has left the ground, nobody has turned back, all have bombed the target, and all have returned home. Sgt. [Raymond J.] Henn, waist gunner, 423rd, was instantly killed by enemy gunfire. Two other enlisted men received minor injuries. This will be the first dead man we have hauled away from this post in 3 months. The bombing apparently was good again today.

March 27 - This has been an inactive week due to weather, but everybody has been glad. It has been a good rest for the fellows. The weather looks good tonight and they will be ready to go tomorrow if called.

I was up at the Diddington hospital this afternoon and was suddenly introduced to no less than the personal representatives of the Surgeon General in Washington, a Colonel and a Lt. Colonel. They inquired about the equipment furnished by them for such stations, and I told them the greatest need in the way of equipment was a stretcher with which one could remove casualties from a B-17, such as the Neil-Robertson stretcher, an RAF item which we were fortunate to fall heir to here, and invited them down for a demonstration. Much to my surprise, they accepted my invitation and immediately came on down and seemed to be much impressed with our demonstration of the need for such a piece of equipment. They even remarked, "You have sold us a bill of goods." And one might say that is something. When one can sell any idea to anybody in Washington in a few minutes it is phenomenal. If that litter is adopted as a standard piece of equipment for heavy bombardment outfits, then I have made my contribution to the war effort for this day. (The RAF NeilRobertson stretcher was indeed adopted and made standard equipment for bomb groups. That is one contribution that the Medical Department of the 306th made to the national war effort.)

March 30 - Stanbridge Earls - Two days ago I reported for a week's duty here, and I must say it is the most wonderful "work" that I have ever done. Stanbridge Earls is a big country estate two miles from Romsey, near Southampton on the south coast of England. It is operated by the Air Force as a Rest Home for Officers of the Air Force, particularly tired combat crews. A doctor is on "duty" here all the time, and that service is rotated a week at a time among various doctors in the Air Force, so it was my turn this week. It is perfectly marvelous. Never before in my 28 years of life have I been surrounded by so much luxury. There is room for about twenty officers. The rooms out-do even the Savoy Hotel, there are several bath rooms, each done in a different pastel shade. They have the same staff of servants that kept the place before the war, the food is simply delicious, including fresh eggs every morning for breakfast. Capt. Morse, the officer in charge, is a former hotel manager in Denver and is skilled at giving service. Mrs. Pam Hanna, of the American Red Cross, is a most charming hostess. The grounds are spacious and perfectly lovely. They have more athletic and sports equipment here than most sports stores have. Everyone seems to have the time of his life here, and I know I am. If I don't get our fellows using this place I am really falling down on my job. There is absolutely nothing here even remotely suggestive of airplanes and would certainly be invaluable for anyone on the verge of nervous trouble or flying fatigue. They even have old clothes for one to relax in. Today I wore a pair of blue tweed pants and a red sweater, the first civilian clothes I have worn in fifteen long months. Boy, it was wonderful.

April 3, 1943 - This is to be my last night at Stanbridge Earls and tomorrow will be the end of one of the most luxurious and most enjoyable weeks in my life. Lelich came down to relieve me this afternoon so my duties are officially over. My entire medical duties for the week have consisted of applying antiseptic to abrasions on two people who had minor bicycle accidents, so I have spent the whole time trying to raise as much hell as anybody else. We have bicycled over the whole country, walked considerably, played badminton, volleyball, touch football, practiced a little archery, shot craps, fished, practically gorged ourselves at every meal, visited at least one pub at least once a day, but most of all just plain relaxed. We all went to a local charity benefit dance last night and everybody had a whale of lot of fun. How can I go back to work after a week like this?

April 4 - Back to the post and the fellows are riding on top of the world it seems. They pulled the finest raid today that we have ever done. This Group sent out 30 bombers, the most any Group has ever put up, three of them turned back, but 27 went over the target and all returned without casualties except minor burns and frost bites. The target was a big truck and tank factory in Paris, and the photographs bear out the bombardiers' claims that the bombing was extremely accurate and completely devastating. They did two other raids while I was gone, one at Rouen where the bombing was also extremely accurate on the marshalling yards, and another one on the docks at Amsterdam where the bombing was not so good. No planes were lost on either raid. That is eight consecutive raids now without loss of plane and with only one man killed.

April 5 - The blow struck with a vengeance today. We sent out 20 planes to bomb an aircraft engine shop at Antwerp. Two of them aborted. The others crossed the target, but fourteen returned here badly shot up and four ships did not return. That is the heaviest loss in planes in one day

Army Air Force Rest Home at Stanbridge Earls. Shuller is seated second from left.
Courtesy of the Thurman Shuller Family Collection.

to date. Furthermore three of these were from the 367th squadron again, which makes their score of losses fourteen. Those lost today were Lt. [Robert J.] Seelos, Lt. [Williams H.] Parker, Lt. [Kelly] Ross, and Lt. [Clarence] Fisher. Lt. Seelos, 368th, was another of our original crews. With him were Lt. [Alexander] Kramarinko (the Russian) and Lt. [William W.] Saunders, whose home is in Bartlesville and who knows Frank [Shuller's brother Frank Shuller]. In Col. Putnam's own words, the greatest loss in fighting strength was Capt. Salternik, the Group navigator who received an awfully bad gunshot wound of the leg. The medical department really did itself proud in saving that boy. He had lost practically all of his blood and was practically pulseless when he got back. Simpson gave him four bottles of plasma before he even attempted to remove him from the plane. He got to the hospital in fair shape after further supportive measures in the dispensary, and he should come around O.K. Blood plasma and sulfonamides are wonderful things in this war.

This tragedy of today is a terrible blow to this Group, but really it may have been a good thing. We were having just a little too good luck and

Mack McKay was an original pilot for the 306th Bomb Group and served as the commanding officer of the 368th Bomb Squadron. He previously flew for the Flying Tigers in China. Courtesy of the East Anglia Air War Collection.

too many of the fellows were getting to feel that we were over the hump and that we were becoming almost invincible. Some of the newer crews have quite a number of missions without ever having experienced the effect of loss of planes. The fellows are really not taking things so hard though except for a few isolated cases. They are really getting battle hardened.

April 7 - Major McKay was ordered back to the States for training purposes today. I sure hate to see him go, but it is a break for him. That is the sort of thing the Air Force should have been doing a long time ago. A man like Mack who has had a lot of combat time and is good at it too can be invaluable in a training unit back at the source. It is usually the man the Commander wants to get rid of who is sent away on a detail like this. That is what's wrong with so much of the poor brains in the various headquarters. If a man is no good, the easiest way to dispose of him is to "kick him upstairs." I am happy that Mack is an exception to the rule.

The whole field is happy that Capt. Salternik is completely out of shock now and is on the road to recovery. No doubt he will be recommended for a high award, he certainly deserves it. Even after his leg was almost shot off, he maintained presence of mind enough to navigate the Group Commander back off the target and give him a bearing to follow back to England before he became unconscious. Lt. Col. Putnam could have paid him no greater compliment when he said that even though we lost four complete planes and crews in the raid, "Salty" was the greatest loss to the fighting power of the Group. It is so seldom that a navigator gets any praise. He is usually an unmentioned man like the guard on a football team. "Salty" for months has had the utmost respect of all his fellow flyers because of his navigation ability, and even though they gave him all the credit, nobody outside the Group ever heard of him. He is quite small, untalkative, retiring, and a most unimpressive person. But this Group always depended on him to lay out all the flight plans and timetables the night before raids. He had that rare uncanny ability to work out time factors and get them accurately. They would start out with a timetable for a dozen points along the course, and time and time again I have stood in the watch tower and watched the planes come back off a four or five hour mission within 30 seconds of the E.T.A (estimated time of arrival). If he was as much as five minutes off, you could almost depend on it that they had run into trouble. It is for these reasons that I am doubly proud of the way the Medical Department handled him. I think nobody but us knows just how close to death he really was. An awful lot of credit must be given to the first aid the crews are able to give to their fellows. It so happened that General Armstrong was riding as passenger on this plane. I reminded "Salty" that it isn't everybody who has the honor of being treated by a General.

April 8 - While I was down at Stanbridge Earls the Eighth Air Force finally got around to setting a limit on the number of missions expected of a crewman in this theatre. The number was set at 25. During the last six weeks I have been agitating for such a move in every way I knew, and Lt. Col. Putnam has backed me up in it. I was advocating 20, but the higher figure of 25 has elevated the morale of the outfit tremendously. I shook so many bushes and raised so much hell about it that I like to think I had a small part in bringing about this action. For the record, I am quoting a letter to the C.O. which he sent on up through Command channels for the benefit of the "big dogs."

Office of the Group Surgeon
306th Bombardment Group (H)
A.P.O. 634
12 March 1943
Subj: Combat Expectancy of Fliers
To: The Commanding Officer 306th Bomb Gp.
 1. The following statement is quoted from an Eighth Bomber Command letter dated 18 Sept 1942, Subject: Enclosed Correspondence-Guide for Care of Fliers, "to the Commanding Officers of 1st, 2nd, 3rd and 4th Bomb. Wings, and signed by Major General Eaker:

"of this I am certain, and you can count upon it, that as long as I retain command of this organization, a combat crew must be told what their combat expectancy is, and further they must be told that when they have completed that period they will never again be required to man a combat crew station in an airplane on operations against the enemy."

2. It should be called to the attention of the Commanding General that although Groups have been operating in this theatre for seven months, this maximum combat expectancy still has not been fixed. As a result of this indefinite state of affairs and in view of our high rate of losses the Group and Squadron Surgeons all feel that the crews in this Group are on the verge of a complete psychological breakdown.

3. In this Group we have lost 20 of our original 35 combat crews in addition to several replacement crews, yet very few have seen as many as 15 missions. This would seem to indicate that the chance of surviving even 20 missions over German territory is very small. Such a figure, though difficult to attain, would offer a far greater incentive to keep fighting than they now have.

4. The fliers are now actually saying among themselves that the only apparent hope of survival in this theatre of war is either to become a prisoner of war or to get "the jitters" and be removed from combat. This has brought about a state of morale that can soon become disastrous. One of our officers who has now been on 19 missions has already said that he is turning in his wings, if need be after completing his 20th mission. And I dare say no Board composed of non-combatant officers could have the nerve to suggest this officer is a coward or that he has not already served his country well.

5. It has been recently rumored that relief from flying in this theatre will be impossible because of lack of replacements. However, it is the consensus of opinion of all our medical officers that the number of personnel lost through completion of a maximum number of missions would actually be fewer than the number brought before the Central Medical Board for reclassification, if a definite policy is not established very soon.

6. It is suggested that 20 operational missions should be a very maximum expected of any man, and according to all our present

data 15 would be nearer the ideal. But even a limit of 20, which relatively few can actually reach, would be an invaluable morale factor in giving these men at least a small hope for the future and a goal toward which to strive.

7. It is the opinion of the Medical Department of this Group that this is a matter of paramount importance and worthy of immediate consideration and action.

Thurman Shuller

Major, Medical Corps Group Surgeon

April 12 - It has been one week today since our fellows went on that tough mission to Antwerp, but they haven't been on a raid since because of cloudy weather. Providence has taken care of us because the fellows really needed that rest. Took a couple short hops yesterday, one to Hanington and another to Norwich. It was swell weather for local flying like that.

April 14 - Briefed today for Antwerp again, but the weather prevented. The first briefing since the last mission nine days ago. That is about the record total layoff this year.

Col. Tracy came yesterday and was going on the mission today if it had been run. I don't know why he is so keen to go, but when he does go, I hope he gets shot at and missed if he is so terribly anxious to experience what the combat crews' experience. He did have the experience this morning of getting all cocked and primed to go and having the take-off time set back a couple of times and then finally scrubbed. That did him good to see how it feels to sit and wait. Personally, I am strictly opposed to medical officers going on missions, and I am sure it isn't because I'm afraid. I'd go tomorrow if I thought it my duty to do so, but I have a feeling these combat crews would a whole lot, rather see us back here on the ground prepared to receive them than trailing along on one of the ships.

April 16 - The fellows raided Lorient again today. All the ships got back to England safely, and nobody was very badly hurt. A lot of the ships were pretty badly shot up though. Col. Tracy got off on this one, and from all indications really got his money's worth. He got shot at both by flak and fighters and had considerable engine trouble so it should hold him for a while. But he's talking about trying to go again tomorrow. He must be nuts. Capt. Salternik died tonight. That is going to be a terrible blow to the officers in this Group. He developed gas gangrene yesterday, had to have his leg amputated today. He died suddenly from a thrombis, apparently. That is such a terrible shame. He appeared to be getting along so nicely. It just goes to prove one shouldn't get too optimistic about bad injuries.

It is rumored today that Capt. Ryan is back in London. Isn't that wonderful news if it is true!

April 17 - This was an all-out effort on the Foch-Wolf factory at Bremen today. You could never have made me believe that we'd ever live to see the day when this would happen to us. We sent out 26 planes. Two returned early. 24 reached the target, of which 10 of our ships failed to return. The blow is staggering. We used to reel and rock with the loss of three planes in a raid, but we didn't believe it possible to lose 10 on one raid. All the fellows say the flak barrage was the worst ever and the fighters were the worst ever, both thrown into one mission. It was such a shameful thing. Almost every one of those pilots had around 20 missions each. It is so terribly sickening to think of those ten pilots with their wealth of experience and hard earned knowledge just thrown away. Their knowledge would have been invaluable back in the States in a training unit and now it does nobody any good. That is just the sort of thing we have been fighting so hard for. There were so many of our old original fellows that I can hardly mention them all. But first of all – Casey [Charles F. Jones]. I didn't believe they would ever get him. He was such a screw-ball, they so seldom get knocked off. The night before he practically drank himself under the table as usual. That same night I sat and argued with him for about half an hour about something or other, our usual thing. With him went Sgt. [Wilson C.] Elliott, an awfully nice kid who started with us from the very first at Wendover. Capt. [Walter N.] Smiley is another great loss. He was a peach of a flier and a most dependable fellow. With him were Lt. [Wilbur W.] Breunig and Lt. [Martin M.] Strauss, both of whom were straining to complete their 25th mission so they could go back to the States to take flight training. This would have been Strauss' 24th and Breunig's 22nd raid. Other pilots were Capt. [Craig J.] Harwood, Lt. [Frank K.] Watson, Lt. [Raymond] Fortin, Lt. [Fred D.] Gillogly, Lt. [Glenn] Lally, Lt. [Robert C.] Miller, Lt. [Theodore] Jankowski and Lt. [Warren] George. Lt. George had become famous as a great initiator of the new replacement crews in telling them of the horrors of war. He used to bring out all the blood stained pieces of flak to show the new fellows and spin some gory tale with it. And now it has gotten him too. With him also went Sgt. [Donald J.] Bevan,[29] the talented artist.

Maxwell Judas air crew in the 368th Bomb Squadron. Front row: Maynard Dix (navigator), Louis Cook (co-pilot), Joe Graziano (radio operator), Gerald Stroud (waist gunner). Back row: Louis Hlavac (waist gunner), Herschel Ezell (bombardier), Elwood Brotzman (tail gunner), Maxwell Judas (pilot), Gerald Barnt (ball turret gunner), and Lee Kessler (enginer). Courtesy of the East Anglia Air War Collection.

In this thing today the 423rd lost one crew, the 398th lost five crews, and the 367th lost 4 crews. That brings the infamous 367th losses up to a total of 18 crews. The Group as a whole now has lost 38 crews out of the 35 [that] we started with. The Group tonight is stunned, but not broken. This sort of thing causes a conglomeration of emotions that just can't be expressed in writing.

April 18 - I flew today with Lt. Wigginton up to Coltishall near The Wash to pick up Sgt. [William R.] Wilkinson who was injured in Capt. Youree's ship. Youree flew the North Sea yesterday with the two motors out on one side and one of the ones on the other side with about half power. He apparently did a heroic job getting that ship home and keeping the crew's wits together. They threw out all their guns, ammunition, parachutes and everything else with weight in order to lighten the load.

The crew was terribly shaken when they got back. We are ordering a week's leave for all of them. Lt. [Maxwell V.] Judas had a particularly harassing experience getting a crippled ship home over the water yesterday too. Lt. Reecher came in with an engine feathered and with a dead navigator, Lt. [Harold E.] Lane, in the nose. All these things I forgot to mention yesterday because of the tense situation in general.

They had a big dance tonight and it was a whale of a success. Everybody seemed to relax and have a big time as if nothing had happened. It was worth a lot. But the feature of the dance was when Capt. Ryan made his appearance after his escape from France. When Capt. Ryan went down over Lorient (Mar. 6) was the only time I have shed any tears over anybody, so you can imagine how glad I was to see him. He was just the same as always except that he has an injured arm, a fracture incurred during the parachute jump. He has some tall tales to tell. He thinks he is going to be retained over here as a liaison officer in the Intelligence Department. He is a very sharp individual, speaks French, and it appears he has brought back more valuable information from France than any other one man has recently. The word has leaked out that he knows more about the Free French than the English do. In fact it may be that he is too "dangerous" to allow to go back at this time.

April 25 - This is Easter-Sunday, but there was nothing today that even remotely resembled Easter except that I went to church and the chapel was crowded for a change.

Our group is still off operations since that big raid eight days ago. We are filled up with replacements again and this time is giving us some valuable time to get started all over again. In addition, a couple squadrons of the 94th Group are here undergoing training prior to going into operation. The 95th Group is somewhere here in England too. It looks like we are going to have a little help over here at last.[30]

A couple of days ago I wrote another letter to Col. Putnam regarding combat crew expectancy, bringing our recent data up to date and further advocating 20 missions as a maximum. I was pleased today to hear that he had personally written an indorsement and sent it forward through channels. I supposed that he would just file it as a matter of information.

April 28 – We are about ready to go back on operations again. The new fellows were flying awfully good formation today. None of the Groups have been on any missions since we were taken off. Will be glad when we get started again, morale will pick up maybe.

A letter came through from 8th Bomber Command today signed by General Longfellow (written by Col. Tracy) that all flight surgeons assigned to bomber outfits should make an occasional operational mission. Personally I think Tracy is all wet. His idea is that in so doing the flight surgeons will elevate themselves in the eyes of the fliers and make them better suited to judge their psychological reactions. Bosh! There is nothing a flight surgeon can learn on an operational mission that he cannot learn on a practice mission. Without exception all the fliers consider everyone a damn fool who goes on a mission who does not have to go. They would much prefer to have the doctors waiting by the sideline for them to come home ready to take care of them when they get back. Since this thing has come out more or less as an order, it will lose all benefit it could possibly have anyway. If we don't go now, it can be said we are "afraid" to go. If we do go, it can be said we went because we "had" to go. Well I suppose we will all start going on missions now.

May 2, 1943 - Writing in this book is getting to be a chore. If only there weren't so many unpleasant things to record. Yesterday the fellows went to St. Nazaire for the umpteenth time. They took off with eighteen planes, three of which aborted. Again three of our planes failed to return, even though the weather was bad and they didn't even hit the target probably. They crossed the target O.K. but on the return trip the navigator was off and they ran right into Brest harbor. They were flying at only 800 feet and the Germans opened up with everything they had, even the 16 inch shore batteries it is said. Little Capt. [John H.] Dexter was doing the navigating and he is feeling awfully low. He more or less holds himself responsible for the whole thing and the loss of all those men. I'm afraid he is about ruined. It has almost completely shattered his confidence. The pilots in the missing planes were Lt. [Edwin G.] Pipp, Lt. [Owen E.] Luby and Lt. [Bart] Wigginton. The one I particularly hated to see go down was Lt. Wigginton. He is one of the eagerest, most likeable fellows I have known. He was awfully friendly and was really a clean good fellow. The last time I rode in a plane a couple of weeks ago was with him. His plane crashed into the Brest harbor, did one or two cartwheels and then exploded and scattered over a half mile or so.

Lt. [Lewis P.] Johnson completed his 25th mission, but it was the toughest one of his active career. A fighter caught him just off Brest, set fire in the tail, and another in the radio room completely burned out everything including the radio equipment, the floor, and buckled the walls of the plane. The tail gunner was badly wounded by gunshot wounds of the chest and lungs, three of his gunners seeing the enormous fires bailed out over the channel and are considered lost. Another of the gunners by the name of [Maynard] Smith, on his first mission, stayed with the plane and extinguished the flames among all the ammunition that was exploding. He should be given the D.S.C. for that.[31] One of the gunners who bailed out was on his 24th mission.

Another stroke of fate connected with Johnson's ship is Lt. [Stanley N.] Kisseberth, bombardier. He was shot in the leg Feb. 16, 2 ½ months ago, over St. Nazaire. He had been grounded all this time but for the last week had been begging to go back. That morning I relented, and let him go to briefing. When he opened the door and saw that it was St. Nazaire again he almost fell through the floor. But being a plucky little devil, he insisted on going. The outcome was that he was again hit by flak, again in the same leg, and again over St. Nazaire, the first time he had been in a plane for 2 ½ months. He will be our first to have been injured twice, the very first one in our eight months over here that any of our men has become eligible for the oak leaf cluster to the Purple Heart.

One gunner was killed, a new man on his first mission. Three or four others were seriously injured and about eight had minor injuries. I think more men were injured on this raid than any other. Very few of these boys I ever heard of even, they come and go so fast.

Diary, do you realize that we have lost 17 complete planes and crews in the last 4 missions? This brings the total losses for the Group up to 41, of which 19 are from the 367th squadron alone. We're getting into a pretty bad state of affairs. There are now several real cases of jitters. Capt. [Chester H.] May, usually a very composed individual was seen crying like a baby in his barracks tonight, just because he is tired and fed up. Lt. [David A.] Steele, a close friend of Wigginton's, is an obvious case of the jitters. Even Colonel Putnam was shaky after the raid last night, Manning said.

With all this excitement I almost forget to mention that Capt. [Richard D.] Adams came back to the field night before last for a few days. I think of very few I might be more glad to see get back from France. He had been gone six months, but he looks well (Nov. 8). He suffered some rather severe frost bite of the feet while crossing the Pyrenees Mountains in the snow. He will be in the hospital at Oxford for a time.

May 3 - My medical practice has developed entirely along new lines to-day. You might say I am specializing in psychological and psychiatric problems. Not one single patient did I see all day, but I have listened to just about every story I can think of. Between the chaplain and me I think I am definitely the winner. If this is the job and responsibility of a Flight Surgeon, then I got plenty of practice today. This is the sort of thing that tests one's judgement and tact. I always feel so terribly incapable and unexperienced in analyzing and advising and encouraging these fellows. God knows I try hard enough. So awfully much depends on just the right words spoken in just the right tone of voice, and I never know whether I have it. I do seem to have pretty good luck getting their confidence. At least I am a good listener. Perhaps they are helped most by just being able to "get it off their chest" to someone whom they figure won't laugh at them or call them "weak."

I started off at 8:00 a.m. with a lecture to the 94th Group on venereal disease (a particularly good beginning in this theatre). Immediately after that one of the young navigators of the 94th came to me wanting help about his drinking too much. I was completely off guard and didn't know what to say. A big percentage of our fellows do drink too much, but it is a rare bird who figures he wants to quit it just now. I had to admit that he was in a very bad environment to try to break something that he already couldn't control. He realizes that it is hurting his job, that he is losing confidence in his own sense of responsibility and losing the respect and confidence of his crew. Reassurance was the best I could do, but realized it was wholly inadequate. Someday maybe we'll discover a vaccine for such cases.

The second case was that of Capt. [Chester H.] May. He was the lead bombardier on the mission Saturday. He was found in his room last night just crying like a baby. He was complaining of just being tired and "fed-up." All week he had been flying quite a bit. Friday he went on a high altitude practice mission. Friday night he sat up most of the night, figuring out the problem for the mission next day, got up early for briefing then flew in the lead ship. He stated that for the first time, he didn't even put on his parachute because it was "too heavy." He said that part of the time he didn't even fire his gun at every plane within range because it was "too much trouble." We put him in the hospital here and will get him off to the rest home for a week tomorrow.

Poor little Capt. Dexter is running around like a chicken with his head cut off worrying about the mistake he made in navigation Saturday. He feels that the whole Group is pointing its finger at him in scorn. Actually, the whole Group feels sorry for him because he feels so badly about it. Everybody knows he is a good navigator, that he did his best, but that something just went wrong. I rather wanted to send him away for a few days too, but Dexter wants to fly the very next mission to try to regain his confidence and that is what the operations officer wants to do also, so we'll give it a try.

About noon Lt. [John G.] Magoffin came in with the story that he was just plain tired and wanted to spend a "day or so in the hospital getting rested up." Mac is considered one of the most stable and reliable fellows in the 369th squadron, and when he breaks down like that there must be something wrong somewhere. Although he has had some harrowing experiences lately, I don't feel that he is suffering from fear at all but that he is having just real flying fatigue. Mac feels it's because they have been flying too many practice missions lately. Everybody is dragging around taking little interest in anything. I took a long gamble and had Col. Putnam come down to the hospital to talk to Magoffin to see if Mac would tell him some of the things he told me about too much flying etc. I don't know whether Mac has the answer or not, but I figure if I can bring the Group Commander and a respected pilot together on neutral ground to talk things over, then I have done my best in trying to get at the bottom of this thing. I haven't had a chance to find out what impression the Colonel got yet. I do have a feeling that we are sitting on top of a bomb shell from a psychological standpoint, and I'm not sure whether it is really fatigue from overwork or simply reaction to the high losses we have had lately.

Another case presented himself today, a Capt. Wright, operations officer of the 94th Group. He was as white as a sheet, trembling and very jittery. His first words were that he was "afraid." He had been scheduled to go on the operational mission today (the mission was canceled later) as an observer. He began to make excuses and so much as said that he would not go. He frankly admitted to me that there was nothing wrong with him physically, simply that he was afraid. Of all the cases of excessive fear that we have had, all have said they'd continue to go if ordered but that they knew they could no longer do their job. There isn't a combat man in this theatre who isn't afraid and almost all of them admit it, but this is the first time I have seen a man refuse to go. He did this in spite of the fact that he realizes that he could be charged with cowardice in face of the enemy which carries the penalty of a firing squad. I don't know yet what the outcome will be. His squadron C.O. wisely wants to give him a few days to re-consider. This man is 32 years old, far above our average age for pilots. He did not take regular Army training but was commissioned on the strength of a lot of civilian time and some service with the Canadian Air Force. He just got here a few days ago and immediately saw one of the squadron commanders in his Group fail to return from a mission, and it apparently struck him so hard that this game is such a hell of a lot tougher than he had ever realized that he was simply overwhelmed before he ever got started.

The above were just a few of the things I was supposed to know the answer to today. Well, I guess a few more gray hairs won't hurt much.

May 5 - The fellows ran a "diversion" mission yesterday and it was completely uneventful. Today they were scheduled to hit an airplane repair shop near Albert, France but the mission was canceled. Everybody was glad and went home and slept most of the afternoon.

Something that is irritating me no end is the fact that they are now calling so many "maximum effort" missions. They are carrying it to the extreme of calling fellows back off their leave in London in order to go on the mission. It is playing havoc with the morale of the fellows. It completely destroys the real benefit of a leave, that of the relaxation in the knowledge that one will not be called on for a period of time. It is irritating me so that I am writing a letter about it to send up through channels.

There is a British officer on the field who gave us the complete story of Lt. [William H.] Warner and his ship which went down on the way to St. Nazaire Feb. 17. This officer was pretending to be a French peasant and was at the scene of the crash. Lt. Warner was hit in the head and killed. Lt. [Lewis H.] Utley, navigator was killed as well as several of the gunners including Sgt. [Colin E.] Neeley whom we practically forced to go on that flight. Sgt. [Eddie F.] Espitalier, radio operator, is a prisoner of war; and Lt. [Robert E.] Kylius, bombardier, Lt. [Arnold R.] Carlson, co-pilot; and Sgt. [Claiborne W.] Wilson, engineer are all loose somewhere in France. He said the bodies were buried by the Germans in a common grave and that they did hold a funeral service for them. The French held a service of their own later and brought huge numbers of flowers, even though it was February and flowers were out of season. He says that the French have placed flowers on the grave every Sunday since. Of all the many planes that have gone down in combat from here, that is the first one in which we have full information as to what happened. It's awfully hard to realize that such a wonderful fellow as Warner is dead. He and Johnston and Brady were all wonderful fellows and wonderful pilots, all dead because of whatever it is we are fighting for. I only hope it is worth it.

May 9 - Guess where I have been the last three days? Went to Northern Ireland three days ago and just got back tonight. Had been wanting to add Ireland to my travel log for a long time and the opportunity came Thursday to ride up with Capt. Smith and Lt. Johnson, who were taking up the old veteran ship "Yankee Raider" for disposition. Capt. Youree took up another old ship and Lt. Magoffin flew another one to bring all the personnel back. Those ship loads made quite a party for the three days we got "weathered in."

I rode with Capt. Smith as far as Wheaton, on the northwest English coast where we landed to let some passengers off. The no. 1 engine had been smoking all the way, and before we took off again Smith put all us passengers in one of the other planes. The engine was smoking so that the tower would not let Capt. Smith take off and like a dope I had left my blouse and coat in that plane. Smith's plane did not get there until 24 hours later and there I was without fit clothes to leave the post. We landed at Langford Lodge, a very beautiful post on the Lough [Neagh] (Lake Lowe), about 20 miles west of Belfast. Our main interest was in getting into Belfast that night because we had heard that there was no black-out, that one could buy thick steaks, etc. etc. just like back home. It was a disillusioned little group of officers who discovered that Belfast was as black as the ace of spades and everything rationed just like here in England. We might have liked Belfast had we not been so disappointed. I had considerable difficulty pretending to be dressed properly. I wore Capt. [John T.] Stanko's trench coat over my leather flying jacket, but that ran into difficulties when we went in to eat. Luckily there were no M.P.'s around to put me out while I was sitting in there eating in my shirt sleeves.

The lodge was very comfortable and all of us were glad that it was raining and that we couldn't leave. The greatest treat of all was that they had all the cold sweet milk we could drink at meal. That is the one food we don't have here that I miss most of all, and it is the first time I had had any milk to drink in over eight months. On Saturday night we also had ice cream—real strawberry ice cream—and lots of it. We had fried eggs on Sunday morning. We bought a few dozen eggs to bring back with us, but somebody stole all of them but 2 dozen. When we got back here we matched for the few remaining and I won them.

The whole post is pretty up there. Vegetation is profuse. It is more of an assembly and repair depot. Lockheed has a big plant there and the Army post is just sort of built around them. They have about 2000

S/Sgt Maynard Smith, recipient of the Medal of Honor at Thurleigh Air Field. Courtesy of the East Anglia Air War Collection.

workers there and they have a modern hospital, beautifully equipped, fit for a city of 25,000. They have a staff of four American doctors, all on fabulous salaries. That's one way of contributing to the war effort.

When we all got piled into Lt. Magoffin's plane coming back there were 20 of us. The big shots back home would have a fit if they knew that many were in one plane. We got back to find that everything had run smoothly as usual in our absence that the weather had been bad here too and no missions run and everything about as we left it. I was glad that I went prepared to be held over a few days. I have learned a long time ago that it doesn't pay to go on that long a plane ride in this region and expect to return immediately.

As soon as Lt. Johnson got back to camp, orders were waiting for him to go back to the U.S., along with Capt. [Roy W.] Howard. Johnson was the first pilot to complete his 25 missions. He's an admirable lad. He's from the mountains of Kentucky, is only 21 years old - yet he has all this terrific combat experience behind him and is really an old man in his field. Imagine that! A veteran of the flying fortress at 21, when most kids that age would still be in college, or just entering Cadet training. In peace time a flier couldn't have thought of sitting on the left side of a fortress cockpit until he had been a co-pilot for several years. He's such an awfully likeable chap and completely unspoiled by the events behind him. He'll be decorated plenty for his performance on his last mission when he brought back that terribly burned out plane. His ball turret gunner on that mission is being recommended for the Congressional Medal of Honor.

If it goes through it will be the first in this Theatre of War. Johnson isn't so terribly anxious to go back to the states now that the time has come, he would just as soon do a little more fighting. It sort of gets him to be reminded that he's an old veteran at 21. One just has to admire that kid. He had a great teacher over here. He flew his first fourteen combat missions as McKay's co-pilot before he took over his crew. He's not the flier McKay is, but he's good enough for me any day.

May 11 - Lt. Col. Putnam became Col. Putnam last night. They say he really "tied one on" last night in celebration. I didn't stay around to see. That's doing pretty well to become a full colonel at the age of 28. He's a very able commander though and is doing a very good job with this outfit. As long as one stays in his good graces he will do O.K. Woe be unto me the day I get on the wrong side of the fence from him.

May 12 - Capt. Robert Williams became Maj. Williams today. He's about the most deserving little fellow in the outfit and it certainly makes me happy to see him promoted. That operations room wouldn't run without him.

The matter of calling crews back off their two-day passes to participate in what Bomber Command calls maximum efforts has been quite a sore spot on my conscience for quite a long time. It reached the boiling point today so that I wrote a letter to Col. Tracy about it today. It lays me wide open to a slap in the face for saying what I think, but it won't be the first time I have been told, "Sit down, little boy. You're talking too big!" I know I'm right even if it does buck a General's policy, although I'll admit a fellow frequently lives longer and is more peaceful who keeps his mouth shut.

Office of the Group Surgeon
306th Bomb Gp.
A.P.O. 634
12 May 1943
Subject: Cancellation of Leaves for Maximum Effort Operations
To: The Surgeon, VIII Bomber Command A.P.O. 639
1. It is requested that strong protest be immediately registered with the Commanding General, VIII Bomber Command, against the calling of combat crews back to the home station from regular passes in order to participate in a so-called "maximum effort."
2. The first such mission was run on 4th April when several of our crews were called back from a two-day pass in London. One of these crews was on its first pass in over four weeks at that time. Although

they were a little vexed at having their well-earned pass broken up, they returned willingly because they felt that it must surely be a most unusual circumstance and that it would not be a frequent occurrence. However, a few days later a maximum effort was called again. It was finally scrubbed, but not until crews had already been called back from London again. On 4th May such a mission was called for a third time, and a pilot, who had gone into London with his crew the evening before for the first time in weeks, was recalled to the base. The mission was later cancelled and the pilot and crew returned to London to resume their pass. The next day, 5th May, a maximum effort was again called and this same crew was recalled to the base a second time in 24 hours. This mission was likewise scrubbed and they still had no leave after two attempts, neither was the mission run.

3. It should not be necessary to point out just how disastrous this practice can be to the morale of the fighting men if this policy is continued. It completely nullifies the real purpose of a pass, that of complete relaxation in the knowledge that one will not be called on for duty within a definite period of time. As a result, our crews can no longer go into London with any more assurance that they will not be called upon than if they were not on leave at all.

4. It has long been recognized that regular and frequent leave is one of the essentials in the prevention of flying fatigue. Therefore, it would seem that it should be an extraordinary case indeed which would interfere with that policy, and especially should the cancellation of leaves after they are already in effect be most vehemently condemned. It would seem that such an effort can be justified only by a target vastly more important than any thus far assigned. It is difficult to see how the advantages the few extra planes operated by such means can possibly, at this time, outweigh the inevitable increase in flying fatigue and the tremendously decreased morale that most certainly will become apparent shortly.

It is requested that operations of "maximum effort" not be interpreted to include crews whose regular two-day passes are already in effect.

Thurman Shuller
Major, Medical Corps
Group Surgeon

✳

This memo was Shuller's second attempt to influence policy and advocate for the air crews who suffered under the existing "Maximum Effort" policy. Unlike his first effort to get a minimum mission threshold established, this time Shuller sent the memo directly to the Bomber Command surgeon. It was a risky ploy.

Major Thurman Shuller with a patient in his office at Thurleigh, March 2, 1943. Courtesy of the Thurman Shuller Family Collection.

Medical officers, 306th Bomb Group, Thurleigh. Left to right: Charles P. McKim, Henry A. Dantzig, Samuel D. Simpson, John J. Manning, Harold D. Munal, Thurman Shuller, Alfred E. Erb, circa early 1943. Courtesy of the Thurman Shuller Family Collection.

Fall out by the ambulances to go meet the planes returning from a combat mission. Courtesy of the Thurman Shuller Family Collection.

The 306th Bomb Group used British ambulances on the airdrome. Courtesy of the Thurman Shuller Family Collection.

Chapter 3

A Doctor at War

May 13, 1943–March 9, 1944

Thurman Shuller opens this next diary chapter with an optimistic appraisal of better times to come. Since the 306th Bomb Group arrived in England in September 1942, four B-17 bomb groups and occasionally two Liberator bomb groups were often beleaguered, alone, and without long-range fighter protection, often suffering heavy losses and sporadic success in attacking Axis targets on the continent of Europe. Between January and May 1943, five new bomb groups arrived in England and were now ready to join the bombing campaign against occupied Europe.[1]

Expanded fighter escort coverage and improved range into Germany is another change that will soon make a difference for the bombers attacking deep into Germany. The key will be long-range drop tanks and the deployment of the North American P-51 Mustang fighter. With increased engine power developed by the British by fitting a more powerful Rolls-Royce Merlin engine to the Mustang, the Americans were moving swiftly to build the new enhanced P-51 in the United States. "By the summer of 1943, Packard Merlin-powered P-51s were coming off North American's assembly line . . . equipped with jettisonable drop tanks," and increased "operational range of more than 1,600 miles." P-51s flown from fighter bases in England "mounted their first long-range bomber escort missions over Germany in mid-December 1943."[2]

The Mustang was a game changer for the heavy bombers in England. The future still included dangerous missions and losses, but the P-51 leveled the playing field for the Allies. December 1943 saw the beginning of the shift in air power that would make all that followed possible. The P-51 was the "first to go with the heavy bombers over the Ploiesti oil fields in Romania, and first to make a major-scale, all-fighter sweep specifically to hunt down the dwindling Luftwaffe." D-Day was still in the future, and VE Day remained two years in the distance, but Shuller had an inkling that the tide was turning.[3]

*

Figure 1
BASES IN EAST ANGLIA
EIGHTH AIR FORCE
1942-1945

1st AIR DIVISION ▲
2nd AIR DIVISION ■
3rd AIR DIVISION ●
DIVISION HQS ◆

Bases in East Anglia: Eighth Air Force, 1942–1945. Courtesy of the East Anglia Air War Collection.

May 13 - I know no better occasion to open up a new book because in the annals of the A.A.F. in the European Theatre, this is a new day. For many months now, four struggling little Groups of B-17's and one or two small Groups of B-24's have been carrying the brunt of the daylight air attacks on Germany. Today three or four new Groups who have been in training here for a few weeks, made their maiden voyage in a raid on a large aerodrome near St. Albert, France. It was a wonderful sight here, but it must have been a terrible sight to Jerry. At one time this afternoon, one could see at least 100 fortresses in the air at one time. It was our biggest showing yet. It was fitting that this should be the date of intensified aerial warfare on Germany because yesterday, the war was over in Africa. The bombing to-day apparently was not too good, but we won't worry too much about that, because we'll be getting more coordinated with the new organizations. We sent out 26 of our ships and 10 belonging to the 94th Group, a total of 36 ships, or six more than have ever taken off from here before. I wonder if anybody knows just how many planes are here on this field now. It must be between 65 and 70. And that's a lot of flying fortresses!

May 14 - It's seldom I make any notes in the morning, but today is exceptional. Our planes took off this morning to go to Kiel, Germany, the deepest penetration thus far. The 94th along with other new units is going to somewhere near Antwerp. This is what we have been waiting for—two blows at different targets simultaneously. Also the B-25's, B-26's and P-47's are in on the show. Col. Putnam at briefing this morning said it was the biggest concentration of the A.A.F. in any theatre to date. It's good weather here at last, and it should bring good results—but dangerous.

But the big reason I am on the pan is because of little Capt. [John H.] Dexter, navigator. He came into my office yesterday almost in tears because he had been grounded and given ground duties. He felt that it was directly because of his mistake on the last St. Nazaire raid that they sailed into the harbor of Brest [by mistake]. He felt that the whole Group is down on him. He has completely lost all confidence in himself, feels that when he is called on to lecture to the new crews that they look at him and say, "Look who's trying to tell us how to navigate. He can't navigate himself." As a matter of fact, Dexter is a good navigator. He just made a mistake and is looking for a chance to rectify it. He was ready yesterday to quit. I tried the old trick of trying to laugh it off with him and persuaded him not to do anything rash until he had slept on it. In the meantime last night, I presented his case to Capt. [William S.] Raper, his [367th Bomb Squadron] C.O., and he agreed with me that he should be ungrounded and given a chance to clear himself. As a result, he is navigating our Group to Kiel today. We're sending a nervous, sensitive kid in the lead ship just to prove our convictions that he is a good navigator and to reclaim him as a useful combat man. That is quite a chance we are taking, which could even be disastrous. I think I'll sit in my office all day and just chew my nails.

Friday night - The bombers came home, all in good shape, bombs squarely on both targets, and only two minor casualties. It was one of the most successful raids this group has been on. The ship building plants at Kiel were squarely hit, something the R.A.F. has failed to do in almost 20 trials. Furthermore, Dexter justified our confidence in him by turning out a fine job. We're picking up speed now with two missions in two days without loss. Other Groups lost 11 bombers today, six of which were B-24's.

May 15 - We're really back in the groove again. A very typical raid. The 306th Gp. sent out 24 planes, and the 94th sent out 13 planes to bomb Wilhelmshaven and Emden respectively and simultaneously. Three of our bombers did not return, and guess who they belonged to—the 367th, of course. That brings their total of planes lost up to 22, out of an original 9 planes. The "Clay Pigeon Squadron"[4] continues to maintain its reputation. And as so frequently happens, they didn't even see the target because of clouds, they dropped their bombs on the island of Helgoland.

The crews are really dragging their rear ends tonight. Three successive days of long missions at high altitude are just too much. Fortunately, Wing Headquarters has used good judgement for a change and declared a holiday for tomorrow. Lt. T.H. Jones, Jr. came into the hospital this afternoon, just on a social call, and he was as white as a sheet and trembling and completely worn out. He, like most of the rest of the crews, got only two or three hours sleep last night after the hard mission yesterday. I'm keeping him in one of our comfortable beds overnight. I wish we could handle all our pilots like that. Junior Jones is one of the most eager little pilots we have, and I have never seen him like this before, so you can depend on it the whole Group is tired. Junior is one of my favorites, I'm afraid. It doesn't pay to have favorites though, they too often fail to come back.

The crews lost today were piloted by Lt. [Alden T.] Mann, Lt. Ritland, and Lt. [Frank B.] Clemons. All of them were replacement crews and I must confess that I didn't know any of them. Manning, their squadron surgeon, knew only one of them. That is really getting tragic. One of the prime responsibilities of a squadron surgeon is to get acquainted with each flier, know them and be in a position to judge their peculiarities of personality, etc., etc. But how can any man know anybody when they come and go so fast. Sgt. [Emil J.] Miller was an old gunner who went down with Clemons. We're going to miss him—the little "screwball." Sgt. Reginald Harris was the only other old gunner. He used to be on Casey's crew and went down today with Mann. His English wife here is expecting a baby next month.

May 17 - In London again at the Hammersmith Hospital again for a week of chest surgery. I wasn't a bit enthusiastic about coming. I would be much happier back at the station with them running so many raids with all the good weather.

I saw the thing last night I have been waiting eight months to see—an air raid in London. But I was so unimpressed that I didn't even get out of bed. I looked out of the window and saw the searchlights and saw the flashes from the antiaircraft, but I was too sleepy to get up. I am disappointed in myself.

May 18 - School was just usual today. Had another air raid, but we're in the west end of the city, and most of the activity is on the other side, I guess.

I went with four of the other doctors to see the play "Flare Path"[5] tonight. It is a story about the wives of the R.A.F. who sit home and wait for their men to come home. It was a good play and wonderfully acted. Almost every line in it, I have seen in real life sometime during the last year. The only thing missing now is that the wives of our officers are not with them. It is a good thing that their absent wives cannot see this play—it would literally drive them mad. It really was wonderfully done.

The papers say that our bombers went to Lorient again yesterday, that the bombing was good, and that four of our bombers are missing. I wonder if our Group lost any more bombers in that wretched place. I wish I was back at the station.

May 20 - Morning - Another air raid last night, the fourth night in a row. I woke up and stuck my head out of the window and watched a few flak bursts. The guns were very close last night, but I didn't see any planes. I heard some overhead, but I suppose they were British. Was asleep again before the all clear sounded. By my own reactions I find that these so-called nuisance raids to keep people awake and excited are a lot of hooey. As much as I have been looking forward to this sort of thing, I find it very difficult to wake up long enough to find out what is going on.

I went to see Noel Coward in his own play "This Happy Breed" last night. It was quite good, and Coward himself was particularly good. I went mainly just to see him. His versatility is a marvel.

The paper this morning says that our bombers went to Kiel again yesterday, and that six of our bombers are missing. I'll never rest easy until I get back and find out what is going on at the 306th. The weather has been so extraordinarily clear the last few days.

May 21 - Back at Camp tonight. The course is over and I'm glad. It was good stuff, but I was too apprehensive about what was going on up here. I don't exactly know why. It's funny, I haven't ever been that way before when I have been away. Everything always runs well.

The two above mentioned raids were run without loss, but they ran into trouble again today. Three of our fellows did not get their planes back. They were Lt. [Robert H.] Smith, 423rd, Lt. [Floyd J.] Field 368th, and, most of all, Lt. [Maxwell V.] Judas 368th. Judas was one of our original crews and had more than 20 missions. With him went Lt. [Foster G.] Daniels who was on his 25th and final raid, Sgt. [Elwood H.] Brotzman who was on his 24th raid and Sgt. [Leland J.] Kessler. Kessler is going to be missed because of his talented artistry. He was always hanging around the hospital because he had been a patient so much. He had crashed into the sea on the way over with Melton off the Irish coast and was getting jittery, but wouldn't give up. Daniels was one of our steadiest and most thoroughly reliable boys. He was an awfully nice kid and more than deserved to get home on this final raid. Those are the ones that hurt worst.

As in the last attempt at Wilhelmshaven, it was cloudy and the bombing was rotten, which makes the losses seem even greater. Lt. Col. [Delmar E.] Wilson is being blamed by all the fellows for poor judgement in leadership today. He apparently carried them through a cloud too long and allowed the formation to get broken up and lost. Some of the fellows are awfully bitter toward him. It's a hard life.

May 22 - Maj. Hastings from Pinetree was here last night on a visit. He is always a pleasant fellow and nice to have around. He gave me some inside dope on just how much of a furor my letter last March regarding Combat Crew Expectancy caused in Bomber Command. I was gratified to learn that it really did cause a stink. I had supposed that it just got pigeon-holed on the way, but it went on up to Maj. General Eaker himself. According to Hastings, that letter more or less brought things to a head. I am pleased to discover that it is possible to make a Maj. General sit up and take notice of a letter from a little fellow like me. Maybe I can do good before I get kicked out for talking too much.

May 23 - This is a happy day for the Group. Lt. [Robert H.] Smith who went down Friday was picked up out of the North Sea after 30 hours along with his entire crew. Major Lambert flew up to the Air-Sea rescue station to pick them up this morning, and when they got back, we found that not a single one of them had any injuries to speak of.

They landed in the drink about 100 miles from shore and were paddling like mad to try to get toward the English shore. It was a remarkable feat. They had carried out every instruction to the letter as far as discipline is concerned in the rafts. They had provisions to last several days.

One of the remarkable things is that they are credited with shooting down eleven enemy fighters. One fighter came in on them, just before they set down in the water. All the guns had been thrown overboard to lighten the plane, except the top turret guns. The top turret gunner had gone back in the belly of the plane to prepare for crashing, so when this plane came in, the co-pilot, Lt. [Robert] McCallum, got up in the turret and shot the plane out of the air. I'll bet there is no other case in the E.T.O. (European Theatre of Operations) of a co-pilot shooting down a plane.

The whole bunch, officers and men are just bubbling over with excitement. We're ordering the lot of them to the Rest Home tomorrow. They've boosted the morale of the Group about 200%.

May 24 - This is a memorable day in my life. I wish the fellows here at the post could have seen it—they wouldn't have believed their eyes. A program was being held in Bedford for an organization called The St. Johns Brigade, a sort of First Aid Group for children aged 11 to 17. A feature on the program was a so-called American Brains Trust, an "Information Please" with Capt. O'Sullivan, Capt Blumenthal and myself as the "Brains" behind the table. The questions had been previously submitted by the children—some pretty good questions too, some of them. They demonstrated their curiosity about things American such as "Why are Americans called Yanks?" "What is the origin of chewing gum?" Also a bit of the sensational such as "Is it true that American girls sometimes marry at the age of 12?" I think we amused them, and I know the three of us enjoyed ourselves tremendously in spite of the suspicion I had of the whole thing before we went. The thing that struck me cold was the fact that all the kids wanted our autographs after the program. I'm sure that's the first time anybody ever asked me for an autograph.

Before the show we had dinner with a Mrs. [Archie] Camden,[6] a very charming person and a gifted song writer. After the show we were invited over for a while to the home of a Mrs. McCorquodale [Barbara Cartland], a writer. It was quite an evening.

*

Speaking in a 2005 interview, Dr. Shuller remembered his stormy relationship with Barbara Cartland. "I had done a little volunteer work with a small unit called the St. Johns Ambulance Brigade, which is similar to our Boy and Girl Scouts, except that it was coed," he said. Shuller participated in a number of meetings with these British children where he "gave them two or three lectures and helped them a little bit with their first aid projects." He also joined in community events to raise funds and interest for this group of

*children. He said, "With my activities with the St. Johns Ambulance Brigade"
in Bedford, "I had occasion to appear with Mrs. Hugh McCorquodale" at several charity events supporting the Ambulance Brigade. "And this Mrs. Hugh
McCorquodale was the one and only Barbara Cartland," who had written
about five hundred books at the time. "She and I sort of tied into each other
so that we didn't particularly like each other because of stress" created during
her efforts to run these charity events. "She was a very dominating woman, as
you can well imagine, and she wanted to do some things that I didn't consider
that I could rightly do as a U.S. military officer." Shuller did not hesitate to
tell her that "so we were on speaking terms, but not too pleasantly."[7]*

*

May 25 - I have just received a most significant letter in answer to the
letter I wrote to Col [Edward J.] Tracy on May 12 concerning the Cancellation of Passes for Combat Crews (noted in Diary previously). The significant thing is that Col. Tracy signs his name to a statement which we
have been aware of all along but have never seen in print, i.e. our original
Groups over here have been experimental, and that we have been driv-
en excessively hard just to prove a point to the doubting Thomases back
home. As it is, the point has been proven as is borne out by the fact, that we
are getting more bombers over here. Col. Putnam told me tonight that my
letter had caused quite a heated discussion at Bomber Command. That's
good even though nothing is being done about it yet. It is a start in the
right direction.

> Hq. VII Bomber Command
> Office of the Surgeon
> 22 May 1943
> Memo:
> To: Major Shuller, Gp.Surg, 306th Bomb Gp.
> 1. Reference your recent letter concerning cancellation of leave or
> passes of combat crew members, I have taken up this matter with
> General Longfellow with little or no satisfaction insofar as getting
> results are concerned. Pressure from higher headquarters necessi-
> tates getting every possible plane in the air on "Maximum efforts"
> and now that we have been getting additional forces over here in-
> stances such as you described probably will not be frequent. General
> Eaker has had a very difficult time convincing the arm-chair strate-
> gists back home that raids by American bombers from British bases

are really worthwhile. The past year has been not only a trying one for the few original Groups that had to bear the brunt of carrying out the convictions of our Commanding General but for General Eaker as well. He fully realized the tremendous load these crews were being asked to carry and certainly is aware that certain measures and means that were used to make the best showing with a small force operating under difficult personnel and supply conditions, were not the best from a standpoint of morale. However he has won his fight for a large force of bombers over here and our original Groups have had to win it for him.

2. I am heartily in accord with the opinions you have expressed concerning leaves and passes for combat crews and am taking the matter up with Colonel Grow to see if we cannot get a policy established that will exclude the possibility of personnel on pass, leave or D.S. being recalled for any reason except a dire emergency.

E.J. Tracy
Colonel M.C.
Surgeon

That letter would be small comfort to our boys down over in France. T.S.

May 26 - A couple of days ago a Lt. [Henry A.] Dantzig reported here for assignment to the 423rd Sq., apparently to relieve Capt [Samuel D.] Simpson as Squadron Surgeon to let him go back to the States to go to Randolph Field to qualify as a flight surgeon. Simpson is walking on air. I hope it isn't a false alarm. Simpson is most qualified and a wonderful person with it and deserving of everything that can be done for him. Hope they don't keep him waiting around too long. Dantzig looks like a likeable chap. However, he'll have a big vacancy to fill because the 423rd Squadron practically worships Simpson.[8]

May 29 - Another raid today on St. Nazaire, about the 12th time on that target, I believe. It seems that all reports indicate that they hit the target squarely this time. For a change they came back all in one piece, no one had even a scratch although there were some planes lost in other Groups. Another way this raid differed was that they went there in force for the first time. They sent 9 Groups of 18 planes each, or a total of 162 fortresses on that one target. A force of at least 3 Groups of fortresses hit Rennes, and two or three Groups of Liberators hit LaPallice, all at the same time. How remarkably different this mission today was from that infamous attack on

St. Nazaire Nov. 28, when Major Holt led four lonesome planes from this Group over that target and one of those, Lt. Isbell, was knocked off. It was a most successful day from the view point of this particular Group. With no mission scheduled for tomorrow, they'll really enjoy this dance tonight.

May 30 - Memorial Day, 1943

Chaplain [Roy M.] MacLeod held a special service at chapel this morning. Col. Putnam gave a short talk. It was quite impressive with all the patriotic atmosphere, a communion service, a big wreath marked "306th," the national anthem, and "Taps."

The service brought a few moments of sadness. It is so fresh in the minds of all of us the sacrifice that some of our fellows have made. Some of them stood out particularly vivid and rushed through my mind in a turmoil. At the very top of the list is Capt. Brady, still unheard of but almost certainly dead, a wonderfully fine blonde handsome youngster, a burning passion for flying itself, a good crew commander, son of a minister in Denver, made attempts at smoking and drinking after a fashion to be "one of the fellows," but could never do it with any degree of enjoyment. Then Lt. Bill Warner, likewise a tall slender perfect specimen of manhood and a very friendly person and a real gentleman, a great captain of his ship and potentially, a great squadron commander if he had lived to get it. Capt. Johnston, another fine physical man, handsome, quiet, reserved, a superb pilot, and also slated to be a squadron commander. The thought of Johnston invariably reminds me of Lt. [Jack A.] Spaulding, the quiet bashful little fellow who was my first roommate back at Wendover, not such a good pilot, but a grand kid—and he was a kid, was nervous, and I should have ordered him to take a rest, that would have saved that collision with Johnston. Spaulding got married just before we left Wendover, and he begged for any tips about married life from a medical view point. That also reminds me of Lt. [Frank K.] Watson, who did the same thing back at Wendover. He was a very enthusiastic little fellow and was very eager about flying on missions. With Spaulding was also killed, Lt. [Gordon R.] Grant, a bombardier, a sad faced little Irishman who was the only man I heard say back at Wendover that he did not expect to come back across the Atlantic.

I shall always visualize Lt. [Bart] Wigginton jumping across the ditch in front of the hospital as he came in for a last-minute check-up on his cold, before he took off on his last mission, and I turned and remarked to Manning, "There comes the friendliest little fellow that I have ever seen."

Wigginton was also an eager little beaver about flying, although not a particularly great pilot. His ship and crew splattered all over Brest harbor that
day they got in there by mistake. Then there's [Walter N.] Smiley, one
of the finest of the original fellows back at Wendover, a marvelous pilot
who also splattered all over the North Sea taking with him Lt. [Martin
M.] Strauss, a most unusual Jewish kid who was really eager about flying,
and was on his 24th mission as a navigator, also he had Lt. [Wilbur W.]
Breunig, bombardier, also with a lot of missions behind him, noted for his
practice of lying in bed reading his Bible from one hand and drinking beer
from the other (a good German Catholic), and more than once was heard
to scream out in a loud voice, "You bastards are going to have to cut out
that goddamn cussin."

It was a sad day when Lt. [Charles G.] Grimes was killed, commanded a
tremendous respect from the whole Group, because of his ability as navigator, was affectionately called "Pappy" because he was older than the rest
of his fellows, and they always depended on him to look-out after them
if they got in trouble or drank a little too much. [Alexander] Kramarinko
(the "mad Russian"), also missing, bawled like a baby about it for days.
Then Lt. [Robert T.] Levy, bombardier, is a tradition in this Group, dressed
up in his very finest pants and battle jacket on his last raid and said, "I'm
going to be the best dressed American prisoner or corpse in Germany."
It's funny about those things. He was shot over his bomb sight and failed
to come back. Lt. [Conrad J.] Farr was also shot over his bomb sight. He
was a quiet little German kid and was once accused of espionage back at
Westover, but proved his loyalty in the end by this, the supreme sacrifice.
[Lt. Robert F.] Dresp, a co-pilot, was wounded badly and wanted awfully
to live, but died after many weeks of terrible suffering. He is the only one
of our many casualties who has really suffered badly. We are to be thankful there haven't been more. [Lt. Clay E.] Isbell is a pilot I always admired.
As a man he was as fine as they come. He had such an awfully sweet but
frail little wife who practically worshiped him. She was about five months
pregnant, but lost her baby just a few days before he was killed in that
four-plane mission on St. Nazaire.

Then I think of Cranmer and his co-pilot [Albert] Brunsting, an awfully fine fellow, being shot down in the English Channel and were mowed
down by the Germans as they tried to get into their rubber boats, and T/
Sgt. Arizona Harris sticking by his guns in the top turret even as the ship
was sinking under the waves, a gallantry for which he was posthumously

awarded the D.S.C. Next there is [Robert E.] Brandon who was on his first trip after he had taken over his own crew, who was lost into the channel with all his men because of bad weather. He was a former football hero and a likeable fellow, but not big enough to handle the trouble he got into. But with him he took Lt. Lemuel B. Smith, that eager little Englishman, navigator, who wanted to get the war over and go back to America to that little girl in Alabama. Also he had with him as a co-pilot that big tall lanky Texan, Lt. J.O. Jones, an awfully nice fellow and friend.

Capt. [John W.] Olson was killed on the very first raid last October. He was a highly respected pilot. It's funny that he knew he wasn't going to get back off the first mission. Lt. [Loyal M.] Felts, who blew up over St. Nazaire on that low altitude experiment, was a quiet reserved fellow and a gentleman. I still have the Newfoundland dime he gave me just before he was killed. Lt. [Edwin F.] Patterson and Lt. [William W.] Ely were a couple of princely fellows who were killed in that practice mission crash before we ever began combat.

And how could one ever forget or fail to mention the incomparable [William J.] Casey. He's the greatest mixture of good and bad that I have ever seen, a typical Irishman, popular, a skilled flyer and a true character in general. I think we miss his inexhaustible repertoire of songs more than anyone who has gone down. We haven't heard from him, but we hope he is safe. He took with him one of my finest friends among the enlisted crews, T/Sgt. Wilson Elliott. I shall never forget the day he insisted that I accept a bar of chocolate from him in payment for some small treatment I had given him, and added that he wanted me for his "family doctor" when we all got back home. He was such a kid. He worshiped the very ground Casey walked on.

Then there are a host of enlisted men too numerous to mention who were just as outstanding personalities, of which S/Sgt. [Colin E.] Neely is a good example—a clean cut intelligent lad, though a little headstrong. He was wounded once in an early raid and got the jitters a little. However, Simpson and I practically forced him to make this flight in which he was killed with [William] Warner. S/Sgt. [James T.] McCloy was an awfully friendly radio operator who went down with Adams in early November. He was a favorite of mine because he was another Arkansan from Mc-Gehee. We heard that he died in a hospital in France. S/Sgt. [Arthur E.] Chapman was one of the most admirable casualties that we had. He was the very first bad casualty; a very responsible and brave patient for which he endeared himself to my medical enlisted men from the very beginning. He was an inspiration to them I think. He lived only four or five days after we transferred him to the hospital.

There are dozens [of] others passed and gone who were just as brave and fine, but there are so many, these were the ones I thought of first. But this is enough of this sort of thing and I shall close this little entry in memory of Lt. Van Vantler Bie who was killed in a crash back at Wendover. One night he saw me make an entry in this Diary and he remarked, "Why keep a diary? I don't want to live in the past, I want to live in the future." It was just a few days later that he was killed. So we will stop all this reminiscing and resolve to strive on to the bitter end, to end this war for which so many of these fellows are giving up their lives. We must dedicate ourselves to live or die for the future, whichever the case may be, just as they have already died for the future.

May 31 - Just before noon today I flew with Capt. [Raymond J.] Check down to Middle Wallop. Capt. Morse, Lt. Firman and Pam Hanna were there to meet us. They took us over to Stanbridge Earls for lunch, then after lunch Check took all of them for a ride. They were simply thrilled beyond words. It was a gesture on Check's part to take them for a ride. They are doing such a wonderful job for our boys down at the rest home and they were most anxious to get a little firsthand experience of the sort of thing their patients do. It was a pleasant day for all of us. Their work down there is invaluable for the morale of our fellows.

June 1, 1943 - Mrs. Leavert, the Red Cross worker here had Maj. Raper, Capt. Manning and me over for a fried chicken dinner tonight. It was simply delicious, the first we'd had in nine months. Did we tear into that plate of chicken!

Major Scarf of 2nd General Hospital came in this afternoon to stay a few days and carry on a little research on frost bite. Unfortunately or rather fortunately we aren't having much frost bite lately. I'm afraid his investigation won't amount to much, but here's to him. We certainly don't know the first word about the proper treatment of frost bite yet.

June 3 - I was pulled in on another English charity last night, and it was some more of Mrs. Camden's workings. She had me down to dinner again, one that she had gone to considerable trouble to fix, and then about 9:30 she took me over to the local school house to give a talk at their "Wings for Victory" program on why they should buy more bonds. I talked about 5 minutes, more or less sob stuff, on the human side of the story. I don't know why I agreed to make that talk—I just couldn't think of an excuse fast enough, maybe. Certainly I'm no talker. We left immediately afterwards, but Mrs. Camden called me today and said that they sold nearly £2,000 ($8,000) worth of bonds after I left. Maybe I did have a little effect on them, who knows. Boy, that sort of thing certainly isn't what I came to England for.

June 6 - It has rained almost every day for days on end. All the fellows are getting restless to be on with their rat killing. Four of us officers went to Bedford to a show this afternoon, the first time I have seen a show there in weeks.

Mrs. Camden's cousin brought out a couple dozen eggs to the hospital patients today. It was a generous gesture on her part and the fellows really enjoyed them. The kids in the St. John's Brigade contributed them. Heard today that Casey is a P.W. Good old Casey! Everybody is awfully glad to hear about it. He'll be coming back after the war with a lot of German songs no doubt, and you can depend on it he'll be teaching the Germans some of his dirty Irish songs. Lt. Miller's entire crew is safe we hear, and all of Lt. George's enlisted men including Sgt. Don Bevin, our talented artist, but we haven't heard from George yet. This is the first news we have had from the 10 crews we lost over Bremen April 17. Somehow somebody got the word that Lt. Frederick who was flying with Capt. Friend has died. (Body was washed up on the Dutch coast.)

June 11 - A fairly big mission today. The target was Bremen, but the target was cloudy and they hit Wilhelmshaven instead. As far as we were concerned it was a very successful mission, no losses and no casualties. A plane from the 379th Group came in here with one man dead and three injuries. That is Maj. Wise's group: They got a baptism of fire yesterday. Their second mission and they lost 6 planes. Their Group is beginning to look like ours used to. Major Scarff, who is trying to see some frostbites was disappointed yesterday, fortunately for us.

June 12 - Flew down to Taunton today to see [Stanley N.] Kisseberth. Poor boy, his injuries, although relatively minor, have kept him laid up in bed for 4 months now and he feels like he has had enough fighting. I am inclined to agree with him and am writing a letter to the hospital tonight urging the Disposition Board to send him home.

I had a considerable word battle with Capt. [Alfonso W.] Nicastro, dentist, yesterday about his lack of work, and my ire has continued over into today. I have put up with him just about as long as I care to, and one of these days somebody is going to get hurt—and I'm not intending that it shall be me. Unless I can get him straightened out, and soon, I'm going to try to "fry" him—and I think I can. I'm sure I won't have any difficulty getting support from higher authority.

June 13 - A repeat on the raid they tried day before yesterday. Struck at the submarine shops at Bremen, but the smoke screen was very efficient and they think they hit the railroad yards and town instead. Lost one plane today, Lt. [William H.] Marcotte, 423rd. I hadn't even heard of him. The fourth wing really took a beating today, they lost 21 planes. 26 planes were lost altogether. The greatest previous loss of fortresses was 16. 26 planes means 260 men, think of that. Capt. [Charles R.] Patten, 423rd Adjutant, was on Lt. Marcotte's ship. It's so foolish for these non-flying fellows to go on these missions, but they will do it. The fourth wing lost one of their Brigadier Generals.

June 19 - I have just returned from a two-day conference at Pinetree with Col. [Harry G.] Armstrong along the line of how better to handle our cases of flying fatigue and flying neuroses (Pinetree was the code name for the 8th Bomber Command Headquarters). Capt. Schumacher and I represented the bomber groups, the fighter groups were represented and also an observation squadron along with four or five psychiatrists. There was lots of talk as usual but nothing was accomplished that I could see. We more or less aired out some of our problems but that is about as far as it will get. As far as I'm concerned the two big problems along that line that need to get settled now are (1) discontinuing the practice of calling combat crews back off pass to go on missions (2) establishment of an Eighth Air Force Consolidated Flying Evaluation Board to dispose of both medical and administrative problems concerning flying personnel no longer desirable for combat. However, it was a very pleasant conference and I enjoyed it very much. But I couldn't understand why I should be given such a prominent part in the proceedings. My opinion was called for repeatedly and they really listened, even the full Colonels—I'm not used to that sort of thing. That hot letter I wrote to General Eaker last March really left its mark up at Bomber Command and I think it's because of that that they selected me to come down. It's funny how a thing like that can make or break a man. It could just as easily have put me in the dog house for the duration. I must surely be having a change of personality at this late stage in life. I didn't used to butt in and speak when I wasn't called on.

While I was gone these two days there has been a complete change of commands including the Commander of this Group. Col. Putnam is being sent up to 1st Wing as operations officer. Who will take his place, I'm not sure yet, but will find out all those things tomorrow. But tonight when I came in I found a copy of a Commendation by Col. Putnam on my desk that has practically made me overcome. I would certainly become stinking with conceit if I did not have to give all credit to the finest, most cooperative staff of medical officers and enlisted men with whom a department head has ever been blessed. It is simply incomparable when compared to the antagonism found in other Groups. But I'm just as proud of that letter as a combat man must be of winning a medal for a job well done. It is double gratifying to me because a doctor so frequently gets so little credit, therefore I consider it a tribute to the whole medical department, 306th Bomb Group. I can't resist copying the body of the letter.

June 18, 1943

Upon relinquishing command of the 306th Bomb Gp. (H) the undersigned desired to confer the warmest commendation on subject officer. He has always performed his duties in a superior manner without complaint or thought of reward. During the nine (9) months of combat in the European Theater of Operations the 306th Bomb Gp. (H) has had over 100% casualties among flying personnel. Many of these officers have been close personal friends of Major Shuller, yet he has unflinchingly carried on in his fight not only to maintain the physical well-being of this Group but also to effect the mental and psychological state required for combat personnel. He has been a jealous guardian of rights and privileges of combat crew personnel, and he has very effectively maintained a high state of morale. The esteem in which he is held by all combat crew members of the Group is a tribute to his professional skill and sound kindly judgement.

It is directed that a copy of this commendation be forwarded through proper command channels to the Adjutant General of the Army to become a part of Major Shuller's permanent record. A duplicate copy is being furnished Major Shuller for his personal file.

(signed) Claude E. Putnam

Colonel AD.

Commanding

June 20 - My man Simpson got his orders to go back to the states to go to the School of Aviation Medicine and he left last Friday. We sure are going to miss him. He was one of the backbones of our little organization here. I think Lt. Dantzig is going to turn out all right, but it will take a superman to fill Capt. Simpson's vacancy. He was awfully popular with his squadron because he was both wise and kindly to the fellows who came to him, he was as near a "family doctor" as I have seen in the Army. He deserves this break and he will make somebody a superb Group Surgeon, though it certainly is a loss on our part.

Col. Putnam had his farewell dinner tonight. Lt. Col. [George L.] Robinson from the 303rd Group is our new C.O. Brig. General Armstrong is taking over 1st Wing and Col. Putnam is going to be his right-hand man in operations up there. Col. [Curtis] LeMay is going to assume command of 4th Wing and my good friend and most capable fellow Lt. Col. Dell Wilson is assuming Command of the 305th Group. Our new C.O. is a nice looking fellow, but I'm afraid he doesn't have the drive that Col. "Put" has. All these changes I believe will add a little more "fire" to the 8th Bomber Command.

June 22 - The big raid today was on the synthetic rubber plant at Huls, Germany on the edge of the Ruhr. It is the first time they had gone to the Ruhr and they apparently did a good job of bombing. The whole force lost 15 fortresses but we lost only one. The pilot was Lt. Johnson; 367th, a new man who had not been here long. I didn't know him, neither did Manning.

The outstanding feat today was performed by Lt. [Eugene G.] Hanes, 369th pilot. He has a promise that he is going back to the States but he almost didn't get back today. It was a real thrill to hear him give his own story at the critique this afternoon. If a recording could have been made of him the public back home just wouldn't believe it. He lost a motor just inside Holland and fell back out of formation and was jumped by a fighter which was knocked down. Other fighters were coming in and he lost the other engine on the same side. He dived the ship for the water level and in so doing lost his life rafts. As he flew low over the water, flak boats shot at him. He ordered the crew to prepare to bail out twice over Germany, but McMann, a gunner on his 25th mission said, "Hell no; let's fly this thing home." He had extreme difficulty all the way across the channel. A waist gunner threw out an ammunition case and knocked off part of the horizontal stabilizer. A third engine was acting up and they prepared to land in the water about six times, without life rafts. When he sighted land he prepared to land at the first airfield but each time he saw one ahead that he thought he could make and finally he hedge hopped home safely on the two engines. It was a real miracle and he will certainly be cited for a piece of brilliant pilotage. Hanes looks about as little like a pilot as any man I ever saw; slight, emaciated and dried-up. One can never tell by looking.

A Major Peck is here for a few days observing "atmosphere" on a bomber station. He is stationed at the 12th C.C.R.C. He is a nice fellow, but I am getting damn tired of entertaining visiting doctors at this post. Why do they always come in on me?

June 25 - They attempted to go in on the naval installations at Hamburg today, but it was a screwed-up detail from the beginning. They said they went through three fronts getting there and couldn't see much of anything. They dropped their bombs somewhere in Germany, Holland, or Belgium, nobody knows quite where. It seems that they must have confused the Germans as much as they were confused themselves. And in spite of lack of results there were a number of fortresses shot down. We lost Lt. [Thomas E.] Logan, out of the 423rd's promising young pilots.

Corporal [Eric S.] Anderson of our Medical Detachment got married this afternoon to an English girl. Six of us doctors and some of the enlisted men went down to their reception late in the afternoon. It was a nice affair. Pvt. [Sigmund R.] Nitka got married earlier in the month. Looks like the medical men are the marrying kind.

June 26 - This was another awfully sad day in the life of this organization. Capt. Check was on his 25th and last mission and was instantly killed right over the target. It was supposed to be an awfully easy target too, just a little diversion raid over the coast of France to the airdrome at Triqueville and there was supposed to be lots of fighter cover. The bombing was perfectly lousy for no good reason at all except for excitement on the part of the lead bombardier. Check's death is a terrible blow to almost every man in the Group. He was one of our original and finest pilots, he was a marvelous crew commander and leader in general. He had taught a lot of our younger pilots most of what they knew about flying. He is one combat man I think it can be said was actually loved by every combat man in the Group, and by many non-combat men as well, and everybody was rooting for his successful completion of his tour of duty. And for him, of all people, to get it on his final mission was just too much. Check was a flying man but not an enthusiastically fighting man. He fought only because

Raymond J. Check, pilot, reported to the 306th Bomb Group at Wendover, Utah, on June 23, 1942. He was killed over Triqueville, France, on June 26, 1943. Courtesy of the East Anglia Air War Collection.

Raymond Check crew. Front, left to right: Raymond Check (pilot), Prue Blanchette (navigator), Ralph W. Jones (co-pilot), Emmett Ford (bombardier). Back, left to right: Nicholas Sawicke (gunner), Charles Wilson (gunner), William Johnson (radio operator), Joseph Uhor (gunner), James Bobbett (waist gunner), and Francis Bowes (engineer). Courtesy of the East Anglia Air War Collection.

it was his duty and he was ready to retire from combat. He had planned to throw away all his high altitude flying equipment the moment he hit the ground. Just before he went out I patted his bald head and wished him luck—maybe I took away his luck. He was one of our favorites here at the hospital and came in to talk a while with us after almost every mission. He liked to take a bath here after he came in because it was more comfortable. Check's memory will be with all of us a long time. It's always worse when a favorite comes back dead than if he didn't come back at all.

Lt. Col. J.A. Wilson happened to be co-pilot of Check's plane. He had long planned to ride with him on his last mission. It was fortunate that an experienced pilot was co-pilot else the ship would not have come home. There had been a big fire in the cockpit and Wilson tried to beat out the flames with his hands and suffered excruciating burns of hands and forehead. Nevertheless he flew that ship home in formation with those agonizing hands. He actually gave the order to bail out over France but only one man, the bombardier, Lt. [Lionel R.] Drew, did so. It was a marvelous piece of flying on Wilson's part and this afternoon changed the opinion of a lot of people about him who have considered him always in a rather unfavorable light.

Major Peck, whom I mentioned on June 22, went on that mission today and happened to be with Check. He comes here from the States very eager and anxious to find out quickly about this war we have been seeing for nine months now. Well, he learned very, very quickly—and all in the space of a three hour trip. He is walking about in a daze and I gave him a couple of Sodium Amytals to quiet him down. He is so violent now against doctors being allowed to go on these trips that he can hardly restrain himself. He wants to sit right down and write Col. Tracy what he thinks of him. It amuses me no end to see how quickly these fellows fresh from the States can cool off. It so happened that I had spent about two hours giving him my views on matters and things concerning a doctor's place. Now he is willing to believe anything I tell him. As much as I personally oppose doctors going on these raids I would like to go on just one—and I'll probably be fool enough to do it one day. I don't want to see our squadron Flight Surgeons do it and I would be setting a precedent that they would follow. Besides I have said my piece in public about the matter and am considered up at headquarters as a champion of the cause of those who are opposing Col. Tracy on the issue. I wish that weren't true because it was not intended at all. If I do go some day it will be in a moment of lapse in

Watching for red flares
as the planes return
from a mission to the
Rheine in Germany,
February 21, 1944. Flight
Surgeon Henry A.
Dantzig, Flight Surgeon
Charles P. McKim, and
Medic Clarence W.
Hoheisel wait with the
ambulance at the ready.
Courtesy of the Thur-
man Shuller Family
Collection.

The injured man gets plasma in the ambulance before removal to the dispensary.
Courtesy of the Thurman Shuller Family Collection.

judgement in an effort to see for myself what this whole thing is about. We are all more or less alike. This war isn't based on common sense, else we wouldn't be fighting a war.

June 28 - Another raid on St. Nazaire. We didn't lose any planes, but a tail gunner was killed. It was Sgt. [Richard J.] Daly and he was also on his 25th and last mission. He was a top-notch fellow from all reports but I didn't know him very well. That 25th mission is just as dangerous as the first. Quite a lot of fellows finished today. The one that I have been sweating out the most is Lt. [William J.] McKearn, one of the originals of the 367th. Capt. [John H.] Dexter finished 2 days ago.

June 29 - Another Bomber Command weather boner today. This is getting to be chronic. The target was Paris and they couldn't begin to see anything for the clouds. Fortunately we had no casualties and the only benefit that this Group got out of it was that it counted as a 25th mission for 12 of our officers and enlisted men. Two of our finest pilots finished, Capt. [John G.] Magoffin and Capt. [Marlen E.] Reber. It was quite a celebration when they stripped off Capt. Reber and Lt. [Luther] Bergen his navigator and threw them in the fire pool. The water was awfully cold too. I was glad to see Bergen finish. He received a severe injury of the abdomen, then came back without hesitating to run off about 15 more missions. Not once was he in the sick quarters for any other illness, except before he ever went on a mission, and not once did he ever show the first symptom of the jitters. Reber is our smallest pilot. One would never suspect him of being able to fly a B-17. But he is not only a pilot but an expert one. His last two missions he led the Group. It is seldom that one gets much praise or wins medals if he doesn't get into a hell of a lot of trouble and shows himself off by bringing a beat-up ship home. Reber is like McKay, conspicuous by his lack of trouble. He's a wonderful little man. Magoffin is a top-notcher also and his squadron is going to miss him. He is our first replacement pilot to finish his tour of duty, he came to us in December. Another outstanding man to finish was T/Sgt. [Chester T.] Wendoloski, one of the finest engineers that this group has had. Another outstanding one is S/Sgt. [Raleigh W.] Holloway, 369th, who has distinguished himself by shooting down 6 enemy fighters during his tour of duty.

Manning and I went to Check's funeral today. Of all the fellows we have sent to the cemetery, this is the first time that I have gone to a funeral, but somehow Check was different. He meant a little more to all of us.

July 2, 1943 - I just heard a story tonight that is as great a piece of sacrifice as can come out of any war. A letter was written back by one of Lt. Fisher's gunners in a prison camp that both Lt. [William H.] Parker and his co-pilot [Charles J. Thelen] were killed in the cockpit (over Antwerp April 5). The plane went out of control but Lt. [Paul A.] Spaduzzi, navigator, struggled to the flight deck, took over the controls, ordered the rest of the crew to bail out, and he himself flew the plane right on into the ground. Not to detract any from the fame that was given Colin Kelly, for his life was worth just as much as Spaduzzi, but Kelly stuck to his controls because he was the pilot and it was his duty. Spaduzzi stayed with the controls not because it was his duty but because he thought of the others first. He was a "washed-out" pilot and took up navigation. Yet the finest pilot could not have made a greater sacrifice at the controls of his ship. However, there are so many similar stories now that each individual one seems almost commonplace. Hitler will have a hard time beating that.

July 4 - Independence Day for the soldiers in Britain as well as elsewhere. George Washington would turn over in his grave. We celebrated by sending the planes out to bomb a big plane repair shop down at Nantes, near St. Nazaire. It was a beautiful piece of bombing, one of the very best. It's one target they won't go back to. Major Raper, the leader, is very, very happy because of the success of the raid. All the planes came back and not a man was hurt. There were eight fortresses lost by other Groups. O'Hara, Junior Jones and Hopkins finished up their tour of duty today. Jones came back and really "beat-up" the airdrome for several minutes before they could get him to land.

Someone called this to my attention that exactly one year ago today there was the first all American raid on German territory when six A-20's took off and bombed the coast of France for the loss of one plane. We have come a long way since that day.

July 5 - It was a real Fourth of July celebration here last night. About 11:30 somebody fired off his rifle. Somebody else came out and answered him, and before it ended there were dozens of them, they were even firing tommie guns. But surprising as it may seem, they ended up by going into the barracks, singing the "Star Spangled Banner" (soberly too) and going quietly off to bed. This is one more place.

July 8 - The feature attraction today was the appearance of Bob Hope and Frances Langford at 1 o'clock for an hour show. It was good entertainment and was appreciated by everybody. Bob Hope has made a real contribution to the war effort in the tremendous amount of time that he has given to entertaining soldiers. Frances is a grand singer and was well received.

July 10 - The boys went on a mission to an airdrome south of Paris today, but the weather was bad and they bombed a secondary target, an airdrome on the coast of France. From the practical point of view it was not very successful, but they completed it without anybody getting scratched. Weather has been very bad lately and it isn't often that they get a fair chance at a target.

July 11 - A very quiet Sunday. Lt. Kylius and Sgt. Wilson who went down with Warner in February came back to camp today. Kylius has a lot of stories to tell. Major Regan had a card from Lt. Judas today. It's the first word we have had from him or his crew. He's in the hospital with a bum shoulder but otherwise O.K. Lt. [Foster G.] Daniels was killed. Remember that was his 25th mission. It's such a shame. He was an awfully nice fellow and a good bombardier. Word has just been received that Lt. Mann died in a hospital. I guess he was just snakebit from the beginning. He crash landed in a corn field coming across. He had all his crew injured on his first raid, and they finally got him. It is also now believed to be a fact that all of Capt. [Walter N.] Smiley's crew is safe—in a prison camp. It seems almost too good to be true.[9]

July 14 - A very successful raid on Villacoublay, France, an airdrome just a few miles from Paris. The target was well hit apparently, all the crews came back O.K. and only two or three minor casualties. Lt. Thomas, 367th, did himself proud by bringing home a plane that had practically the whole vertical stabilizer blown off.

The 369th Squadron is still going strong. They have now run 38 consecutive missions without loss of an airplane. That is a record nobody can challenge.

July 15 - We called the war off today to have a big ceremony. Secretary of War Stimson came here to present the Congressional Medal of Honor for the feat that I previously mentioned May 2. It was nothing but a big day, it's not every day that a Congressional Medal of Honor is given out. In fact I know of no other in this Theatre of War. Smith is generally known as "Snuffy" and it's about the best name for him. He's a screwball and is quite an uncontrollable little rascal. Major Lambert has had him on K.P. the last few days because of indifference to attending lectures, meetings, etc. Movie people were here a few days ago to get pictures of him doing K.P. He's said to be the only recipient of the Congressional Medal of Honor in the history of the U.S. who has been put on KP. He hadn't received the medal of course, but the orders were already published. He did do a fine job on that ship, however, and nobody can deny that. Whether it deserved so high an award I question, but any man who continues to go on any mission should be awarded. He did stick by the ship when all the others were leaving it around him and got in there to fight the fire with bullets going off all around him. It is rumored that he even urinated on the fire. It might be said that he did what he did in order to save his own neck. Maybe so, but he was a cool little cookie for a man on his first mission.

Yesterday I sent Sgt. [Soloman] Werlin to the hospital for mental observation. It's a bad situation when one of our own medical fellows starts going wacky, but he was getting definitely psychotic. He is our pharmacist and a very essential man in our organization, and I sure hate to lose him, but it happens to the best of them sometimes. I'm afraid he won't be back with us. He suddenly developed a terrific persecution complex, and I believe he is hallucinating. Too bad.

July 17 - The fellows started out to raid the big rubber plants at Hanover, Germany today and got as far as the Dutch coast and returned on account of weather. It was a wonderful set-up and was the biggest and best planned show that the A.A.F. has ever attempted here. They did go far enough to get one of the bombardiers injured.

This afternoon I went for a little flight and it was the wildest and scariest flight that I have ever made. It was with Lt. [Leroy C.] Sugg who finished his 25 missions and is going up to the replacement pool in preparation for return to the U.S. It was his farewell flight and [he] was hell bent for "beating up" the airdrome and hedge hopping everything between here and Burtonwood. He even got down on the ground in the open fields and climbed up over the trees at the edge and down again on the other side. He climbed up over a 100 foot chimney and down again so steeply that it threw us up to the roof. That sort of thing is just a little too risky for me. It just isn't proper to fly a plane weighing over 25 tons at 200 miles per hour at a low altitude like that. I don't think I'll ride on any more of these "farewell" demonstrations.

July 21 - We have been visited for two days by Dr. [Howard C.] Naffzieger, neurosurgeon from the University of California. Major [John Edwin] Scarff came with him. He came to this field mainly to get "atmosphere" of a tactical flying outfit, and was interested particularly in flying equipment,

Leroy C. Sugg finished his twenty-five missions at Thurleigh and returned to the United States as a flight instructor in B-17s. He was killed in a bomber fire and crash on June 2, 1944, twenty miles from Clovis, New Mexico. Courtesy of the East Anglia Air War Collection.

combat positions and flying and living conditions. He was very interesting, and we were honored to have such an outstanding personality.

July 22 - I found it necessary to crawl all over Lt. Dantzig's skin this morning and pointed out that I wanted a little more work out of him. I think he is potentially a good boy and a good squadron flight surgeon. We will see.

July 24 - The planes went out for the first time to bomb Norway. They went after a big aluminum and magnesium plant at Heroy, near Oslo. From all reports they hit it squarely. It was an 8 ½ hour trip, the longest our group has yet made, and they went in at only 15,000 feet.[10] The fourth wing has wing tip tanks (Tokyo tanks), and they were sent even farther, a twelve hour trip to Trondheim. From all reports it must have been a very successful day. Lt. [Stanley R.] Stedt, navigator, 423rd, got an awfully nasty compound fracture of his left-elbow from one of our own bullets in the plane ahead of him. I don't see why it doesn't happen more often. Capt. [David W.] Wheeler's was the only ship that took a beating. His navigator, Lt. Bollenback, received a bad brain injury from a 20 mm shell, and his tail gunner was shot. Two engines were shot out and his hydraulic system useless. On landing he didn't have any flaps, no brakes, he had a flat tire and the plane ended up by ground-looping at the end of the field after narrowly missing another plane. They had thrown out everything expecting to have to land on the water, but since they couldn't move Bollenback, Wheeler gritted his teeth and brought it on in. Wheeler collapsed almost completely after it was all over and tonight we have him and several of his crew here at the hospital "snowed under" with Sodium Amytal. Wheeler gave a wonderful demonstration of skill and good judgement before he cracked on us. He is one of our most experienced and skillful pilots at the present time, but he has been quite sensitive and nervous for weeks. I hope we can bring him out of it.

July 25 - The planes started out to Hamburg today, but they got all screwed up today and several Groups, including ours, got lost and came back. Somebody will probably be in for trouble.

July 26 - A big raid today to get those rubber tire factories at Hanover, Germany. I don't know yet what the bombing results were but it is thought that they were good. Two of our planes did not return, Lt. [Wesley E.] Courson and Lt. [Norman] Armbrust, both 423rd. I didn't know either of them. These are the first planes we have lost in over a month. They were badly hit by flak over the target, but fortunately fighters did not attack them because some of the ships that returned were terribly shot up. One came in on two engines, one with the whole nose out, one with the left aileron completely knocked off by a falling bomb from one of the other planes. When they landed they were shooting flares all over the place. However, nobody was critically injured and only three were even hurt bad enough to send to the hospital. Lt. [Alphonse M.] Maresh ran out of gas due to flak holes in his fuel tanks just ¼ mile off the English shore. Several of the fellows got minor cuts and bruises but all got out into the boats safely and were rescued about 10 minutes later. I think we are going to run into some more psychological trouble tomorrow, we'll know better the extent of our damage then.

We sent Capt. [David W.] Wheeler off to the hospital for narcosis treatment today. He's still in a nervous state. I'm hoping he'll respond to treatment though.

Four of us officers went to Dunstable near Luton tonight on another of those "Brain Trust" programs. It was a lot of fun and a pleasant evening in general. I suspect we didn't give out much information though.

July 29 - Went up to the 30th General Hospital at Mansfield to a medical meeting a couple of days ago and came back today. Drove up with Col. Tracy and Lt. Col. Streeter. It was a very good meeting, an excellent program, lots of doctors I knew and a lot more that I met and they entertained us royally. The only thing I didn't like about it was the suspense of knowing that our Group went to one of its toughest missions yesterday, and I was anxious to get back and find out what was going on.

The 423rd did lose two more planes yesterday, Lt. [Stephen W.] Peck and Lt. [Jack] Harris. In addition Lt. [Woodrow W.] Thomas and Lt. [Lawrence W.] Kooima crash landed on the coast. There were several bad casualties. Lt. Thomas is the remarkable story of the day. He had two engines out over the target and had to drop out of formation. He came on home by himself in a straight line right across Germany and right across the middle of the Ruhr valley and wasn't even shot at either by plane or antiaircraft. His outstanding crewman was Sgt. St. Louis. He was shot in the head last May and sustained a skull fracture with a slug in the brain and a paralysis of the left arm. The arm recovered and the slug was left in. He was offered a chance to go home but having made only one mission he wanted to fight some more. This was his third mission yesterday, he shot down a fighter and made the third crash landing of his career. If we only had more like him.

Today they went to Kiel again. They were so terribly tired. This was the fifth mission in six days. They had to get up at 1:30 this morning and I doubt that some of them had slept any at all. The maintenance crews are tired too and they can't keep the planes in shape for so much combat. Five planes came back because of engine trouble which left the group weak and they lost four planes over the target. It's all a vicious circle resulting in poor flying by the pilots, poor bombing by the bombardiers and high losses. There is a human element to this thing that Bomber Command seems to fail to consider. There finally reaches a point to human endurance where further activity is no longer profitable even if weather is good. The crews lost were the two Flight Officers, [Merryman H.] Brown and [Carl D. Brown] in the 367th and Lt. [Keith] Conley and Lt. [Donald R.] Winters in the 369th. That breaks the lucky winning streak of the 369th consecutive missions without loss at 41. That's a formidable record for any squadron to shoot at. It was a remarkable thing that of those who returned there was not a single injury of the slightest degree. Eight planes we have lost in the last week, but still morale is fairly high. The boys are just plain tired.

July 31 - Hooray! Bomber Command finally got a little sense in their heads. They granted a 3-day holiday to let the fellows rest. The weather is awfully good too, but that can't be helped. They are having a big dance here tonight and I guess some of the fellows will be knocking themselves out.

August 2, 1943 - The three-day holiday was a wonderful thing for the fellows, they are already in fighting shape again and were anxious to resume the combat today but the weather is bad now. Looks like the weather may extend the vacation indefinitely. Manning went to a big conference at Bomber Command Saturday and came back with news about having to make out a bunch more medical reports. My God, don't we have enough of them already?

Aug 7 - Still no more combat missions since the last effort. Weather bad and no prospect of it being better soon. But I have been chewing nails since yesterday. They are planning a maximum effort and they called back everybody, including two crews in the rest homes. I got in everybody's hair from Bomber Command on down about calling those boys back. That is one place where they should be immune from duty of any kind. I wrote a strong letter to Lt. Col. Streeter at Wing this morning, and he called and said the General has decreed that it shall not happen again. I do hope so. But now that it has happened, I am not going to say any more about it. It apparently is a really big effort that they are going to try this time. It's one that they have been practicing for for weeks. It is generally known about the post as "Target A," that is all that we know about it. It is supposed to be one that the R.A.F. have stood off from for two years. We are to go there in the late afternoon and pave the way and start fires to guide the R.A.F. for an attack the following night. Nobody but the big shots know what it is but it must be important. Every bomber the Air Force can get in the air is going to participate. They make no bones about its being a dangerous mission and everybody is on edge now with fear and anxiety just waiting for a good day.

Aug 10 - They briefed this morning on Target A [Schweinfurt], but then they called it off on account of weather. I can't understand, and neither can anybody else what was in Bomber Command's mind to brief that show when there was so little chance of being able to carry it out. Now the cat is out of the bag and all of the element of surprise will surely be gone. It is going to be an awfully tough mission at best. Target A is a big roller bearing factory way in south of Berlin. It is at the very limit of the Fortress range and there will be enemy fighters in numbers unable to count. It's just too bad they couldn't have gone ahead with the show once they started.

Aug 11 - A letter came down from the Commanding General of 1st Wing that combat crews would not be called away from rest homes for missions without specific permission from the Commanding General himself. That is the direct result of a letter that I wrote the Wing Surgeon. I'm not exactly sure how the Commanding Officer will like that, but we'll see.

Aug 12 - They pulled a stunt today that we have all been curious about and that the crews have been dreading. They went after a target right in the heart of the Ruhr. Someone said the flak was so thick that you could let down the wheels and land on it. They couldn't see the target which was a big synthetic gasoline plant, because of the smoke and clouds. However, they dropped their bombs on a big plant of some kind and destroyed it, but they haven't any idea what it was. Our group lost only one plane, Lt. Cunningham, 367th, Sq., but there were 25 bombers lost for the whole show. That was just one under the maximum loss and they don't know what they bombed! Some days this bombing game doesn't seem to pay so well. It seems the pressure is so strong from above now that they are forced to try to bomb even though they know before they go out that their chances of being able to see the target are very remote.

Capt. Wheeler came back from the rest home today following his course of treatment at the hospital for the "jitters." He looks mighty well and appears to be quite steady. If he holds up well now he is going to be an awfully good advertisement for the treatment we doctors have been advocating to the commanding officer. His condition at the time he left was so bad that even they were concerned about it.

Aug 14 - A couple of days ago I remarked to Capt. Erb that I had a feeling of impending disaster. Last night I found out what it is if it goes through. Longworth told me that Lt. Col. Streeter is going to be thrown out on his ear next week, and that I am one of about three who are being argued over to take his place with me leading at the present. I can't think of a worse job in the Air Force than being Wing Surgeon, except being medical inspector. It would carry a promotion, but I would much prefer to be a major in my present job than a Lt. Col. in that job. There is absolutely no contact with either flying personnel or sick patients. It is purely an administrative job, and a poor one at that. I did something that I have never done before. I wrote Col. Putnam this morning to use his influence to keep me from being sent up there. I don't know whether or not that was

Major Alfred W. Erb, flight surgeon with the 367th Bomb Squadron, 306th Bomb Group since August 8, 1942, at Wendover, Utah. Courtesy of the East Anglia Air War Collection.

a mistake. One who tries to interfere with assignments in the Army usually comes out at the little end of the horn. But we'll see what happens. I sure wouldn't be happy about going up there.

It was learned last night that Lt. Col. Terry is being transferred out up to 101st Combat Wing staff. I sure hate to see him go. In the opinion of 95% of this group he is the brains of this organization at this time. He has made remarkable advancement in this organization because he has demonstrated his abilities again and again. He'll go still farther.

Aug 15 - The blow fell today! As of noon today I am 1st Bomb Wing Surgeon. I just didn't think this could happen to me, not so soon at least. I am just simply sick. I could scarcely keep tears out of my eyes this afternoon. For 16 whole months now I had been a member of the great 306th Bomb Group. I have grown up with it, have seen a host of wonderful fellows come and go. I had outlived most all the officers in the Group. I have humored those flyers and tried in a million ways to keep them flying most efficiently, and I'm going to miss that sort of thing awfully. A lump came in my throat tonight as I sat in my room up here at Wing. There was a roar overhead and the fortresses were coming home from a raid on Brussels. I could hardly stand the thought of not being there to see them come in. Over sixty times now I have been there to see them come home—or fail to come home—while I was with them 56 ships and 560 men did fail to come home. About 10 came back dead and countless ones injured. It's going to be awfully hard getting accustomed not to be there. It was a priceless experience this 16 months with the 306th Bomb Gp. I shall do the best I can with this new job, but as yet I can't see where there is much job to it. I do distinctly remember 13 ½ months ago that I felt almost as badly about leaving the Squadron to become Group Surgeon, and it turned out to be a gem after we got into combat, so who knows? This job might turn out O.K.

Aug 18 - I have now been Wing Surgeon for 3 days and already I am finding it not so bad as I expected. It is a very responsible position as I am finding. It is going to be a difficult job to really be fair to the Army and still stay in the good graces of the medical officers who are working under me. Already they have thrown in my lap some recommendations for promotions and return to the United States to assume greater responsibility which I have been forced to veto in the interest of the Army. I hope I shall not run into too much trouble on that score.

I went in to pay my respects to General Williams this morning. And he greeted me with, "Oh yes, I hear you didn't want to take this job." I don't know who told him. He went on to say that he didn't give a damn whether I knew how to treat a scratched finger or anything else. What he is interested in is the mental and psychological state of the flyers, and he wants me to keep him informed. He said he got me up here because he figured I could do it. That's where all those letters I have been writing have finally caught up with me. That is absolutely the reason why I am here. It didn't occur to me until today, however, just how many people were bypassed in putting me here. They sacked Lt. Col. Streeter who has been in the regular Army for 12 years, and jumped me over three regular Army Majors within this wing, each of whom have three to five years in the Army, and me just out of an internship and with exactly two years in the Army. But I'm not going to stick out my chest over it until I find if I can hold down the job. It is there for me now and is a real challenge and I'm going to bust a gut or make a go of it.

Yesterday was that big mission on Target A [Schweinfurt] that we have all been waiting for with fear and trembling. It was that big ball bearing plant deep inside Germany. It was by far our biggest and toughest effort and our losses were much the highest. The 91st lost 10 planes, and the 381st lost 11.[11] There were 36 planes lost in this wing alone, and the 4th Wing losses were high too. But the old 306th rode on the crest of the wave. They put up a maximum number of planes, didn't have a single abortion, every plane bombed and hit the target, and every ship returned to base and not a man was injured, a 100% raid on the toughest target to date. That is really a feather in the cap of Major [William S.] Raper who led that show for them. And by the way he has just been made executive officer of the Group, replacing Terry, with [George R.] Buckey taking over command of the 367th. All of us who were on the inside were really sweating out that choice but are very happy about it. Raper has really come through where it counts.

Aug 20 – I have made calls to four stations in the last two days sort of in the manner of getting acquainted. The General sent me over to see what the psychological status was in the 91st and 381st Groups yesterday following their heavy losses on the 17th. Capt. [Marlen E.] Reber flew Major Wright and me over there. It was an enjoyable trip and was the first time I had been in anything other than a fortress since we all almost cracked up in that old B-18 back at Wendover 14 months ago. I found the Groups not too alarming in spite of their losses. The 381st is a little shaky and a little worse off than they think they are. They lost another plane yesterday on what was supposed to be an easy mission.

Today I visited Talbot of the 384th and Wise of the 379th. They are in good shape as far as I can see, even though their losses have been high.

I can see right now that the General is going to expect me to create a job here. It's going to keep me humping to keep a jump ahead of him. It'll take a while to get used to supervising these 70 or so medical officers.

Aug 23 - I made the rounds of two more stations today, Polebrook and Molesworth, and of the 160th Station Hospital. I learned more new ideas about what can be done than [at] any other stations I have been on. [Major Lewis J.] Nowack is really doing a wonderful job as Group Surgeon up at Polebrook. He deserves a lot of credit.

Also I met Capt. Clark Gable for the first time today. Nowack had to go over to his room for something today, and I went with him not knowing where I was going, and when he busted into a room and introduced me to a big strapping fine looking man I was surprised to discover who it was.

Captain Clark Gable (right) and Captain William R. Calhoun after a mission, 359th Bomb Squadron, 303rd Bomb Group, Molesworth, England, April 5, 1943. Courtesy of the East Anglia Air War Collection.

He was dressing and had nothing on but his shoes and his girdle. Yes he was wearing a girdle, but my guess is that he doesn't have too much of a paunch at that. He is a beautiful specimen of manhood. He was most cordial and seemed like a real guy. His room was littered with more junk than most officers have around. He would be just another good Army officer if he were not prevented by his fame. He does pretty well as it is.

Aug 25 - U.S.O. camp shows presented "G.I. Gang" composed strictly of soldiers here tonight. They were really a marvelous bunch of musicians. The leader was a saxophonist and vocalist named Hal Craig. I know I have seen him somewhere with a big band. The pianist, Bill Bartlett from Brooklyn, was the smoothest accompanist that I have ever seen. I want to remember that name. We'll be hearing of it again one day.

Aug 31 - Capt. Manning got his orders to go back to the States today along with Allan, Lame and Ross from each of the other old groups. It is a great break for them because all of them want to go back so badly. However, they may be delayed a few days until there are replacements for them. Munal will become Group Surgeon at 306th. I'm a little afraid that Munal will not be a very good organizer, and most of all he is lazy; but this may be just the thing that will make a man out of him.

Sept 1, 1943 - I have just had one of the hardest days that I have ever had in my life. I called Major [Garfield P.] Schnabel, one of my Group Surgeons [381st Bomb Group at Ridgewell], up to my office today and told him that I was relieving him from his job, and why! That is the first time in my life that I ever had occasion to fire anybody and it certainly isn't in my line at all. The biggest reason it was so hard was because he is a Major and I am a Major, he may even outrank me. Just a little over two weeks ago we were group surgeons together and on the same status. Today I am taking his job away from him.

Furthermore, he is possibly the most hard working of the nine group surgeons within the wing—he has tried harder. Perhaps he has tried too hard. He has completely alienated himself from every single medical officer under him. They have even gone so far as to express contempt for him. They have a thousand and one petty grievances against him, most of them justified. The enlisted men have no respect for him. But worst of all, he is not on real conversant terms with any of his flyers. That is my sorest grievance. A flight surgeon who is not the best friend a flyer has is not worthy of the gold wings he wears. Schnabel tries hard, but he just doesn't have the personality it takes to be a group surgeon in a fighting outfit.

I didn't sleep more than an hour night before last when I was trying to make up my mind about this. This is the penalty of being in a responsible administrative position. The next one will be easier, I guess.[12]

Sept 4 - Went to a meeting at Pinetree today. There was a lot of talk pro and con about flying equipment but I can't see that we got a great deal accomplished. I do believe that the equipment officers are working up a little enthusiasm for their jobs at least. We're going to cut down on our losses from frost bite a great deal now.

Sept 6 - They sent the planes in to bomb Stuttgart all the way across France into Germany today. Preliminary results seem to be very poor bombing and tonight it looks like this wing lost 27 airplanes. Most of the groups didn't even see the target because of clouds. The strange part of it is that they found the weather just like it was forecast. I suppose it will remain one of the mysteries of this war why Bomber Command insists on sending planes out on hard missions like that when they know that the weather is bad. The 306th has two planes missing I believe—Lt. [Wesley D.] Peterson of the 368th and Lt. [Martin] Andrews, 423rd.

Tonight I attended the planning conference on the mission scheduled for tomorrow. It was interesting, but I had no particular business there and shall not go very frequently.

Made a little visit down to Thurleigh this afternoon. Collected my pay and enjoyed a little bull session with the fellows at the hospital.

Sept 8 - Right now almost to the minute it is one year since I first touched Thurleigh. If I live to be 100 I shall never forget that night. It must have been about 11:30 p.m. and as we got out of the trucks there were some big chandelier flares hanging in the sky that had been dropped by a German reconnaissance plane. We just knew that the Germans were watching the movements of the 306th Bomb Group and were preparing to personally give us a hot reception. That is absolutely as close as the 306th Bomb Group has ever gotten to this war except in taking the war to the Germans. A lot of things have happened in those 365 days, probably a wider experience than I will ever have in any one span of 12 months in my whole life.

This was a good day for an anniversary too. Italy threw in the chips and called it quits. It's going to be interesting to see what takes place in the next few days.

Another milestone for an anniversary occasion is the fact that tonight a squadron in the 305th Bomb Group is scheduled to make its first night flight over enemy territory. That is another new experiment that is going to be interesting to follow. From where I sit I'm waiting on that one with fear and trembling.

Sept 9 - The first night mission last night was a success. Five planes took off, successfully bombed the target on the coast of France and all returned safely without difficulty. Of course that was a short trip and a puny effort as far as numbers go, but it was a successful experiment, and is a beginning just like July 4, 1942 when those six Bostons (A-20's) were the first organized All American effort against German held France.

They ran a successful early morning mission against an airdrome in France today, and they had another scheduled this afternoon but it was scrubbed on account of weather. That is another record breaker; the first time two missions have been scheduled in one day for the heavy bombers, even though one of them was not run.

Capt. Reber flew me over to Ridgewell today. Went over to see how things were coming along under the new Group Surgeon. I'll swear I've never seen such a change in a bunch in my life. They were very happy about the change, were really putting forth some effort and show signs of developing into a first class medical organization under Major [Ernest] Gaillard. Even though it was a painful task to have to remove Major Schnabel as group surgeon, it is one of the best things that I have ever done.

Sept 12 - There has been a fog all day. This, I guess, is the beginning of the foggy season. It will certainly be interfering with the business for which we are here for many weeks to come.

Was invited to a dinner over at the Camden's last night. It was a sort of farewell party to Capt. O'Sullivan who is being transferred to Hq., E.T.O.U.S.A. The Camdens have certainly been nice to us.

Had a sweet letter from Mary Opal yesterday. She has always seemed more like a sister than a sister-inlaw. She talked at length about their boys. I wish I could see them. She mentioned about Ruby coming to see them. I always scan through Mary's letters rapidly to see if she does mention Ruby, and when she does I wish she hadn't. Oh, well.

Sept 14 - The new Table of Organization that everybody at this headquarters has been so anxiously waiting for came through approved today and I suppose there will be much mad scrambling to get everybody promoted up to strength. The thing calls for a full Colonel as head of the medical department. On the surface that means that when and if I become a Lt. Col., I will then have another bump to work for after serving in the new rank for one year. However, I have a little fear. This job is just a little too juicy with rank to go unnoticed by some of the regular Anny big shots and some of them are going to look upon it with covetous eyes. I'm really going to have to deliver the goods to be able to hang on. Not being in the regular Army, having so little Army experience and being so young puts me at a distinct disadvantage, but I'm going to bust a gut doing my best to make a go of it. If I can hold onto this job in the face of the regular Army, it would give me no end of satisfaction. The 1st Bombardment Wing is no more. From this date we are known as the 1st Bombardment Division.

Sept 15 - A fortress belonging to Alconbury crashed in northern England on the way to Scotland yesterday killing several of the essential men in their group and also Major Williams in the personnel section of this headquarters. The loss of this one officer is a great loss to this organization. He had more brains and energy than almost any two other men around here. It's a shame that fellows have to get killed like that. They were just on a pleasure trip.

Sept 17 - Our division bombed the submarine installations at Nantes yesterday with a great deal of success and the day before they practically wiped out the airdrome at Romilly. The Romilly raid was made at about 7 o'clock at night (dusk) so as to try to catch all the flying personnel and mechanics in their barracks. The living areas of the airdrome were completely covered. The planes did not get back here until nine o'clock and it was pitch dark. It was the second time that our planes have gotten back to the home station after dark and this time without mishap except for one crash landing at Polebrook.

Sept 19 - Spent the night at Thurleigh last night and attended the big anniversary dance. It was held a week late because the enlisted men had their dance last week. It was not as wild an affair as I anticipated. Everybody enjoyed himself. About all the old original fellows from the 306th were there who still are in England, but there weren't many of us at that. There are lots of faces we would have enjoyed seeing.

There was a Division holiday today to allow for a little relaxation and hell-raising throughout the division.

All the groups enjoyed it. We are expecting a raid tomorrow.

Sept 21 - I never received such a surprise in my life as when this afternoon the door of my office opened and in walked Coy Kaylor. He was the last person I expected to see. He is a Major and group surgeon in a fighter group [of] P-38's and is stationed near here. He stayed two or three hours. It sure was good to see and talk to him again.

Sept 22 - It is worthy of note that for one whole day of daylight there was not one cloud seen in the sky. That is rare indeed. However, there were no missions today. It must have been cloudy over Europe. Tomorrow I suppose this clear spot will have moved over Europe and it will be cloudy or foggy here. It is awfully cold. We are not supposed to start burning coal for a month yet, but we sure need the heat. I have been cold all day, and furthermore a lot of us are catching colds.

Sept 24 - They ran two missions yesterday. Both of them were sent to Nantes with a submarine tender in the harbor as the target. Both formations hit everything but the submarine tender. This makes three missions they have sent out for that one boat and still haven't hit it. This is another new deal for our air force to run a morning raid and an afternoon raid. It was tried once before but wasn't carried out.

Sept 27 - Today was another new experiment for us. They sent out a complete force to bomb Emden with complete overcast. It is the new technique of bombing through the clouds on a target located by a Pathfinder plane using radar equipment. We don't know yet just how successful the mission was because they haven't seen the target. This is a new thing for the A.A.F., this indiscriminate bombing.[13] The target was the center of the town. Only three planes were lost from this division, all from the 91st Gp. That was pretty cheap if the bombing was any good. It represents about 150 planes. The third division put up about the same number.

Sept 28 - Had a meeting of all group surgeons in my office today. It lasted for two hours and I can't see that we accomplished much, but it allowed the fellows to get a lot of hot air off their chests—which after all does a lot of good.

Sept 29 - Had a U.S.O. show tonight featuring Billy Gilbert, the big fat radio comedian. It was a good show and was well received.[14]

Sept 30 - Today is pay day, but I am not collecting it because I failed to get all my flying time in this month. So I'll just let it accumulate until next month. I've been on flight status for sixteen months now and this is the first time that I haven't gotten my time in. I lacked about 45 minutes this month. I am ashamed of myself.

Had an anxious consultation tonight. A young Second Lieutenant came into my room for advice about his wife who has just had a 10 pound baby girl, but he wasn't at home at the time he should have been according to his calculation of when conception must have taken place. I suppose this is just one case of many that we'll be seeing before this war is over. This poor man was almost prostrate. By the way, I'd hate to see what happens here in England when the Eighth Army gets home. I hope our soldiers are not here to face them.

Oct 1, 1943 - Longworth and I went over to Lilford Hall tonight [in Northamptonshire, south of Oundle and north of Thrapton]. The 160th station hospital has left and a new hospital unit, the 303rd station hospital has taken over. It is commanded by a Lt. Col. Smith, who seems like an awfully nice fellow. We went over for supper and afterwards I was asked to talk to the medical officers about medical problems as we meet them in the air force. I think they are going to be a big help to us. They were most courteous and I think they will be very cooperative.

Oct 5 - Have just gotten back from London tonight. I went on official army travel to attend the Inter-allied Medical Society at the Royal Academy. Got there Sunday in time to see the musical show "Strike a New Note" which was given free for members of the Eighth Air Force. The meeting was only moderately interesting. The morning was largely taken up with medical organization during the Tunisian campaign. The afternoon devoted to Russia, and there were four talks by surgeons who had visited Russia recently about the glories of Russian surgery. It was so colored with obvious propaganda that it stank, but was amusing. I stayed over another day just to relax and enjoy a little leave.

I heard a sad bit of news today. It is confirmed that Lt. Robert Smith (referred to May 23 as having been fished out of the North Sea after 30 hours) has been killed. He went back to the states a few months ago largely for advertising and training purposes. He was killed in an air collision in Florida. That is such a tragic ending for the grand record that he made for himself over here.

Oct 6 - I did something today that I once swore I'd never do. I submitted a letter to the Commanding General requesting permission to go on an operational mission. The reason that I am abandoning my crusading against medical officers going on missions is that Col. Tracy has practically given me a direct order to do so. Anyway, I am more inclined to want to go since I have this job. It's the lack of intimate contact with the fliers that does it, I think. I'm rather looking forward to it now with a great deal of anticipation.

Oct 8 - Our division made a heavy raid on Bremen today. Bremen is always a tough spot. The flak there is terrible. The division lost 13 ships today, seven of which were from the 381st, the group that has taken over the old hard luck of the 306th. Their losses have now been enormous. About 7 weeks ago they lost 11 planes on one mission. I shall never forget the first raid the 306th made on Bremen last winter. We lost 10 planes then. The 306th lost 3 planes today, one of them [Lawrence W.] Kooima, the hard luck pilot, on his 23rd mission. He had landed in the Channel once, made a bad crash landing once and has had to land away from the home field innumerable times. It's too bad to have to lose a good man like that so near his goal. He had Capt. George the group equipment officer with him. Lt. [Thomas D.] Ledgerwood, whose father used to live south of Ozark, a cousin of Ralph and Othel, is also missing. The other pilot is Capt. [Dean C.] Rodman, 423rd. It is now believed that the bombing was good, however. Maybe it was worth it—I hope so. There is a notable change the last two missions from the (German) single engine F.W.190 to the twin engine

Me 110, a more inferior ship. There is much speculation whether or not the enemy may not actually be feeling the pinch of our strategic bombing. In a few more weeks we should be able to know definitely.

Oct 9 - One year ago today my entry in this diary contained an account of the 306th first operational mission—the hardest and longest one the A.A.F. had ever made in this theater. They went all the way to Lille, a mission that is now considered nothing but an early morning milk run. We lost Capt. "Swede" Olson.

It is befitting that for an anniversary raid the division made the longest and perhaps the hardest raid that it has ever done. They went all the way to Poland on the Baltic Sea. The division lost 20 planes, bombing results are unknown. The results yesterday are not so good.

Oct 10 - The results at Gdynia, Poland and at Anklam, Germany yesterday were really good. The F.W. plant at Anklam is almost completely destroyed.

They went out again today, the third day in a row. The target was an industrial and railroad center just north of the Ruhr. Most of the groups missed their primary target, but they dropped them on German towns anyway so they did a lot of damage. They have claimed over 350 German fighters shot down in the last three days. The third division caught the fighter attacks today and lost about 30 planes. Our division lost only one plane.

Oct 13 - The weather has been stinking for the last few days. The usual fall and winter fog. It was really a blessing though because the personnel could hardly stand up to so much continuous activity. However, it is estimated that the German air defenses were probably more strained after that three day attack than our force was. I suspect the folks back home wonder why we don't go out and bomb every single day. But not only is it too hard on personnel, but the weather here in England just doesn't permit. In only two different months have the Americans made as many as 10 raids in one month.

I have two new roommates now, Maj. [Bernard] Card and Maj. [Manvel H.] Davis. I am glad to get permanent roommates. This room has been a tourist camp lately.

Oct 15 - Yesterday, 14 Oct. 1943, was the bitterest battle in the history of aerial warfare. Every AAF bomber organization in England was sent against Schweinfurt to get those ball bearing factories again, and they really met some opposition. They met opposition last time but they didn't hit the target very well. This time they literally blew the target off the map. But we paid for it with the loss of 60 of our fortresses, our own division lost 46. The 305th and 306th groups were the heavy losers. The 305th put 15 over Germany and got only two back. The 306th put 15 over and got 5 back. Several other groups lost six or seven. It is estimated that the Germans had approximately 600 enemy fighters against us. They met our boys with F.W. 190's, Me 109's and even a lot of twin engine stuff. But they used a new tactic. They are now sitting out on the tail just out of range and lobbing rockets into the formation. It is a deadly new weapon and it looks as if the Germans have at last found an answer to our high altitude formations. We have the answer in the P-47 fighter, but unfortunately it won't go far enough. It is said that the P-38 will be able to go all the way. If so, there will still be lots of competition when they get into service.

General Anderson made quite a pep talk at the critique this afternoon. He succeeded in making the arm chair strategists here at headquarters feel that the Hun is staggering much worse than we are. However, that is small comfort to the boys back on the station. Some of them are pretty badly shaken up as one can well imagine. I am at a loss to know just how to go about handling the morale situation. I know that I will run up against a stone wall from command because they are getting pretty blood thirsty now. I'll have to do a little more thinking and scheming.[15]

Oct 19 - I received quite a compliment from Col. Beaman, our executive officer, today. He called and said that he had just read my weekly activities report and that it was the best one that had ever come out of the surgeon's office since he had been here over a year. I was overwhelmed. He is such a hard cuss usually. But I had put a great deal of thought into the writing of that report which concerned mainly my estimation of the psychological and morale status following the Schweinfurt raid.

I have pretty closely checked the 305th, 306th, and 384th groups, three of the ones with the heaviest losses, and they don't seem to feel so badly about it. They are low of course but feel that they can make a rapid come-back provided they can get rapid replacements. We won't know the full effects of all those heavy losses for another two or three weeks. What bums me up and is also burning up the combat crews even more are the statements being made by our high ranking generals here and by General Arnold to the effect that the destruction of Schweinfurt was worth the loss of 60 fortresses that we could well afford [to lose] them. General Arnold made a statement to the press that it would be profitable on a raid like that even if the losses were 25%. Our losses within this division were actually 40% and most of our flyers know it. But fortunately losses like that are not expected often. It is now believed that the Germans had good advance notice of that raid. They must have because they were perfectly organized.

General Williams scribbled a note on the face of my report that he wanted to talk it over with me. At least it indicates that he read it and that something rubbed him one way or other. I'll be seeing what is on his mind.

Oct 20 - Yesterday Col. Tracy told me that he would be transferring out a couple of our group surgeons to another air force. So I spent the entire afternoon checking up on who we can best afford to let go. I have settled on [Abraham] Black and Spangler provided I can talk Tracy into it. Personnel troubles are still my biggest headache. Replacements are not in sight at the moment. After kicking Capt. Trach out down at Podington, I just about had things set. Of course there is the stinking situation up at Molesworth, but I had resolved not to interfere with it. But when Black leaves the thing will spring from smoldering embers into a raging inferno or else it will die out completely.

Today Major Reber flew me down to Coombe House, the new rest home for officers located in south England. It was a very pleasant trip. I navigated the trip (by pilotage, of course), and we didn't get lost once. Coombe House is larger but not so luxurious as Stanbridge Earls. It has just about as much facilities for recreation. It is more like a big fraternity house there. It is really swell.[16]

Oct 21 - I went in to see what General Williams had on his mind today and found him very receptive to my recommendations that two missions in two consecutive days is the greatest number that can be run without resting the crews. I honestly believe he is one commander who has the physical and mental interest of his men at heart. The matter of prolonged continuous operations and lack of leave has long been a sore spot with me and he is the first one in real authority that I have gotten to agree with me. My theory has always been that one can put more bombs on the target with 100 alert crews than one can with 200 tired and exhausted ones. General Williams did go so far as to say at four o'clock this afternoon that there would not be a mission tomorrow on account of weather. The usual procedure is to plan a mission and scrub it at the last minute. Maybe General Williams is going to have a good influence on General Anderson.

Oct 22 - I spent the day at Pinetree today. Spent a couple of hours at Col. Tracy's office and the rest of the time with Jackson and Hastings. It's the first time I had ever been in Col. Tracy's office, and I have been in this job over two months now. At least no one can say that I am trying to play up to my superiors. Most of my conference with him was taken up with the problem of making personnel changes. I will be losing eight of our best medical officers within the next few days.

Had a most interesting session with Hastings as usual. He and Lt. Wright have written up some of their findings and conclusions from a psychiatric standpoint that they have made in the last year. Lt. Wright has just completed a survey of about 150 officers and men who have completed their tour of 25 missions to determine just what their physical condition is after having completed a tour and to try to determine if possible just what the factors are that go into the making of a successful combat man. He found that 95% of them suffered from nervous symptoms due to operational exhaustion, a third of them severe. He made one interesting observation that considerably flattered my ego. I recall how Col. Armstrong, the assistant air force surgeon, pricked up his ears and looked at me as if to say I was a damn fool and an ignorant rascal at the conference last June 18 (four months ago) when I came out with the statement that my observation of the men who were successfully completing their tour of 25 missions did not bear out the present standards of selection as far as background is concerned; that some of our poorest specimens as far as history and environment goes were the ones who were finishing. That was a nasty thing to say to Col. Armstrong who is the outstanding research man in aviation medicine and one who has been influential in setting up the standards. But Lt. Wright in his survey which I read today reveals that about 50% of the fellows who finish have something bad in their history which would ordinarily have disqualified them for flying training if a complete psychological and psychiatric history had been taken at the time of admission to the air force. His conclusion is that combat itself is the real test of who will be a good combat man. So that is one time that I jumped at a conclusion and hit it right on the head.

Oct 24 - I went this morning over to Molesworth to have a session with Col. Stevens concerning the loss of both Major Black and Capt. Lame, or rather the possibility of such. It's a funny thing that Commanding officers in general don't seem to pay much attention to what the medical department does until one tries to take some of them away and then they scream to high heavens. The thing is that he does not want to lose both Black and Lame. Lame is supposed to go back to the States this week in accordance with the policy of rotation of officers, but Col. Stevens says he is not going, and Col. Tracy says he is going. I'm betting on Col. Tracy, but I'm talking up both sides to see a good scrap. I hope that Col. Tracy does win out and that Lame goes home. I want to try to get McKim in here as group surgeon if I can. There may be trouble any way the thing falls and I've tried to maneuver the thing so that the group commander is fully responsible if trouble does break. I've been trying all sorts of schemes to try to get Col. Stevens to do what I want him to and still have him think that it was his idea. It is a crazy deal—this being in a headquarters. It's shameful the politics that has to go on, but if one doesn't look out for the interests of his own men, nobody else will. It's amazing how many jobs are given out and destinies determined by the flip of a coin or the position of one's name on a roster. If I can get out of this shift in personnel up at Molesworth without making any enemies, I shall say that I am learning fast.

I had an exciting few minutes tonight. About the middle of the afternoon, Col. Putnam was taking Pam Stannard back to her station by plane about 100 miles north of here. Major [Hugh G.] Ashcraft was flying the plane and they had invited me to fly along with them. The way up was uneventful except for some nasty weather on the way. We started back just before dark but it got dark on us on the way. About 2/3 of the way back the entire electrical system went out. There were no dashboard lights, no radio, no landing lights. Luckily an airdrome that was lighted was close by. Oh yes, half of the spark plugs were out (those that are operated directly from the battery), the wheels had to be cranked down and the flaps would not come down. The Lord be praised, Ashcraft made an excellent forced landing right on the correct landing strip, but since we had no radio or lights, the control tower did not know that we were landing and Lancasters were landing all around us. One almost chewed off our tail but not quite. Things happened so fast I didn't have time to get scared and really didn't realize how serious things were until afterwards. We came back to base by automobile, about 30 miles, and got here almost at midnight. Life in the Army is pretty dull in spots, but there are some interesting moments.

Oct 25 - McNeil, our new division dental officer who reported last week, and I made the rounds of Bassingbourn, Nuthamstead, and Ridgewell today. Kaylor is at Nuthamstead, but he was not at home. Had quite a nice session over at Ridgewell. I feel that we accomplish quite a lot just sitting down for an hour or two and "passing the time of day" with the medical officers and finding out what their problems are. It helps to gain their confidence. Sometimes there is not much I can do about it, but at least I give them a chance to blow off steam.

Oct 29 - Came back last night from a two-day pass. Went to Bournemouth, on the south coast. The Red Cross Club, the Ambassador Hotel, for officers is just about the swankiest thing in England. It is just the thing for a rest. My purpose in going there was business as well as pleasure. Was checking into the facilities for sending more of our flyers there on leave. They have wonderful beds, good food, grand climate and all sorts of recreational facilities. It is truly the playground of England. The only trouble, I didn't stay long enough.

Our troubles over at Molesworth are still brewing. It seems that Col. Stevens and Col. Tracy reached a deadlock and they compromised by deciding that Capt. Lame would leave and Major Black would stay. I'm still waiting for those replacements to show up to let those four medical officers go home. Things sure are happening awfully slowly.

Nov 2, 1943 - Today I interviewed a couple of fellows from the 91st Group who are being charged with lack of moral fiber because of too many abortive missions. Both have completed 13 missions. One has aborted 10 times and the other 11 times. One is wearing the D.F.C. One is a particularly nice chap of 21, married, a really fine pilot, but one who just won't take a ship into the battle zone unless it is 100% O.K. The other one did 18 missions with the RAF before joining the A.A.F. and completing 13. He has turned sour after getting married last June. I haven't so much sympathy with him as I have for the other one, but both of them in my opinion should not be disgraced. In the same group two or three weeks ago, a pilot had court martial charges initiated against him for refusing to go on a mission after having completed 19 missions. We got him off to the hospital. That stops him temporarily. That is too many experienced pilots from one group. I'm suspecting that there is more trouble somewhere in command over there than there is with the pilots. I'm going to make it my business to find out. We doctors are sometimes accused of defending these fellows too much. But I do not believe it. I am just as opposed as the next one to a man who really lays down on the job. There were three other cases that came up from the 91st Gp. whom I shall not turn a hand to defend. But some of those fellows have given a lot and I shall not stand by and see them crucified just for the sake of making an example of somebody.

Nov 6 - A British Wellington bomber crashed right in our back yard only about 50 yards from some of our enlisted men's barracks tonight. It caused quite an explosion and really shook the house. We thought at first that we were being bombed. We picked up the bodies of four R.A.F. men and one W.A.A.F.A crash like that makes a nasty mess.

We are still battling those reclassification cases from Bassingbourne. Lt. Cobb is working himself up into a lather trying to determine whether it is the men or the group Commander that needs reclassifying.

There was a raid Nov. 3 on Wilhelmshaven and another yesterday on the Ruhr [Gelsenkirchen, Germany]. They bombed on Pathfinders through the overcast and it is not known what the results are. Pathfinder bombing is "area" bombing, and too much is really not expected. If the bombs don't fall in open fields then it is considered good. Losses were not great.

Nov 8 - Those two pilots whose skin I have been fighting to save were finally disposed of today by transferring them out of the 91st Group to other outfits. Lt. [Robert S.] Gerald is going to our old 306th and Lt. [Winston M.] Cavaneau is going to the 303rd.[17] Col. Putnam wanted me to come over to his office to interview them with him, but he did all the talking. He gave them the most beautiful piece of dressing down that I have ever had the privilege of listening to. Col. Putnam is a very gifted man in more ways than one. He took time out to do what Col. [Clemens L.] Wurzbach,[18] the C.O. back at Bassingbourne should have done. There wasn't any doubt that Lt. Gerald should be given a new chance. But Lt. Cavaneau has the nastiest attitude of any pilot that I have ever seen. If it weren't for the fact that he is an extraordinary good pilot, he wouldn't have a chance in the world. Some of his combat abortives definitely look like retreat without cause. Col. Putnam was undecided about him, but I wanted to give him another chance although I almost had to agree with Col. Putnam that anyone with a disposition like his is practically hopeless. I'm hoping that Col. Stevens over at 303rd Gp. can bring him out of it. These boys have just got to make good, else my opinion on matters that didn't concern one much in the first place will become almost valueless. It's just that there has got to be somebody who will act as a buffer against the cold hard military demands that are made upon these boys and the medical officer frequently can fill in where the chaplain doesn't have a chance. We've got to be able to see and appreciate both sides equally. But some of these flyers are pretty young and immature yet in spite of their 21 years. A good sound tongue lashing like these two boys got this afternoon is often worth much more than anything else in not only saving these fellows from possible injustice but also saving their valuable experience for the Air Force. It goes without saying that I shall keep a watchful eye on them because my own reputation as a Flight Surgeon and a psychologist (amateur) is at stake.[19]

Nov 13 - There has been very little excitement lately. The planes went out yesterday but returned before reaching the target because of clouds reaching up to 32,000 feet. The radio this morning stated "American Fortresses continued their daylight offensive against Munster in western Germany yesterday" and went on to describe it as if it were a highly successful raid and that only five fortresses were lost. The facts are that of the approximately 350 fortresses that started out, our whole division of about 180 planes returned early and only about 50 planes from the third division reached the target. Plus the fact that bombing results were unobserved because of cloud cover. In all due respect to our publicity agents, they are not always exactly truthful in the impressions they give on a lot of these efforts. But one score that is infallibly accurate is our announced loss of fortresses over enemy territory. The number of enemy aircraft destroyed are obviously subject to question but are just as accurate as it is humanly possible to make them. The bombing results, which are after all the important thing, can make headlines only when they have the photographs to prove it.

I am happy to record at last that our four medical officers who have been scheduled to go back to the United States for so long have at last received their orders and have as of yesterday morning taken up residence in London awaiting transportation. My man Manning is one of them.

Nov 14 - Yesterday they had one of the greatest screwed up details in the history of the 8th Air Force. There was an unsuspected and unpredicted storm which appeared right in our area just after takeoff and several of our ships crashed because of the weather. One of them just disintegrated in the air and others iced up. They all got lost and had difficulty getting in formation. Most of them didn't even leave England. The third division got about 75 across the target and lost only 3. The Liberators got about 50 across the target and lost 12 to fighters. The P-38's ran into about 300 German fighters and lost 7. Our 1st division didn't even get out of England and lost 5 fortresses and 29 officers and men due to weather only. My old 306th group lost two of those. One complete crew piloted by Lt. [Floyd O.] Scudder, 368th Sq., was wiped out. All got out of the other plane except the pilot, [Lt. Clyde W. Cosper],[20] 367th, whom I did not know. I think the Germans would be very proud of our effort for that day if they knew all the details.

Col. Putnam is acting C.O. of this division for the last few days. General Williams is up at Bomber Command while General Anderson is in the hospital.

This has been a stinker of a day. There was a little ice this morning and there has been a strong bitter wind all day. This morning at 8:30 the sun was shining, the moon was shining and it was snowing. It has been bad for days. It is always bad either here or in Germany these days. There have been several attempts at bombing during the last month, but the bombardiers have not seen their target since the big Schweinfurt raid, exactly one month ago today.

Nov. 15 - Went flying today with Major [Hugh G.] Ashcraft in an A-20. As long as I have been in the Air Force that was my first ride in an A-20. They really are smooth ships, cruise along at 220 miles per hour. But from the nose the ground sure does come up in a hurry when the thing lands at 130 M.P.H. I have ridden more different kinds of airplanes in the last two months than all my life before put together. They had a bad crash over at Chelveston today. A midair collision which instantly killed 21 men. It was just after takeoff on a practice mission. Those things are getting a little more frequent than is necessary, it seems to me.[21]

Nov. 17 - A very successful raid yesterday, the first really good one in over a month. They sent over 300 planes to southern Norway. They lost only 2 planes for all three divisions and hit two targets square on the head. One was the molybdenum plant and the other a large power station. There was very little opposition.

Nov 20 - Came back from a 48 hour pass in London yesterday. It was a very quiet time. Saw two stage shows. One, a very excellent play, "Junior Miss." It was one of the funniest most enjoyable legitimate plays that I have ever seen. The other was Irving Berlin's soldier show "This is the Army." There was certainly a lot of talent in it. I recall that I was unable to get seats to see it in New York 15 months ago. Irving Berlin himself got the biggest hand just because he is who he is, but his was just a minor part of the show. However, he almost ranks up there with Bob Hope in the time and effort he has put into the entertainment of the troops. There were some really outstanding acts. Furthermore, it was clean enough to put on in a church. The number that got the biggest hand was his rendition of "My British Buddy," a piece he wrote about 10 days ago after he came over here this time.

The weather today was perfectly lousy. There is a great deal of ice and the fog was so thick you can't see 25 yards. The fog actually froze on the vegetation. Several of us were disappointed when the fog prevented us from going to a big dance at our old home group back at Thurleigh.

Manning, Ross, Allen, and Lame actually did leave London for the good old USA on Nov. 18. I happened to be in London that night before and bade them good bye. I'm glad that they are really gone, they have looked forward to it so long. However, they are all very apprehensive about the assignment that they may get when they get back. I had been working with Manning for 23 months—that's a pretty long time. He is one of my very best friends and a wonderful person as well as a fine doctor. He had gotten married only 3 weeks before leaving the States. He's from Chicago. I wonder if I will ever run into him again.

Nov 25 – Today is Thanksgiving. Except for a most excellent dinner work went on as usual. We had turkey, cranberry sauce, with all the trimmings, and a big dish of ice cream for dessert. We didn't feel like doing anything much this afternoon and fortunately there was very little to do.

My most important patient of the moment is the General [Robert B. Williams, First Air Division commander] himself. He has a mild case of the flu such as is running through this division in a more or less epidemic form. Chelveston admitted 25 cases to the hospital at Diddington three days ago, and yesterday when I was over there they were getting 12 ready to go. It has sent our non-effective rate soaring upward, but fortunately few of the cases are severe.

The most exciting news of the moment is the devastating raids that have been inflicted on Berlin by the R.A.F. In three raids within a week they dropped 5000 tons of bombs from 1598 bombers for the loss of only 76 planes. That is perhaps the best bit of bombing in a concentrated way during this war by the R.A.F. Our boys were scheduled to go to Berlin in daylight day before yesterday, but it was scrubbed because of weather. The bad weather during daylight hours has really worked a hardship on us this month. We still haven't had a really good show since Schweinfurt six weeks ago (except Norway). It is staggering how rapidly replacements are coming in now. Since we lost those 60 planes we not only have filled up that hole but have another entirely new group of 36 planes (the 401st group) and have perhaps 150 or 200 additional crews assigned throughout the rest of the division. Along with the B-26's we would have no trouble at all putting 1000 bombers over Germany in one raid. My heart almost skips a beat when I think about our pitiful little force over here just one year ago. We were operating four groups of 35 crews each, we couldn't get replacements for either planes or crews, and after the first three raids each group could get 12 to 15 planes in the air. Many is the time the great 8th Air Force went across the target with less than 60 planes altogether.

The worst news of the moment, in my opinion, is the scandal that has developed about General Patton. I have heard a great deal of criticism of Drew Pearson for publicizing it in the manner that he has, but I do not agree with that argument. It is proper that it should be brought out in the open. But it should be aired and dropped. It looks now like the public is going to demand that Patton be busted. But the Army and the United States has too much to lose by throwing away a commander of his abilities. I believe that he should be given a public spanking and sent back to duty. This all goes to prove that a man is only as great as his weakest moment.

Nov 27 – There was a heavy raid on Bremen yesterday. The 8th Air Force dispatched the greatest force of planes in the war. Our forces sent well over 1,000 bombers and fighters. There were over 600 heavy Bombers alone. They bombed Bremen through 10/10 clouds,[22] but it is believed that the results were good. There were 29 heavy bombers lost, 19 of which were from this division.

Nov 30 – This was pay night, but I neglected to sign my pay voucher until only a couple of days ago so my check was not ready. But I do not mind. It seems so funny but money doesn't seem to mean anything. There isn't much now that it can be used for. I draw it, send most of it home and then don't spend what I do keep. Only three years ago there were so many things that I could have done and fun to be had with just a little money, and now with money there is so little to buy.

The general is still ill, but he is better. He has been in the hospital for two days. Just a case of flu, but he got pretty sick—in fact just about our sickest patient. It would have to be the boss who had the worst case. Guess I'm not such a good doctor!

The crews were ordered out on a mission beyond the Ruhr today and one yesterday over Bremen, but both were royal screw-ups because of weather. A few bombs were dropped in some German cow pasture yesterday, no doubt, but no attempt was made to bomb today. To make it worse there were several crews lost. Bomber Command is still impatient to get something accomplished it seems.

Dec 2, 1943 - Our division went out to hit at a small town east of the Ruhr again yesterday. It was another case of bombing through 10/10 clouds so they didn't see the results of their bombing. But still our division lost 20 planes and the second lost six. The third division stayed on the ground. About four of those crews were picked up out of the channel. One almost amusing incident was one of Thurleigh's ships which crashed. Capt. George Reese was on his 25th mission and was trying to assemble into formation when he ran into a thunderhead which threw him out into a spin. They all put on their parachutes and looked around again. It didn't look so bad so he tackled it again. This time it threw him out with his ailerons missing so they all bailed out. The only tragic thing, one of the men's chutes failed to open. Of all people to have such an experience one would almost have guessed that it would happen to Reese.

Dec 4 – General [Malcolm C.] Grow[23] was here today. I went with him to Alconbury, Molesworth and Deenethorpe. Lt. Col. Stone was with him. The General was interested mostly in some new equipment he has up at Molesworth. He is quite a fellow. I have mixed opinions about him, but he has undoubtedly done a great deal for the Air Force. I like Lt. Col. Stone very much.

Dec 5 - Today was another milestone in my life. This morning I learned that I am a lieutenant colonel. Boy oh Boy! That is getting up there in rank far beyond my wildest dreams at the time I joined this man's army. I recall seeing a 29 year-old major at Las Vegas when I first got there, a West Pointer in the Air Corps. We all thought that was quite a record. At that time a 29 year old lieutenant colonel in the medical corps was absolutely unheard of. And even now I don't know that I have ever seen one. Of course we have a 23 year old full colonel in charge of a fighter group. I really feel foolish with silver leaves on my shoulder. I know full well that I don't deserve them at all, and I am almost ashamed to show myself among all the captains who are far better medical officers than I. Nevertheless, I can't help feeling a deep sense of pride. I didn't ask for this job in the first place and they promoted me after the very shortest possible lapse of time. In spite of the unreasonable rapid advancement that I have had, I have never yet asked for, hinted for, or otherwise maneuvered for a promotion or a transfer. I am more proud of that record than anything else. The obligations in line with the customs of the service hit my pocketbook pretty hard tonight, but it's not every day that one becomes a lieutenant colonel.

Dec 6 - General Williams is ill again. He's having a hard time with his case of flu. I think it is going to be necessary to send him down to the rest home for a week. He is going to scream bloody murder, but I believe he can be managed. There are few commanders who don't feel that things will go to ruin if they take off for a while.

Yesterday they took off and flubbed around over France for a while and returned because of weather. One of the planes from Deenethorpe crash landed on takeoff right in the village. It caught fire and burned for about 20 minutes before the bombs went off. It practically wiped out the village of 102 population, but due to quick thinking and action on the part of the M.P.'s all the villagers were evacuated in time. One amusing incident in connection with it was the old 75 year-old Englishman who was wandering around that afternoon saying, "This village has stood here for 600 years. Now the damn Americans come along and blow it up."

Dec 9 - Went down to the hospital last night to see the General. While there I saw the worst case of frost bite that has ever occurred probably in the history of aviation. He was in an R.A.F. hospital for several days and they had never seen anything like it. It was the case of a navigator from Molesworth. The nose of his ship was blown off and the bombardier was killed. He was knocked unconscious and rode for a long time at temperatures around −45° C. His entire face was frozen, also his hands. He will lose all fingers up to the last knuckles. His entire face is gangrenous and will lose much of his forehead, probably his eyelids and nose and much of his cheeks. His neck was swollen so bad a tracheotomy had to be done. It's too bad he wasn't killed also.

Dec 12 - There was a very successful raid on Emden yesterday. Almost 300 planes went out from this division and only one was lost. It was a visual target this time, aiming only at the center of the town. The pictures reveal that much of the city was wiped off the map. It was really a successful mission.

Dec 15 - Have just gotten back from a couple of days in London on pass. I really relaxed and enjoyed that pass. They had another very successful mission on Dec. 13 while I was away. This division sent out over 300 planes and again lost only one. They bombed Kiel and Bremen through the clouds so the results are unobserved. With the force that was sent over something must surely have been hit.

Col Putnam has been sent down to the 91st Group to take command, Col. Wurzbach [is] relieved. Lt. Col. [Henry W.] Terry is to be his [Putnam's] executive officer. That is a good swap and am pretty happy about that. The old 91st has been slipping bad[ly] in recent months, and I believe the Putnam-Terry combination[24] will really put them up where they belong. I predict that within three months that will be the outstanding group in the division.

Dec 19 - Yesterday I heard a humorous story that I must record. Capt. Stroud, one of our finer flight surgeons from the 384th Group went along on one of the combat missions a couple of weeks ago. On the way home, the plane developed engine trouble, but the pilot was unable to feather the propeller. It vibrated so much that he feared it would tear off the wing and ordered the crew to prepare to bail out over the channel. Capt. Stroud said no, he didn't care to bail out in the water and drown so he'd just go down with the ship if he were going to be killed anyway. So it was decided to try to bring it down on the water—and they actually did get it to England and land on the coast. But during the time they were expecting to land in the water any minute, Stroud was having many thoughts, the most important of which was the conviction how foolish he was to be on this mission anyway, since he wasn't required to go. This thought gathered momentum in his mind as he sat in the radio room until his emotions turned to anger at himself. He admitted that he said a prayer for his wife and two children, but was so mad, he wouldn't pray for himself.

General Williams got off to the Rest Home today. I hope he likes it there, he better with all the salesmanship I gave him. He will go from there to take over Bomber Command for a couple of weeks. General [Robert F.] Travis is in command here in his absence.

Dec 24 - There have been three raids in the last five days, one on Bremen, one on Osnabrock, and a huge one today just across the coast of France from Dover. The losses on Bremen and Osnabrock were just average and the results just average. The targets today were the rocket gun installations in France that are aimed at London, each group having a different installation. There were over six hundred heavy bombers and over two hundred medium bombers. There were enough fighters to make a total effort of U.S. planes on France of almost 1500 planes. That's the biggest show yet. I think they'll be going back again until they actually destroy those installations. No planes at all were lost today.

Dec 25 - This is the completion of our second Christmas in England and the third one in the Army. Today has been by far my best Army Christmas. A couple of days ago the officers gave a party here for the kids of Brampton village and they had a whale of a time. They were served ice cream. Some of them liked it very much and asked for a second helping. Others didn't know what it was and wouldn't eat it because it was too cold.

I started off by going to the office today in the usual manner, but the medical section had a little Christmas party this morning which included punch which we must confess was spiked. It was intended only for us and the Ordnance section which occupies the same hut with us, but the word spread, and we invited more people, until we had someone or several there from every section. It just sort of gained momentum as it rolled along and there just wasn't any stopping it, but nobody tried very hard. Therefore, the medical section did not one speck of work today. At noon we had a perfectly wonderful dinner with as much of the best turkey that one can ever hope to have. There was pie a-la-mode for dessert. Immediately after dinner I went down to the Camdens and took my gallon of peanuts for roasting, the ones mother sent me. I got there in time for dinner and they forced me to help them eat their chicken. Then we went to their church with them, (Munal and Erb were there), after which we had tea. Tonight there was a double feature movie down in the lounge, which rounded out a very full and enjoyable holiday. Tomorrow we should be ready to get right back into the swing of things.

The crews were told last night that they'd have the day off today. Perhaps both sides took a rest today.

Dec 31 - Have just gotten back today from another meeting at Pinetree, called at the request of Col. Armstrong for the purpose of discussing disposition of combat crew failures. It was a Snafu mission from the beginning. First of all, I was sent to Widewing by mistake and was about three hours late getting to the right place—which was all right by me because the meeting was no good anyway. Besides I got to see 8th Air Force Headquarters which I had never seen before. The discussion ended where it began with Col. Armstrong and all the psychiatrists on one side, and Col. Tracy, Major Haigler and me on the other. Col. Armstrong's attitude is that nearly all our fellows who fail to make good in their first few missions are mentally sick and should be found physically disqualified for flying, or in other words an attitude of leniency, and expressed that what the administration did with them after that was none of our business. The three of us got right crossways with him and expressed our opinion that it was very much our business as Flight Surgeons what the ultimate disposition of these men was inasmuch as it could affect the morale of the other crews. My opinion is that they should not be put in a position where they can be rewarded, whatever the outcome is.

A fairly successful mission to Southern Germany on the 30th.

Jan 1, 1944 - Little did I realize a year ago today that I'd still be stationed less than 15 miles from where I landed in England in the first place. There have been an amazing lot of things happen in the 8th Air Force, and it is being climaxed at the end of the year by a change in command. Lt. Gen. Eaker is going to Africa and Maj. Gen. [James] Doolittle is going to take over our old Eighth. We're all wondering what that will mean. The Eighth Air Force is at least getting a lot of publicity in all the magazines and there are at least a couple books about it on the market. It's at last recognized as the powerhouse of the U.S.A.A.F. It has been a revelation to see it grow almost from scratch. The 8th and 9th Air Forces in England put 1500 fighters and bombers over Germany one day this week.

There are plenty of headaches scattered throughout the headquarters today. The big New Year's Eve dance last night was a huge success from all appearances. But most of the fellows conducted themselves admirably. The only one who passed out cold was an old 60-year-old British civilian from the neighboring village of Brampton. I took him home in the ambulance on a stretcher. That can be chalked up as credit against Anglo American relations.

The last operational mission of 1943 was run against the coast of France along the Bay of Biscay yesterday. Results were poor because of clouds. The 351st Bomb Group took a terrible beating with the loss of eight planes, which included their C.O. Col. [William A.] Hatcher, a squadron commander, the assistant Group operations officer, some of their best bombardiers and navigators. I don't believe any one group has ever lost so many important people before. It's a blow that will be hard to recover from. However, nobody here at headquarters feels as sorry for them as they ordinarily would other groups because they have been so cocky all along. They have just run through their luck at last—that's all. No one organization is ever invincible.

Jan 4 - This afternoon I went over to Molesworth to lecture to the division physical training officers. There were about 15 of them, and my comments were along the line of the importance of physical training for combat crews. I fear my comments were rather dry, but I bored them for about an hour. After that I went by the 303rd Station Hospital to meet the new C.O. and chief of surgical service who came in only two or three days ago. They seem nice enough.

Jan 6 - The groups went out on Jan. 4 to Kiel and they repeated it again yesterday. Losses were moderate, but the tragic thing is that we lost four planes from this division before they got out of England. A Molesworth plane ran into a Kimbolton plane, both going down and taking another Kimbolton plane with them. Also a Thurleigh plane crashed on takeoff. In the four planes 36 men were instantly killed. That's a lot of officers and men to expend for no good reason at all. They took off before daylight. It's quite a problem and an accomplishment to get over 500 heavy bombers into formation over the eastern section of a small island like this in the cover of darkness. Formation flying at night was unheard of anywhere a few months ago.

Longworth was promoted to major today. I had no idea when I came up here that I'd be promoting him, but he's really done a splendid job for me. And although it goes against my principle of not promoting fellows in higher headquarters who did unsatisfactory work in the lower echelons, I hope that I have not made a mistake this time.

Yesterday was a full day for me. The entire morning was spent on a board which gave commissions to six enlisted gunners.

In the afternoon the equipment officer and I had a meeting of all Group Surgeons and group equipment officers. The primary purpose was to map out some procedure for cutting down the number of deaths we have been having due to oxygen failure. We have had eight fatalities in the last month, which is entirely too many. The fault lies in improper training primarily because the fellows are either careless or ignorant in the use of their equipment. It is hoped that we can do better. Col. Tracy came up for the meeting.

The latter part of the afternoon was the most enlightening and amusing. Capt. McNeil, the dental officer, and I went over to Bassingbourne to act as a sort of reception committee to Major General Mills, the big shot dental officer from Washington. In fact he is the only general dental officer in captivity. He is an old fuddy duddy from the word "go." He is in his upper fifties, has a belly like Will Hill used to have, and can talk more about nothing sensible than anybody in such a high position that I have ever seen. The pay-off was when he went in to see Capt. Nicastro's dental set-up. Nicastro had gone to a great deal of trouble to remove the foot pedal from the old G.I. machine and install an electric motor. Nick was going to a great deal of length to explain how he had taken a small electric motor from a B-17 generator and hooked it up to a battery series and with a foot rheostat had made quite a satisfactory electric unit. Nick had not even finished when the old General turned up his nose and said, "Why don't you pedal it? A lot of awfully good dentists have pedaled their own machines." Someone almost asked him if he came into camp in a horse and buggy. His parting remark on the side was, "He could have filled a hundred teeth while he was messing around with that electrical stuff." Needless to say, the dentists are no longer proud of their high command and now understand perfectly well why the dental corps has advanced so slowly during this war.

Jan 10 - Lt. Col. Card is being transferred to the Detachment of Patients at 2nd General Hospital in preparation for boarding back to the U.S. He is a typical case of neurosis. So we'll be having another new roommate I suppose. Major Davis is now Lt. Col. Davis.

Jan 12 - Yesterday the 1st Bombardment Division was party to the greatest air battle yet. Even the Germans describe it as such. The main force of the attack was on Oserschleben, about 80 miles west of Berlin, a big F.W. aircraft plant. It was murder, but they did apparently hit their target solidly. After takeoff there was a sudden change in weather and the forces were ordered to return. The second and third divisions did return, but our division was already within 20 minutes of the target so they continued. The re-call was responsible for the fighters turning around and going home also so it left our forces over there fighting for three hours without fighter support 700 heavy bombers, the biggest force yet, was dispatched but only a little over 300 went on in. A total of 59 heavy bombers did not return, of which 42 are from our division (the Germans claim they got 124 of our heavies). Molesworth, the old steady 303rd Bomb Gp., finally at long last caught it in the neck. They lost 10 ships, Ridgewell lost 8, and others lost from 6 on down. I don't know whether anybody can be blamed or not— probably it was just circumstance, because the bases in this section were closed in when they returned and most of them landed elsewhere. Jerry just put up everything in the book, and we didn't have the fighter cover there to take care of it. It just emphasizes again that Jerry is a long way from being whipped and should be taken as a lesson for all the optimists we have back in the States. However, even with the extremely high loss, we weren't hurt nearly as bad as we have been in the past: All the groups have 70 crews and the loss of 10 crews out of one group doesn't mean so much, unless it includes a commander or other leader. Six months ago the loss of 10 from any one group would have been a third or more of its strength. I think a tour of duty of 25 operational missions still can hardly be considered too few.

Jan 13 - Spent the entire day out visiting Ridgewell and Bassingbourne.

They didn't seem to be in bad shape in spite of their losses. Major Gaillard, our group surgeon at Ridgewell is getting married next week to a British girl.

Heard Lord Haw Haw tonight, and he still sticks to his claim of a major victory over the American air forces two days ago and that the Americans lost a total of 136 planes. It's the first time I've ever heard him. He sounds very convincing if one didn't know better.

Jan 14 - Today I saw France! No, I didn't go on a mission, I just saw it from this side of the channel. It was a most delightful afternoon. The weather was wonderful and I went flying with Capt. Thomas and several others in the "silver queen," the General's old B-17 which has all paint removed as well as both turrets and all guns. We went down to Beachy Head at 13,000 feet and watched the formations go out at the same altitude to bomb the area back of Calais, the rocket gun nests. The French Coast was plainly visible in spite of a ground haze, and I must say it just looked like some more of England and looked so friendly and peaceful, just like a next door neighbor. Of course, I knew all along how close we really are to the enemy coast, but there is no impression so impressive as a visual one. My first thought was of the fact that we were down there in a ship that could no longer defend herself, but then I thought that the German fighters had their hands full at the moment right over their own territory, so the thought was quickly forgotten in a smooth and sightly flight. We descended rapidly doing steep "wing-overs" which must have looked to one on the ground like the plane was completely out of control, then we buzzed a couple of airdromes on the way back. Thomas is a very excellent pilot and its grand fun doing things like that with one you have complete confidence in.

And by the way, the early reports on the mission today sound pretty good, and only two planes were lost from this division. This was the 100th raid for the dear old 306th group. Lt. Col. Bill Raper led it. He was on the first one on Oct. 9, 1942 also. That boy has seen some rough ones in that interval, but I bet there's no one any steadier for having gone through it.

Jan 16 - They had the critique today here at headquarters on the last 3 missions. General Travis made everyone sick trying to maneuver things around so as to be in the limelight for the raid and be in a position for a high citation. The high point of the critique was a major from Deenethorpe who was practically violent in his praise of a P-51 pilot who alone and unassisted, protected an entire combat wing of about 50 bombers over the target of Oschersleden against something like 30 enemy fighters. He was over them, under them, and on all sides of them and shot down several of them (the major swears at least 10). From the facts brought out it will probably be written up as the greatest piece of pursuit flying in this war. He is a Major [James H.] Howard, a former Flying Tiger. He no doubt will be recommended for and will receive the Congressional Medal of Honor. His feat is what that medal is really meant for.[25]

Another boy, however, who is getting a lot of publicity who shouldn't be is Lt. Watson, the World Series buzzer. On 11 January he ran into trouble and lost two of his engines. He didn't believe he could make it so he bailed his crew out over enemy territory, which General Travis says was over water, and then proceeds to bring the plane on home. The consensus of opinion is that Watson is just a young fool. If his crew did hit land then he's O.K. But if he bailed them out over water and they're never heard from again, he's going to hear a lot of contemptuous things from their families back home. A pilot really has a lot of responsibility on his shoulders, nearly a half million dollars' worth of equipment and 10 lives.

Jan 20 - I am making plans for an 8 day leave. Lt. Col. Davis asked me several days ago to go with him on a trip with the British navy on a destroyer for two or three days. I hadn't imagined myself going on a leave with him who is more than twenty years older than I, but it sounds like a good idea and am making plans accordingly. This will be my first official leave in England, or anywhere else, for that matter. The trip on the destroyer is being arranged through Commander Horley, a retired British naval officer attached to this headquarters.

Jan 24 - My leave actually began today but the Judge and I left Hq. last night and came to London. At the Jules Club I ran smack into Lt. [Lionel R.] Drew, the bombardier who bailed out over France when Capt. Check was killed last June 26. He was the only one to leave the ship. He stayed in France almost six months before he got out.

Early this morning we struck out for Sheerness expecting to be sailing on the high seas by afternoon, but learned that we would not embark until tomorrow, and that even then we would only go across the harbor to spend the night. So with nothing else to do we went down to Dover to see what was there. On the way we went through miles and miles of apple, plum, and cherry orchards. I didn't realize England had that much fruit, but discovered that Kent is quite famous for its fruit. The weather in the Straits of Dover was ferocious, rain and wind of gale proportions. We decided then that we were glad the convoy didn't get out on schedule. We saw the white cliffs of Dover, but no bluebirds. The whole water front was littered with barbed wire, and there are huge caverns in the cliffs which could very easily sprout some big guns, no doubt. The formerly beautiful hotel row along the waterfront is now either empty and decaying or occupied by one of the services, The thing that impressed me about Dover is that there is an air of "business as usual." No one was the slightest concerned that the Germans had been shelling them a couple of nights before.

Tonight we are holed up in the most delightful little old hotel at Sittingbourn. It is called "Ye Olde Bull Hotel" and bears the date 1540. The conversation around the fireplace tonight bore out the findings at Dover that the enemy doesn't worry them much anymore. Three nights before Jerry had made his biggest raid in that vicinity in months with incendiaries dropping everywhere and the people were all laughing about it and apparently enjoyed and welcomed the excitement again. You can't lick a spirit like that.

Jan 25 - Early this morning we went back to Sheerness, but again we were disappointed. We were told to be back there at 8 a.m. tomorrow. Today we went over to Canterbury and are spending the night there. The whole town centers around the Canterbury Cathedral which is absolutely monstrous. It is very beautiful and most interesting, but like all these old churches it has very little seating capacity in relation to the general expanse of things. A couple of weeks ago when we were flying over this section the cathedral stood out in the center of town just like a huge centerpiece on a table. Had tea at the Pilgrim tea shop.

Jan 26 - We are finally off as guests of the British navy on His Majesty's destroyer, the Pytchley. Boarded her at 8:30 and at 9:30 went over on the other side of the Thames estuary to South End. At 1:30 p.m. we weighed anchor and began our escort of a convoy of 10 small freighters through the channel, along with one other destroyer, a Norwegian ship. Just before dark we were joined by 4 motor launches. Things looked right for a little excitement, but by the time we reached the Straits of Dover about 7:00 p.m. the sea was getting pretty rough, making E-boat attacks unlikely. I marveled how the convoy could keep any semblance of formation in the pitch blackness of the night.

The Pytchley is 185 feet long and displaces about 900 tons. It has a crew of 10 officers and 110 men. It is commanded by Lt. Commander Hodgkinson. The engineer's name is Lt. Wickham and the First Lieutenant is a lad named Welby, both of whom are particularly nice. Was surprised to learn they had their own ship's doctor, a 23 year old lad named Assinder, a very friendly chap.

Jan 27 - We tied up in the harbor at Portsmouth at 10 a.m. after an uneventful voyage. We saw not a single thing that looked suspicious. I stayed up on the bridge until after midnight. We were probably in the way a little, but they didn't seem to mind. They were most anxious to show and explain everything we asked about. The latter part of the night I slept for a time on a small couch in Assinder's quarters. The gentle rocking of the ship put me to sleep very quickly, but about 8 a.m. the violent pitching woke me up much quicker by almost throwing me out on the floor. Will have to admit that when I sat up I felt a little weak around the middle for a while and decided against eating any breakfast which was a good thing, but I didn't actually get nauseated.

When I got up on the bridge again, the bow was making frequent plunges completely under the waves and the ship did most of its forward motion on one side or the other.

At Portsmouth, Wickham took the Judge and me ashore to see the naval yard. A thing I shall always remember was a trip through Lord Nelson's old flagship Victory, on which he was killed at Trafalgar. It is a wonderful old wooden warship launched 179 years ago, but beautifully preserved and restored. At least half of it is in the original state. A lot of the original guns and rigging are still there. The poor old ship's doctor must have led a dog's life along with the rest of them. His sick quarters and surgery would make a modern doctor's eyes stand out on stems. He, however, was in charge of the ship's rum stores, which was a good idea because he probably needed a lot of it himself. Another amazing feature was the ship's stalls where a small number of livestock were kept for eating purposes. I saw there the biggest rope that I have ever seen, the anchor rope measuring 24 inches in circumference. I have always wanted to see one of those old wooden warships, and there is perhaps nowhere in the world where another is so well preserved nor so famous. It was only as a guest of the Royal Navy that I was privileged to see it in wartime.

At 12:45 we weighed anchor again and started our return journey with a small convoy of 8 ships together with the British destroyer the H.M.S. Albrighton. It is noteworthy that a couple of British destroyers accompany a convoy of many ships through the channel sometimes, while the Germans now have to use a convoy of many warships to accompany a couple of freighters. The wind tonight is high, but it is to our back and the waves are with us so it won't be so rough.

Jan 28 - We arrived back at the harbor at Sheerness just before noon today and remained on board for lunch. We had been just over 48 hours with them. For a while last night it looked like trouble was brewing. They picked up evidence of German E boats on the radio, but by the time we had reached the Straits, the sea was pretty high again and they probably couldn't attack. The Captain ordered his men to action stations about 9 o'clock last night, and they stayed there the greater part of the night. However, when prospects didn't look so good, I turned in about 1:00 a.m.

We are back in London tonight after a treasured experience, one that doesn't happen to every officer. The following are some of the things that impressed me most on the trip. (1) The dependence on radar equipment. I knew that radar is now extensively used by the navy, but I didn't realize how important it really is. It is operated constantly and is used not only to detect enemy ships, but also to determine the position of the ships in the convoy. That is indispensable on a dark night. It can determine direction, distance, and relative size of ships, buoys, mines, etc. within a reasonable range. (2) The discipline of the crew. Never in my life have I seen a group of men function so smoothly. Every man was always where he should be at the precise moment. Not once did I see the Captain raise his voice or call anybody down, but with a look or a gesture he had absolute control of his men. To them the trip was just another hunting expedition and they were sincerely disappointed when the hunting turned out not to be so good. Perhaps our navy has the same brand of discipline, but I'm sure much of our Army hasn't. (3) The hospitality. Never in my life have I been treated better. One might say they rolled down the rug for us. They made no unusual effort to entertain, however, because they were busy with their jobs. The food was good, they gave us free run of the boat, they did everything to make us feel at home and one of them, and they acted as though they felt it were an honor to have us with them.

It has been a privilege to have this two days with some of the finest of young England. Except for the Captain and the engineer none of the officers were over 23. They are a welcome contrast to the usual Englishman we see around who is ordinarily a fugitive from one of the services. I came back much more impressed with England, and thankful for a rare and interesting experience.

Jan 29 - Had a very pleasant and educational afternoon: At noon we joined a party which made a tour to Windsor Castle. This Castle during wartime is open only to members of the Allied forces in uniform. The place is magnificent and enormous. It is difficult to imagine such an immense place being designed for the convenience of one family. I was most impressed by St. George's chapel. There probably isn't a more beautiful or elaborate church in England. It was started by Edward IV in the last of the 15th century and finished by Henry VIII in 1528. Dear old Henry left his mark at Windsor as well as on England in general. The remains of him and his favorite wife, Jane Seymour, his third, occupy a very prominent place in the very center of the chapel floor. All the rulers for the last 500 or more years are buried in St. George's Chapel or in the Albert Memorial Chapel. Windsor Castle was begun by William the Conqueror in 1070. They didn't let us into the royal suites of course but they took us all around. The king and queen spend most of their time in winter at Buckingham Palace. Most of the royal finery is stored for the duration so we didn't get a true picture of the magnificence that the place really has.

The Castle is really a little city unto itself with all the guards and domestic help, the family and innumerable hangers-on, the Royal Knights of Windsor (retired Army officers of high rank), and even the choir boys for the cathedral. The clever old guide who showed us around is an obvious fan of Henry VIII.

After the tour we had tea with Mrs. Williams, the wife of the superintendent at Windsor. It was a delightful little interlude. She is a very ordinary but most pleasant little woman and not at all like one would expect of high ranking attendants to royalty. She was most generous with answers to all our enquiries about the royal family and other things. She obviously thinks that Queen Elizabeth is just about the most wonderful woman alive. That, I might add, is concurred in by all our Air Force Officers who have had opportunity to meet the queen on various occasions. The king lacks much of her charm, but apparently he is just as genuine.

After leaving Windsor Castle, our guide kindly consented to take us through Eton school which is only about a mile away from the castle. Eton was founded by Henry VI early in the 15th century; and it cannot be denied that the place shows its age. It isn't as well maintained as Windsor Castle, of course. It being late in the afternoon, all the little boys were out in town in their top hats, tails, and white ties. That certainly looks funny to us of the western hemisphere, but nobody can deny that they are distinctive, and that's what they wish to retain, I suppose. Eton enjoys a wonderful tradition, has a remarkable history behind it, but I am unable to appreciate all the things they value so dearly and am very, very glad that I had the opportunity of going to a good old American public school. However, we were only Yanks at Eton.

Jan 30 - The paper this morning said London had its heaviest gun barrage of the war last night. It happened while we were in a movie and we didn't know a thing about it until it was all over. I'm disappointed.

Jan 31 - Arrived back at the station tonight. The rest of my leave was just spent in London relaxing and seeing an occasional show. Am glad to be back and go to work again.

They have had a couple of very large and apparently effective raids on German targets while I was away. On one the 8th A.F. put out over 800 heavy bombers on Frankfort, the largest yet. A year ago the 8th A.F. still hadn't ever put up 100 bombers at onetime and they didn't even have any fighters, compared with the 600 or so they send out now. The other raid was on Brunswick with a slightly smaller force. Our losses on both raids were moderate. Bombing results are believed to be good, and enemy fighter losses were high.

Feb 4, 1944 – The mission on Wilhelmshaven was successful yesterday as far as losses were concerned. Only 4 bombers were lost, 2 from this division. The bombing results are not known yet because they bombed through 10/10 clouds.

Yesterday afternoon I took an R.A.F. medical officer over to Polebrook for a week's stay and in exchange we are giving Major Bergener to the R.A.F. for a week. This is a new experiment we are trying to see if we or they learn anything by exchange of ideas.

Yesterday afternoon I also stopped in at Glatton to check on the new fellows up there. They are getting things set up very slowly, but they are progressing. One of the squadron surgeons is a Capt. [Walter Woodrow] Crawford who interned at Charity Hospital the same time I did and was on the O.B. service at the same time. The biggest complaint was with the mess facilities. They are messing 2000 men in a mess constructed for 800. The engineer went out there today at my request, and it is hoped that they can give them a little additional construction to alleviate the situation. It seems like an awfully nice bunch that we have up there. They are eager and cocky like all new groups, but a little combat will drive them in line with everybody else.

Last night I went to an anniversary party over at Molesworth, celebrating the end of the second year of their organization. It was a stag party and a not altogether quiet one. They had undoubtedly the sorriest stage show for entertainment that has ever been shown on any stage. One strip tease "artist" came out on the stage the drunkest that I have ever seen a female stand on her feet. She made such a fool out of herself that everybody got a good laugh out of her.

Feb 5 - Went out to Podington this morning and then over to Thurleigh for lunch. Stayed to see the planes come in about 14:30. It was good to be seeing them come home again. It was a relatively uneventful trip to an airdrome in France. Only one plane came back with battle damage, a direct hit on the wing tip and the radio gunner injured. They were on Frankfurt again yesterday. They are working the boys pretty hard now and I was just sort of checking up on them to report to the General how they were coming along.

At Thurleigh I was confronted with some bad news that was quite a shock. I learned that late yesterday afternoon Lt. Michael Roskovich was killed in a crash up in Scotland. He was one of my favorites. He was the first combat man to finish a tour of duty here in the E.T.O. That was as an enlisted man, a radio gunner in the 423rd Sq. back with the 306th last spring. He wanted to become a cadet and take flight training, but somehow none were being taken from here at the time, so upon the recommendation of his C.O., he accepted a commission as a 2nd Lieutenant as gunnery officer. Even then he still wanted to take flight training. He didn't do too well in his first assignment at Kimbolton because of that and was transferred to Alconbury, but was still unhappy. Even after completing a tour of duty he slipped on planes over at Kimbolton without permission and went on about four more missions. He just wanted to fly one way or another. I stuck my nose into the complicated mess and arranged for his transfer back to his old squadron. He had already gotten permission to do five more missions. He had only gotten back there about a week before, and his squadron was overjoyed to have him back. They gave him a real homecoming and morale went up 100%. I do feel somewhat a sense of responsibility in this thing, but I don't feel very sorry about it because it is exactly as Rosky would have wanted it. If he could have changed it, he would only rather have died in actual combat against the enemy instead of just a routine training flight. The pilot was trying to take a fortress off an 800 yard grass airdrome on three engines. That extremely foolish pilot error accounted for his own death and three others. It's too bad Rosky couldn't have had his flight training. He was only 21, very fine looking and extremely enthusiastic. If only our Air Force had a few more Roskys than they have the war would be over much sooner. I almost never write a mother of boys who are killed over here, but I do intend to write Mrs. Roskovich.

Feb 7 - The planes went to France again today, but most of them did not bomb because of clouds. This makes nine briefings the fellows have had in ten days, six of which were run as planned. Some of the crews flew all six of those missions, four of which were the last four consecutive days. Most groups, however, have enough crews now that they can rotate them so that they will not be overworked. Some commanders don't seem to use so much judgement. I have conducted a survey of how the crews are standing up and find that they are not as tired as they were after a similar period of activity last July. I think it is because they are not having so many losses now and that this reflects upon their decreased anxiety in the air and better sleep and rest at night. The wonderful fighter support is a great help in this bombing effort. The report of my survey has been sent to Gen. Williams and Col. Tracy, not that I expect anything to be done about it much. It's the same old story. Gen. Doolittle, being new here, has to make a good name for himself—hence a big force, whether an effective force or not. At least my report upholds my reputation for bitching, but I didn't feel it necessary to make it as strong as usual.

Feb 9 - They had a poor mission on Frankfurt yesterday with a small force of 124 planes from this division. Today, however, this Div. started 357 out toward Leipzig, but they were recalled on account of weather about 1 ½ hours in the air. That is the sort of thing that breaks down morale. This one today would have been a tough one.

Feb 20 - Have been neglecting you, diary, the last few days, but there has been nothing recently of much interest. Longworth spent four days down at Thurleigh waiting for a chance to go on an operational mission but none was run because of very poor weather all week. Last night I attended the first dance and opening of the Officers' Club at Glatton. It was a very nice affair. They are awfully eager to get to fighting up there. They'll get that taken out of them in due time, however.

Feb 21 - I have been reading a few chapters in the new history of 8th Bomber Command called "Target Germany." It describes at length those long hard pulls we were having just a year ago and a month or two before

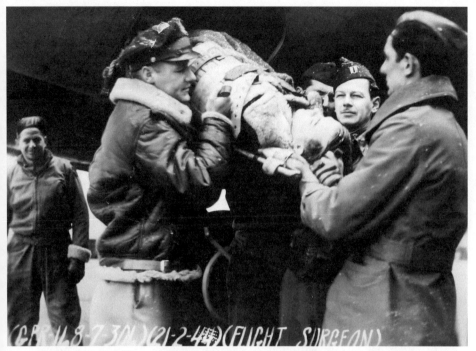

Charles P. McKim, Henry A. Dantzig, Clarence W. Hoheisel, and John A. Buccelato
remove an injured man from the nose of a B-17, February 21, 1944. Courtesy of the
Thurman Shuller Family Collection.

that. Those were really lean days when it was really a struggle for four
groups of B-17's to get 60 planes into the air for an all out effort. That is in
contrast to yesterday's effort when more than 1000 bombers took off for at
least a half dozen German targets. Most went to Leipzig to get the aircraft
factories there. It was a wonderful show. Only 22 bombers were lost out of
the whole show to pay for a superb bombing job on a number of targets
and over a hundred German planes destroyed in the air, besides many on
the ground. They were very lucky. It was to have been a particularly rough
raid and had been planned for at least three months. They were just waiting for perfect weather. The night before the R.A.F. had sent about 800
bombers to Leipzig so that the German fighters were probably tired and
scattered. Also there was heavy snow on the ground in the target areas
which may have hindered their getting off the ground. Everything was so
perfect that General Williams, when being driven to work this morning,

insisted that his driver must drive very carefully because he feared they used up all their luck yesterday.

Several heroes were made yesterday. One Polebrook plane came back to England with the pilot and copilot both killed. The navigator and engineer flew the plane over the field and bailed out all the remaining crew except themselves. They crashed and were killed in attempting to make a landing. In a Kimbolton plane, the pilot was killed and the co-pilot badly injured. Others flew the ship back to the field but the co-pilot returned to the cockpit to land it. He was deathly sick when he was taken to the hospital and at operation they removed a whole armor piercing-incendiary bullet from his abdomen, a German 13 mm, and they resected three portions of torn bowel, sewed up several other holes in his bowel and two big tears in his bladder, and removed a reasonable amount of pieces of flying clothing from his belly. This morning on the ward he was laughing about it.

Feb 25 - They have been really giving Germany a royal pounding the last few days. They hit the ball bearing plants at Schweinfurt with much success again yesterday, a number of aircraft factories a couple of days before that, also with much success. Today they hit Stuttgart and Regensburg. The fellows are getting tired again having made five raids in six days. But I rather suspect the Germans are getting more tired than our fellows. I suspect the German doctors are having a much harder time than we in handling neuroses.

The Germans are getting a little mad themselves. London is no longer the place to go on leave. They bomb it rather heavily every night now. A couple of nights ago a near miss damaged the Jules Red Cross Club beyond use.

Had a big meeting today of all group surgeons, the other two division surgeons and Col. Tracy. Capt. Bond was also up here from Pinetree. It was about a three-hour meeting all together. There was a lot of discussion about the proper handling of neurotics and lack of moral fiber cases, all of which brought no definite conclusions. It was a rather enjoyable session however.

March 3, 1944 - Arrived back from London tonight after having been gone for three days. The real purpose of getting away was that I had been called on to speak to the class of newly arrived flight surgeons at Pinetree at the Central Medical Establishment. I started out talking about Rest Homes, but wound up talking about the management of psychological problems of flying personnel as we have encountered it over here. They appeared to be listening to me. I hope it wasn't too bad.

Bombing hasn't been so successful during the last week. They turned around and came home today because of high cloud, they bombed something or other through the clouds yesterday, and two or three days before that they sent a small force to the targets at Calais with poor results. The sort of bombing they were doing last week happens only once during a war, apparently.

Before I left for Pinetree, I had spent three or four fitful days at the office and was really ready for a day or two off. Longworth was gone on leave and everything seemed to happen. The ground work was laid for three changes in personnel which required more diplomatic maneuvering than I have been called on to do before. Col. Tracy is taking Major Talbot, one of our best group surgeons up to his office. Instead of letting us promote a very deserving squadron surgeon to take his place, he is forcing us to accept a major fresh over from the States in exchange for him. The major is one [John Francis] McGregor, a young fellow I interned with at Charity and a very nice fellow. However, it's hard to expect a station to accept him when they want to promote one of their own. It's most unfair to expect our good squadron surgeons to keep on indefinitely without any hope of advancement. We'd prefer that they kept their Majors back in the States.

The other big problem was the selection of a couple of Captains to be permanently assigned to a secret mission going to some other country. I had no difficulty making the selections, but had considerable difficulty getting the C.O.s to release them, particularly Capt. Minor. The whole thing required much telephoning and personal visits. Col. Stevens wasn't quite so hard to talk into releasing Capt. Newell. His going should relieve a little of the tension over there in the medical department.

March 4 - Learned that the target yesterday which they didn't reach was Berlin. The target for today which they also didn't reach was Berlin again. It is rumored that about 25 planes from third division actually did go on in to the briefed target, but the rest dropped their bombs early on anything in Germany and came home. General Spatz seems to be getting awfully eager here of late.

Exactly 18 months ago this morning we took off from Westover Field, Mass. and headed east. That has been a long time ago in a relatively short period of time.

March 6 - Longworth and I spent the entire day at the 7th General Hospital, or at least mostly on the way there and back. Went up there to advise on the disposition of some of the Air Force personnel. They seemed plenty willing to give us everything we asked for, but I only hope they can get away with it. S.O.S. headquarters is now getting unreasonable about sending casualties back to the States, which is what we want any time a man is grounded from combat flying.

At 2:30 this morning I got up and went with Capt. Schapp and Lt. Col. Davis to a briefing at GraftonUnderwood. It was the first briefing I have attended since coming to this headquarters. The target was the ball bearing plant at Berlin again for the third time in succession. Such determination was never had by anybody but our high command. Haven't heard the result yet, but hope it was good so it won't have to be gone after yet fourth time.

On getting back here tonight, Lt. Hicks gave me the startling news that we have a new 8th Air Force Surgeon. Col. Tracy is going to North Africa and Col. Armstrong is taking his place. That makes me very uneasy in my position because I have never made any particular effort to get along with Col. Armstrong, in fact we have more or less locked horns more than once. I have utmost respect for his scientific and analytical mind, but in my opinion, he has neither the force nor practical application to make a good Air Force Surgeon. But we shall see. I shall get along with him if possible, who knows it may work out much better than we expect.

Col. Beaman, our beloved Chief of Staff, today became Brig. Gen. Beaman. That is one promotion that is unanimously heralded by all the personnel of this headquarters. It is a rare thing indeed that an officer in his position of power can be so universally popular and at the same time so extremely capable and efficient. Gen. Doolittle came down to headquarters to pin the stars on him. Was sorry to be absent.

March 8 - The crews are resting today following strong attacks against Berlin yesterday and the day before. Monday, Mar. 6, was a great day in the history of the 8th Air Force. Berlin was hit with a great force of about 700 bombers for the first time in daylight. The target was the ball bearing works, but they were obscured by clouds and they dropped on other industrial targets in the suburbs of Berlin and according to reconnaissance photographs inflicted enormous damage. There was excellent fighter coverage and one of the greatest air battles ensued with the German fighters.

We lost 68 bombers and several fighters against over 180 of their fighters. It was much cheaper and much more successful than anyone dared expect the first great Berlin raid to be.

Yesterday, March 7, was another extremely successful raid on Berlin. The ball bearing plant was solidly hit this time as well as other areas in the suburbs. We lost only 38 bombers against 125 of their fighters. It is beginning to look like Berlin is not going to be such a difficult nut to crack after all. Our intelligence reports say that German fighter production following recent raids on their aircraft factories is only about 300 fighters per month. We have destroyed over 300 of them in two days. We are on the downgrade at long last.

March 9 - They went to Berlin in force again today with Pathfinder

Bomb Group Surgeons, First Air Division. Sitting, left to right: Major Mulmed (401st BG), Major Gaillard (381st BG), Major Bergener (305th BG), Major Longworth (Hqs, 1AD), Lt. Colonel Thurman Shuller (Hqs, 1AD), Major Walker (91st BG), Major Henry (92nd BG), Major Haggard (457th BG). Standing, left to right: Captain Hicks (Hqs, 1AD), Major Stroud (384th BG), Major Zampetti (398th BG), Major Wise (379th BG), Major Munal (306th BG), Major Black (303rd BG), Major Schumacker (482nd BG), Captain Goodman (Hqs, 1AD), Major Nowack (351st BG). Courtesy of the Thurman Shuller Family Collection.

Fighter Group Surgeons, Sixty-Seventh Fighter Wing, Thurman Shuller, seated at left. Courtesy of the Thurman Shuller Family Collection.

ships because they expected solid overcast. They do not know what they hit of course because of the cloud. However, a startling thing happened. Only one enemy fighter was seen all day long and not a claim was made. Of over 600 bombers that went over, only 5 were lost due to flak. This indicated no fear or change in policy on the part of the Germans, however, because it is believed that none of them could get off the ground because of fog.

Went to Pinetree this morning to give a talk again to a new class of Flight Surgeons. That is getting to be a nuisance. We won't be having another class for a month however. While there I dropped in on Col. Armstrong at the surgeon's office. Apparently he is going in with his sleeves rolled up. We're all wondering from the top to the bottom just where we stand with him. I brought back a replacement medical officer with me for Molesworth.

Yesterday I went to Thurleigh to pin the gold leaves on Munal. He was the happiest man I have ever seen in my life.

Chapter 4

A Doctor in the ETO

March 10, 1944–December 30, 1944

When Lt. Col. Shuller began this new volume on March 10, 1944, it was just three months until the invasion of Europe at Normandy. Losses were still heavy, weather still wreaked havoc in getting raids to target, and combat fatigue and what to do about it continued to plague the surgeons and the headquarters staff.

While the losses remained high, with some missions just as costly as those in 1942–1943, Shuller's perspective changed on two levels, from a group surgeon's viewpoint to one that held a much broader outlook at the First Air Division. He was no longer a group surgeon with personal connections to every loss. Shuller's relationships that began at Wendover and continued at Thurleigh were close and personal, with many of the officers and enlisted men in the group. As the 306th endured the combat struggles month after month over occupied Europe, the group at Thurleigh became a close-knit community where combat losses became a fact of everyday life. The high frequency of casualties and the personal nature of the losses soon grew overwhelming for Shuller and everyone else in the group.

Much had happened during the war since Shuller's first assignment to Las Vegas in 1941. The Japanese attack on Pearl Harbor triggered the United States entry into the war and ushered in the beginning of a difficult time for all Americans as the Axis powers seemed to sweep across the world unchecked. By the time that Shuller reported to the 306th Bomb Group at Wendover in April 1942, the momentum began to shift against the Axis powers. In June 1942 the Battle of Midway marked the turning point of the war in the Pacific. In the following months the war saw a reversal of Hitler's successes in North Africa and Russia, with Axis and Allied troops at a stalemate in Europe. Germany's failure to mount the cross-channel attack on England led to a series of Hitler's strategic and tactical failures that left Britain's defenses intact. Soon England would become the staging ground for massive air campaigns against occupied Europe and the ground invasions of Italy and Normandy in 1943 and 1944. By spring 1944 the buildup was well underway, as the Eighth and Ninth Air Forces were expanding the air war over Europe. As D-day loomed ahead, the Allies were poised to take advantage of the opportunities at hand.

By the time Shuller moved up to Division, most of the 306th's original crews were gone, either dead, captured, or missing. Shuller observed that "almost never do I know one of the fellows who is killed or missing in action, and it gives the whole thing an impersonal aspect." His diary is now filled with entries about missions and losses that reflect how many losses the division, not the group, had in comparison with the other air divisions in the Eighth Air Force. The one-to-two thousand four-engine bomber raids by the end of 1944 proved to be a vast change over the early days.

*

March 10, 1944 - This is no momentous day with which to open up a new volume, but I did do something this morning that I have been waiting many, many months to see. One morning in August 1942, at Westover field, Col. Overacker at the breakfast table in a sort of whisper, told about a new bomber, then already in production, which would carry 10 tons of bombs, fly thousands of miles without refueling and go comfortably to 40,000 feet in a pressurized cabin. It was to be called the B-29. After many months of expecting, I finally saw one at Bassingbourne today, there on tour. It is simply magnificent and out of this world. It contains all the known aids and improvements and really makes those B-17's, of which we have been so justly proud, seem just a bit out of date. It is not believed that they will be used in this theater.[1]

Received a poem from Cousin Fred McWhorter today which was sent Dad on his recent birthday. It is no literary gem, but it packs a wallop of sentiment. I liked it so well that I can't resist copying it here:

Birthday Tribute

Every milestone marks advancement
In our daily human strife.
Each should make us feel we're winning.
On the battlefield of life.
There's a deal of satisfaction
which rewards true parenthood,
When a couple can look backward
On the past - and find it good.
So it is with Ed and Sarah
Parents of "the Shuller boys."
For each son has added something
To the home's domestic joys.
Now, with silvering hair, the father
And the mother take their ease;
Spend long days and happy evenings
At exactly what they please.
There were years of earnest effort –
Long hard days of honest toil,
With Ed setting the example –
Tilling native Ozark soil.
Saturdays the boys quit early;
Feasted on home-made ice cream
Sunday was a day of worship -
No work done by man or team.
Sacrifices were there, surely,
Ed and Sarah did their best
To give every son the training
That would help him meet the test

of a life of worthwhile service.
The results the world can see:
Six tall sons - each one successful;
Each as fine as he can be.
Frank and Albert, Edgar, Elbert,
Herbert, and the youngest son,
Thurman, who is now in England –
Serving till the war is done.
Each son more than six feet standing,
Strong in character and mind,
Each in presence as commanding
As you'd ever, ever find.
In the fields of education,
Medicine and business, too;
In the ministry, in flying,
They have shown what they can do.
Serving in two wars for freedom,
Serving God from day to day,
Truly, there's no set of brothers
More commendable than they.
So on Mr. Shuller's birthday,
Let us join in wishing him
And his true companion, Sarah,
Years ahead, filled to the brim
With the joy and satisfaction
Earned by their fine parenthood;
As, together, they look backward
On the past - and find it good.

Thurman Shuller, representing the First Air Division, presenting a silver cup to the Great Barford division of the St. John's Ambulance Brigade for their "promotion of Anglo-American friendship." Captain W. C. Knight received the cup from Shuller as Mrs. McCorquodale looks on, Bedford, England, March 11, 1944. Courtesy of the Thurman Shuller Family Collection.

Yesterday this area was filled with visiting dignitaries. Gen. Kirk the Surg. General, Gen. Grant the Air Surgeon, Gen. Hawley the Chief Surg. ETO, Gen. [Malcolm C.] Grow Surg. USSTAF; and others were at the 49th and 303rd Station Hospitals and later went to Molesworth. They were here primarily interested in surveying the medical care to Air Force personnel with possible consideration of establishment of Air Force hospitals. I happened to be at Pinetree again talking to another class of flight surgeons at the Central Medical Establishment and missed seeing them. Longworth followed them around.

March 11 - Had an interesting experience today. I presented a silver cup at a big meeting in Bedford to the Nursing Division of the St. John's Ambulance Brigade of Great Barford for "doing most toward making our service men feel at home in their country." It was a very fine occasion. There was a very excellent revue put on by the cadets under the very able direction of Mrs. Archie Camden. The cup was bought and paid for by Capt. Jerry O'Sullivan, to be given anonymously to Great Barford. Mrs. McCorquodale jumped at the opportunity to make a big show of it and decided it should be given "by the 8th Air Force." The 8th Air Force, however, decided it should be given by a lesser unit and that the words "Anglo-American Relations" were not to be used. I had a regular word battle with Mrs. McCorquodale about it last night, and I fear I was very nasty with her and should be sorry. She is a most intelligent, capable and influential woman, but she is head-strong and overbearing, and I dislike over-bearing women and as much as told her so. However, everything went off very smoothly this afternoon and we all said a lot of nice complimentary things and everybody smiled broadly and cheered. Whatever I may have said in that little presentation, or however I may have said it, the thing that would have spoken the truth would be "Oh! You wonderful English! You have been so nice to us. We are going to give you a prize." Aw, nuts!!

March 12 - They have now officially increased the number of missions from 25 to 30 to constitute a "tour of duty" in heavy bombers in this theater. The crews are not going to take to the idea readily, but frankly I have been expecting it a long time now. Losses are still high and a man's chance of finishing a tour of duty is surprisingly low yet, but it is better than it was, and they have a better chance of finishing 30 now than 25 eight or more months ago. This scheme goes into effect on March 15.[2]

March 15 - Went riding with the General today for the first time in the seven months I have been here (that's right, I have been at this Hq. 7 months today). He is quite a fellow. His glass eye apparently sees well enough, because he's still an excellent flyer. We were just cruising around in a fortress this morning over the various stations in the division. We were scheduled to go up and observe the results of Major [Frank K.] Corbett's experiments with some new sky markers dropped from another plane, but just before takeoff one of the smoke bombs blew up in the bomb bay of the ship and burned out the inside of the whole ship until it sagged in the middle. Fortunately the gas tanks didn't catch on fire. It was rather funny because Corbett was working so hard to get the Legion of Merit. This was a $300,000 experiment. What the American taxpayer wouldn't say about that. However, it seems that expenditures are so staggering now that the bigger the figure the less it registers.

March 17 - Today, I spent the entire day trying to salvage one flying officer. The 91st Bomb Group is trying to reclassify a co-pilot, a 2nd Lt. Camosey. After talking with him for about three hours this morning, Longworth and I came to the decision that the lad was O.K. at heart and needed a little prodding. After we had made perfectly clear to him the fate of one brought before the reclassification board, he decided definitely that he wanted to continue combat flying. In the afternoon I took him down to Bassingbourne and had a talk with Col. Putnam who was persuaded that he might make the grade but would not let him continue in his group. So I'm going to try to sell the 306th Group on the idea of taking him. I'm sticking my neck out on this case again, because everybody at the 91st Group except Col. Putnam is against me on this case and insist that he is worthless. Lt. Col [Robert P.] Hare says the only thing that may save him from a similar fate over at Thurleigh is being shot down. But I've accepted the challenge, and he better make good. We have just recently had final results on the other three cases from the 91st Group whom we rescued from the wolves. Lt. Evans, the 19 mission man who was going to be court martialed has completed a tour of duty. Lt. Gerald one of the pilots who was accused of cowardice manifested by excessive early returns has also just finished his 25 missions at Thurleigh. Lt. Cavaneau did not turn out so well because he didn't finish any more missions but he was given credit for a tour of duty by counting his RAF sorties. This tickles me good. I suppose that's largely because it gives one's ego a little stimulation to be able to prove somebody in authority terribly wrong. But also, if a $25,000 pilot can be rescued from the scrap pile, that isn't to be sneezed at.

March 19 - A big raid to a southern German airdrome yesterday. Small losses, but also probably small results. They made an easy raid to Calais today. Haven't heard about results.

Had more medical practice last night than I have had in many day. A car load of our officers and men were in a wreck last night and they got me up about 2:30, after going to bed at 1:30, to treat them. Sewed up three of them before taking Lt Col. [Eugene P.] Roberts to Diddington with a fractured knee.

March 22 - Lt. Fleischer, Div. equipment officer, and I went to Third Division Headquarters today to attend a meeting of the surgeons and equipment officers of that division. Olson had the staffs of the nearby hospitals in on the meeting also. All went off very well. They are really jealous of us as far as equipment and training goes, however there is no reason why they should be because they are as well or better than us at the present time. We are flattered that they consider us worth beating. We will accept the challenge.

A big raid on Berlin in force today. It was cloudy over the target as usual today, but there were enough breaks in the clouds to see that they hit the city solidly. Losses were very low, only 4 from this division and only 13 bombers from the Air Force. The German fighters did not come up for attack. Cause unknown.

March 23 - Another nice big effort on Germany in the region of Munster. Three airdromes were the target. First of all, nobody can understand the reason for the targets because it seemed an awfully long way to go just to bomb an airdrome. Second, it was solid cloudy over the target when they got there. Third, they dropped their bombs somewhere in Germany, God only knows where. Fourth, the enemy fighters engaged in force today and our fellows found that the German forces most definitely are not knocked out. They knocked off six of our planes, 5 of which belonged to the 92nd Bomb Gp. Third division lost 17. This raid reminds us of a lot of those a year or more ago, high losses with no bombing results to show for it.

March 25 - The above mentioned raid turned out much, much better than was first suspected. They didn't even attack the primary target at all because of weather, but individual wings went around looking for anything at all to hit, and pictures reveal that some of them did extraordinary bombing on targets they have repeatedly missed before. The marshalling yards at Hamm, for instance, was completely knocked out including two hits on an essential railroad bridge over a river. Yesterday they did similar type bombing again, but weren't so successful this time. Losses were only three for this division, two of those due to collision over the target. However, they had plenty of trouble getting off. A plane crashed on takeoff at Ridgewell, killing the entire crew. Another crashed on takeoff at Chelveston and it killed not only the crew, but the plane plowed into a barracks and a civilian house killing eight other soldiers and two small children. I don't know whether flying is here to stay. Capt. Schapp and I had gotten up at 2 a.m. and started to Podington, but got lost on the way and ended up at Chelveston shortly after the crash.

March 26 - I went over to Nuthampstead this afternoon to see Kaylor. It was just too pretty a Sunday afternoon to stay in. We are making arrangements to take over that station for bombers in about three weeks.

The bombers returned to the Pas de Calais area again this afternoon. Longworth went along with the 306th. He says it was a screwed up detail again. He saw one ship go down out of his group and he himself had a piece of flak cut his pants leg but didn't scratch him.

March 30 - Have been gone for three days. Yesterday I was at a big surgeon's conference at 8th Air Force with Col. Armstrong. All the Command and Division surgeons were there. It was quite a long session, it being the first. We are to have them once every two weeks. Nothing particularly new or startling was brought out. Major Olson, the third division surgeon is going home to go to Wright Field in the experimental laboratory.

Spent Tuesday and today in London. Spent a quiet time as usual and saw a few shows, none of them particularly good.

March 31 - Pay day. Didn't get my flying time in last month so I collected two month's pay. It seems like quite an event when a country boy like me gets a check for over $700. And nothing to spend it for. Less than three years ago at New Orleans, I would have been able to enjoy some of that. It seems the opportunity to spend and the ability to spend just don't go together.

April 2, 1944 – This has been one long dreary day. Rained all day for the first time in ages. I had almost nothing to do this afternoon. Longworth is on pass. This morning I went over to Kimbolton to discuss for an hour or so their problem of flyers quitting. They have had three or four fellows permanently grounded and they are creating quite a problem. Ordinarily speaking, we have absolutely no use for them if they cannot be used for flying.

April 5 - Went to the 7th Gen. Hosp. for consultation today. They had several men whom they wanted a little advice on in the matter of disposition of flying personnel. Lt. Col. Roberts, our personnel officer who is up there following transfer from the 49th Sta. Hosp. is doing only fair. The General is most anxious that he come back at the earliest possible moment for duty and his leg does seem to be doing satisfactorily, but his general condition is not what I would like to see. He is running a little fever, has no appetite and is losing weight. I hope he is getting proper care. Lt. Col. Davis and Lt. Col. [Guy V.] Whetstone went with me.

April 6 - Had a meeting of Group surgeons today and invited the commanding officers, chief of medical and surgical services and the registrars of the 49th and 303rd station hospitals present. All were called on to make any criticism and comment on improvement of relations between the stations and the hospitals. I was gratified to discover that there were no serious complaints on either side. About an hour was taken up with purely business matters pertaining to the Air Force doctors. It was one of our best and most profitable meetings. We had no frostbite cases at all last week and have had only 10 during the last three weeks. I wrote a commendation for the unit Equipment officers and Flight Surgeons for their recent improvement in anoxia and frostbite, and it was sent out to all stations over Gen. Williams' signature. A little pat on the back for a good job gets more work done than criticism a lot of times.

April 7 - Col. Armstrong and Lt. Col. Cobler were here from Pinetree today. It was Col. Armstrong's first visit since he became 8th Air Force Surgeon. His greatest concern at the moment is in assigning a medical inspector to this headquarters. He doesn't know exactly what he expects to inspect for, but he believes we need more inspections. Maybe he is right. One thing that is going to be done in the near future apparently is the institution of training with the use of tent hospitals in case we should move to another theater which, of course, is likely. In that case we will need plenty of inspecting in connection with the training program.

T/Sgt. Gordon, formerly from the 305th Gp., gave a most interesting lecture this afternoon on his experiences in German territory and in German prison camps. He is the first American to return from a German prison camp and he really has a yarn to tell. He escaped from the Germans three times before he made a successful get away. The second time he disguised himself as a Hitler youth and rode a stolen bicycle all the way to the Swiss frontier before he was captured hiding in a hay stack. The third time he escaped as a French laborer. He is small, only 120 lb. and full of mischief and no doubt gave the Germans plenty of trouble. They are perhaps relieved to be rid of him. He spent about a year getting out.

April 9 - Today is Easter Sunday. As far as the war goes it is just another day because they sent out a maximum effort today to bomb Marienburg, Gdynia, Posen and all the other aircraft factories on the German-Polish border. That is their longest and hardest raid. Part of our Division failed to assemble properly because of weather, but the five groups that went across did excellent bombing.

The day was different today in that I went with Lt. Col. Davis to the Easter service in the little village church here in Brampton. It was the first time I had ever attended a service of the Church of England. It seemed to me very cold and revealed a lack of enthusiasm. I was unimpressed. I thought of the thousands of beautiful Easter services back home.

April 13 - Arrived back last night from another trip to Pinetree. There was nothing at all remarkable about the meeting this week. Tuesday night was spent in London, but I arrived there too late even to go to a movie. Was billeted in the Cumberland Hotel, and I did immensely enjoy the luxury of lying in bed just as long as I liked yesterday morning.

The crews have been working every day now for five days. After that extremely long effort Sunday, they had an easy one Monday on airdromes in Belgium. Tuesday they went for airdromes and aircraft factories in the Berlin vicinity. Yesterday they started for Schweinfurt but were recalled because of weather. Today they hit Schweinfurt, apparently pretty well, however one combat wing failed to get off because of weather. Losses have been pretty high but in return they have been giving the German fighters plenty of hell. The 92nd Group caught it Tuesday with 8 lost. Today the 384th lost 9. The Germans can still destroy any group they choose to destroy, although they cannot ever turn back any force of bombers. Losses and graduations are now exceeding our replacements. I fear they may extend the tour of duty even more, but Gen. Williams says there is little likelihood of that soon.

April 15 - This afternoon we held a big meeting instigated by me which included all Group executive officers, all Group surgeons and S-1 officers. Capt. Bond was here from Pinetree to explain the interpretation of 8th A.F. memo 35-6 which has to do with disposition of personnel who are no longer fit for combat flying. I was surprised to note that there were few questions asked. Lt. Cobb explained the administrative red tape and Lt. Col. Davis, the Judge Advocate, explained the limitations of court martial for fellows who refuse to fly. A case in 3rd Division which was convicted six months ago for refusing to fly on a combat mission has just had the decision reversed. The one case we have had in this division received the same sentence after 4 months review that he would have gotten in 8 days with reclassification. For that reason I have long advocated reclassification instead of court martial, and I hope this meeting left that impression with all concerned. Second division has just had a man sentenced to death for refusing to fly, which decision also will be reversed, it is presumed, and will make everybody connected with it look silly. The purpose of the meeting was to work up a little better understanding between administrative people and the medical officers. I hope it accomplished its purpose.

CHAPTER 4

April 17 - Alas! Alas! The W.A.C.s have at last invaded my domain. One Strauss was assigned to my section today. W.A.C.s have been at this Hq. for some weeks now, but none had been assigned to my office. We needed another clerk typist so she is it. Immediately the problem arose as to the proper way of addressing her. It was agreed that we should simply address her "Strauss," which is her last name. That seems a little awkward, however, because she is married, has a son in the service and is at least 50 years old. She is a Private. She will be a valuable addition to my staff. Her age and lack of beauty will have a sobering rather than disturbing influence on the lustful wandering eyes of young male members of the office.

April 19 - There have been a couple of nice days for bombing. Yesterday a big force went to Berlin and suburbs. About half the groups could see their targets and bombed aircraft and other factories quite successfully. The rest of them bombed the city itself through the clouds. Our division lost only 3 planes, but 3rd Division lost 14. It was still classified as a successful mission.

Today they all went to numerous targets at Kassel and other towns just beyond the Ruhr. They were after aircraft component parts and repair depots. Only five planes were lost for the whole force and the bombing, generally speaking, was very successful. Opposition has been only moderate the last two days. The Germans still have a mighty Air Force in spite of publicity to the contrary, but they are certainly losing their ability to replenish it.

Everybody has been expecting the Second Front hourly the last few days, but there is still no sign of it. Leaves, passes and furloughs have now been cancelled for about two weeks, except for combat crews.

April 20 - Had a nice letter from Sullenberger today. He is home on a 30 day leave after being in South America and Puerto Rico for 17 mo. I really envied him when he began telling about the good things they still had back there and about going to the races at Hot Springs. He sent me a clipping from the Ark. Gazette about the presentation of the cup at Bedford. It labeled me a full Colonel, misspelled my name and said I spent one or two evenings every week with those kids. Boy Oh Boy! If there wouldn't be a laugh over the true story.

April 22 - Gen. [Bartlett] Beaman has been in an uproar today about the way one of our crashes was handled. A Kimbolton plane crashed on the coast and had a couple of unexploded bombs aboard. They recovered all but three bodies, but couldn't get the others until the wreckage was moved. The Second Air Depot Area was then made responsible for moving the wreckage and the English bomb disposal people were also involved in removing the bombs. There was too much split responsibility and as a result those bodies stayed in the wreckage for ten days before they were reclaimed. Gen. Beaman is rightfully upset about the whole thing. As a matter of fact those bodies were just as dead 10 days ago as they are now, but it wouldn't look very good in print. Somebody is going to get scorched over it.

April 23 - Last night I was invited to a cocktail party at the Hon. Mr. and Mrs. Michael Bowes-Lyons' home. Was taken by Mr. and Mrs. McCorquodale and Mrs. Camden. It wasn't nearly as stuffy an affair as I expected—was really enjoyable. Both Mr. and Mrs. Bowes-Lyons are just ordinary sort of people and there were several other real interesting people there. I was highly flattered to be a guest in the home of the queen's brother. I was the only American there out of about fifty, other than three Red Cross people. We left after about 1 ½ hours fortunately. I had a date for the regular monthly dance back here at the club. It was a rather full but enjoyable evening.

Yesterday our crews really did a magnificent job of destruction on the Hamm marshalling yards. Losses were relatively low too. They were given a rest today after an early morning briefing which was scrubbed because of weather.

April 25 - Our division took an awfully bad beating yesterday. We lost 27 planes, one crew was rescued out of the channel. My old 306th Group caught it again for the loss of 10 planes. That now makes three times my old group has lost 10 planes. That is a bitter pill. It was in April last year, I believe, that we lost those first 10 over Bremen. The other divisions didn't lose so heavily yesterday. The targets were repair depots for aircraft in the vicinity of Munich, and I believe the strike photos were the best we have ever had. Destruction will really be severe. The fellows don't grieve over the losses so much when so much can be accomplished. In spite of all the current ill-conceived publicity the Luftwaffe is most definitely not whipped as any combat man will testify.

Today they went out again to airdromes in France near the German border. Losses were light today. Don't know the results yet.

T/Sgt Starr, my chief enlisted man pulled a rare crack today. He's always good for at least one. Longworth, Hicks and I got sore at Major Packard, the station commander, for some reason and were discussing his unfavorable points with considerable gusto in the presence of Starr. Long-worth sarcastically remarked that we shouldn't be criticizing a superior officer in the presence of an enlisted man (which is proper military procedure). Whereupon Starr remarks, "Oh, Excuse me. I'll go out so you can call him a son-of-a-bitch, then I'll come back in."

We let our W.A.C. go today. We got a new enlisted man from the pool, Corp. Stone. Stone is a particularly good lad, apparently, and we wanted to keep him but couldn't have both. Strauss was an awfully swell person and was working in beautifully with the boys. She almost cried when we told her we were going to let her go, she really wanted to stay. Hicks was anxious to keep the new boy. I hope we did the right thing by letting Strauss go.

Our final new group came in Saturday. It is the 398th group and is situated at Nuthampstead. Major Zampretti is the Group Surgeon. He was in my class at Randolph Field. It looks like they are really a swell outfit. Capt. Miner was sent over there from Bassingbourne to help them get set up and they are getting started off with a bang. It is rumored that no new Air Force units of any kind will arrive in this theater after the last of this month.

April 28 - Day before yesterday I made the regular run to Pinetree via London in one day only. That is a hard day's run. The best thing we accomplished at the meeting was the announcement that the meeting would be held monthly instead of every two weeks.

Yesterday I made the run up to the 7th Gen. Hospital. Lt. Col. Slagle and Lt. Col. Johnson went with me. Saw about 8 patients in consultation, visited awhile with Lt. Col. Roberts and then went on in to Lincoln to see the cathedral there, which is one of the largest, oldest, most beautiful and best preserved cathedrals in England. A few man hours were spent in building that thing.

Today was spent mostly in the office, but ran up to Glatton for a little session with the doctors up there. They are having a little administrative shake-up there with Major Councilman, the executive officer, leaving. It is hoped that it will improve the efficiency of the group a little, but personally I think the top man is the one who needs some changing. Lt. Col. Luper is a little too West Point and G.I. to get out of the fellows in combat what is desired. At least something is wrong with him.

They are working the crews unmercifully now. Day before yesterday it was Brunswick through the clouds, yesterday for the first time in our history there were two missions in one day. The first in the morning to the Pas de Calais area with rather poor bombing, as usual. The afternoon mission went to airdromes at Nancy, France again with good results. Today a small force went to airdromes beyond Paris. It hardly seems that the choice of targets justifies the sustained efforts because of exhaustion of personnel and planes, but fortunately the losses have been low the last three or four days. From what we can see the sustained effort has no bearing on any immediate second front. The restriction on passes which has been in progress for three weeks has now been lifted.

April 30 - Yesterday was quite an affair. I took off at 9:00 a.m. for London to attend the wedding of Major Sam Haigler, the 3rd Division Surgeon, to Margaret Malloy, an American nurse. The wedding ceremony was Catholic and very boring. Sam himself thought he got cheated and got the $1.00 ceremony instead of the $5.00 one. But the reception afterwards at the Senior Officers' Club on Park Lane was much, much more interesting. Then after that Major John Talbot and I met a couple of his girl friends for dinner afterwards. But I was a good boy and was sleeping on a hard bed in the Red Cross Club by 11 o'clock. Got up early and arrived back here by 9:00 this a.m. It was one of the best "days off" I have had in several weeks.

Yesterday the bombers went to Berlin for a loss of more than 60, our division losing only 10 and not many from any one group fortunately. The bombing was not very good in spite of glowing reports in the papers. Today was a small effort on an airdrome deep in France. This makes nine raids in eight consecutive days and there is no sign of let-up yet. This weather is incredible.

May 1, 1944 - At 5:03 this afternoon I became a combat man. That was the moment we crossed the Belgian coast on the way to Reims, France. For several months I had fully intended to go out with the boys but the occasion never seemed to be right. Today they planned an attack on the French coast in the morning, but it was unsuccessful because of clouds. They then hurriedly planned one for the afternoon. At 1:15 I learned that I could get away. At 2:15 I arrived at Thurleigh and at 3:15 we were in the air. Of course I wouldn't have thought of doing my first mission with any group other than my old beloved 306th. It was only a small effort. Only one squadron, the 368th, participated. A similar squadron from each of two other groups made up a composite group. There were only a little over 100 planes from this division out and a similar number from the other two divisions.

My pilot was Lt. Paulsen, a fellow I did not know, but he turned out to be an excellent pilot. My friend Lt. Col. (Willie) Williams took care of that. He is a veteran of 25 missions and he gave me the smoothest formation ride that I have ever had. All his crew were old timers and were a swell bunch.

The plane really groaned with its heavy load on take-off from the shortest runway. It had 6-1000 lb. bombs and 2100 gal. of gasoline. We climbed singly up through the overcast and broke out at 4500 feet. The formation assembled at 10,000 feet near our home base. The climb after assembly was gradual and we crossed the enemy coast at 17,000 feet and ascended slowly to the target and bombed at 20,000 feet. We were on oxygen 3 1/2 hours, which is a relatively short time by present standards.

My reactions fooled me throughout. At no time did I suffer any anxiety or nervousness. That is partly due to the fact that I went on so short notice that there was no anxious period of waiting. The only thought I noticed giving to the possibility that I might not come back was that I several times went over in my mind that in case I had to jump I was determined to make a delayed jump. I was just a little anxious as we crossed the coast into Belgium because of the sudden realization that for the first time I was in the land of the enemy. I at least expected some flak, but when none appeared and then a few miles in our escort fighter planes pulled up alongside, it gave complete confidence that everything was running smoothly. We flew east almost to the Belgian-German border to the south of Brussels and then turned southeast to Reims, which is southeast of Paris. The target was the huge marshalling yards there. I was rather disappointed that there was no excitement, not any enemy fighter or a burst of flak anywhere in the sky. After turning at the I.P. and heading for the target with the bomb bay doors open I was momentarily expecting something to happen, but it was only just about 15 sec. before "bombs away" that the first burst appeared. Flak came bursting up immediately below us and in front of us, mostly in bunches of four to six. The bombs were gone and we were turned off the target before anytime, and then I looked back and saw that they were shooting at the group behind us and heaved a sigh, "Well, that's over." After turning off the target it was clearly visible and smoke was boiling up heavily from all over the target. It had really been hit solidly (confirmed also by pictures). After getting out of sight I recalled that I had intended to have a look at the beautiful and famous Reims cathedral, but I had forgotten to look for it. My subconscious mind must have said, "Thurman, you have seen a lot of famous old cathedrals but you haven't seen any flak—you better watch the flak." After passing the target the fellows began remarking that the flak was very accurate and close, though not particularly heavy. I had actually expected that it would be closer, although I did see one burst right under a plane in the next squadron with no apparent damage from a distance. However, on landing we did find some flak holes in the wings. Perhaps I was too ignorant to be scared. The return trip was uneventful. Friendly fighters were all around. Two things added to my discomfort. First, I wore too many clothes and was actually hot most of the way. I was dressed for about −35 C. and the temperature was only about −20 C. However, I was determined not to get frostbite considering all the preaching I have been doing about frostbite due to carelessness. Secondly, when I started to put on my heavy gloves up in the air I discovered that both were for the left hand. I still can't figure it out because I swear I've had them on before.

We started letting down right at the coast after having been in enemy territory about 2 1/2 hours. We landed something after 8:00 p.m. It was an experience I wouldn't take anything for, but as for learning something that would make me a better flight surgeon, I didn't. In fact, it may have given me an entirely distorted viewpoint because I had the privilege of choosing my mission, I didn't have to "sweat it out" and it was considered an easy one. I am still in no better position to judge first-hand the experiences of a man suffering from psychic trauma as a result of combat hazards. Well, anyway I got my flying time in on the first day of the month, which is considerable improvement over what I usually do.

I would now like to see bombs hit a German target.

May 4 - Has been remarkably quiet the last three days. For two days no planes took off at all for combat for the first time in ten days. Today they started for Berlin but returned because of weather. One combat wing bombed an airdrome in Holland on the return, however.

Longworth will be away all this week for school at Pinetree, but I haven't let it keep me in much. Yesterday I flew with Capt. Thomas down to a field south of Oxford. It was a lovely trip over a very pretty section of springtime England, but the weather was rough as a cob. Today I made professional calls on Nuthampstead and Bassingbourne.

May 6 - This is another milestone passed, have reached the ripe old age of 30. Thirty years old, unmarried, and no immediate prospects. That means I'm not making much of a contribution toward upholding the race. Of course, there isn't much I can do about it now, but time's a wastin'. Am spending a very quiet evening at home tonight—wrote a couple of letters. Received a perfectly wonderful box of homemade candy from Mother yesterday. Of all people, Joan Carter remembered my birthday with a small box of candy the other day.

May 8 - They have now gone back to work in earnest after a few days rest because of weather. Yesterday they bombed Berlin on Pathfinder through 10/10 clouds and again today. The new 398th Group made its maiden voyage to Berlin yesterday without loss and also today without loss. Our division lost only 6 yesterday and 7 today. But 5 of those today were from the 306th, 3 due to a collision over the target. That is a heart sickening thing. Apparently the bombing was good in spite of the fact that it was blind. They sent out one combat wing this afternoon late just across the channel and they lost 3 ships to flak, I understand.

May 12 - The raids they are running now are proceeding with monotonous regularity. The weather is superb and each day about 700 to 900 bombers go out to various marshalling yards, airdromes and factories all over enemy territory. Results are pretty good, although they have had no targets assigned lately of any tremendous importance, although they all add up. Losses have been minimal. The only really important losses lately were at Chelveston a couple of days ago. The 366th Sq. there had gone almost 60 mission without loss of life or plane. Then on one mission that one squadron lost 3 planes including both their squadron commander and their squadron operations officer. That was really hitting where it hurt[s].

I'm certainly having a lot of changes in medical personnel all at once. [John F.] McGregor of the 384th is going to a hospital as a flight surgeon consultant, which will allow [Henry H.] Stroud to move up to group surgeon. [Alfred W.] Erb at Thurleigh and Lihn at Deenethorpe are going back to Randolph Field. Keany at Chelveston is going back to the States for emergency reasons. Alexander at Nuthampstead is being transferred to Pinetree. It's the biggest shift we have had in a long time, but it serves to keep things from getting too monotonous for the boys.

The brilliance of some of the officer material of this great Army is well illustrated by one at Thurleigh the other day. There was a crash just off the field and the flying control officer called the dispensary and requested Major Munal to send an ambulance to the crash immediately, which he did. After things had settled down, Munal inquired of the control officer why he didn't send the ambulance which was sitting right at the control

Shuller rowing on the Avon with "Porky," his radio operator. The Shakespeare Memorial Theater is in the background. Courtesy of the Thurman Shuller Family Collection.

Pausing at the Swan's Nest Hotel on the banks of the Avon before attending a play at the Shakespeare Memorial Theater. Left to right: Milgrom, Welter, Ludtke, Shuller, Johnson. Courtesy of the Thurman Shuller Family Collection.

tower, whereupon the control officer replied, "The regulation says that an ambulance is to stay by the tower at all times." Small wonder we are stalled in Italy.

May 14 - Today I have just completed a 24 hours that I have been planning for over a year. Took a day off yesterday and flew over to Stratford-on-Avon for a little breath of Shakespeare atmosphere. The party was composed of Capt. Johnson, pilot; Capt. [John B.] Mazanek, navigator; Lt. Ludtke; Squadron Leader Bumpers and myself, as well as two enlisted crew members. It is only about a 20-minute flight by fortress, but it took a full hour to land because of a thick ground haze. We made eleven passes before we made a successful approach. The weather eased our conscience when we decided we wanted to spend the night there. Stratford is a picturesque little town which straddles the Avon River, but there is not an awful lot life around. The sleepiness adds to the atmosphere, I suppose. We intended to see an afternoon play, but they were completely sold out and we had to see the evening performance. There is a large modern theater built overhanging the river devoted exclusively to Shakespeare productions during the summer season. We passed most of the afternoon by "punting" on the river (to pole a small boat). Traffic was particularly heavy and those punts are particularly hard to keep straight so we merrily bumped into everybody and everything. The locale is enjoying a great surge of prosperity at the moment because of the multitude of service men who go there. His Majesty's swans, which are numerous on the river, looked upon us with utter disgust and contempt. In the latter part of the afternoon we paid three pence admission to see Shakespeare's house and the room where he was born. I hope we held our mouths open with the proper amount of awe and respect. It was really quite interesting and remarkably well preserved for a house over 400 years old. About the next hour was then spent in trying to find beds for the night. The Red Cross was full.

The play we saw was "The Merchant of Venice." I shall have to admit that it is the first time I have ever seen a Shakespeare play on the stage and was prepared to be positively bored with it all. My real purpose in going was just to be able to gloat over the fact that I had nonchalantly done what any English teacher back in the States would have given half a year's salary to do. But I must admit that I found the play intensely fascinating and interesting. It was remarkably well done. The characterization of Shylock was particularly well acted and I shall remember it a long time. Guess I'll have to admit that Shakespeare was pretty clever. It was almost noon today when we got back to base and I shall remember that trip a long time as a very pleasant 24-hour pass.

The combat crews were given rest today after a long trip to eastern Germany yesterday and to Leipzig the day before. Bombing was only moderately good but losses for this division were not heavy. They are bombing with such regularity now that it is almost worthy of comment when they do not go out.

May 16 - I spent an exhaustive day accompanying a couple of high ranking British medical officers all over the airdrome at Kimbolton. They were guests of Lt. Col. Morton down at the 49th Station Hospital and he asked me to arrange for them to see an airdrome. They were Major General Overby, surgeon for the North African Campaign, and Brigadier Cairns, neurosurgeon for the British Army. They were remarkable gentlemen and were very friendly and wanted no fuss or flurry. The executive officer, Lt. Col. Short, and Major Wise devoted about six hours of their time to showing them anything and everything. They saw the operations block and the intelligence room. They were all over a fortress and all through it. General Overby even got in a ball turret in the gunnery room in spite of the fact that he is a huge man, they saw the sick quarters and the method of evacuation of casualties, they went to a presentation of awards and to a critique, they had lunch and in the middle of the afternoon had coffee with Col. Preston, the C.O., and saw a bunch of photographs before and after bombing, and they asked a million questions about everything. It was quite a day!

May 17 - There have been no operational missions for two days, but nobody is complaining.

This afternoon I went to Thurleigh to see the Air Force movie "The Memphis Belle." It was not a great movie, but it was far better than most similar shows. It didn't glamorize anybody or anything but just showed some plain facts. It didn't even glamorize the fortress "Memphis Belle" or her pilot, Capt. [Robert K.] Morgan (the damn reprobate). It simply presented the Belle as just a typical ship in a typical squadron of a typical group in the Air Force, and it was about her 25th mission to Wilhelmshaven. It had a bunch of real combat action shots and they mixed up some of the scenes among several of the stations. It is a picture for the folks back home to see. (Memphis Belle was also in the 1st Bomb Division.)[3]

May 21 - They did a little run into Villa Coublay today with one combat wing without loss, they tried the Pas de Calais area yesterday with little success but without loss, and they bombed Berlin through the clouds the day before with the biggest force ever from this division - 400 planes. They couldn't see the bombs hit, they just dumped them out over the city. This division lost only 8 planes. Today for the first time they flew a new 12-ship formation instead of the classical 18-ship group. It is designed to concentrate the bombs a little better, I believe, but I don't know how it works exactly yet. The old 54-plane combat wing formation composed of 3–18 plane groups has been flown consistently without the slightest change for 15 months now. It must have been good or else it wouldn't have lasted so long. Everyone expected the Germans to find a way to break it up long before this.

Everybody is getting awfully impatient for the invasion to start. I personally don't believe the invasion will make much difference on the activity of the heavy bombers, but some think so. The 9th Air Force fighters and light bombers are really doing a bang-up job strafing over in France now. Every night almost the transports and gliders fly overhead in droves in their exercises.

General Williams got all excited about the diarrhea we had at a couple of the stations the last week and wanted the messes at four of the stations given a special thorough check. There were a few diarrheas all right, but not more than will occasionally occur at any large mess. However, it hit in a vulnerable spot in that it caused a total of about 10 planes to return home early because of sick men. That was not a good thing! The messes did need a little brushing up, and perhaps they will do better.

May 23 - Today I went up to 7th Gen. Hospital to see Lt. Col. Roberts. It has been two months since his injury and his knee is coming along O.K., but it will be weeks yet before he walks on it. He is needed back here awfully bad in the A-1 section. It is rumored that Lt. Col. Fleming will be leaving the section before long. It was a wonderful day for the trip. Lt. Col. Packard and Lt. Col. Johnson went along. Major McGregor who has taken over his new duties there as Air Force advisor is tickled with his new job.

The raid on Kiel yesterday stank! As usual on that target they killed all the fish in the Kiel harbor and canal. The weather was not good. Losses from this division were only three planes.

T/Sgt. Tropeano and Sgt. Hinkley, a couple of my old enlisted men at Thurleigh are in trouble. When Capt. Erb went home he took with him a couple of letters from each of those men which he had to surrender at the port. They contained a lot of censorable matter as well as admissions in the letters that they would get in trouble if caught. They are now up for court martial for violating censorship regulations. Tropeano has been riding for a fall for a long time, but Hinkley is really a top notch boy. I hope they don't catch too severe a penalty, but it may be serious.

Yesterday I went up to the casualty section and looked over some of the "Missing in Action" cards and I came away depressed. Even though we should be hardened to it now, it's still rather shocking to read the notice "changed from M.I.A. to K.I.A. by letter order, 8th A.F. dated __." My boy, Lt. McCallum, co-pilot for Lt. Johnson when he got shot up on his 25th mission, and Snuffy Smith won the Congressional Medal of Honor, also co-pilot for Lt. Smith who ditched in the channel and the whole crew rescued after 30 hours; whom I nursed through two recurrences of V.D. and wouldn't respond to anything - is now officially "killed in action."

And while I am recalling the good old days, we have received word that Major [Mack] McKay, one of our finest pilots we've ever had and whom I have praised many times (see Mar. 10, 1943), has been in a mental hospital back in the States for two months. But the heart sickening news is that Capt. Pervis Youree has been given a dishonorable discharge for flying formation with a commercial airliner back in the States. Youree was the 7th officer in the old 306th to finish his 25 missions and that was back in the days when it was a real distinction to live to tell about it. On several occasions he was very badly shot up and on his 21st missions almost didn't make it after which he cursed all flying and swore he'd never fly again, yet within a week was at it again and finished up in spite of a real case of operational exhaustion. He died a thousand deaths for his country just like a lot of other fellows. But now a court of officers back in the States call him a disgrace and a dishonor to the service because he daringly flies close to an airliner. As a man, I disliked Youree more than any pilot we had because even though he was an excellent flyer, he had little judgement, he was absolutely immature and irresponsible and delighted and bragged about his excessive and tragic exploits with women (which was not exaggerated). But he did an excellent job in the capacity for which he was trained—fighting the enemy. And it would seem to us over here that it would take more than flying near a civilian plane to make him a dishonor to his country. He is not a good officer and perhaps they were justified in letting him out of the service to keep from wrecking it; but they could have done it without disgrace. The Gov. of Oklahoma has appealed to the President to set aside the sentence and I hope he does.[4] This seems to me

Pervis Youree (leaning against the box) with some of his air crew. Courtesy of the East Anglia Air War Collection.

just another example of increasing tension between the chair borne Army back home and the soldiers returning from overseas. However, I realize a lot of our returning heroes are making too many demands on a suffering public back home in a number of instances, but it works both ways. I'm pretty blue about the kind of society we'll be having back home after the war with all the millions of men who have seen action in battle all trying to make a decent adjustment. We have spent three years now and billions of dollars training our lads to be killers and to live by their daring. Is it reasonable that we can expect them to return home and become good little boys again overnight—or ever?

May 25 - Sat on a direct appointment board today and interviewed 10 Flight Officers for appointment as second lieutenants. We passed all of them except F/O Jackson whom I saw once before. He's a 20-year-old kid from the 306th Group who was jittery and wanted to quit. I more or less talked him out of it about a couple months ago, or at least tried to, but his C.O. failed to put him right to work again and after he brooded some more, he was worse than ever when he came up this time. He was very slow thinking and had difficulty assimilating ideas. He couldn't even think of his Group Commander's name even though he has been there at least four months. I believe the lad is on the verge of insanity now. He's a pitiful case. He's been flying a plane since he was 16 and loved it. Now he dreads the sight of a plane. I believe there is something behind it besides fear.

Lt. Camosy, the young officer whom I salvaged from the 91st Group and sent to Thurleigh to try it some more as a co-pilot after having been discarded by the 91st as no good, is now missing in action. He was on one of the three Thurleigh ships which collided over the target a few days ago. I believe he would have made it. (Correction—Camosy was co-pilot on a plane which dropped out of formation and disappeared with all crew over Kiel. This was before the 3-plane collision.)

May 26 - Last night I went over to Polebrook to a dance. It was the first time I had been at one of their socials. There I ran into Dale Alford, one of my classmates at Med School. He's doing E.N.T. for the 160th Station Hospital.

Capt. Thomas flew Hicks and me down to Stanbridge Earls in the A-20 today. It was a grand day for a little ride and "Tommie" really gave the old "flak house" a royal buzzing. Capt. Morse was his same old jovial self and Pam Hanna as sweet as ever. Pam and Roy Furman have just announced their engagement to be married next month. Roy is a lucky dog. The house was full and the fellows were thoroughly enjoying it as usual. It is literally worth its weight in gold. There is no spot in England which seems so completely divorced from the war where the fellows can so thoroughly relax for a week.

The planes went out in force to the Leipzig area yesterday. They did a good job of bombing but our division lost 12 of which six were from Polebrook. Last night I had to do a little psychological therapy on Capt. Hartnett, our new flight surgeon over there. He was much grieved over four crews lost from his squadron. Today they went out in force to near Ludwigshafen and hit a synthetic oil plant solidly enough as well as some airdromes and marshalling yards. Our division lost 17 this time out of less than 300 of which 12 were from only one combat wing, the 94th. Polebrook lost 5 again which will really make them realize at last there's a war on. The 401st Group lost 7. They lost one complete squadron except for the leader. Tactically, the results justified the losses, they say.

May 30 - This morning I took off a couple hours and attended the

Memorial Day service at Cambridge American Military Cemetery. It was only a short service with a couple prayers, the 23rd Psalm, the laying of wreaths by Lt. Gen. Lee for the Ground forces, Lt. Gen. Spaatz for the Air Forces, and by various high ranking British Generals. Then the benediction by the Archbishop of Ely, and taps. There were four platoons of troops in review, an RAF platoon, one from the American Air Force, a Negro quartermaster outfit, and a British infantry outfit. It was very simple but impressive, and with plenty of rank.

I recall that last Memorial Day I went into a long list of reminiscences about friends brought back to memory by this day. However, there is little of that this year—only one year has made all that difference. It's the difference in my job. Now, almost never do I know one of the fellows who is killed or missing in action and it gives the whole thing an impersonal aspect. A year ago I was just a little contemptuous of those who were only in a position to say or cared only to say, "One of our aircraft is missing," when to us it meant, "Capt. John Doe was shot down today." But now I am placed in just that spot. I glanced down all those long rows of neatly placed white crosses and few names did I recognize, although nearly all of them had died in heavy bombers. But I'm glad it's that way. One can't spend very much time thinking about the dead when there is so much to be done for the living.

The air battles are still progressing at a fever pitch and with very strong forces. At long last they finally got that big F.W. fighter plant at Posen, Poland yesterday and completely destroyed it, along with numerous other aircraft plants and airdromes. Today they went into the middle of Germany for more airdromes and assembly plants. The weather has been superb for several days, and one combat wing usually gets a beating from the German fighters, but they are paying an awfully heavy penalty for it and are still not turning our bombers back. We're losing quite a number of planes, but the losses are really paying dividends now. The combat men maintain a much better state of morale when they see real results, even when losses are relatively high.

June 1, 1944 - Have just returned from London tonight after going to the regular monthly meeting at Pinetree. The meeting was its usual speed, but there were several things of interest discussed. It afforded me the usual opportunity to stop over for the night and spend a day in London.

This morning I diverted from the usual a little and went out to Kew Gardens, which is one of the greatest botanical gardens in the world. It was enormous. Although the numerous large green houses did not open until after noon, there was an awful lot to see on the outside. There are over 300 acres and it contains just about every tree and plant that can be grown. It was too early for most of the flowering plants. But the rhododendron was in full bloom and was everywhere in all colors of the rainbow. I have never seen anything like it. They also had a marvelous collection of iris in full bloom, including some of the most peculiar shades. I should like to go back there in about six weeks when there are more blossoms and stay longer—and take lunch—and feminine company.

This afternoon I went to the theater and saw "While the Sun Shines," which is one of the funniest current plays of the season, involving a young and handsome as well as rich British Earl, a very typical American bombardier in London on leave, a very suave French lieutenant and of course some girls. An Englishman wrote the play but he makes some wonderful cracks at the British as well as brings out a lot of things about American officers that amuse the British.[5]

Tonight on the train I heard a very casual remark that explains very well why England is so far behind the times in many respects. The discussion got around to roads, and the old duffer who was sitting across from me remarked, "The road between Cambridge and Newmarket is very straight and dull and uninteresting." As a matter of fact, when I drove over that road several weeks ago, I thought it the only good road I had seen in England. It is straight and wide and is well kept with trees planted on the side. I didn't tell him what I thought, it wouldn't have been good for Anglo-American relations. They are content to leave this small island one huge antique shop. That's O.K. by me. I must confess it looks very pretty, but it further emphasizes the fact that our countries are just as foreign as any among the brotherhood of nations.

June 2 - Back at the office today there was almost a foot of papers stacked up in the basket. It is amazing how much junk can pile up in an office in only two days. I wonder how they fought the Civil War without typewriters. And it is said there is a paper shortage!

Nine new dentists reported in today which will bring our strength up to 3 per station. One of them is a Captain Owens who has just come from the Air Field at Las Vegas, Nevada. He went there after I left, but it was just like seeing a long lost friend to talk with someone who knew some of my old friends and familiar places back there.

June 5 - A reasonable portion of my day at the office was spent in receiving and talking to one of my medical officers, Capt. Genglebach and a dental officer, Capt. Bresden. Both were similar cases and required the same treatment. Both have been here 18 months or more, both want to go home, both are having domestic troubles back home and both are developing psychoneurotic symptoms from it. It was my duty as on numerous other occasions to gently, but firmly show them that they had no honorable way of getting out of their situation and that to continue on the best way they could was the least distasteful course in the long run. I've had an awful lot of experience at that sort of thing in recent months, but I am never satisfied that I have said the right thing in the right manner. But just to get it off their chests to someone who will listen is sometimes all that is necessary. Our ground personnel are beginning to really show signs of theater fatigue in a lot of instances. The incidence is not alarming, but it will be in another six months.

For the last four or five days our bombers have gone out regularly twice a day to bomb coastal positions along the French coast. Most of that bombing is done through cloud. It must be done for a purpose.

June 6, 1944 - This is it! This is the day we came to England for 21 months ago. Paratroops landed last night and our ground forces landed on a wide stretch of the coast of Normandy this morning following a heavy bomber bombardment. This will be a real day in history, however it was just another day at this headquarters, except for intense interest in listening to the radio news. By ten o'clock this morning the 8th Air Force had put up 1,895 four-engine bombers in two waves. That is stupendous. It, according to Gen. [Lawrence S.] Kuter who is here from Washington in the plans and training section, exceeds the Washington expectation by almost 500. However, there was overcast and a lot of them did not bomb. In fact, we were disappointed that the Air Force was not used to its maximum. We had expected every flyable ship to make 3 trips on D-day, and we only sent out a moderate force this afternoon. There was absolutely no enemy air opposition this morning. That is something that was undreamed of. The news tonight is very optimistic about the landing in general and says that casualties were very light beyond all expectation. We are eagerly looking forward to tomorrow's developments.

It is strange to us that there was so little German opposition in general. Last night there were: no German planes over any part of England and none of the invasion force was attacked. The invasion seemed to be a pretty closely guarded secret. As close as I am to the inside, I was fairly sure that it would come within the next 10 days but I had no idea that this was D-day until the radio announced it.

June 8 - On this, the third day of invasion, the Air Force part is a sort of anticlimax to all the pre-invasion buildup. They sent out a couple of moderate sized forces today and they sent out one big force this morning but none this afternoon. The reason is weather. There has either been solid overcast or patchy clouds ever since the thing started and they are not so inclined to bomb French civilians indiscriminately. They dropped through clouds on the coastal defenses even on invasion morning. Even this morning some of the groups brought their bombs back. Some of them were lucky however and did some wonderful bombing. The losses have been extraordinary. In the three days this division has flown about 2500 sorties in fortresses and not one single man is missing. One plane landed in the channel and the crew was rescued. One man has been killed and a few have been slightly injured. The other divisions have lost only a few. The Jerries slipped over and knocked down 3 forts as they were coming in for landing after dark. They were prepared for terrific air battles and there has been no opposition except some moderate opposition to the 9th Air Force's low level stuff.

June 9 - Because of weather not a fort got off today for combat. That is heart breaking. Those poor men over there on the beachhead are fighting their hearts out and critically needing the overwhelming air support we are prepared and anxious to give and we are grounded. From all reports they are pretty well holding their own for the moment but that isn't sufficient. Every combat man we have would gladly fly three missions a day for a week if he could. After all the big expectations of bloody air battles, these last four days have been the easiest four days the crews have had in weeks. The official communiques are optimistic, but I can't help feeling that the loss of the air support they counted on may be critical. Fortunately the Luftwaffe is not doing much either.

Last night Lt. Hicks and a couple of the enlisted men in the office had all my office staff out to dinner at the Lion Hotel in Buckden, a little village a couple of miles down the road. They were celebrating their first year in the E.T.O. There were nine of us in the party, four officers and five enlisted men. It was the first time we had ever had any sort of an affair together, and we did have a very enjoyable meal and bull session. They're a grand bunch. In no other Army in the world could officers gracefully sit down to the same table with enlisted men and get away with it, and to advantage under proper circumstances.

There was an amusing incident at Staff meeting on Tuesday that is worthy of mentioning. It was 8:30 and the first news was out about the beginning of the invasion, everything was very solemn and grim, everybody was straining an ear to catch every word that might be said about the momentous history-making events that were at that moment taking place. Lt. Col. Coleman made a remark about the great beginning, Lt. Col. [John B.] Wright told how the almost 1900 airplanes had already been dispatched by the 8th Air Force, and Col. [Charles E.] Marion made some remark about it from an operations viewpoint. When the Special Staff was called on for any remarks of interest only one officer had anything to say. Capt. Clarenback got up and said, "Yesterday Kimbolton won the 8th Air Force barbershop quartet contest."

June 13 - For the last three days various numbers of forts have been going over to bomb bridges and airfields with varying degrees of results. The weather continues to hinder good visual bombing. The bridgehead is one week old this morning and it is firmly established at 60 miles long and 15 miles deep. For the first time all commanders and correspondents seemed to be completely satisfied and optimistic today. All are agreed that it is a good start even though conditions were not perfect. I rather suspect that the heavy bombers will soon again leave the tactical bombing to the 9th Air Force and go back to bombing Germany.

June 16 - On the 14th the 8th A.F. had over 1400 planes out in one wave, 502 of which were from this division. That is the biggest force yet in one effort, and certainly more than this or any other division has ever put up, and that with two of the groups stood down. Several of the groups put up over 50 planes. That is phenomenal. Thurleigh's 54 planes got off in 24 minutes and that's something! For the last three days, the targets have been the same—airdromes and bridges in France. Because of clouds, all bombing is done in the early morning only. Results for the most part are phenomenally accurate. The bombing of bridges, particularly, has really upset the German transportation system in France. The beachhead is almost at a standstill the last 24 hours.

Last night we had the 2nd anniversary dinner-dance for the 1st Bomb Division Headquarters. It was really a successful affair. We had fried chicken with chocolate ice cream and strawberries for desert. There was also a breakfast after midnight with two fresh eggs. It was swell—the band was also good.

June 19 - Yesterday they went to Hamburg, the first time to Germany since the invasion began. This was again a new record for this division, 520 planes. There were 1300 planes (four engine bombers) from the 8th A.F., but because of weather some of them chose other targets. The destruction in Hamburg was terrific. Whole city blocks were knocked down, factories, railroads, utilities of various sorts, a large cargo ship in the harbor, and terrific explosions and fires in the oil storage and refinery areas. It was the most widespread area destruction that I have seen on American photographs. And it was cheap too as far as numbers of planes lost—only 4 from this division. But in personnel our losses were out of all proportion to the number. They included Col. [Ernest H.] Lawson, the Commanding Officer of the 305th Bomb Group and Major [John G.] Weibel, the operations officer of the 398th. Col. Lawson's ship took a direct hit by flak and blew up in the air. He is the second group C.O. we have ever lost in this division, Col. [William] Hatcher from the 351st being the other last Dec.

The weather over Normandy is still cloudy. This ends two weeks since the invasion began and there hasn't been really a good day for high altitude bombing yet. Things along the invasion coast are considered good. The Americans yesterday extended themselves on across the Cherbourg peninsula. Casualties are really pretty high. Hospitals in a lot of areas are filling up rapidly both with American and German wounded.

It was announced a couple of days ago that the tour of duty for this theater had been further increased to 35 missions. Naturally the combat men take a mighty dim view of that, but it is to be expected, I suppose. I agree that there should have been a rearrangement of the tour, but I agree with General Williams that they should be graduated on points, grading each mission on its length and severity. I'm looking for some repercussions from this one.

This afternoon I attended the opening of the Bedfordshire service arts and crafts exhibits in Bedford. It was one of those many things sponsored by Mrs. McCorquodale, and she insisted that I come. It was opened by H.R.H. the Duchess of Kent. The duchess is as beautiful and charming as she is reputed to be, but she looked terribly bored with the whole thing, and I didn't blame her. Mrs. McCorquodale had a tea afterwards at the

Swan Hotel which I attended. It was a miserable afternoon, but I am always amused at all the fuss and flurry of the social butterflies which kept me entertained.

Night before last Dean Munal and I paid off a social obligation to Mrs. Camden and Barbara Wormington by taking them to see "Skirts," the sensational 8th A.F. Variety show that was playing in Bedford last week. It was really a bang-up show of professional quality and about equal to Irving Berlin's "This Is the Army." I enjoyed it thoroughly even though I had seen it three nights previously.

June 22 - This business of bombing every day or sometimes twice a day is getting pretty monotonous. The crews, both air and ground, are becoming perfectly exhausted. Weather is better and they are trying to make the most of it. On June 19 they hit at French airdromes in the vicinity of Bordeaux with excellent results. On June 20 this division went back to Hamburg and perhaps did the most extensive bit of destruction done by a bomber force in this war. The results were phenomenal. The targets were the numerous oil refinery and storage plants. All were hit solidly and all produced violent explosions and fires that rapidly spread and which were still burning yesterday. There is no doubt that Hitler has much less oil than he had a couple of days ago. There were literally scores of violent explosions. Yesterday, June 21, they went back to Berlin in force just to let the Germans know we hadn't forgotten about them there and that the invasion was "going so well we now had time to go back to them." From the looks of things that is just what was planned, because most of the Berlin targets were residential districts, at least that is what they hit. However, there was plenty of industrial destruction, particularly a couple of big railroad stations and a big clothing industry. Today the efforts were much lighter, only a small one this morning to the Pas de Calais and another small one to the battle line on the Cherbourg peninsula. Today's results were not good, particularly this morning.

Yesterday was the first time that English-based bombers made a shuttle run into Russia. Third division sent about 160 forts against an oil plant east of Berlin and then landed them in Russia. That same thing was done by the 15th A.F. from Italy about three weeks ago.

The German pilotless aircraft or flying bombs have been causing quite a stink for five or six days. Their releasing platforms over on the coast of France account for the innumerable missions to the Pas de Calais that we have made in the last three months. They are really doing a pretty vicious job on London with those things, being able to send in 25 to 75 per day, each carrying a 2200 lb. bomb. However, the defenses against them are improving and fewer than half of the ones launched ever make land fall, being shot down in the channel by antiaircraft or by fighter planes.

This morning I went over to Podington for the first time in some weeks to see how things were percolating. Watched the planes come in and talked to some of the crews. They have a wonderful spirit, they are just tired.

June 23 - Gen. Williams came to work this morning wearing two stars. It has been rumored for some time that he had been made a Major General and it is now confirmed. Everybody at this headquarters has been "sweating it out" for him a long time. It is one promotion that every officer and man at this headquarters unanimously applauds. It is unusual for the general of a command like this to be so universally respected and admired. In our eyes, at least, he is a great general. He is absolutely sound in judgement and has an acute feeling of responsibility for the men who are doing the job, both combat crew and ground crew. He has his feet solidly on the ground.

Visited Chelveston today and paid a little social call on the medical officers over there. Lt. Gasper is just back from several weeks special duty in which he spent several days on a troop landing ship in connection with the invasion, even spending three or four days on the French coast. He has some nice stories to tell.

A couple of the combat wings went over France today on a short mission but clouds were again bad and some of them brought their bombs back. It was more wasted effort at a time when it could be better spent resting or getting ships in shape. Battle damage from flak has been terrific lately even though plane losses are relatively low. Of some 800+ planes assigned to this division, over 300 are grounded due to battle damage. The poor mechanics are really catching hell now.

June 24 - They are once more releasing combat crewmen to go home after completing a tour of duty after having discontinued it during the invasion. It was announced this morning that over 300 officers and 400 enlisted men are being transferred out as having completed, and about 85 officers and 250 enlisted men are going home for 30 days leave and return here for a second tour. That makes over 100 complete crews who will be leaving. It may mean that we won't be putting up 520 crews from this division at one time again soon.

They ran three missions today of various sorts, none of them very successful, mostly cloudy again. They did knock out a couple of bridges. The results now are certainty not worth the exhaustion they are heaping upon the crews and ground personnel.

June 29 - Returned this morning from my monthly visit to Pinetree. It has been a long time since I have been away overnight so I left a day early and stayed over in London. As a matter of fact I missed my train on Wed. evening and spent a second night there. That was because the meeting with Col. Armstrong dragged out about three hours. Col. Armstrong did much more talking this time, it was really quite a good session.

I went to London expecting plenty of excitement from the flying bombs, or doodle bugs as they are affectionately called. Hadn't been on the street more than 15 minutes before one came over Piccadilly Circus going like a bat out of hell. It was the only one that I saw, and I heard only three or four explosions altogether, although there were innumerable alerts. The people in London are awfully jittery, and although those buzz bombs are most effective for their nuisance value, they are actually doing an awful lot of damage. They have a terrific blast effect and have caused quite a lot of casualties. The most pitiful sight that I have seen in this war was when I rode the underground train this morning before 7:00 and saw thousands of poor people sleeping on racks or on the floor of the crowded subway stations. They all had their blankets or bed rolls. Small children and dogs on leashes were sleeping there too. It must be pretty fitful sleeping there, but some of them are exhausted and can sleep soundly even with the racket of the tube trains.

The most interesting hour in London was spent at the Jules Red Cross Club shooting the breeze with a couple of young glider pilots who had just arrived back in London from Normandy after having landed there in the early morning of the invasion. With just a little pumping they flowed like a gusher and had some wonderful stories to tell. It was obvious that they hadn't had an easy time of it, but they didn't seem any the worse for wear.

Their praise for the toughness and fighting ability of our paratroopers was unlimited. The Germans had been warned that paratroopers do not take prisoners, and the Americans didn't do anything to disillusion them, so apparently blood flowed freely on both sides. One of them had captured a German officer who inquired of him why they didn't arrive the night before as they had planned. Practically all of the gliders crashed and a high percentage were fired upon just before or immediately after landing. The Germans had placed poles in most of the open fields. Some fields were clear, however, except for grazing cattle, which also indicated that there were no mines in the fields, but when the gliders landed they were met by German 88s firing from the surrounding woods. The Germans hanged a number of the Americans the first morning which only infuriated them. The American paratroopers were guilty of taking some of the German prisoners away from M.P.'s the first couple of days and shooting them. So our side makes a few fouls too, but when the game is kill or be killed, the rules don't mean very much.

Saw one play while in London; went to see the Lunts[6] in "There Shall Be No Night" by Robt. Sherwood. It was an old and monotonous theme about life in a Nazi overrun country at the beginning of the war. So I didn't enjoy it too much although the acting of the Lunts was superb. There is nothing on the London stage at the moment that can touch them.

June 30 - Last night my experiences were added to by doing something else I had never done before and something that one with the slightest bit of diplomacy about him would never tackle. I judged an English baby contest. Capt. Hance roped me in on that. There were about a dozen of them, some fat, some undernourished, one mental defective, one wet, some squalling and one or two smiling. We hauled off and picked one out of each of two age groups and awarded the prize of 10 shillings to each of the two mothers. Two women were happy about the whole thing—I hope I never meet any one of the other 10 again. But it was fun. The occasion was a garden fete for the Prisoner of War Fund at the estate of Sir Ernest Shepperson, a member of the House of Commons who lives near Huntingdon. He is a very interesting old codger who is very fat and has the gout. The old manor house dates back several centuries. The nicest thing about the whole affair was the nice buffet supper with a large bowl of fresh strawberries for dessert. We all got into a big discussion about post war peace problems. It was evident that Sir Ernest was much concerned whether or not the Americans were going to be willing to pay their share of the expense of maintaining a peace police force. That, of course, I could give him no help on. But I did note slight evidence of pain when I brazenly prophesied that the English and Americans were going to have a bit of a falling out when we started demanding certain Pacific island bases after the war. I think the English distrust us, but the feeling is probably mutual. But along that line Russia isn't even to be mentioned.

July 2, 1944 - This is another G.I. Sunday and I worked harder than I have for a long time. Besides disposing of a lot of things at the office, I visited three stations during the course of the day. Went to Nuthampstead to check on some sanitation problems in connection with the mess halls down there, then came back to Bassingbourne for lunch and a short discussion with Walker. After coming back here to headquarters it was necessary to go up to Glatton for a little session with Col. Luper about moving one of his medical officers. He has an overage by virtue of the fact that he had an old acquaintance transferred in, and now he wants to boot out a perfectly fine man to make room for him. That is against the wishes of Major Haggard, the group surgeon, and is also against my better judgement. But Col. Luper is a tough man to do anything with and it is not yet clear which way he will jump. But I did recommend that he take the advice of the squadron commander concerned. I'm afraid he's going to break up a right smooth running medical organization with his meddling.

Operational flying has hit a very low ebb here of recently. Almost every day we have been struggling to get a small force out in the weather to bomb something or other but with very little success. During the last month there have been enough holes in clouds that some of the groups have done extraordinary bombing, but except for the marvelously successful raid on Hamburg on June 20, it has been a month since every group has been able to see its target. It is raining again tonight. In spite of the weather the low level fighter bombers and strafers [fighters] have been doing a wonderful job on the German concentrations in Normandy. It's too bad the heavies cannot be utilized to good advantage too. But it has allowed them to get rested up for a change.

July 3 - Spent most of the day on the station at Ridgewell following around a bunch of engineers and two British civilians from Air Ministry. The problem was whether or not to install two ventilating fans in the post theater and one in the briefing room, such plan to be adopted for all stations in the Air Force. One would have thought it a conference to discuss plans for construction of a new airdrome. English construction methods are completely beyond me. Someday I hope to see an Englishman who is impressed with something or shows a reaction to something. If the day gets three ventilating fans out of them, I suppose it will be worth it, but the question still is, "Do we get them, or don't we?"

Have a most urgent request from Major Gaillard at the station to remove his dental officer from the station without delay having yesterday observed him indulging in an act "unbecoming of an officer and a gentleman." Personnel problems are mounting again. Things have been too quiet for a month now. But that's what makes this job interesting.

Personnel problems reminds me that Capt. Bresden (mentioned on June 5) is now much improved by virtue of the fact that we have sent another dental officer down there to work with him who is just over from the States and who is already more homesick than Bresden himself. Both are disgusted with the other and each insists that he is not as bad off as the other, so both are feeling better. It takes all kinds.

July 4 - This was no holiday that I could see. There were a couple of missions today and all work went on as usual. The only celebration is a dance at the 49th Station Hospital tonight.

This morning I was chairman of a direct appointment board which interviewed about six flight officers who were recommended for commissions as second lieutenants. All were approved, as they usually are. After that I digested the stack of papers on my desk. The activities this afternoon were equally far removed from the practice of medicine. Spent the entire afternoon following Major Laidlaw, our public relations officer, around getting things squared away for a visit by the king and queen to Thurleigh day after tomorrow. We were running down some molds to freeze ice cream in. Mrs. Camden provided those, and while we were there, she gave us some invaluable tips. The king apparently has had an intestinal operation and cannot eat a heavy diet. Furthermore, he refuses to eat soup. So the main dish is being switched from steak to chicken. Mrs. Camden is always giving us valuable suggestions like that. Anyway, I suppose everything is now under control. The occasion is to be the christening of an airplane by Princess Elizabeth. It will probably make a big splash in the papers back home. She has never done this sort of thing before. Laidlaw told me this afternoon how it all came about. He was down at Thurleigh one afternoon out on the line when he ran into a sergeant line chief who had just been checking over his brand new fortress and was all greasy and grimy as they usually are, and when he recognized Laidlaw he said in a Brooklyn brogue, "You want to do something for us boys? We want to name this ship after the Princess Royal and we want Princess Elizabeth to christen her." Whereupon Laidlaw informed him that the Princess Elizabeth was not the Princess Royal. But he insisted, "Well, she's royal ain't she?" Laidlaw also thought it a good idea, so it was arranged through the proper channels. That is how the heir apparent to the throne of England came to be christening a fortress "The Rose of York" day after tomorrow morning.

July 5 - The dance at the hospital last night was none too lively, but it was pretty lively as far as dances at the 49th Station Hospital go. I can just about imagine how one of the bomber stations would have done it up with the availability to all sorts of flares that they have.

This afternoon I had all the Group Surgeons up here for our infrequent pow-wow. We were honored to have Col. Armstrong here and he really contributed a lot to the meeting. He allowed us to cut loose at him with any questions that we liked and it worked out to the benefit of all concerned. I do believe it was worth something to all the fellows. Col. Armstrong is an awfully nice fellow and is trying to make a good job of it, but I do wish he would rear back on his heels and scream a little louder for some of the things he knows are right and that we should be doing. He was here for lunch and had with him Col. Dyke and Major Anderson from the 91st General Hospital at Oxford.

Gen. [Bartlett] Beaman called me up to his office this morning to explain the complaint I had made in my weekly summary report against a couple of the group commanders in this division. At briefing for the last Berlin raid, one of the C.O.'s made the statement at briefing that it was a reprisal raid against the Germans for their use of pilotless aircraft against London (which it was, and a very successful one too). Also one before that had casually remarked after briefing a target that if it was cloudy and they couldn't see the aiming point, to drop on anything in Germany "and kill off the women and children." There have been a lot of such raids where it has actually worked out that way, but they don't have to remind the boys about it. After those remarks there was considerable discussion and indignation among the crews. And although none actually refused to fly on those days, some were on the verge of it. Last week I saw a sergeant at the Central Medical Board from another division who had refused to go under similar circumstances because it was against his Catholic religion. The whole thing was unnecessary because the lad wouldn't have known the difference or thought anything about it if it hadn't been called to his attention. It was an entirely needless combat crew failure. To brief any target as anything other than military target can serve no possible useful purpose and can do untold damage to the morale of the combat men. Gen. Beaman agreed, and it was not intended that such things should have happened. This incident just further proves the thing we have observed

Princess Elizabeth, with 306th Group commander Colonel George L. Robinson, Thurleigh Air Field, July 6, 1944. Courtesy of the East Anglia Air War Collection.

Princess Elizabeth is introduced to the crew of the Rose of York, with 306th Group commander Colonel George L. Robinson, Thurleigh Air Field, July 6, 1944. Courtesy of the East Anglia Air War Collection.

Princess Elizabeth, King George VI, Queen Elizabeth, and General James Doolittle pose below the B-17 Rose of York, Thurleigh Air Field, July 6, 1944. Courtesy of the East Anglia Air War Collection.

from the beginning, that the American air crews are not really mad at the Germans. I think it is one of the great wonders of this war how our flyers have fought so magnificently and successfully in this war having the war psychology that they do. But it is not only the flyers, the same applies to the ground forces. I have just seen a news reel of a Sgt. Kelly getting a rousing hometown reception after getting the Congressional Medal at Salerno. His statement for the audience was, "The fellows over there are fighting to get home." Even our fellows over there would relish the opportunity to kill off a few Japanese civilians, however.

July 6 - Took off and went down to Thurleigh to see the christening of the "Rose of York." It was a nice little ceremony. The Princess Elizabeth is quite a cute little girl and made a very nice impression. It was her show and the king and queen stood in the background until she had done her do. It was the first time that I had actually seen any of the royal family, although the king had been at Thurleigh on two occasions while I was there. Photographers were thick as locusts, of course, but it burned me up because they wouldn't let us take pictures. The only hitch in the whole thing was the formation of planes which came over in salute arrived exactly on the second, but the royal procession arrived about 30 sec. late after the formation had passed over. M/Sgt. [Edward S.] Gregory whose idea was responsible for this thing will now be hard to hold.[7]

Tonight after supper Lt. Col. Johnson, Capt. Cargill, Capt. Goodman and I bicycled down to the farm of a Mr. Brown just south of Buckden. It was a swell ride of about four miles. Mr. and Mrs. Brown are extremely hospitable people and made us feel right at home. Mr. Brown was found repairing a wagon loaded with hay. The smell of new hay almost made me homesick. Even after staying a couple of hours we are still back long before dark.

It is believed that the bombing on airdromes in France was good again today for the first time in many days. We'll know when we see the photographs tomorrow morning. For a long time they have been piddling along with little forces of only 70–90 planes, and then they frequently could not see the target and brought back the bombs. One day 3–4 days ago there wasn't a single 8th A.F. bomber or fighter off the ground. Some good weather would be a blessing now, though this bad weather was also a blessing in allowing the crews to get rested again. They are ready and anxious to go back to work.

July 9 - Mr. [Winston] Churchill has at last come out and relieved the silly restriction about information on the flying bomb. The folks back home will now know that it isn't just a bunch of foolishness. London has been taking much more of a beating lately and the people are really getting jittery. People are leaving there by the thousands. The recent cloudy weather has been to their advantage because they cannot be attacked either at their launching sites or in flight.

There was a large successful raid on Leipzig yesterday, 450 bombers from this division and over 1100 in all. Some of the targets were missed but there were enough bombers that there was plenty of destruction on airdromes, airplane factories, marshalling yards and other industries. The weather was rugged over England and Grafton-Underwood had an air collision before they got out of England killing all but four [men] out of two ships [aircraft]. Our division lost 7 other ships to flak, second div. lost 28 to fighters and third div. lost 2 to flak. Yesterday was the greatest air battle in over a month. We are claiming 117 of the German fighters. A good stiff battle like that which destroys their planes in the air as well as their factories is now paying real dividends against the Luftwaffe. The bombing of the French airdromes the day before, which at first looked good, really stank. It was a wasted effort. A medium sized force went out very early this morning to the flying bomb sites in the Pas de Calais but they couldn't see them and brought all the bombs back. What weather! We'd be better off if the heavy bombers forgot all about France and stuck to industrial Germany. Eisenhower couldn't have picked a worse month as far as we are concerned. A second mission was scheduled for this afternoon but was scrubbed on account of____[blank line appears in the original].

Today I went into the intelligence office and had a look at the photographs of our Russian disaster. Of the 160 forts which went from England to Russia on June 22, 53 were destroyed that night by German incendiary bombs on the ground. Fortunately only two or three were killed. But it was sickening to see picture after picture of those poor burned out airplanes on that vast Russian airdrome at Poltava. The remainder of the planes went to Italy and 75 only arrived back here in England day before yesterday. I suppose now as a result of all that screwed-up mess the third division will get another Congressional citation.[8]

July 11 - This afternoon I had the opportunity to go flying with the general [Williams] in the Silver Queen. We stopped off first at Glatton, then flew out to the coast to see our planes come in from bombing Munich. Clouds were prevalent and we were under them, over them, through them and around them. All the way from 1,000 feet to 13,000 feet. I didn't feel too comfortable going through the clouds when we were expecting our planes coming from the other direction, but after much stooging around we never did find them. We then returned to Polebrook and watched them land. Gen. Williams then interrogated Col. [Eugene A.] Romig and the other lead teams. They bombed through 10/10 clouds and the Pathfinder equipment was not working too well, but they think they hit the city solidly. At least the German radio was howling about our bombing their women and children. There were about 1100 bombers on Munich today, which should make quite a splash.

The General handles that old fort like it was an AT-6. But I feel perfectly safe with him. He's only been flying forts for about 10 years, and he should know what a fort can do if anybody does. If he wants to loop the thing even, it is O.K. by me.

My conference with Col. Luper 9 days ago has paid off in a moral victory. By giving him a week to reconsider the decision he was wanting to

Having just completed their first shuttle bombing mission from England, these B-17s were destroyed on the ground in a perfectly timed and well-executed attack by the German air force on the night of June 21, 1944. Courtesy of the East Anglia Air War Collection.

make concerning kicking out one of his medical officers to keep one of his friends, he has hung himself and came around to our way of thinking. That man is reforming, I do believe.

July 15 - On 12 July they sent a big force of bombers to Munich for the second straight day and dropped their bombs through 10/10 clouds. They hit everything except Munich and did a lot of late spring plowing for the German farmers. It was an awfully sorry show. On the 13th they went back to Munich for the third straight day with over 1000 bombers and dropped again through clouds and nearly all the bombs hit squarely in the city, and incendiaries at that. The Germans sent all the firefighting equipment from all southern Germany. Devastation is thought to be terrific.

Last night Laidlaw and I were invited down to Mrs. Camden's for dinner. It was a swell meal and a nice evening in general. We later went over to Mrs. McCorquodale's at her request – "because she wanted to meet Laidlaw." When we got there it became clear why she wanted to meet him; she wanted some publicity for a big tea that she was giving for the women of the services. Really she is a disgusting social hound, but she and Laidlaw became a riot.

Tonight we are having our monthly dance. I am expecting my usual lady friend from Bedford.

July 17 - Three years ago today I reported to Camp Joe T. Robinson (North Little Rock, Arkansas) for my physical examination for entrance into active duty. It doesn't seem that long, but when one mentions it in terms of 3 years it is entirely too long, particularly at my age. It has been a very interesting three years and very pleasant most of the time, but a lot of it has been time wasted. There are experiences however that should be most valuable. I hope that I shall not have to spend much more than one more year in the Armed Service.

For a change, they had good visual bombing in France today for striking at several important bridges. Results were therefore excellent.

Capt. Cargill, the Division Bombardier has just received the bombing results for last month by comparison with other divisions. Again our division led the nearest other division in bombing accuracy within a 1000 foot circle of the aiming point by 10%. That is good bombing.

July 20 - Received a wonderful letter from Ell and Anita today along with a half dozen pictures made at home in June. I have never appreciated pictures so much as those. Particularly the one of the house, and the front view. I found myself showing them to everybody in sight and look-

King George VI speaking with pilot Henry Terry on a visit to Thurleigh on November 13, 1942. Colonel Charles Overacker is at right in the background. Officer at left of the king is unidentified. Courtesy of the East Anglia Air War Collection.

ing longingly at them. Guess they gave me a little spell of homesickness. They're the first pictures I've had of home since coming to England.

Our bombing efforts are quite tremendous and consistent lately. Today they blasted at Leipzig and adjacent localities. Ran into heavy fighter opposition today and lost 15 planes from this division. The 91st Bomb Gp. lost 8 of those. This was an awfully hard day for Col. Henry Terry, the new C.O. Not only did his group take a beating, but he also got married to an English girl today. Henry is an awfully sharp combat man and a good commander. He has to be good, he's one of our old original 306th boys.

Yesterday they did wonderful bombing in the Augsburg area, mostly on aircraft factories and airdromes. The day before they did a perfectly marvelous job of bombing on the experimental station and factory area for the flying bombs, which is located on the Baltic Sea. The day before that was bridges in France, and the day before that the fourth heavy attack on Munich in six days. The 15th A.F. from Italy attacked Munich yesterday which would make 5 big attacks on them in a little over a week. That is a pretty terrific pounding on the old Nazi capital. I think the Germans realize by now that we have enough planes to support the invasion in Normandy and to continue to strike Germany at the same time. The morning our forts went to the Baltic, the R.A.F. sent to the battle front 1,100 Lancasters followed by 600 U.S.-Liberators and 500 U.S. mediums which all dropped 7,000 tons of bombs in a 4-hour period. It must have been terrific. The most amusing sight to us is to watch the R.A.F. now trying to fly formation and in daylight. They have been flying at night so many years they have lost their day vision. The Luftwaffe is really in a bad way when the R.A.F. would dare send 1100 bombers out in daylight.

July 21 - Longworth was out of the office inspecting all day and I had more telephone calls and paper work than a few to dispose of. Col. Armstrong wants a report from all the stations about fatigue—among certain ground crews and other personnel. Gen. Williams wants one of those new plastic eyes they are making over here [Williams lost an eye during the Blitz while serving as an air observer in late 1940].

Col. Armstrong wants Major Nowack to be transferred up to his office, and a million other things. After some degree of checking up, I learned that the Gen. won't like one of those new eyes, if he gets one, and after going to Polebrook to talk over prospects with Nowack, he will be happy to get the new job if there is a promotion in it for him.

Nowack was full of glowing tales about the visit of Major Gen. Kirk, the Surgeon General, to his field a couple of days ago. He did have his place all shined up nice and put on a good show for him. As luck would have it, Polebrook had more severe casualties returning from the mission that day than they had ever had in one day before, just as though it was a show especially for the Surgeon General. Mr. Stimson, Sec. of War, was there too and personally commended Nowack, so Nowack was one proud little customer. Nobody can absorb praise quite as well as Nowack, but in spite of that, he's a swell doctor and has done a grand job as a Group Surgeon. He deserves the advancement if it comes.

July 22 - Joyce Camden pulled a damnable trick on me and practically coerced me into judging a baby contest down at Great Barford today. After much hesitancy I did go, and did go through with it. They were having a big Red Cross fete at that village. A more distasteful task I cannot think of and swear that I won't do it again. I hope the mothers took it good naturedly.

There was a terrific bombing effort today. The entire 8th A.F. sent out 10 forts (all from this division, they could hardly spare them) to bomb Kiel, Bremen, and Hamburg with over a million leaflets. This great force was

General Robert B. Williams, commanding the First Air Division. Courtesy of the East Anglia Air War Collection.

General Robert B. Williams, inspecting 303rd Bomb Group units at Molesworth Air Field. Colonel Kermit D. Stevens, group commander, follows General Williams on the inspection. Courtesy of the East Anglia Air War Collection.

escorted by 35 fighters, all of whom made an uneventful journey. They are striking with propaganda while the iron is hot over the attempted assassination of Hitler. Weather prevented additional activity.

July 23 - This afternoon the officers' club gave a party for the evacuee children[9] from London who are at this village of Brampton. They were shown a movie, then were taken into the mess and stuffed with popcorn and ice cream and cake. The eyes of those little kids just stuck out on stems and before they were through many of them had unbuttoned their coats. Then as they went out the door, each was handed a sack containing at least a half dozen bars of candy and some chewing gum. There were 56 of them. One of the officers overheard one little boy about 8 remarking to another, "I shall always love the Americans." And he probably meant it. The Americans have always made a good impression on English kids. Chewing gum has been a mighty weapon in promoting future Anglo-American friendship.[10]

July 24 - Longworth is in the process of writing the Division medical history and histories have been submitted from the groups. One reported in his history the incident of a bombardier who got out of the nose of his ship which crash landed after coming home on only a wing and a prayer. The first thing he did was to get down on his knees and kiss the ground. The Chaplain happened along and remarked, "The good Lord was certainly with you this time, wasn't he fellow?" To which the bombardier replied, "You're goddamn right he was, Chaplain."

July 27 - Have just returned from Pinetree to attend the monthly surgeon's meeting with Col. Armstrong. I got in a heated argument with Col. [Olin F.] McIlnay over the disposition of combat crew failures. Fortunately, I had the support of most of the others, particularly Capt. Bond. After all the discussion nothing was accomplished. The most amazing news came to earth in Col. Armstrong's office. Sam Haigler over at 3rd Division is being given the boot in order to make room for Lt. Col. Cobler who is in Col. Armstrong's office. That is because Col. Cobler is a personal friend of Gen. Partridge who is over there. I feel awfully sorry for Sam because he has really tried hard at the job and hasn't done badly. I like Col. Cobler also. My man Nowack is taking Cobler's place at 8th A.F. and 3rd Division is to give me a major to replace him. That's where I get dragged in on this ungodly situation. I've never yet seen one move initiate so many other moves and stand a possibility of making so many people mad. I'll be glad when it's all settled. I stand to lose any way it goes.

On my arrival back here, I was swept off my feet with the announce-ment that our Bombardment Division has now become an Air Division and now has a Fighter wing assigned which is composed of 4 P-51 fighter groups and 1 P-47 group, also a sub depot. This will bring our strength up to over 50,000 officers and men. That gives me the knee shakes when I think about it; but I'm not admitting it to anybody else. In fact with Sam Haigler losing out over in 3rd, it makes my position seem even more inse-cure. After all, it just isn't reasonable to have a 30-year-old Lt. Col. respon-sible for the medical care of an organization of that kind when a ground division of 12,000 men has a full Colonel medical officer. I shall not be surprised if someone else does get my job one of these days, although I do have the advantage of being at a headquarters whose policy is not to make changes as long as a man is doing a reasonably good job. I can handle the job perfectly well as long as we remain here in England, but I have some question about being able to hold down a separate organization set up in China, or where have you? But you'll find me hanging on until I'm kicked out, which is a very simple procedure in this Army.

Last night Sam Haigler and his wife had me out to dinner. Maggie, his wife, is going to Normandy next month. She is on V.D. control work.

There was no operational flying today. Yesterday and the day before they bombed just in front of our lines in the Cherbourg peninsula. Quite a number of the bombs fell among the American lines, not without loss of life. Gen. Williams told me this afternoon that when the British bombed in front of their lines, the ground troops withdrew 500 yards for the attack The Germans closed in and the English fought for 2 days regaining their 500 yards. That, apparently, is the success of heavy bomber support of ground troops. They should put them back to bombing industrial targets which they were meant to do in the first place.

In London this time I didn't see as much evidence of the buzz bombs. In the two nights I only heard one explosion and heard one fly overhead. There were fewer in the underground stations. Hundreds of thousands have been evacuated from London. I learned last night that a week or so ago a barracks was hit in London, killing 75 U.S. soldiers. That is still on the secret list as yet.

July 29 - I have just completed my most difficult long range person-nel maneuver to date. For a long, long time I have wanted to improve the efficiency of the enlisted men in my office. I was supposed to have only three men but have actually had four for a long time. I transferred out

T/Sgt. Starr, the chief clerk, then promoted the other three and traded one of them to the 306th Bomb Group for T/Sgt. Hinkley to be in charge. I really had to fight with Major Munal to get Hinkley but finally won. For months I have had my eye on that boy for my office, but it took months to lay the ground work for the change. Hinkley until a couple of months ago had been a buck sergeant for over two years, now he has suddenly become a T/Sgt., and that after having been court-martialed a couple months ago for breaking security regulations. He was acquitted on a technicality, although he was guilty as sin. He had written a letter home to be delivered in person by a returning officer, but it was intercepted at the port of embarkation. In it he had written a beautiful glowing account of the location of his station and all about their activity. He was tried because they had to do it, but everybody secretly praised him for the literary characteristics of his letter. As a result he has been "discovered" and rapidly promoted. T/Sgt. Tropeano, at the same time, committed exactly the same crime, was convicted, sentenced for six months and busted to private. Such are the fortunes of war.

Aug 1, 1944 - T/Sgt. Hinkley reported for duty today at the office. I'm going to be awfully disappointed if he doesn't turn out to be a most valuable addition. The other men seemed to take to him right off.

Longworth left tonight for a week's duty at the rest home. That is going to make me work a little for a while. He had just completed the division medical history. It is a pretty good one too.

Yesterday the crews went to Munich and dropped their bombs through clouds again. Results are believed to be terribly bad. They went to airdromes in France today, and I have an idea that the results were no better. They have just changed Commanding Generals over in 2nd Division and it wouldn't surprise me if Lt. Col. Hecker's head will not fall. The position of a staff officer is never secure, particularly when one is disliked by as many people as Hecker is. We shall see how long he can last with a change in command.

Aug 6 - For several days now they have been having excellent bombing weather in Germany and have been taking full advantage of it. They've been hitting the usual targets of airdromes, assembly plants, and oil refineries as well as another trip to the flying bomb experimental station at Peenemunde on the Baltic. They've been having some excellent results, all of which proves that they can hit the target if they can see it.

The news from our troops in France is awfully good. They are now going into Brest like a house afire and have completely cut off the base of the Brest peninsula. And with the Russians just before entering German territory and Warsaw in the east, it may not be so long after all.

For the last three days, I have been so busy I haven't had time to get my breath. Col. Wright was here two days getting some data on morale of the combat crews, a survey which was requested by Gen. [Hap] Arnold because some of the guys who landed in Sweden made some statement to the consul about how bad conditions were over here. But after making the rounds of several stations with him, we found that morale is now better than it has been in a long time. Those jokers are just trying to cover up for running out on the war. With Longworth gone and all the monthly reports coming in at this time there has certainly been plenty to keep one busy in my "spare time."

Aug 7 - Attended the Ground Executives meeting today by command of Gen. Beaman and sat through a lot of dull talk. But there was one rich one that deserves recording. Capt. Nelson, our division M.P. officer reported the incident of a couple of Majors walking down the streets of Kettering when they met a soldier all armed up with his girl. He was challenged by one of the Majors for failing to salute whereupon the soldier got real huffy and replied, "Sir, I am willing to forget this whole incident provided you apologize to my girl." It goes without saying that that immediately landed him in the clink to give him time to consider the question of military courtesy. It is admitted that the American soldier isn't famous for a lot of saluting and heel clicking, but it is hoped that this soldier is not representative. I couldn't help being amused, though it is a reflection upon the U.S. Army.

I almost forgot to mention the lovely afternoon I had about four days ago. Lt. Col. Johnson, the Division Adjutant, and I took off at 3 o'clock in the afternoon and bicycled about 8 miles over to St. Ives to see Mr. Claude Smith, an antique dealer over there. He is quite a character. He is at least 70 years old, has only one eye, and has built up a reputation throughout England as an authority on antique silver, and he thinks much more highly of his reputation for honesty that he has built up over a period of about 50 years than he would ever think of any additional money that he might make out of his antique shop with a few misrepresentations and shady deals. His advice is sought far and wide by individuals who are preparing to sell their old silver, paintings, or furniture. He expresses frank disgust at the high prices that antiques are selling for now during wartime and admits that most of them are not worth the price. In fact he seldom buys at a sale anymore because it hurts his conscience to resell at the necessary prices. He had very little in his shop that one would want, but he did ask us to tea over at his house. We gladly accepted, so he just closed up his shop tighter than a drum, and we went off to tea. His wife was also most hospitable, and we thoroughly enjoyed at least an hour with them. She dragged out some of her personal collection of valuable old silver as well as other treasures, thousands of dollars' worth of it. She certainly had a beautiful collection. We then went back to his shop and a bought a few real nice little trinkets, the very few that he did have on hand, and came back in the clear cool afternoon about 8 o'clock along the bank of the River Ouse feeling considerable refreshed and feeling that we had enjoyed the hospitality and friendship of an Englishman.

Aug 8 - Went to see the enlisted men's movie tonight since I won't be here to see it in our lounge tomorrow night. The reason I couldn't afford to miss it was because it was "Four Jills in a Jeep." And the reason that particular film was of interest was because it was about the trip Kay Francis, Martha Raye, Carole Landis and Mitzi Mayfair made over here in the fall of 1942 a couple months after we arrived. They will always be remembered very kindly by us old-timers because they were our first big time show over here and came at a time when our losses were high and our spirits low. They really did a lot toward picking us up. I was very curious to see how much of the facts they put into their show, but it hit only the very highest spots and put out some very good entertainment. It did well to leave out those things a lot of us know, particularly the escapades of Carole. Her violent love making, even on the night of her fake wedding to a poor sap in a fighter outfit, is no secret to the old bomber boys.[11]

The bombers went across the Normandy line at noon today and bombed opposite the British line. It is the first time in several days that we have directly assisted the ground forces. The weather for a week now has been perfect for bombing, so our fellows bombed Germany while the 9th A.F. tackled France. But today again they worked together. This is what we have been waiting for.

Aug 9 - Gen. Williams had his very worst day yesterday. He flew along to observe the bombing of the German lines. He returned in fair spirits, but he had no more landed than Gen. [Jimmy] Doolittle was on the phone trying to find out what two formations bombed the British troops behind their line. So very much care had been used in briefing the crews on where to bomb and where not to bomb. Gen. Doolittle entrusted this particular job to the 1st Division because their bombing has been more accurate in recent months and he figured that they would do it better. Some of the weaker units in this Division did excellent bombing, but the two units who bombed our own lines were the two groups most outstanding for accuracy, Kimbolton and Deenethorpe. Gen. Williams was shaken to the very core. He said that all the hard-earned prestige this Division has come to enjoy in recent weeks was all thrown away in a few minutes by those two groups. The trouble was that they had much more flak than they had had recently and the bombardiers just got excited. Gen. Williams proceeded to get skunk drunk before dinner. He took it awfully hard. He says very little about it, but he has a tremendous pride in his command. I do hope his prestige will not suffer as a result.

Aug 10 - I ran across this report submitted by Lt. Harvey G. Tidwell, 381st Bomb. Gp., concerning his return to the U.S. for a 30-day leave after completing a tour of duty here and prior to starting a second tour. It is so typical of a young flying officer that it deserves remembering.

"My Return to Civilization"

On a black day in April, Wed. the 18th, way back in 1944, the officers and men of Lt. MacNeill's crew, departed on a voyage back to the "Promised Land," the "Utopia of Civilization," the U.S.A. They told us we were going for rest and recuperation, but we had other plans.

We left this base in the "Joker" #888, more commonly known as the "Old Whore." A short time afterwards we arrived at Burtonwood, a few miles from Liverpool. I needn't say that it was raining when we did get there.

Disappointment number one was our failure to fly the "Joker" home. Our bond-selling tour was therefore cancelled. Hard luck!

Then came our most unpleasant night, the crowning glory. We had to spend a night at 12th R.C.D. Early in the morning they routed us out of our hole in the wall, and we were on our way. It was a cold misty morning, typically British, as we boarded an old, but romantic ship. (All old ships are supposed to be romantic). Then came day after day of anxious waiting and praying. Again and again, the skipper was fearsome of mutiny. Six knots an hour just wasn't fast enough. Then after a long and tedious voyage, the "Mayflower" pulled into "Plymouth Rock," and we waded ashore and planted our flag and our corn.

Next came the march up to the guardian of America's shores, Fort Hamilton, in dear old Brooklyn. We went into a room, stripped, coughed, and took the first door to the right. The goal was at hand. The long awaited moment was here, for down the road a piece, American beer was being served. Far into the night, the lines of "My Wild Irish Rose" and other tavern tunes were very audible.

Morning saw us off to AAFRS #1 at Atlantic City, NJ. We were met by buses and given the key to the city. We stayed at the Ritz Carlton Hotel. From here we were off to our various homes all over the country within 24 hours.

Reported to Fort Wayne for 20 minutes. Saw something of the "Beat You To the Bar" battle, which is being fought on many fronts in the States. Luck was with me on my arrival home, for I got there on "Mother's birthday."

Now a short break of 32 days, all of which were spent in laughter and gaiety. Some were spent in Tennessee at Reelfoot Lake (wonderful bass fishing). Some were spent in Chicago (oh for another day at the races). Of course, I became engaged (almost married). The "two hours" from May 4 to June 5 were very memorable.

The mission completed, I trudged back to Fort Wayne (where I experienced the invasion). From here to Atlantic City. God bless Atlantic City—twelve days wait. It was another leave. New York was next, with Fort Hamilton, and thirteen days of "Jack Dempsey's," "Coney Island," the "Astor Roof," "The Paramount Theater" and, of course, "Girtie" of room 712 at the President Hotel. Good old Girtie.

The time had come to say "So long, Uncle Sam—I'll see you soon," so I said: "So long Uncle Sam—I'll see you soon." We did pretty good time coming back. We did six knots an hour.

Total casualties for the nine-man crew were: 2 married and 2 engaged.

Aug 11 - Had a pleasant afternoon. Got in some of my flying time by riding with Col. Marion and Maj. Ashcraft down to Zeals in southern England. It was such a wonderful afternoon for flying. It was awfully rough at lower altitudes, but there was a thin cloud layer at 4,000 feet with a lot of peaks about it and just as smooth as glass on top. It was real fun darting in and out of those cloud peaks in the new Beechcraft plane that the headquarters has.

Aug 12 - They have been doing some awfully successful bombing of tactical targets in France the last 2 or three days. They are hitting at strong points: gun emplacements, road junctions, marshalling roads, fuel and ammunition dumps, and airdromes and bridges. There has been clear weather. The 9th A.F. is really raising hell with their fighter-bombers. Their toll of locomotives and rolling stock is simply terrific the last two days. Air supremacy is now unquestioned in France. There are plenty of flak guns, however. Evidently they are saving their fighters for Germany, because they never fail to send up some resistance there.

General Williams and General Beaman went over to France today to have a look at the damage we did to the British when we bombed them last Tuesday. It is now believed that the loss of life as a result was not too great. Perhaps the advantages gained by those who were successful outweighed the damage done. After all, the artillery frequently shells its own infantry also.

Aug 13 - Last night three of us started out on our bicycles about 8 o'clock just for a refreshing ride and went to St. Neots and back up a back road to Offord on the way home. Got back about 10:30 after a nice 20-mile ride and a couple of stops on the way. It was a wonderful opportunity to see an English Saturday night. Near Offord we stopped at a couple of pubs, "The Black Bull" and "The Black Bell." Both of them were full to capacity with local village folk in for their evening quaff of pale ale or a mild and bitter. The second had an ancient piano which was played by a very jovial R.A.F. chap and all joined in the singing while the inevitable game of darts between some of the older blokes was proceeding in the next room. I was amazed that each one of the really enthusiastic dart players brought his own darts, one proudly showing me his set which he had been using since before the war. Men and women alike were all enjoying their pints of beer which, because of the present rationing, was available at these two pubs only once in a fortnight so we really got in on one of their regular community affairs. The English pub is a wonderful institution and an essential part of the English community life. There is nothing comparable to it in America. Our drug stores are frequented more by the younger individuals. The English pubs are regularly patronized by the aged as well as the rest of the whole family.

Aug 14 - Went to Pinetree by automobile with Capt. Cobb today. My visit was purely social and to pick up any information or rumors possible. I was particularly anxious to get any information on the proposed reorganization with the fighter outfits which is now scheduled to take place next month. Little was available. The forecast medical personnel change over in 2nd Division has now taken place, that of Col. McIlnay being transferred from the Fighter Command to 2nd Division, following Maj. Gen. Kepner who recently assumed command there. That throws Lt. Col. Hecker out on his ear. Everyone has wondered for a long time why that has not happened before, but it is just one of those things one never quite figures out in the Army. That leaves me as the only one of the three surviving young division surgeons. The $64 question now is how much longer will I last. A change in command has meant a change at the 2 other places, and it is probable that a change in command will do the same here. That is the price of being on a general's staff.

Col. Armstrong was not there, had gone to Italy a couple of days ago. Had a nice visit with Talbot and Nowack however. They are fine fellows, and we are most fortunate to have them in the office up there, they sort of keep things on an even keel.

Yesterday afternoon I finally planted Major Lyday over at Polebrook after much hair pulling with Lt. Col. Bowles, the executive officer. Col. Bowles had tried to block our move and had violated our agreement with Col. Armstrong to replace Nowack with another major by shoving one of his squadron medical officers in there behind our backs. However, with the support of this headquarters, we made Col. Bowles back water and accept him. I hated awfully bad to do that to the other medical officers at the station because they have little or no chance of advancement, but I'm convinced it will be better for the group in the long run. The morale of the medics on that station is worse than any combat crew I have ever seen. I hope they recover.

Aug 15 - Today a year ago I reported for duty at this headquarters, a very bewildered and disgruntled young fellow. It seems only two or three months ago. I hated coming up here and leaving my old Group so awfully bad. I got the call that I was to be in charge up here at 12:00 noon and was instructed to report by 4:00 that afternoon. It was the greatest shock that I had ever received. But it has fortunately worked out O.K. for me and am glad that I came.

After spending a busy morning in the office getting caught up on work that piled up from yesterday, I spent most of this afternoon doing my "duty" flying. Flew with Col. Wurzback to Bovington where we each bought some clothes, then we went down over London and had a look at the barrage balloons that are placed south of London. They just absolutely form a solid wall as protection against the buzz bombs. All the balloons have been removed from London proper. No enemy aircraft ever come over England now days anyway. I did the navigating for him and didn't get lost but once for a short interval. That was an achievement for me.

It was most welcome news about the new invasion in southern France today. The noose is drawing rapidly much tighter around Germany. I have a feeling that something big is brewing. Gen. Doolittle frantically called Gen. Williams and the other two Division Commanders together for an emergency meeting this afternoon. Things may now pop thick and fast for a while.

Aug 18 - Last night Sgt. Hinkley and I were invited to a dance in Bedford given by the medical department at Thurleigh. Maj. Munal had Maj. Wise come over with some of his enlisted men and cover the post while all the resident medics went into town to celebrate the approaching end of 2 years in the E.T.O. It was a wonderful idea to have a function like that for all the officers and men together, and I was honored to have them invite me after having been gone for a year. They did have a good time.

T/Sgt. Spry and S/Sgt. Thomas, those lovable characters whom I had in my medical section at Thurleigh and whom I have mentioned before as having played many practical jokes on various individuals, me included, have made history again. They transferred from the medics to the Air Corps soon after I left Thurleigh and after a period of training became very successful combat aerial gunners. They were on the same crew, Spry as engineer and Thomas as ball turret. About five days ago Spry, who had run off his missions faster than Thomas, was on his last mission when the plane at take-off got into some prop wash in the fog of the early morning and crashed about 300 yards from the end of the runway. Five of the crew were instantly killed, four escaped with slight injuries. The four who escaped were the pilot and co-pilot and Spry and Thomas. Those boys just have charmed lives. Spry was given credit for having completed his tour of duty and Thomas is in the hospital. Spry was the life of the party last night and for all practical purposes is still considered one of the medical men. There will never be another like him.

Today the bombers did an excellent job on several bridges in Holland

and Belgium. Guess they are anticipating heading off the escape of the Germans across the Seine River. Progress in northern France is certainly heartening. Yesterday for the first time in many weeks the entire division was told the night before that there would be no mission. An advance stand-down has come to be just about a thing of the past. The weather recently really has been remarkably good. The two successive days before yesterday saw us doing extraordinary bombing of airdromes and aircraft factories and assembly shops in Germany proper—but not without some cost. The first of those days Molesworth lost nine planes and the second day Bassingbourne lost six. The Germans still make some semblance of protection of the fatherland and are still able to take out any one Group they care to. Fortunately they have little opposition to spend on more than one Group at a time, which makes it hard on somebody, but good for the team as a whole.

Aug 19 - Blackie, the pet crow around here, is getting to be quite a bird. He was raised from a tiny foundling by one of the soldiers over at the sick quarters, and now that he is full grown he is just as much a pet as ever. He used to go over to the sick quarters regularly at mealtime and flap his wings against the door until he was let in, but he has graduated now and comes to the officers' mess hall. The other day somebody set a spoonful of ice cream up on the window sill for him. He tasted it suspiciously at first, then approvingly started gobbling it down in huge gulps. He was given a second spoonful and he tried to carry it off to bury it along with the rest of the food he buries. Of course it promptly spilled out and when he saw what had happened he just threw the spoon out the window and went back to eat the cream. He has very definite likes and dislikes among the personalities here. He will always respond to a definite sort of whistle by Capt. Miller or Capt. Schapp and will come to them anytime. Schapp was walking across the pasture the other day, and Blackie picked him out of all the other officers and went to him unexpectedly and lit on his arm. When a crow can distinguish individuals at a long distance it seems peculiar to me that we should expect them to be afraid of scarecrows. He has a trait of mischief about him too. A couple of weeks ago he made a dive bombing attack upon a W.A.C. who was riding her bicycle down the road, then lit on her shoulder and it scared her so badly that the first thing she knew the bicycle was riding her. It is a favorite stunt of his to ride down the street on the handlebar of the bicycle of someone he knows. The pets that can be collected around an Army post know no bounds.

Aug 23 - Have just completed another very unpleasant job. Got a call at 3:30 this afternoon that Lt. Col. Gerald Price had been killed in a crash. He had been buzzing the hospital down at Diddington when the thing apparently exploded on him in the air as he was pulling out. It was a P-51. The plane was scattered all over the countryside for at least a quarter of a mile, and Jerry with it. Most of him was in one piece, but then I went around with a blanket and picked pieces off the bushes and out of the grass. It isn't so bad as it might seem, however, because it is more like picking up just messy pieces of meat rather than attending to the body of a friend. It isn't nearly so hard when it is messed up so badly it can't be recognized. Jerry was a cracker jack of a pilot. He was a squadron commander with the 305th Bomb Group for a long period of time and did a lot of our experimental work on night flying. He then worked at this headquarters for months and has recently been doing some special work in fighters. His loss struck a blow around here.

It was announced today that Paris has fallen to the French troops. The American troops are advancing rapidly on both fronts. The news is now everywhere so consistently good that it is almost getting monotonous. We are not contributing much to the success at the moment, however. Our bombers have been grounded on account of weather for five days. That is some sort of a record in recent months.

Two important developments at staff meeting this a.m. Lt. Col. Whetstone became the first ground officer in the history of 1st Division to become a full colonel, and had his eagles pinned on by Gen. Williams himself. The other development was that it was announced that leave and furloughs are again in order for the first time since April 1. Look out Scotland—here I come.

Aug 28 - Has been hard getting down to writing the last few days, but there is really no reason. Haven't been very busy. Will be going to London on pass tomorrow and to Pinetree the next day.

They stayed on the ground today because of weather but they did get in three days of German bombing with moderate results the days before that. The flak over there is really getting fierce now. Scarcely a ship ever comes back without at least one hole in it.

Aug 31 - Have just returned from my monthly trip to London and Pinetree. The meeting at Pinetree was better than usual and I do believe we actually accomplished something. Most of all we are getting some of the power away from the Central Medical Board and giving more to the stations in the disposition of their personnel. There were no arguments and no fuss for a change and everything was fine.

The stay in London was rather dull. There were no buzz bombs at all. Spent all one morning visiting antique shops looking for that silver tea set that I'm trying to find. Did find one I wanted but the price was too high. London is not the place to buy antique silver. The price to Americans is unreasonable. The one unusual thing I did was to go to an opera, my first. It was the Sadler's Wells Opera Company, which isn't in the running with the Metropolitan but is fair. They did "The Barber of Seville" and sang it in English rather than Italian, but I was glad of that because I wasn't familiar with it. I did rather enjoy it.

Sept 1, 1944 - This afternoon I had a group surgeons' meeting here and spent about two hours talking to them after which we had them over to the club for about 1 1/2 hours. It was a full, but profitable afternoon.

Tonight several truckloads of us went to Alconbury to see Bing Crosby's show. He was well received as he always is. He doesn't quite rate with Bob Hope in the number of troops that he entertains, but as a singer he has no equal. There is a rich sweetness to his voice that no living man can imitate, and there can be little doubt that he is the greatest singer of popular songs of all time. He's truly a remarkable person.

Sept 2 - This was a stinker of a day with a cold rain. A fire tonight feels good. No flying today. The mission to Manheim yesterday was recalled over Germany before they got to the target because of very high cloud, and there was not a ship in the 8th A.F. up the day before that. The fellows are beginning to feel that they are not contributing as much as they might to the momentous things happening over in France. The 9 o'clock news tonight was awfully good. Patton is 11 miles from Germany, the British troops are 75 miles from Brussels and the Canadians have triumphantly entered Dieppe. That must be a glorious day for them to avenge that horrible beating they took in that Dieppe raid experiment 2 years ago. There is tremendous satisfaction in reading the names of those northern French towns that have fallen in the last week, names such as LeBourget, Villa Caublay, Rauen, Romilly, Reims, Amiens—all of them targets where our fellows have bombed repeatedly in the last two years and whose names have been written in the blood of our bomber boys. These victories really mean a lot to some of the old timers—the few that we have left. Patton is making the old battle line of 1918 look sick. Verdun and the Argonne and the Marne mean no more to him than somebody's backyard.

Optimism is running high in all quarters now, but nowhere quite so much as at the 91st Bomb Group. They are quite convinced that they are scheduled to return to the States in short order and are quite violent with anybody who says that they are not. Major Walker and some of the other medical officers were insisting on betting that they would be moved from Bassingbourne before Nov. 1. I do not consider myself a betting man, but I am perfectly willing to accept the challenge when someone makes foolish bets.

Sept 8 - 11:00 p.m. It has just occurred to me that at this moment exactly 2 years ago we were piling out of the G.I. trucks for the first time at Thurleigh. We had just set foot on England in the late afternoon at Grafton Underwood because the airdrome at Thurleigh was not ready. It was cold and wet, the blackout was rigid and was pitch black, we stumbled into all the ditches and hit all the mud puddles trying to find our barracks. There was that large chandelier flare in the sky which was dropped by a German reconnaissance plane and knew that "this was it." This was the real war zone, and we all had our pistols by our side. It's a strange thing that I saw about as much of the war that night as I have ever seen since. The German plane was shot down only three or four miles away from camp. There was no doubt in anybody's mind that the Germans knew that the 306th had arrived and would be paying us a visit in the next couple of days.

I marvel when I think about what has taken place in these 2 years. At the time we landed, the old 97th Bomb Gp. had made a half dozen sorties out as far as the French coast. The entire aerial war by the Americans in this theater was ahead of us. Today practically all of it is behind us. Mere words can never describe the heartaches, the simple pleasures, the mistakes, the victories, the losses, the progress, the lessons learned by us of the American Air Forces in Europe during those two years.

Sept 10 - Last night Longworth and I along with a number of other officers went to the big 2nd anniversary party at Thurleigh. It was a knock down and drag out in more ways than one. It is said that they spent £2,000 on that party and I wouldn't doubt it. The group was stood down for the day and all the officers and enlisted men really cut loose. Capt. Nugent from Bassingbourne was over there to take care of the medical situation while the local medics joined in the celebration. And there were plenty of medical situations too. A jeep turned over and cracked a skull, there was a broken clavicle, all sorts of cuts, bruises, and bloody noses; and to top it all off one boy committed suicide. It isn't known what was behind it, but it is said that he put on his best uniform, went out into the dispersal area and shot himself. He was a 2-year man. There were so very few there who started out there with the group two years ago. It would have been so awfully nice if we could have had our fellows back from the German prison camps for that party. In later years when veterans get together and discuss the various parties that were held in the E.T.O., the 306th can top them all with all the "cutting and shootin'" they had at their 2nd anniversary party. May the next one be held in the U.S.A.

I wasn't worth two hoots all day because of anticipation of starting my leave. We planned to fly up to Edinburgh this afternoon but couldn't get a plane that could go in that direction. Instead of going to work this afternoon I flew with Capt. Thomas down to London and back. We will try again tomorrow and if weather does not permit, we will start out on the train.

Sept 11 – Today I actually got started on that leave that I had planned almost 13 months ago and which my transfer up here interrupted. Tried in a feeble sort of way to get away yesterday afternoon, and with more pressure upon Capt. Thomas this morning, we still couldn't get a plane from his headquarters because Col. [Charles E.] Marion outranked Thomas out of the only available plane. But with some quick action and considerable scurrying around arrangements were made to go with Capt. Witt from Thurleigh who was taking some fellows from that station. I am with Capt. Hance and Lt. Garvin from this headquarters.

We originally planned to go to Edinburgh, but the plane was coming to Aberdeen which suited us just as well. The weather couldn't be better for flying, for which I was thankful in view of all the tragedies we have had in connection with flights to Scotland during cloudy weather. Things just couldn't have worked out better, and in only 2 hours had made a most pleasant trip to northern Scotland that would have taken 13 or 14 miserable hours by train, if lucky.

We had been warned about the crowded conditions in Scotland, and had even failed on all our attempts to get advance reservations, but we had not been impressed until we arrived and every hotel said they were booked up until the 1st of Nov. One of the hotels referred us to a private home which turned out to be a miserable sort of place and turned it down in favor of a travel agency which kindly referred us to the home of Mrs. Massie, who didn't exactly have a palace either, but at least it was clean.

Aberdeen is a clean and beautiful city. All the houses are built of white granite and look as if they would last another 5,000 years. Right away an entirely different atmosphere from that of England was very apparent and it was remarked how much like Americans the Scots looked (the first thing one learns in Scotland is that the people are Scots and not Scotch). They were well dressed and showed no signs of stress, worry or war weariness such as the English do. One also could almost spot an English kid by his peculiar look, dress, and mannerisms, but the Scottish kids look like the youngsters in anybody's backyard back home. We immediately ran into hospitality and friendliness such as we had not seen in this country before.

But in spite of the good intentions of the Aberdenians, our stay here got off to an awfully bad start, and the four hours we spent trying to get a place to lay our weary bones for the night put us in a very bad humor, but the natives were genuinely sympathetic. This left little time for seeing the sights about the city. After walking about five miles and spending a reasonable amount of time at the "famed" Caledonian Hotel, we went to our rooms fairly early. Accommodations here are not such that it would pay us to tarry longer here.

Sept 12 – At 9:00 a.m. we caught a bus from Aberdeen for Inverness. There hasn't been a cloud in the sky all day, which is unheard of in Scotland at this time of year. The trip took five hours and the scenery was perfectly gorgeous all the way. It was mountainous and of a formation that somewhat resembled the Ozarks except that they were not so rocky and all the peaks were a lovely purple with heather in full bloom. This is also the first time since coming to Britain that I have seen beautiful swift, clear mountain streams.

We had considerably better luck with our accommodations in Inverness. Obtained a hotel room on first try. Had a very late lunch and after shopping around for a while, we just aimlessly wandered over to the famous Caledonian Canal and followed it down to where it runs into the salt water at the junction of Beauly Firth and Moray Firth. On the dock we ran into an Australian doctor named Jamaison who is a Wing Commander with the R.A.F. stationed at Inverness and a Mrs. Green who is serving with the British Red Cross. They were getting ready to go sailing and kindly invited us to go along. Theirs was about a 15-footer, and quite sturdy. There was a light cool breeze in the bright late afternoon and we sailed merrily along against both the wind and the tide to a little pub on the other side of the Firth a mile or so. I still can't understand the mechanics of sailing. We came back across the Firth just before sundown and left W/C Jamaison and Mrs. Green after thanking them profusely for a rare experience (my first attempt at sailing) and went on back to the hotel for dinner. While we were eating, however, the two of them came over to the hotel and insisted that we go out to the R.A.F. officer's club for the evening—without excessive persuasion, of course. The whole bunch were very hospitable and treated us royally. It was almost midnight before he took us back to the hotel.

At the club we had a chance to observe a bit of real Scottish atmosphere and attitude. There was one girl there who was a "Highlander" from way back and she minced no words about her opinion of the Lowlanders. But when the word "English" was spoken she fairly flew into a fit. She pretty well typified the Scottish feeling of that particular locality. They have no lost love for the Irish either. They are still a very clannish bunch, and our Civil War feeling doesn't even hold a light to it. It was quite evident, however, that their talk is mainly bluff.

Sept 13 - We crawled out at 7 a.m. to catch the train. I'm tired of having to get up so early while on leave—we can do that back at camp. Am also getting tired of rushing about and traveling on crowded buses and trains, but after a rather dull ride of about four hours, we arrived at Callander between Edinburgh and Glasgow. Our stop for the next three nights is the Trossachs Hotel about 9 miles from Callander. After many vain attempts to get a taxi to bring us out here, we finally caught the school bus and are now most comfortably settled. It is a perfectly marvelous place built like a Scottish castle and situated on Loch Achray near Loch Katrine. We arrived in the late afternoon, but they had saved a cold lunch for us. Later we walked up the mountain for a short distance and picked some heather which I shall try to send home. After dinner they had a fine piano and violin duet which played some excellent dance music and everybody joined in. Queen Mother Marie of Yugoslavia is a guest here with her youngest sons, and she came down for a while but took no active part. I didn't meet her, but perhaps could have. She didn't seem to be meeting anybody. She was chewing gum and looked very friendly and agreeable. She is a huge masculine looking woman of about 44. I swear I had the urge to go up to her and ask her to dance, but didn't quite have the gall to do it. She would have declined of course, but I bet she would have been amused and passed it off as just another crazy American who didn't know any better. I did, however, meet Prince Thomaslov, the brother of King Peter who looks to be about 20. He did take a very active part in the dancing and tried to be quite nice, but he seems like a queer sort of duck. The whole family is rather defunct as far as royalty goes.

I am writing today's entry sitting up in the most comfortable bed I've seen in months, with super soft inner spring mattresses. Boy, this is really rough!!!

Sept 14 - Such luxury! Such solid comfort! This morning the maid woke us up with a cup of tea at 8 o'clock and then we continued to lie in bed until 9. There is nothing quite so flattering and nothing which makes one feel so completely a man of leisure as to be served something in bed. Until today we had been dashing madly about from one place to another so we almost welcomed this rainy day which forced us to more or less stay in and relax. I read a book until noon. After lunch the three of us walked the two miles over to Loch Katrine which is the setting of Scott's fine poem "The Lady of the Lake." We stood on the bank and gazed at Ellen's Isle, but since it was misting we didn't take a boat ride. The mountains rose a couple thousand feet above the clear waters of the lake and the beauty of that scene is indescribable. I was so disappointed that the weather was unsatisfactory for making pictures. There is no spot in the British Isles which surpasses this in beauty. After the evening meal the evening passed very pleasantly and quickly with other of the guests here. There are some awfully interesting people here to talk to. This place takes only about 50 or so guests so that one quickly gets to know most of them. A large portion of them are elderly but there are enough young ones to make it worthwhile. I'd like to know the background of some of these individuals.

Sept 15 - This is our last night here at the Trossachs Hotel. It poured rain all day, and I didn't even get out of the house. However, I have thoroughly enjoyed every minute of it just leisurely sitting and reading and talking. Tomorrow we will be on our way to Edinburgh and start another mad scramble to find a place to stay. That is the only unpleasant thing about this whole trip.

There are plenty of pranksters around this place, but one of our practical jokes backfired on us tonight. There is a young lieutenant here who very closely resembles Gen. [Dwight D.] Eisenhower. One of the older ladies, whose intentions are perfectly good but who is a sort of busybody to the annoyance of everybody, was very "confidently" informed that he was a son of the General. She promptly spread the news and everybody was getting a terrific bang out of it until she actually started arranging with the hotel manageress and the lady-inwaiting for him to have an audience with Queen Marie. That, of course, was going a little farther than was intended and when the manageress learned that it was all a hoax, she thought the whole thing was most unfunny because it made her look foolish too, since she had been sucked in on it, and she is trying so awfully hard to impress the queen. As a result she has ordered the perpetrators of the story to leave the first thing in the morning. I hope her anger will not be carried on to Americans in general because this is too nice a spot for others to miss. I'd give most anything to know if the queen found out about this. If she did, she was no doubt amused. It's the lesser individuals who surround the larger personalities who can't appreciate such things.

Sept 16 - The sun was shining briefly early this morning when we left the Trossachs, but it was too early to get good pictures, and I made only one of this whole area. Caught the bus at Callander and stopped at Stirling for a couple of hours, most of which we spent inspecting the castle which is the oldest in Scotland. Most of it was built in the 9th century. Both it and the Edinburgh castle have natural fortifications that should have made them impregnable to all but the modern forms of warfare. This castle was the seat of government before the Edinburgh Castle took over.

Upon arrival in Edinburgh we learned to our disgust that this is another of those blasted British holidays and that most of the stores closed at noon today and will not open for two more days. I had so depended on doing a little early Christmas shopping here. Furthermore, the hotels were all full and so was the Red Cross Club. The crowds of Americans on Princes Street makes Piccadilly look sad. Am sure the people here must get sick of Americans. I would like to be able to get away from them on this leave myself. The Red Cross found us a place in another private home, that of Mrs. Laughton at 36 Alva Street. She is most friendly and hospitable (which I have found to be a true Scottish characteristic).

After a very poor afternoon tea we walked up to the Edinburgh castle but found it was also closed until tomorrow afternoon. That was the last straw. It's not that I cared so much about going in because I'm really getting a bit sick of cathedrals and castles; it's just that we seem to be thwarted at every turn here today. I was, however, able to find a few stores open and bought a few things.

After a nice dinner at the Royal British Hotel (with music by a dilapidated old trio) we went out to see how Edinburgh operated at night, but again everything was closed up by 9:30 even though it was Saturday night. In disgust we went back to our room where our greatest delight of the whole day was the enormous tea that Mrs. Laughton served us.

Edinburgh is one of the cleanest and most beautiful cities in the British Isles. I should like very much to see it sometime after the war under more favorable conditions.

Sept 17 - This being Sunday morning (not that it really made much difference) we lazily got up at 9 o'clock, had the biggest and finest breakfast since our leave started, and caught 11:25 train for York. This terminates our stay in Scotland, but I leave very much impressed with Scotland and its people. I like the Scots very much.

York is an old and proud industrial city in the north of England. We are staying at the Station Hotel and had no difficulty getting in. One thing I discovered on this trip is that contrary to our own country the railway station hotels are usually the best ones in town. The cathedral is the proudest landmark in the city, but there are other points of interest. The old Roman wall around the older part of the city is very interesting. Tonight at the hotel we found the atmosphere immediately much less friendly and more reserved.

Sept 18 - We spent most of this morning shopping and after lunch started for home. That was one of the most miserable train rides I have ever had. Changed trains twice and stood up all the way in the aisle which was crowded like a cattle car. I'm glad to be back—it seems like I have been gone a month. But it was a most enjoyable week and I feel much refreshed.

Sept 19 - All hell broke loose in my absence. The plane losses in this division were terrific last week. One day they lost over forty planes. Another thing, there were four deaths due to anoxia all in one day. Of course there was nothing I could have done about it, but it sure doesn't look good. Losses were higher than the apparent results. The 9th A.F. has made their huge paratroop landing in Holland a couple of days ago and it looks like the war is progressing nicely on all fronts. On the 15th they announced that the 67th Fighter Wing is officially ours, so that adds a little more work. It was terrific the amount of paper that is piled up in my basket. It will take a couple of days to clear it out.

Sept 20 - They showed us the movie "Target for Today" this afternoon.

That is the one they were making here about nine months ago and concerned a typical 8th A.F. mission. It is an exceptionally good film.

Major Anderson reported for duty from Fighter Command today. I expect to use him as medical inspector.

Letter as Written:

Dear Colonel Schuller. We are having a violin recital on Friday Sept 29th at the Red X. Officer's Club at 8 p.m. with Miss Jelly D'Aranyi playing. The Queen of Yugoslavia will be present. It would be so nice if you were able to come—I know she would like to meet you. I hear from Barbara you have been in Scotland for a holiday. How are you. I hope well. Do bring some friends with you.

Yours very sincerely

Betty Bowes-Lyons

Sept 24 - Why, you could have knocked me over with a feather when I received the foregoing letter from Mrs. Bowes-Lyons. Why yes, of course, I shall be delighted. How would one go about refusing an invitation from the sister-in-law of England's queen to meet the Queen of Yugoslavia, anyway?

Longworth has gone on his leave for a week now, and I shall have to do a little work myself. Maj. Anderson, my new assistant, has immediately gotten a case of atypical pneumonia so he will be no good for three weeks or so.

The planes were grounded yesterday and today and the other missions that have been run this past week have been pretty sad, most of it being done through clouds. The poor paratroop force in Holland is having an awful hard time of it and the weather prevents our doing much about it.

Sept 26 - Last night I was invited out to dinner at the home of Sir Earnest Shepperson (where I did my first baby judging). It was strictly social this time and no official duties to perform. It was a very nice meal and was a pleasant evening in a large barn of an English home. Went with the two lads who were with me on leave. They are particular friends of Rance's.

Sept 28 - Received a letter from Mother today that they have purchased a little house in Ozark and expect to move there about the first of the year. It does come as quite a shock when faced with the reality that they are leaving the old home. It just doesn't seem possible. I can't imagine them being anywhere else. But I suppose it has to be. All the other boys are sure that it is the proper thing, and all of them insist that nobody can be gotten to stay with them out at the farm. If that can't be done, then of course there is nothing else they can do but move into town. They have always spoken about doing that in their old age, but now that the time has come I wonder what the psychological reaction in them is going to be. It can either be very good or very bad. I wish I were back there during this change, but it's probably just as well that I'm not.

Sept 29 - Spent the entire day over at Ridgewell trying to unravel another personnel problem, but I think I lost. Col. [Harry P.] Leber, the C.O., has suddenly developed an adversity to Major [Ernest] Gaillard, the group surgeon. That distresses me very much because he has been one of my very best group surgeons up until recently, but he has lost out badly in the last two or three months. It was my first distasteful job when I came to this hq. to remove the station surgeon over at Ridgewell and put Gaillard in, and now we are having to move him out. His trouble dates from soon after he got married 5–6 months ago. It's not that he has exactly neglected his duties at the sick quarters, but he has progressively given more time to his wife and less to his association with the fellows off duty. He has his wife in a little house about three miles off the post and has taken innumerable small irritating liberties with transportation, food, fuel and other things, but over a period of time has developed into a mounting fury. It's not too difficult to see that no small part of the difficulty is jealousy of the married fellows who are themselves homesick for their wives. But Col. Leber has given his order that he will no longer tolerate him on his post, so moved he will be. Am going to get a Maj. Blouner to replace him.

During the last two days our losses over Germany have been very severe. On both days they were heavily jumped by fighters who attacked only a small number of groups. The weather still isn't in our favor either so there is question whether their losses are worth the results at the moment. The 303rd Bomb Gp. is the heavy loser with eleven planes. Jerry still can take out any group he pleases if he chooses to fight. The command is trying to send out too many bombers for the fighter coverage that we have available.

Sept 30 - Last night we really flew high—and then some. It was the night that I accepted the invitation of Mrs. Bowes-Lyons to attend the violin recital at Bedford Red Cross Club, played by the noted French violinist Miss Jelly D'Aranyi. She gave a very exceptional program and it was much enjoyed. I would much rather have heard Yehudi Menuhin who played at one of our stations the night I arrived back from leave, however—too late. The officers who went with me were Col. Whetstone, Lt. Col [Manvel H.] Davis, Lt. Col. Roberts, and Maj. Robert Johnson. The queen of Yugoslavia was there as guest of honor and Mrs. Bowes-Lyon went through with her bargain to present us to her. As I had suspected, she is a jolly old soul and very congenial. After the concert there was a buffet supper, and Mrs. Bowes-Lyon sat me right down by the queen's elbow. We re-hashed our experience at the Trossachs and eased my curiosity by asking her what she would have done had I asked her to dance and she replied that she never, never danced. We talked for a while about various insignificant prattle— what does one talk to queens about anyway? Then I reminded her of how well her mother, Queen Marie of Romania, was received in America some years ago. And she reminded me that her mother was a very, very fine woman. I agreed, but didn't remind her that I didn't think so much of her brother Carol of Romania, or her son King Peter of Yugoslavia (she doesn't either, by the way), or several other of her not so esteemed relatives. She is an ugly old so and so, but she is nice. Mrs. [Jan] Camden was indirectly responsible for our getting in on the "inside" like this. Boy, oh Boy, this old Arkansas hillbilly was sure out of his territory last night. But I was anxious to see if I could do it. 'Twas fun while it lasted.

Late this afternoon Lt. Col. Robert P. Johnson, Maj. Nelson and I went down to Chelmsford to a tea-dance given by the local citizenry for the American officers stationed in Essex. It was a nice affair, as nice as such affairs ever are, but it was such a long ride, and we didn't stay long, but we were there "to represent the General." I hope all my "social" obligations are paid for a while and maybe I can settle down to work. Longworth is just back off his leave tonight and we will have to start work in earnest again.

Oct 1, 1944 - Last night we fulfilled a very important obligation—collecting our pay. It was a very special pay day for me because it amounted to $886.00, the biggest check that ever had my name on. I am indebted to Frank for reminding me that I can collect full longevity pay on all the time that I was in the National Guard in college. It amounted to about $500 back pay since 1942. That is a joke and a graft that I really feel almost ashamed to accept. My pay at the time I was in the guard was $8.00 a month for drilling twice a week. Now as a result of that, my present pay is increased by almost $22.00 a month. I owe Frank something nice for reminding me about it.

Tonight for almost the first time since coming to the E.T.O. I heard a half-hour program by my old favorite, Guy Lombardo and his "Sweetest Music This Side of Heaven." He is very soothing after listening to most of the jive that is forced upon us.

Oct 3 - Mother's latest letter brings the information that they have sold the old home to Grady and Fannie Yates. Will have to admit that the thought of it stuck in my throat, and I could hardly keep from shedding a tear or two, but it seems to me almost as much a part of the family as Mother and Dad themselves, and it is certainly a loss of something very, very dear. But it is just one of those things which happen that can't be helped and which are necessary in the course of events. I shall have to get used to the idea, myself, of not having the old home to go back to, and it is a painful thought. Every man in this war is living and fighting and dying for one thing and there is one thing that is upper most in the conversation—to get back home. Mother and Dad sense that, I know. That's a big reason why they have been so resistant to moving. It's not that I would ever spend much time there anymore, because I won't. But I'm awfully glad for their sake that they have decided to do it if they think they can be happy in town. That's the only thing that really matters. There is nobody better to whom they could have sold the old home than Grady and Fannie.

Oct 9 - The air battle has been going on more or less half-heartedly for some time with the weather the limiting factor, but it bit a mounting fury the last couple of days. Day before yesterday there was extraordinary good results in destroying some oil, rail and power targets on the Baltic near Stettin. There was a loss of only about three planes too. But yesterday was a rough one. They went back to the same general area with a big force, about 480 from this division alone. Results were again good, but this division lost 23 planes (48 in the whole air force) all to flak. The flak was heavier and more accurate than it was ever known to be before. Those losses included Col. [James R.] Luper, the C.O. at Glatton, and Major [Gordon H.] Haggard, the Group Surgeon. Haggard is the first medical officer to be reported as missing in action from this division. He is one of my very best medical officers, and I sure hate to lose him. It was a needless loss, too, because he had gone on at least 14 operations and kept on going. He is the only medic in this division who has gone on more than six, which is too many. It brings up a problem now as to who will take his place. I have some schemes of my own which I shall try to sell to the new C.O., whenever he is appointed.

This afternoon I went to Deenethorpe to coordinate the transfer of

Captain Henry A. Dantzig, flight surgeon. Courtesy of the East Anglia Air War Collection.

Capt. [Henry A.] Dantzig from Thurleigh to Deenethorpe. He is doing a very poor job at Thurleigh and I'm hoping that Maj. [Earl I.] Mulmed can straighten him out. This is his second chance which I'm giving him before giving him the ax. I would have killed him or straightened him out long before this if I had remained in control down at Thurleigh.

This past week Thurleigh had a peculiar death due to anoxia which occurred about 12 hours after first unconsciousness and another which almost died several hours after apparent recovery. These are something new in our experience over here and are very interesting. There is an awful lot about anoxia that we do not know.

Oct 11 - The shifting of personnel is still occupying most of my time at the moment. Maybe I take it too seriously but I actually worry over that sort of thing much more than anything else. But I'd much rather get the fellows properly placed and then do less supervising of their work. A responsible man doesn't desire too much heckling anyway.

Charles P. McKim, flight surgeon with the 306th Bomb Group since the beginning at
Wendover, Utah. Courtesy of the East Anglia Air War Collection.

Yesterday morning Capt. Dantzig came up to protest his transfer. I had
firmly made up my mind that I was not going to be swayed by any degree
of persuasion, but I weakened. Never before had I ever seen a grown man
plead so hard and make so many resolutions so quickly. He practically had
tears in his eyes all the time. My bargain with him was that I'd reconsider
if his squadron commander and the station surgeon were persuaded to ask
me to keep him there. That forced him to make the same pledges to them
that he did to me. They did just that. So we really have him over the barrel
now and if he doesn't come through with his bargain, he is in for a hanging. I think I did right by reconsidering.

But the question that is closest to my heart at the moment is the selection of the Group Surgeon up at Glatton [457th Bomb Group]. The new
C.O. was assigned today, Col. [Harris E.] Rogner from the 94th Combat
Wing. I went to work on him this morning and gave him my best sales talk
on why the medical section there will get the necessary strengthening by
transferring in one of the older and more deserving squadron surgeons
from another group. It is really the preference of the people of the station
to have one of their own men promoted. I did persuade him, however, to
interview my old friend Capt. [Charles P.] McKim from my old group, the

306th. McKim is having dinner with him tonight, while I have my fingers crossed. It's not only that McKim is a personal friend of mine, but he is the oldest squadron surgeon in this theater (in experience) and I believe him the most capable of all the prospects. I have felt very, very badly because I have never been able to do something for him before. The numbers of medical officers of superior quality who are permanent captains is a crime against this Army.

Oct 13 - This is Friday the 13th and something really happened. Late yesterday afternoon, the adjutant sent word around to all sections that it was desired for all officers to attend staff meeting this morning. Gen. [Bartlett] Beaman got up and stated that Gen. Williams had something of vital importance to say. Gen. Williams started out by stating what a smooth running organization this one is and then made the startling announcement that he has received his orders to assume command of a B-29 Air Force and will be leaving in about a week. You could have heard a pin drop. He has been in Command here about 15 months now, for longer than any other commander and it is inevitable that changes will take place, but he is going to be badly missed. Never before have I been associated with a man who had been so respected, so loved and who has so completely commanded the devotion of so many. He is not a politician and does not kiss anybody's hand regardless of his position—yet his superiors are bound to recognize his quiet efficiency and wise judgement. The consistent superior bombing record over a long period of time is proof enough. This headquarters will always look upon Maj. General Robert B. Williams as its greatest leader. Brig. Gen. [Howard M.] Turner is coming up from the 40th Combat Wing to assume command.

My efforts up at Glatton have borne fruit and Capt. McKim is assigned as Group Surgeon and has reported for duty there this afternoon. That is an obligation and a desire that I have wanted to fulfill ever since I have been here, and I feel like it is almost like a major triumph. I did not notify the people up at 8th A.F. until after the complete transfer had been made. They screamed to high heaven when I asked for a captain as a replacement, but they will come across. They still have a bunch of majors they are trying to place.

Oct 18 - Yesterday Capt. Thomas flew me down to Furzedown House[12] which is one of the Air Force Rest Homes we have in south England. For a long time I have been wanting to visit it. We intended to stay for lunch and come home in the afternoon, but it started pouring down rain, and it was

General Robert Boyd Williams. Courtesy of the East Anglia Air War Collection.

General Howard M. Turner. Courtesy of the East Anglia Air War Collection.

impossible for us to fly back, which of course did not make us mad at all. There couldn't have been a better place to get weathered in. Furzedown is as nice as Stanbridge Earls almost. It just doesn't have as much sentiment and tradition, but it's really top notch. We flew back early this morning. Our division is supposed to share it with 9th Air Force. But they are not using it, so I'm going to see to it right off that there will be no vacant beds.

The thing of greatest interest to me was the boxing tournament we attended at Winchester last night. I had heard something about English boxing but even so I was perfectly amazed when I saw it. As for the two contestants themselves, it is just as it's done at home, but the startling thing is that the referee sits in a chair on the outside of the ring. The crowd is instructed to remain perfectly quiet during the round so that the contestants may hear the referee, but may cheer wildly at the end of the round. When they get into a clinch, he tells them to break and they break. When one fouls the other, he calls one over to the edge of the ring and tells him, "Naughty, naughty, you mustn't do that." The fights were done well enough, but I'd just love to see a fight managed like that in Brooklyn.

Oct 20 - Went to Walcott Hall[13] today to attend a meeting of the Fighter station surgeons. It was the first time that I have met any of them except one, I'm sorry to say. It was a good meeting, and I hope not a bad introduction. I must get out on their stations soon and find out how they are running things, more to learn than to instruct them.

Oct 22 - Had the disagreeable task today of accompanying Major Stroud over to the 305th Sta. Hospital to register a complaint against Lt. Col. Bateman for a couple of herniaplasties which he did and which have turned out extremely bad. This is the very first time that I have ever entered or had occasion to enter a complaint against the surgical proficiency of any one of our hospital surgeons, but this one bears plenty of investigating. The hospital C.O. is now investigating it thoroughly. I hate very badly to put somebody else on the pan like this, but good treatment can be had in the Army, and we are going to have it.

Oct 26 - Arrived back for duty this morning after two days in Pinetree and in London. The meeting with Col. [Harry G.] Armstrong was about the same as usual with very little accomplished but a lot of argument. In London I spent a few hours shopping about for a bit of silver that might be used for Christmas gifts. Saw a couple of plays, one called "No Medals" with Fay Compton.[14] It was about the role of the housewife in war time. Fay Compton played a very convincing part and is truly a finished actress.

I think she is perhaps the finest actress that I have seen on the English stage. The other was an operetta called "The Lilac Domino" which had some very nice music but the cast of singers was terrible.

Have just learned that we have taken over another station called Harrington. It is rumored to be a stinker. They have been doing some special low-level stuff with B-24's, but it is anticipated that they will within the next few weeks be converted over to B-17's. Their station has been sort of bounced around from one command to another and really isn't much good for anything at the moment, so they say.[15]

Went up for my introductory session with Gen. Turner, our new Commanding General today. He seems nice enough and had nothing particular to offer in the way of suggestions or criticism. I only hope that I can maintain a status quo with him.

The bombers today went out and bombed Germany by Pathfinder today as usual. The weather is still stinko over the target. They haven't had a real good visual target in over a month. One wonders if the bombing effort is really worth it at the moment.

Oct 27 - Went flying with Maj. Johnson this afternoon in the A-20. Flew up to Norwich and went downtown for a short while. Norwich is one of the older cities on the east coast, and it looks it. It wasn't a particularly good day for flying, but there was a beautiful sunset.

Oct 28 - Made my first call on the new station over at Harrington today. Contrary to previous reports, I find the medical organization in splendid shape. Major Gans, the group surgeon is a good man, and he has what appears to be a nice bunch around him. Their only problems of any great concern at the moment is their abnormally high rate of V.D. I think that station is going to be O.K.

Oct 31 - Today one of our B-17's flew out over the Wash to jettison some bombs because they were unable to land with them, and as they were coming back over the English coast the British ack-ack opened upon it and shot it down from 5000 feet. Fortunately, the crew all bailed out safely. It was a stupid thing for them to do, because they had been properly notified that a friendly plane was approaching the coast, but at the same time there was a flying bomb alert and apparently they became confused due to the clouds. It gave the British gunners some good practice, but it was a little expensive and ruffled up the tempers of the crew which was shot down. I suppose this will be quietly smoothed over.

Nov 3, 1944 - Yesterday our division really caught hell. The German fighters came up in strength for the first time in weeks. There were about 400 of them, and they took out about 27 of our B-17's. Our escorting fighter wing took out over 130 of them and other bombers about 30 more. It was really a royal fight from all reports, and the results of the bombing is unknown because they bombed Merseburg through clouds. The entire Air Force had up over 1100 bombers and 900 fighters. Our losses were about 60 bombers and fighters to their 208 fighters. All records for individual claims were broken yesterday.

Nov 8 - Last night I arrived back from London after having attended the Inter-allied medical meeting on Tuesday plus a day off yesterday. The meeting was a good one, and they had some good lectures, particularly about the medical service in France. Spent most of yesterday shopping about ending up my Christmas shopping.

There certainly are a lot of soldiers in London now. When I went to eat out at the "Willow Run" officers' mess at the Grosvenor House it seemed to me as though it were just as crowded as it was just before D-day. Perhaps some of them are on leave back here from France, but most of them didn't seem to be. It is a perfectly amazing thing how they can serve 2000–3000 officers there within the course of a couple of hours.

At the meeting the other day I ran into three of the fellows with whom I interned at Charity, Maj. [G.F.] Schroeder, Maj. [Blaise] Salatich, and Capt. Chaney.

Nov 9 - Last night all the medical personnel at this station had a party out at a little village near here. Capt. Austin from Molesworth came over with six of his enlisted men and covered the medical service for the station in our absence. We had goose for dinner which was black market and about twice its value, but it was the best outing that some of our men had had since they have been on this station and was well worth it. Corp. Ross, who is getting married in a week or so furnished as material for joking.

Nov 10 - I have been having a lot of difficulty tonight getting my Christmas packages packed. They are very late getting mailed.

Our planes continue to go out regularly every day, but regularly every day they have to bomb through 10/10 clouds and can only do area bombing. It does serve to keep the Germans jittery, perhaps, but one wonders if it is worth it.

Nov 11 - This has been a poor Armistice day. As far as we were concerned there was no such day. But it is Mother's birthday. I've been over here so long I've lost track of how old she is.

Tonight I worked harder than I have in a long time building some boxes to ship my Christmas packages home in. It felt good to get a hammer and saw in my hand for a change. The Army is creating a helpless bunch out of its officers by providing someone to do all the manual labor for us. I am worn out after packing, boxing and wrapping eight packages.

Nov 17 - This has been a perfectly filthy day, low fog and raining a slow drizzle constantly. Lt. Col. [Thomas B.] Morrow and I spent the day, or most of it, driving up to Cottismore to investigate why they still have not recovered the bodies from the wreckage of one of those Molesworth planes that collided in mid-air a week ago. It is another of those situations where there were bombs aboard which did not explode and are in the wreckage. The R.A.F. bomb disposal people cannot get the bombs out until the wreckage is moved and the wreckers cannot move the junk until the bombs are disposed of. Both crews are English and are under separate commands, neither of whom are particularly interested in how soon we recover the bodies. It is hoped that our expressed anxiety over the matter today will stimulate a little action and that our wading mud to our knees and getting wet was not in vain. These mid-aid collisions certainly do make a mess.

Yesterday this division sent out over 500 planes to bomb in front of our lines near Aachen. There were 1200 from the three divisions. They took off in fog and bombed blind through clouds. The infantry asked for it that way and they got it. That is certainly blind faith. But apparently the bombing was successful and the armies are advancing. The bases were closed in though, and they had to land elsewhere on return. That was the first time in several days they have attempted to go out on account of weather. There is certainly no doubt that the weather has been the greatest friend of the Nazi in recent weeks.

Nov 22 - The planes went out in moderate strength yesterday for the first time in 5 days. The weather was bad over Germany as usual, and they didn't see what they bombed. The 398th got off all by themselves above the clouds from everybody else. Thirty enemy fighters made just one pass through them and knocked down 8 of them. This Div. lost about 16 in all. A pretty rough fight for questionable results.

Today I flew with Maj. Thomas up to Atcham in the A-20. We expected to pick up a Cub to fly back, but it was not there. It was a nice flight anyway with "Tommie" rocking that old ship all over the sky dodging Col. [Charles E.] Marion in the P-51. They had a nice dog-fight and lots of fun.

"Tommie" is an excellent pilot, a bit on the conservative side, but he can put enough thrills in it to suit me.

Nov 23 - Today was Thanksgiving Day, or rather Tranksgiving. The dinner was postponed until tonight, but it was worth waiting for. There was lots of good turkey and dressing, peas, potatoes, celery, cranberry sauce and apple pie a-la-mode, also apples and candy. The quartermaster finally let the secret out about why the turkey has been so short here in the E.T.O. on the 2 previous Thanksgivings. Mrs. Roosevelt was over here in 1942 and gave most of it to British hospitals. Last year the Germans sank a big lot of it. This year the program went according to plan.

Nov 24 - Today I made a rather long trip to two of our Fighter Stations, Bodney and East Wretham. Also I stopped in at 3rd Division headquarters on the way back to see Lt. Col. Cohler. It was my first trip to each of those two stations and found them in very good shape. There are still two stations that I have not seen.

Dec 1, 1944 - Have been away for three days including two at Pinetree. Monday I took the day off and spent most of it in London. On Monday night I went on to Pinetree and got in on a big dinner that the medical section at 8th A.F. threw as a going-away party for four of the officers there who are leaving, three of them back to the States. On Tuesday there was a conference on recommended changes in Tables of Organization and Equipment for all our organizations. As usual there was much discussion and little decision, but I did enjoy the evening again when I sat and listened to Lt. Col. Jackson telling about his experiences with the Air Force contingent in Russia for at least four hours. However, I realized after it was all over that, as usual with him, I didn't know what to believe and what not to. So I decided not to repeat any of it. He is convinced, however, that we'll be fighting Russia one day. It was quite evident that the Russians received them with suspicion and showed little tendency to cooperate. I will record one statement he made just to see how it turns out, that the much publicized Crematorium in Poland where several hundred thousand people were systematically killed is just a big hoax and a Russian propaganda story. (Col. Jackson was wrong.)

Next day was the regular monthly meeting which was up to its usual standard, but I did enjoy the morning going through the underground operations building. It is built in a huge cavern excavated into the side of the mountain. It's no different from our operations room however except a little bigger and more elaborate. Spent the following night in London and caught the early morning train back here.

Dec 3 - We are now faced with some far-reaching reorganization. They are now making the combat wings administrative which means they will have some medical officers. That means that some more doctors will quit practicing medicine so they can do paper work and tell others what to do. Along with that we are now going to make some of our sergeants into medical administrative officers. So we are going to have plenty of commotion. The only thing I hate about it is that Sgt. Hinkley in my office is wanting to become an officer which means that I will be losing him. That breaks my heart too because I had just gotten my office force organized exactly like I want it.

A couple of days ago I was given the privilege of choosing an officer for a most enviable assignment, to accompany a plane load of patients back to the States and also receive a 10 day leave there. I could just as easily have submitted my own name, but then I consider myself "indispensable" to my job. I gave it to Maj. Bergener who has been here the same length of time as I and who has a wife and two small children. He has at times recently had some spells of pretty bad depression and he really needs it.

A day or so ago I heard a little story that is so typical of an Englishman's lack of demonstrable emotion. A lady in Bedford had not heard for weeks from her husband who is a Colonel in Burma. But last week she received a cable containing these five words, "Left leg amputated; damn nuisance."

Dec 5 - This morning I called on two Combat Wing Commanders to get their reaction to whom they wished placed into the medical section of their new organization. I knew already whom these two C.O.s wanted so that was easy enough. The next two are going to be the tough ones. I know that neither one of them will have a particular preference, and I'm going to have to recommend. The trouble is I haven't worked it out in my own mind yet. I think I shall sleep on it for another night or so. I'm going to be a lucky man if I can get out of this without making a few enemies among my medical officers.

Dec 11 - Am stalling as much as possible on making recommendations for the new Bomb wing surgeons, but I went to Thurleigh to see Col. [Anthony Q.] Mustoe today about an officer for him. I don't anticipate any difficulty with him. I shall not be making any recommendations on the fourth officer until Gen. [William M.] Gross gets back from the States and starts in picking his own men.

Dec 14 - Col. Mustoe called today and said he was going to ask for Maj. Longworth as his wing surgeon. That shook me for a moment, but it shouldn't because I recommended him to him. It puts me on the spot to try to find myself a good assistant when and if Longworth goes. A good man who would willingly take that job is not going to be too easy to find. I immediately thought of my friend Bill Bunting over in 3rd Division. He's going to come over tomorrow, and I shall feel him out on his attitude when and if. If this change should come off, it is really going to shake my little playhouse with Sgt. Hinkley possibly going about the same time to get a commission as an M.A.C. officer. However, today Gen. Beaman informs me that the wings may not be reorganized so rapidly after all.

Dec 15 - Received Mother's letter of 3 Dec. which stated that right after the sale on Wed. 29 Nov. she and Dad drove into town and have taken up temporary residence with Jewel. Even though I have been trying to get used to the idea for weeks, it still came as quite a shock. At that moment I realized that I do not have a home. Not that it makes any real difference because practically speaking I have no use for one, and if Mother and Dad stayed on the farm indefinitely, I would still never go there for more than a short visit again. But the sentiment attached to it is quite a formidable force. All fellows have something to hang on to and fight to get back to the States for. Most have wives, or children or sweethearts. Mine, of course, has been to get "home"—home meaning primarily the family, but the old farm as well. It is so very difficult to imagine Dad and Mother in any other setting. No matter where they live it wouldn't be home as far as I am concerned. At that moment I realized that I had suddenly joined the ranks of those whose "home is where the hat is." It's so silly, but I just couldn't help shedding a tear. The loss is purely a sentimental one, and it wouldn't make nearly so much difference if I hadn't been thinking for 27 months now about someday getting back home, and actually living for that day. Even though I have been home so little in recent years, I think I have had a greater attachment to going home than most. It is difficult to imagine just what Dad and Mother's emotions were as they drove away that Wednesday afternoon—I can only guess. I shall not forget how I cherished those photographs of the place which Ell sent me six months ago. That was before I heard any talk about moving. But fortunately, as for myself, I will have several months, at least, to get used to the idea before I go back to the States. I expect a prompt and complete recovery.

Dec 16 - Lt. Col. [Manvel H.] Davis, my favorite roommate, left yesterday to go home because of ill health. He has been wanting to go for so long, and it is well that he's on his way. But I did rather hate to see him go. He has been a most pleasant and interesting companion. Major [Martin J.] Her, who is being assigned in his old job, has moved permanently into Col. Davis' bed.

The weather is most foul again, or I should say still. The planes were stood down today, they struggled out yesterday, they were down the two days before, and always they have to bomb through clouds. It would seem that they would find a target they could see just once again.

Last night I accompanied Mrs. Camden to a party at the officers' club at the British Ordnance headquarters at Biggleswade. There weren't many there I knew, and it was a rather stiff affair as far as I was concerned, but it wasn't too bad.

Dec 23 - Lt. Col. Ragan, C.O. of the 303rd Station Hospital invited the station surgeons of those posts which send patients to his hospital, Maj. McNeil and myself to dinner last night, and then had a business session afterwards. It was a good session because we got several things ironed out which should be to the interest of both them and us. Mostly however, it was a gesture on the part of Col. Ragan to have us smoke a peace pipe with him and meet his new chief of surgical service, Lt. Col. Kendall. That is the final result of that campaign I started two months ago to get Lt. Col. Bateman unseated because of lack of surgical proficiency in the job he was holding. It took a lot of pressure to do it, but it was finally brought about. I had three conferences with Col. Ragan, two with Col. Morton and one with a Col. Gardner as well as some of my own officers. I feel very badly about having had to do this, but there is no use having the man there if nobody trusts him. Col. Kendall seems like a very nice fellow and is reputed to be a very capable surgeon. We're all happy about the change, as well as the junior surgical officers at the hospital.

We're right in the middle of picking our new Medical Administrative Corps officers. We've now interviewed about half of them or more. There are some surprisingly intelligent lads among them. It's an awful job to make a fair decision on some of these fellows. We're sure to make some mistakes, however. T/Sgt. Hinkley, in my office, stands right up in there with the rest of them and there is no doubt in my mind that he will make a good officer. We hope to have picked about 14 of them by next week.

Dec 25 - This is the end of my third Christmas in the E.T.O., and it has been a good one - considering. I got an enormous number of gifts from the folks back home which I finished opening last night and things were lively enough around here. A couple of days ago the lounge was thrown open for a party for the kids of Brampton. Each was given a big bag of candy, more than they had seen in years, each made up from bars contributed by officers from PX rations and Christmas boxes. This morning our medical section put on the dog by whipping up a batch of eggnog and inviting over practically every officer and enlisted man in the headquarters starting off with Gen. Turner and all the section heads. The eggnog was really good and turned out to be very much appreciated by all concerned. At noon today the enlisted personnel over at the dispensary here (mainly the WAC's) invited all of the medical officers and EM's over for Christmas dinner. They had moved the beds out of one of the wards and set up a real banquet table and served a wonderful meal with candles, mistletoe and all the trimmings. They even had a little gift package for each of us. The girls really did a good job on it. Tonight we had our Christmas dinner at the mess, which being the second dinner for today might be called sufficient. Furthermore, I was scheduled to go to Mrs. Camden's for dinner at 8 o'clock this evening, but it was scrubbed because of the terrific fog tonight. I didn't mind though because one more dinner would have been just too much. I forgot to mention that this is a white Christmas—the fog is freezing on the fences and vegetation.

For the last three days operational missions have really been rough. They have been taking off in the thick fog and returning as best they could to their home or other bases. For the first time in many weeks, day before yesterday they saw their target, but it was a small force. Yesterday the 8th A.F. sent up in the fog the biggest force of bombers in history. 2,005 four-engine bombers were dispatched, 554 from our division alone. Fortunately, again, the weather was clear over the targets which were tactical targets in the area of the big German counterattack (the "Battle of the Bulge"), bridges, roads, railroads, supply dumps, etc. But none of our bombers came back to this division because of weather. It must be disappointing to the crews to be stranded away from base at Christmas. Some of them have been away from base as long as five to 8 days now without any items of personal equipment at all. Of course that is not as rough as the boys on the line on the ground have it. A note of sarcastic humor was registered by the operations officer at the 67th Fighter Wing who ordered his pilots this morning (Christmas) to be prepared to land away from base and to take

1944 Christmas Party, Headquarters, First Bomb Division Medical Section, Thurman Shuller, seated, third from left. Courtesy of the Thurman Shuller Family Collection.

with themselves 2 blankets and 3 days K rations. Then at the bottom of the order he wrote, "It's tough boys, but that's the way it is—Merry Christmas." K rations for pilots on Christmas day! Those boys must have been fit to be tied. But there's no doubt about it, those boys in Belgium need every bit of support today they can get.

Dec 30 - For several days now we have been back to bombing tactical targets behind the German advance through 10/10 clouds. Even so, they seem to be doing a little good.

Yesterday our board finished up action on making officers out of some of our enlisted men. We approved 12 of the 24 who actually applied. It is now hoped that higher headquarters concurs with our recommendation. Following the regular monthly meeting at Pinetree on Wednesday, I had all the station surgeons up to this headquarters for a real pow wow. Never in the history of human endeavor has there been a meeting of doctors where there has been discussed so little medicine and so much paper work.

Hostilities Cease

January 1, 1945–October 20, 1945

As 1944 turned to 1945, Colonel Shuller began recording the final months of the war in Europe, and the impact that events had on his world in the First Bomb Division, soon to be renamed the First Air Division. His diary entries provide a special window on changes brought about by the closing combat operations of the war.

During January and February 1945, weather persisted to create obstacles for the large-scale missions against occupied Europe. Despite the increasing experience gained from months of operations in the ETO, the opening months of 1945 brought additional casualties from midair collisions, crashes on takeoff, and other fatal mishaps over the skies of England and Ireland, and Shuller's diary presents his continuing frustration over these losses.

By the turn of 1945, the ground war on the continent began to have a significant impact on Eighth Air Force operations, in the air and on the ground. Shuller served on a board selecting soldiers for the Infantry Officers' Candidate School. All across the Eighth and Ninth Air Forces, commands were at work during the first two months of 1945 to satisfy Eisenhower's demands for transfers to the infantry.

Events on the battle line in the previous months revealed serious discrepancies in supporting the coming push in Europe to end the war. Earlier in 1944, Eisenhower recognized that the flow of infantry replacements to the ETO had slowed and worried that he might not have sufficient replacements for a final spring offensive against the Germans. He reasoned that if he did not have adequate replacements in the pipeline, heavy losses along his lines in the coming spring might give the Germans an opportunity to break out and threaten the Allies' final push into Germany.

On December 16, 1944, Germany mounted a counteroffensive against the Allies, and the "ensuing 'Battle of the Bulge' came at a time when the replacement system in the Zone of Interior [United States] was strained to the utmost." Washington signaled Eisenhower that additional replacements would come from the United States, but added that he would have to draw on forces already in the ETO to meet his needs, primarily from support troops, many of them Black soldiers, other ground units, and from the Air Force.[1]

Eisenhower ordered Lt. General John C. H. Lee, who commanded the Communications Zone, to move twenty thousand men from his command to the Ground Force Replacement Command (GFRC) for conversion training. Lee proposed to use volunteers from Negro units in his support commands to provide about a quarter of the twenty thousand needed. To make up the rest of the twenty thousand required, a levy from other Army Air Force and support units across the ETO needed to be implemented. Eisenhower approved the plan and gave Lee instructions to proceed. Lt. General Ben Lear arrived from the United States to take charge of the retraining program for the replacements coming from the Eighth and Ninth Air Forces and other ETO commands. These transferred soldiers would receive infantry conversion training and then be made available for assignment to infantry units on the battle line.[2]

By April 1945, Shuller's diary entries revealed the growing scarcity of bombing targets in Germany. "We are definitely running out of targets. For the first time, we have come to the realization that the mission of the 8th Air Force has already come to an end!" For Shuller, the end of the war in Europe seemed eminent.[3]

Meanwhile, rumors and scuttlebutt circulated the First Air Division about what the future held for the division. Shuller's diary revealed that little had been done in planning for the tactical deployment of the "Occupation Air Force" (OAF as Shuller called it), and what was to be done about the combat air units at every level in the ETO. As spring moved into summer and fall, the confusion was apparent at every step of the way, and Shuller's observations give important clues to the decisions made and not made regarding how the Eighth Air Force, and the First Air Division in particular, would be used in the occupation of Germany and possible operations against Japan in the Pacific. Shuller was part of the senior staff team that traveled many times to Germany to select headquarter sites and plan for the occupation. His movements throughout the period reveal much about the continuing reorganization of the division for postwar Europe.[4]

By early 1945 the Army Air Force was still dealing with the question of air crews and combat fatigue. Shuller had little patience with the inability of command to set a clear and concise policy on combat fatigue or how to handle the problem at division or group levels. Shuller writes of the political pressures coming from changes "in Army Regulations which [state] that only *psychoses and major severe psychoneuroses" diagnoses "will be considered basis for physical disqualification for flying in those individuals who crack under the stress of combat." Shuller's reaction to the politics resulting from this new directive illustrates his confidence and successful experience in dealing with the issue.[5]*

Perhaps Shuller's greatest contribution in this chapter are his observations of reactions to the surrenders of Italy, then Germany, and finally Japan at headquarters and with Shuller's American and British friends and acquaintances in England and elsewhere. His diary entries vividly describe the reactions behind the scenes as the war winds down and the unknown future lies before him.

*

Jan 1, 1945 - This is a good time of the year to start a new book. Little did I realize when I started out on this project that it would become so long and time consuming. The war wasn't supposed to last this long in the first place. I fear the character of these notes has changed a great deal since the beginning, also. At the start I was in such intimate contact with individuals and events that it had a much more personal touch. Now I mention things more or less in generalities. That is unfortunate.

The old year was properly rung out last night at the dance here at the club. It was a remarkably well behaved bunch last night, remarkable because some of the fellows who were celebrating their third New Year's Eve entered into the evening with definite malicious intent.

The year 1944 certainly gave us a lot of changes in the war situation, but I believe the most pessimistic of us thought the war would be nearly over on this date. It is hoped that 1945 will see the end of hostilities in Germany and that we will be back within the limits of the United States before Jan. 1, 1946. That is our toast to the New Year.

Jan 3 - An order has been published that effective yesterday, the 1st Bomb Division will be officially known as the 1st Air Division. That is a good thing because it has become embarrassing to be known as a Bomb Division when we have so many fighters and other units. At the same time, it was announced that we were taking over Alconbury and Cheddington. That brings the number of our stations to 23 and the total strength of the Division to approximately 55,000. That is a sizeable number of men in any Army.

We have suddenly had nine M.A.C.[6] officers descend upon us unexpectedly direct from the States. That may knock us out of getting our sergeants appointed. But that's the way the Army works. I do hate to see all that work go to waste and hate worse not to see some of our deserving sergeants get a break.

They are having considerably more luck bombing the last few days and the losses have been comparatively low. For the last 3–4 days, they have been hitting at railroads visually with considerable luck. This was either the eleventh or twelfth consecutive day with 1000 or more heavy bombers out. Our division averages about 300–400 each day.

Jan 6 - Today Gen. Turner and Gen. Beaman asked me to accompany them up to the 307th Sta. Hosp. near Coventry where Gen. Turner had been invited to present some medals. It was very cloudy, so we drove up—over a 2-hour drive—and arrived just in time for an excellent lunch. Lt. Col. Stinchfield really put on a show for us. It is used as a rehabilitation center for men who have been injured, and they have always over 3000 "trainees." They grade their inmates in classes down to E and as they work up to more strenuous tasks, they are finally placed in class A which means they can do 20 mile hikes with full pack, run the obstacle course, etc. After lunch they showed us first through the Air Corps training set-up which had all sorts of elaborate gadgets including complete B-17, B-24, B-26, A-20 fuselages, complete motors, all sorts of radio equipment and flying equipment. The infantry training school had all sorts of rifles, carbines, mortars, field telephones. They had a remedial gym with rowing machines, stationary bicycles, and exercise machines of all sorts. The physiotherapy department was excellent. All the patients who could walk filed out for the dress parade and review—24 companies of them, and they really put on a swell review. In fact the whole thing would sort of knock ones eye out. Gen. Turner presented four medals and then met all the company commanders. Gen. Turner was tremendously impressed, and I have to admit, it was a wonderful demonstration. But after it was all over, I had the burning desire to steal away from the inspecting party to talk with some of the patients and find out what it is like. I'm very curious to know if they are really doing a job there or whether they are set up to impress inspecting generals.

Jan 8 - Went to our new station at Cheddington today to get acquainted with the medical personnel there and look over the plant. They have only a couple of squadrons there, together with the service personnel. Capt. Mozersky is in charge of the medical organization, and I was delighted to find it in excellent shape. Don't think I will have any difficulty there, except that Mozersky wants to be promoted. It snowed on us part of the way back.

Jan 11 - There has been marvelous weather (local) for three days. It has been snowing at irregular intervals all this time, and there is about three inches of it. It is cold, dry and crisp—the only time in six weeks the air hasn't been saturated with fog. It is more snow than we've had before in England since we've been here. This morning my bike slid out from under me, and I suddenly discovered me picking myself up off the middle of the road, but no injury other than a bruised hip. That's the first fall off a bike I've had in months. The fellows who are from the deep south look upon the snow as a great curiosity.

Yesterday, they ran a mission in spite of the snow and ice and there were five crashes on takeoff. It certainly isn't good flying weather, although it is pleasant on the ground. They are still unable to give visual air support to the fellows fighting in Belgium.

Jan 13 - A light drizzle or mist has completely done away with the snow yesterday and today.

Yesterday afternoon, I attended the meeting at the 49th Sta. Hosp. on trench foot. There has certainly been created a major problem there, and nobody seems to know much about handling it. It doesn't concern us directly, but it is very kin to frostbite which did concern us greatly up until 10 months ago.[7]

This morning I was wakened by the village air raid siren and about a couple minutes later, a buzz bomb came putting along about 500 feet directly over this house. It went on and exploded about 15 miles from here. It is O.K. by me if they turned those things loose in another direction. The V-2's are getting pretty bad in London now.

Jan 17 - We had a new sort of meeting today. Col. Armstrong was here with Maj. Bond, Maj. Powell and Maj. Berger from his office. Instead of calling in the Group surgeons for a meeting as usual, we called in at least one squadron surgeon from each station, the idea being to give the captains a chance to do a little talking and listening and see what makes the wheels turn upstairs. As far as that was concerned, I think the affair was a success. We had them all down to the club afterwards for refreshments for about an hour which gave them all a better chance to get at Col. Armstrong. They seemed to like it.

There has been a recent change in Army Regulations which states that only psychoses and major severe psychoneuroses will be considered [a] basis for physical disqualification for flying in those individuals who crack under the stress of combat, and those who had symptoms not justified on the basis of severe combat stress even though severe will be found physically fit for flying and handled administratively. All of which means that he is physically qualified, but he is not really qualified. That makes no difference to me particularly, because it is not expected to change the way we have been doing it much as far as final disposition is concerned. However, Col. Armstrong wants us to say flatly, "physically fit," which I know will not be satisfactory to the unit commanders, who will want additional explanation. Therefore, I differ rather sharply with him on the subject. After some rather heated words on the subject I, in effect, said, "yes sir!", but actually meant that we in this Division are going to do it the way we want to until told in writing to do otherwise. One day I may get court martialed for insubordination, but as long as they are as confused upstairs about how to dispose of combat failures, we shall continue to do as we have in the past, which has worked wonderfully well in recent weeks.

Jan 19 - Am having a hard time getting my flying time in this month since I have to do double time for not having gotten off the ground last month. So I went to Thurleigh today and took a ride in a B-17. It was supposed to have been a practice bombing mission, but the weather closed in and no bombing was done. In fact, a pretty heavy little snow storm came up.

Yesterday and today I have completed arrangements to send Maj. Munal, 306th Bomb Gp, back to the States on a hospital plane. His father died a few days ago. It is fortunate that we have this means available for getting some of our medical officers back in case of emergency, but it is too bad that it now has to be an emergency before we can do it. He is to have 15 days leave in the States.

Jan 21 - I wouldn't take a months' salary for my experience this afternoon. Right out of the clear sky, Col. Marion asked me to go flying with him in the P-51 which someone has rigged up for piggy-back flying. There was a couple inches of snow everywhere, and the country was beautiful. We flew out to the east coast to watch the bombers come in off a mission to Germany. That old mustang made those bombers look like they were standing perfectly still going around, over and under them. Col. Marion wasn't feeling too well, so he didn't attempt anything violent—only one snap roll—but it was wonderful fun. After flying in so many big planes it seemed strange to be up there with practically no wing at all for support.

Harold D. Munal, the group surgeon with the 306th Bomb Group, had known Colonel Shuller since they were classmates at the School of Military Medicine. They both later joined the 306th Bomb Group at Wendover, Utah, in April 1942. Munal later succeeded Shuller as group surgeon at Thurleigh when Shuller was promoted to Chief Surgeon at First Air Division. Courtesy of the East Anglia Air War Collection.

Then, too, that big plexiglas blister over the cockpit allows perfect vision everywhere except straight ahead. Coming home, he flew at 200 feet at 300 miles an hour for several minutes. At five miles a minute things go by pretty fast. Never in my wildest dreams did I ever think I'd be flying in Uncle Sam's finest combat fighter plane—at least, the best one in action at the present. I really don't blame most bomber pilots for wanting to be fighter pilots. They're more dangerous, but more fun.

Jan 23 - There was a bad crash out at Kimbolton this morning. A Fort loaded with 10-500 lb. bombs stalled on take-off and crashed into a living site. Fortunately, the bombs did not explode for about five minutes so that most of the crew and the fellows in the barracks got out before the bombs went off, but it did an awful lot of damage. There are still some unexploded bombs which prevent full investigation yet, but seven were seriously injured and several killed.

This crash was just one of several we have been having lately. At takeoff it was snowing heavily and visibility was very poor. It was weather that experienced pilots would not be allowed to get off the ground in at home. But over here, the policy is to take chances, knowing there will be some crashes. When they are in such a dangerous game anyway, I suppose they are right. The object is to get the bombs on the target. To do that, they have to face flak which always claims a certain percentage of them. Therefore, the high command figures it is profitable to try to get bombs on the target, knowing also that weather will claim a certain percentage of them too.

Day before yesterday there were five fatal crashes on landing, which represents about 350 planes in the air. I suppose that is considered good at that when these lads flying these big four-engined planes, most of them at least, are 21 years old or less, are less than one year out of flying school, and have less than 500 hours in the air. Kids like that wouldn't be allowed off the ground back home if there were a cloud in the sky. It isn't uncommon to takeoff here with 200 yards visibility and have to go on instruments immediately from the ground up. They're a good bunch, at that, but they fear that weather much more than they fear flak and fighters.

It is doubtful how much good our bombing lately has been doing. Nearly all of it has been through cloud and the targets have been too small to hit blind, mostly railroads and communications centers. Yesterday they destroyed a synthetic oil plant that was already inoperative due to previous bombing. However, it looks good on the home front to be able to write a headline that 1000 heavies went out again today to attack the Reich oil supply.

Jan 29 - Today is the first chance I've had in some time to get out on the stations. Went to King's Cliffe, a fighter station, and Deenethorpe, a bomber station. Today was the first time I have seen fighters landing after a mission. They usually put on quite a show, but it was slowed up today by the heavy ground haze. It is remarkable how much better is the morale of the medical officers with a fighter group. It is difficult to give an adequate reason for that. All of the doctors at King's Cliffe profess to be happy there and not kicking at the traces to go home. Amazing!

Have been having a little trouble with Lt. Col. Green of the Fighter Wing the last couple of days over some equipment he wants to let one of the fighter groups take which is being moved to France. I leave him strictly alone to administer the medical organization of his five stations. He rather resented my bucking a deal he was making this time, but it will do him good to meet a set-back for a change. And I think he will recover. This is the first group to move from England to the Continent from this division. It is altogether possible that all the fighters may eventually move. Perhaps that is a long way off.

Stations within this division have been called on to furnish 600 men to the infantry as reinforcements. This, no doubt, is just the beginning.[8]

There has been snow on the ground for well over a week now and it is snowing again tonight. Also the temperature has been well below freezing all this time. The papers say it is the coldest winter in 25 years. The bombers went out today and yesterday, in spite of the snow after having been grounded for four days.

Feb 3, 1945 - Rain has driven away the snow, and today was fine. To celebrate it, the bombers today gave Berlin its worst daylight bombing of the war. Over 2,000 tons were dropped on Berlin alone, and there were other targets. There was cloud all the way until they approached the target, and then they had the first entirely cloud-free target in about 3 months. They got eight direct hits on the Air Ministry building, and other buildings were hit, including the propaganda ministry, as well as several rail stations and many blocks of thickly settled residential districts. With Berlin in such a turmoil with several million refugees from the Russian front, the damage must have been terrific. I wouldn't be surprised if this wasn't the worst blow of any kind that Berlin has ever had. Out of about 500 planes, the 1st Air Division lost 18, but some of those may turn up tomorrow.

The news from the Russian front is awfully encouraging now. With the Russians well into German territory and practically all of East Prussia overrun, it's hard not to become a little over-optimistic.

Feb 7 – Returned last night from three days in London. One day of it was on "duty" to attend the Inter-allied medical meeting. The other two days were just on pass. I enjoyed it very much. Col. Slagle has been after me to take more time off anyway, not that I need it, but those were the first days I have taken off in over a month. Major Stroud was in London, and we went to a play together on Monday night—saw Noel Coward's "Private Lives" which was light and amusing, but rather unenlightening. Then we went to dinner at the Landsdown Restaurant and met Capt. Vivian and his date. The next day went to see the movie "Since You Went Away." It was a real tear jerker in spots, but I genuinely enjoyed it. I don't know what there was about it that impressed me so, unless it was the vivid portrayal of some real home atmosphere back in the States. Other than that most of my amusements were shopping and sleeping.

The morning session at the medical meeting was most instructive—concerned medical care of the German Army as observed by prisoners of war and by medical officers who have inspected captured German hospitals. All four speakers reported that German medicine now literally stinks. As one expressed it, their medical care of wounded has degenerated back to the pre-Crimean state of deplorable sanitation before Florence Nightingale. One reported that of 1,500 injuries he saw in a hospital, every single one of them was infected and that pus was literally dripping off the beds and running down the floor. They used huge drainage tubes in all wounds and allowed them to drain into kidney basins. One German medical officer told him that they had found modern surgical methods inferior and had gone back to 1914 methods. Dakin's solution irrigations[9] and regular morphine were the routine for all wounds. They did not use the sulfonamides except in rare cases, and had not heard of penicillin. It is difficult to realize a Germany who has been such a leader in medical advances in modem times has sunk to such a sorry state of medical science. All four speakers agreed that they did not learn one single thing from the Germans that could be applied to our advantage in medical care of the wounded.

Feb 14 - Longworth has been gone to London for two days, and it is keeping me humping to run the office and keep up with the outside work too. I am right in the middle of an investigation as to why this division runs a higher non-effective rate due to illness than Second and Third Divisions. This is at the direction of Gen. Turner who is much concerned about it. So am I, for that matter, but am having a very difficult time explaining it. Personally, as a professional man, I secretly revolt at the idea of having to worry about rates when the rates depend so much upon professional judgement, which is something we want to preserve. But still the fact remains, we have more men in quarters and hospital than the other two divisions, which should not be so. I have visited all the stations but three investigating this, and hope to have some sort of answer for the General in a day or so.

One never ceases to be amazed at things these kids on the station can think of. The other day on one of the bomber stations, a bomber was being taxied around the perimeter track when for some unknown reason an English workman was struck by one of the moving propellers and instantly killed. It being the common practice to indicate enemy fighter planes shot down by a particular plane by painting swastikas on the nose, this particular plane made its appearance next day with two swastikas and one teacup on the nose. Needless to say, the teacup was removed when the C.O. saw it.

We have now been giving sulfadiazine on a compulsory basis ½ gm per day as prophylaxis for colds for about 3 weeks. Naturally with anything new, there are bound to be all sorts of objections and complaints attributed to the drug. At one station they weren't using it enthusiastically because it was found it made the flyers sleepy during their afternoon classes. The adjacent base wasn't using it because it kept the men awake at night. It has been responsible for poor landings, loss of weight and marked obesity as well as being accused of being responsible for conditions of much greater concern to a virile young man. But the prize one came to my attention today. A lad at Kimbolton was AWOL because he missed his bus due to shortness of breath from having taken sulfadiazine.

Feb 15 – We had another major incident this morning when the planes tried to take off in the fog. A Chelveston plane crashed into a living site very similar to the one over at Kimbolton three weeks or so ago. As at Kimbolton the bombs did not go off until a few minutes after the crash; so everybody got out of the site except those few actually hit by the plane itself. Only 8 were killed, but about 13 were injured enough to be sent to the hospital. It's getting unsafe even to stay on the ground around these bomber bases. They had two other take-off crashes this morning in the fog. Those three crashed planes alone, less lives and property damage cost almost a million dollars. That's a costly take-off in any man's Army. But I don't know why I should be getting mercenary. Wars are not run on economy.

Feb 16 - This morning I flew with Gen. Turner and Gen. Beaman in the General's fort out with the bombers. We were intending to follow them in as far as our lines and watch them bomb without actually crossing into enemy territory. But it was cloud covered all the way—not one single hole in the clouds. Since we would be unable to see anything, we turned around and came back 12 miles from the French coast. It was a pleasant trip but very monotonous. I was disappointed that we didn't see France. I haven't seen France since last May 1 when I went with them to Reims.

Feb 18 - We are being further drained for the infantry. This month 744 enlisted men were taken from this division against 612 last month. In addition a board is meeting twice a day to select men to be sent to Infantry Officers' Candidate School. I was on the board today and we interviewed 10. Some of them were really sharp and eager lads and will make excellent officers. This drain on personnel is going to cut down on some of our comfort around here. It may even take away the officers' orderlies. There will really be some screaming if that takes place. But actually I don't know why it is essential that we have somebody to sweep our floor and make the beds. When there is a war on, I suppose we can do some of that ourselves. We as officers are getting too soft and dependent. I am ashamed to say I tore a big blister right in the palm of my hand just using a screwdriver the other night. British are much worse though. They have a "batman" for every officer.

Feb 21 - The orderlies have actually been taken away. There is plenty of bitching and moaning around here. We started making our own beds and sweeping out yesterday. As a matter of fact, we should all be thankful we have a bed to sleep in. A few million infantrymen aren't that fortunate. We'll survive, no doubt.

Two of my recent personnel problems came to a temporary conclusion yesterday. I went down to Nuthampstead and had a man-to-man talk with Lt. Col. Lewis P. Ensign, the new C.O., [398th Bomb Group] there about his group surgeon, Maj. [Herman A.] Zampetti. Col. Ensign had called me up a few days ago and requested that Zampetti be removed. However, after discussion yesterday, it was agreed that Zampetti would be left there on trial for a few weeks after the C.O. had called him in and told him what is to be expected of him. Zampetti is Italian, is somewhat obnoxious in his personal appearance, being grossly unkempt most of the time. It now behooves us to get Zampetti on the ball, because I'd sure hate to have to move him. He has never recovered from having been jerked out of a favorite group of his in 1942, and to move him again would ruin him. I greatly admire Col. Ensign for his attitude in the matter. He isn't afraid to look a man in the eye and tell him just what he thinks and what he expects. One of my greatest grievances is a C.O. who snipes at one of his men behind his back and never calls him in on the carpet and tells him where he stands and what is wrong with him. Too often it has been my painful duty to have to do the C.O.'s job by calling the man up to my office and laying the cards out before him. No doubt Zampetti will still be an obnoxious Italian when both Ensign and I get through with him, but it is hoped that we may get him at least to clean himself up a little as well as his dispensary.

Another group surgeon problem has been Maj. [Edward R.] Schumacher, a problem I inherited with Alconbury on Jan. 1. He had gotten into trouble by getting orders to go to France and overstaying his authority by five days. His C.O. who was justifiably unhappy about the whole thing preferred court martial charges against him for A.W.O.L. On the basis of his past excellent record, we got the charges dropped, and he was given only a reprimand. It was hoped that he would react favorably to that, settle down, laugh it off and continue to be a good man. But instead he developed a persecution complex and has soured on the world to such an extent that his C.O. has asked for his removal. No suitable assignment could be found for him in the 8th A.F., so we had to trade him off to USSTAF for another major. When Schumacher found out about it yesterday morning, he got very angry because he was not given a chance to pick his assignment and blames me for giving him the "works." The very audacity of him, who is now hard to place in any job, to feel that he is in a position to pick his assignment. As much as I hate to be really offensive to anyone, it became necessary to tell him to go to hell—"or in words to that effect."

But it's not all personnel war. They are still fighting with the Germans too. They blasted the pants off Nuremburg yesterday and went back there today in cloudy weather. We make a common practice of sending up 432 planes from this division now. That's 36 planes per group. Losses are very low lately—no fighter opposition much.

Feb 23 - There was a most wonderful bomber mission yesterday. There were over 1,400 heavies out (432 from this division) and they hit dozens of different railroad targets in the area between Berlin and Hamburg. The results were excellent, and the losses were very, very few. They bombed from the extraordinary low altitude of 10,000–16,000 feet because there was cloud above that level but perfectly clear below. They evidently caught Jerry by surprise because no fighters came up to meet them, and they missed most of the flak areas. It was a most successful effort in every way. It is said that these particular targets were ordered yesterday by Gen. Eisenhower himself. If that is true, we may consider it a prelude to an offensive in north Germany. It was just the sort of activity which preceded June 6.

I am just now in the midst of writing up some efficiency reports on about 27 medical officers, the ones immediately junior to me. It is a job too to write original descriptions of each officer's personality. I am trying to be perfectly truthful with each one even if it points out a few defects.

I just learned a few days ago from Capt. [Carroll D.] Briscoe, an old

306th pilot who has returned to England after 15 months back in the Z.I., that Lt. [Leroy C.] Sugg was killed in an aircraft accident back in the States. I am the last one to be surprised. He was the pilot who scared me so badly buzzing the airdrome at Thurleigh making his farewell salute to the field in July 1943. In this flying game, the reckless all catch it sooner or later, and that is still the wildest ride I have ever had in an airplane. (Z.I. = Zone of the Interior. That's the U.S.A. to your civilians.)

Feb 24 - Yesterday the boys went back after railroads, again with good results and low losses. It announced on the radio very late last night that an offensive had been launched on the 1st and 9th Army fronts. The rumors about Eisenhower ordering these targets is now confirmed.

Feb 25 - This afternoon I complied with Mrs. McCorquodale's request to make a little speech at a meeting she was having of all the St. John's Officers of Bedfordshire, in spite of a resolution I once made that I'd never have anything else to do with her or any of her functions. I swear I haven't found out yet how to tell that woman, "NO," and make it stick. I had lunch with them, and after the program, there was tea. However, I really enjoyed it. The Great Barford division presented me with a nice antique silver apostle spoon. It was certainly a pleasant surprise and much appreciated. On the night of the 22nd, I went to Bedford to see the Great Barford Cadets put on a musical adaptation of Cinderella. Their voices weren't very good, but they certainly showed a lot of training under the direction of Mrs. Camden. She had a lot of original music in it which was quite good, too.

Feb 26 - The movie tonight was "Rhapsody in Blue," the story of George Gershwin's life and music, and was marvelous. I don't know if it followed the true story, but the music was certainly well produced. I have a great deal more respect for Gershwin's music after seeing that show.

Eighth Air Force has directed that we furnish two medical officers, captains, to be transferred into the 3rd Army. That is going to be a job to make those selections, because anyone who is selected is going to resent awfully being pulled out and sent to the infantry. Here is another time where a man's fate may be decided by the flip of a coin. There is no other really fair way that it can be done, and that by tomorrow noon.

Feb 27 - The two medical officers have been selected for the infantry and their names submitted. I shall be away from the station tomorrow and the next day. I hope I am away when these two find out about it.

March 2, 1945 - Back from London and Pinetree last night. The meeting at 8th A.F. was much the best one we have ever had. Col. [Olin F.] McIlnay was not there and there was less argument. Col. McIlnay's successor, Col. [Joseph A.] Baird, who is relieving him at 2nd Division was there. He is the very image of Col. [Arthur L.] Streeter. That meeting was followed up by our station surgeons' meeting here this afternoon. It was very long and drawn out, but very interesting and instructive.

March 4 - I have made no mention of operations for several days. They have been run off with monotonous regularity on similar targets in a similar manner ever since the offensive west of the Rhine started.[10] This is the 14th consecutive day they have put more than 1,000 bombers (usually 1,400) on railroads, bridges and oil refineries in Germany. Most of those have been visual bombing and with good results. Losses remain around only about 1%, but they have again sent up some fighter opposition the last couple of days with a few planes lost to fighters. Our escort fighters claimed about 60 in the air day before yesterday. The combat crews are not particularly tired, because we have enough crews to rotate them, but the airplanes and ground crews are getting awfully tired.

Jerry sent a couple of bombers over here last night. They dropped one bomb on Bodney, our one station which has been evacuated. It was obviously just a nuisance effort for Goebel's benefit. It has not been definitely known why Jerry has been putting so few planes in the air lately. Every reconnaissance photo of German airdromes shows them filled with airplanes. Maybe they are short of fuel—some say they are short of pilots. They have even lost a lot of their training fields in the Russian drive in Silesia. Besides, it has been unsafe for them to get training planes into the air over Germany without fighter cover for a long time now.

It has just occurred to me that exactly 30 months (2 ½ years) ago tonight I was sitting in the Officers' Club in Newfoundland, having made the first leg of one of the most exciting trips in my life. I well remember how we could hardly sleep because of the anticipation of our arrival in the "theater of war." We reached England wearing our .45's on our belt and fully prepared to handle any Jerry who showed up. We couldn't understand why the English laughed at our gun toting, and we were thus convinced the English didn't know there was a war on. But we were fully prepared to show them how a war should be fought. Things have changed since then. These 2 ½ years now put me in the category of "old-timers," but I'm willing to lose that title any time they say now.

March 6 - The winning streak was broken at 15 missions. Today the 8th

A.F. was stood down partly on account of weather, but mostly on account of need to allow maintenance crews to catch up. There have certainly been a lot of bombs dropped the last two weeks.

March 11 - The bombers have been going out regularly every day after taking only the one day off. Day before yesterday, they had visual bombing on an oil plant, but mostly it is blind bombing. As a general rule, there is very little air opposition, but about a week ago was the last real effort. Unfortunately our night leaflet bombers were returning a few nights ago at the time and place where Jerry planes were crossing into England. The British antiaircraft opened up on them and shot down Lt. Col. [Earle J.] Aber, [Jr.], the commanding officer who has been with them since the beginning. Eight of the crew bailed out, but Col. Aber and his co-pilot went down into the channel. I hope the British were as accurate with the ones they were supposed to shoot down.

All week the appointments for the MAC officers which were recommended 2 ½ months ago have been coming through. That has included my own man, Sgt. Hinkley. I am very happy for him, because he really is a most deserving and sharp young lad. He was sworn in day before yesterday, and we have been enjoying seeing him going through the painful process of being transformed from an enlisted man to an officer. He doesn't feel like he belongs with either bunch now. The enlisted men the first day really gave him a beating by their superpolite "Lieutenant, sir" as a prefix to every statement. But he has taken it well. Tonight he was given the job of escorting the enlisted men's liberty truck into Cambridge. The men will probably give him fits tonight and may want to see how a two-day old officer conducts himself. His being commissioned certainly plays havoc with my office. In the seven months he has been here, we have thrown more and more work to him, and we have depended heavily upon him because he is a lad who can accept responsibility. But one can't stand in the way of advancement for a lad like that, even though we ourselves are worse off. Capt. Hicks and I interviewed 5 sergeants today from each of five stations, but I'm not too hopeful of getting a man of Hinkley's caliber. Unfortunately, the other really smart boys within the division received commissions also.

On the night of the 8th I attended a party given by the medical department from the old 306th Bomb Gp., held at Bedford. It was a nice affair, and I was most proud of my old outfit that night. They were the neatest dressed and best behaved bunch of enlisted men that I have seen in a long time. They continue to have a lot of pride and spirit, even after 30 months in the E.T.O.

March 14 - Yesterday afternoon I drove with seven other senior officers to London to see a private showing of "The Fighting Lady," the documentary Navy film showing the activity of an aircraft carrier in the Pacific. The whole thing is in Technicolor, and the action shots are simply terrific. Maj. Zegart practically went wild when he saw it, because the Air Force has never been able to get any color film. A lot of our Air Force action shots are just as good, but the color makes the difference. The Navy this time has far outstripped anything we have ever done in the way of photography. It's a truly marvelous picture. It is said to have been cut from 3 ¼ million feet of combat film.

March 18 - Yesterday was a typical English day, overcast sky and a great deal of ground haze—not a very good day for flying. But I went on a most enjoyable trip which included three European countries other than England. With Lt. Col. [Hugh G.] Ashcraft as pilot, Maj. [Richard P.] Barry, Col. [Charles E.] Marion, Lt. Weber and myself as passengers, we took off from Kimbolton at 9:20 and landed at LeBourget airdrome just outside Paris at 10:50. Upon circling the airdrome on the approach, it occurred to me that there weren't as many people there to meet us as met Lindbergh at that airdrome 18 years ago. In fact nobody gave two hoots whether we landed there or anywhere else. There were quite a number of French laborers cleaning up around, and some working on a couple of the hangers. The whole place is certainly the worse for wear. Huge craters are everywhere, the runway and perimeter track have been repaired, the control tower and all five of the big hangers, have been bashed around plenty. There was a huge pile of wrecked German planes, but there were also a couple dozen German planes of various shapes and sizes in good working order parked around all sporting new French insignia. We had hoped to eat lunch there, but upon inquiry of the R.A.F. officer who was running the control tower about the possibility of food, he very delicately replied in the negative by saying with a sheepish grin, "You know the Americans are not here anymore." After dropping Col. Marion and Lt. Weber, we proceeded on to Luxembourg. Ashcraft took us over the center of Paris. In spite of the ground haze there was a good view from an altitude of 1500 feet. It was easy to see why everybody raves about Paris—the beautiful wide streets, the big substantial buildings—like nothing at all in England. We flew right down between the Eifel tower and the Arc de Triumphe and over the cathedral of Notre Dame. It all looked just as clean and un-battle-scared as LeBourget was beat up. The only other large place we passed over was Reims, which is also a very lovely place centered by that huge lovely cathedral. The marshalling yards I saw bombed last May 1 showed no signs of damage, though they were bombed many times since. The most battle damage we saw along the route was usually some farm house or small village at a big road junction. Occasionally a patch of woods would look somewhat unhealthy as a result of gunfire. For the most part, however, we saw very little battle damage from the air.

We landed at A93 airdrome a few miles from Luxembourg about 1:00 p.m., or rather I should say landing strip because it is only a bunch of steel matting on a hill top, but it is the only landing strip in the whole of Luxembourg. There were a few tents around, and the control tower is operating in a truck. Having missed our lunch we drove into the city to have a look around. It looked not unlike an American city, and it was only there that it occurred to me that the cars were driving on the right side of the street. I almost got hit looking the wrong way. We found a shop which sold delicious ice cream and cakes, so that held us over for a time. The people didn't seem the least bit concerned about the progress of the war. Only three or four months ago, the Germans were there just as our soldiers are there now. Luxembourg has been overrun in its history so many times that it has just learned to thrive on invading armies. In spite of the fact that only a couple weeks ago, before the Germans were pushed over the Rhine, the front was only 12 miles to the east, it was most evident that there was business as usual. There were a lot of American soldiers around all with tin hats and carrying guns; but a lot of them are now getting ready to move on up with the front. In this whole war, yesterday is the first time I have worn a tin hat—and I had to borrow it.

We picked up Maj. [Roberts P.] Johnson, [Jr.], who had been on temporary duty over there for a month and took off at 4 p.m. The trip was a little longer coming back due to head winds. We flew right over Lille coming out, and over Abbeville going in. Both of those places were well beaten up. At sight of Lille, I thought, of course, of our first operational mission at the 306th in Oct, 1942. In that vicinity were also several V-bomb sites which operated before our occupation. The landscape is certainly churned up with bomb craters all around. We also flew over southern Belgium on the way back, mostly the coal mining district. Having landed first at Honington to drop off a passenger, we got back to Kimbolton about 6:40 p.m.

The trip was exciting to me, not so much for what I saw, but because of all the first hand stories connected with these places that I have been hearing these 30 months. It's marvelous to think of covering all this territory in the course of having a day off. I think aviation is here to stay.

March 23 - For several days we have been having the most remarkable weather. They have been sending out daily a force of around 1,400 bombers (about 450 from this division) and bombing railroads and airdromes visually. They are doing an awfully good job when they can see the target.

Things are looking awfully good on the western front. The first Army bridgehead at Remagen is growing rapidly, and the most amazing thing is the way the 3rd and 7th Armies are completely bottling up and destroying the German armies west of the Rhine. We are all terribly amused at the British newspapers now. With Montgomery sitting quietly in his little sector while all the brilliant fighting is going on, the reporters are hard put to keep Monty's name before the public. But they managed it today. In a small lined column, the Remagen bridgehead was described as well as the "incidental" destruction of a mass of some 100,000 German soldiers in the Saar basin by Patton's army—the headline across the top of the page read, "Monty Has Greatest Smoke Screen in History." We all got a big kick out of that. I wonder if any of them ever stopped to consider how funny that seemed to an outsider. But of course, our own newspapers do the same thing for the Americans back home. After all the British and Americans are about two of a kind on that score.

Tonight I had my first introduction to golf. Capt. Dunbar and I bicycled over to St. Ives after supper and played about 4 holes before it got too dark. We got much more exercise from the bicycle ride than from the golf, but it was a swell moonlight ride home, about 16 miles round trip. I'm hoping to do a little golfing this summer.

March 25 - At last Monty has again captured the imagination of his countrymen. The long awaited airborne invasion came off yesterday in invasion weather. About 40,000 airborne troops were supposed to have been landed across the Rhine opposite Monty's command. But even so, this morning's radio headline went, "Monty throws American 9th Army across Rhine to establish a firm bridgehead." However, there is silence from the English sector, and it is probably that they are in there pitching too.

Our bombers made two trips yesterday for the first time since last summer, and such a marvelous job too. The pictures this morning showed terrific strikes on some six or eight airdromes which our Division attacked.

They will be completely neutralized for several days at least. There is no doubt that our bombers have made a real contribution to the success of this landing. The two days previously, they had dropped huge concentrations of bombs squarely on numerous large German troop encampments in that area, using fragmentation bombs. There's no question that part of their decreased opposition is due to an increasing casualty list.

I believe for the first time in the European war the weather was on our side before and during the big air offensive or any other big thrust. The weather yesterday was supposed to be the finest March day England has seen in 50 years, so said the radio this a.m. But it came off just in time—the weather closed in today, and all the bombers were recalled after take-off.

March 30 - The news on the western front is electrifying. All armies are advancing beyond the Rhine—even Montgomery's. There seems to be no organized resistance anywhere. Only the limited facilities for getting supplies across the Rhine seems to be a limiting factor. Our bombers went after the submarine pens at Bremen today. They were grounded yesterday because of weather. A couple days before that, they scrubbed a mission 10 minutes before they were ready to take off for Frankfort. The trouble was that Patton had gotten ahead of himself so far, they didn't know exactly where he was and were afraid he was already in Frankfort. Every paper now contains the names of a dozen or more German towns captured which have been favorite heavy bomber targets for months—Mannheim, Munster, Ludwigshaven, and all the cities in the Ruhr are now just about cut off.

The last two days in London, including the monthly trip to Pinetree, passed very quickly. March 28 will always be memorable to me for an extra special reason.

April 2, 1945 - Yesterday was Easter Sunday, but it sure didn't seem like it. It might have been just most any other Sunday. Military religious services of any kind are not the best, but an Easter service is most unsatisfying. Hope I celebrate next Easter at a civilian church.

Today was my first experience at skeet shooting. On the first round my score was unmentionable, but the second showed some improvement. Improvement—that's the important thing.

April 3 - For about two weeks, I had been working up to this trip today. For some time I have had the urge to go on another operational mission, and I got permission from Gen. Turner on Sunday. Last night I got word that there was chance of a good one, and upon checking at operations at

11:00 last night, found that the target was Kiel, Germany and that weather was expected to be good. I immediately called my friend Col. [William S.] Raper, who is C.O. at the 303rd Bomb Gp. and made arrangements to go with his group. He was hoping to go himself.

It was an early mission, I got up at 2 a.m. after 2 hours sleep, shaved, went to Molesworth for a 3 a.m. breakfast and a 4 AM. briefing. Take-off was scheduled for 7 a.m. At briefing, Raper learned that the wing C.O. vetoed his going on a mission, but he arranged for me to go with a Lt. [Thomas F.] Kahler and was introduced to him at briefing. He was small and mousy looking and looked not at all like a pilot, but I trusted Raper's judgement. We were briefed for Kiel; bombing altitude 26,000 feet, which suited me fine because there were supposed to be over 100 heavy flak guns at the target and there was supposed to be little cloud over the target. The only thing I didn't like about the trip as planned was that extremely long trip over water. The thing I did like was that we were to be over actual German territory only 55 minutes. One can't have everything to his own choosing. After briefing, Kahler helped me check out some electrically heated flying clothing from the equipment room. I had all the other equipment already. He then went to the ship, and I went back to the mess hall with Raper to have a cup of coffee with him to help pass away the time till take off.

At the mess hall, I was subjected to the usual stress of combat because while there, a call came in stating that the time schedule had been set up 6 ½ hours—6 ½ hours, no one had ever heard of such a time change before. That would make take off time about 1:30 p.m. Raper took me over to his quarters, and I slept until 11:00. And strangely, I slept soundly without the least bit of nervousness of anticipation.

I went out to the plane about 12:30 and found the crew in the tent next to the dispersal area, all of them already dressed. So I hurriedly got dressed and went into the tent to meet the crew. It began to drizzle rain a little, and some of the fellows expressed the hope the whole thing would be called off. For some reason the crew all seemed a little apprehensive about this trip.

But it was not called off, and at 1:17, the plane roared down the runway and heavily lifted its load of 6-1000 lb. bombs off the runway. We climbed steadily and at 5,000 feet started up through overcast, and it soon became heavy instrument flying. Eight minutes later, we broke out into clear sunshine at 8,000 feet, and in the meantime I had gained confidence in my pilot because of the smoothness and certainty with which he handled that heavy plane on instruments. In 12 more minutes we were on oxygen at 11,000 feet and beginning to pick up some of the other planes in the formation.

At 2:45, we were scheduled to be assembled and start toward the east coast, and we did, but some of the planes did not get in position until well on the way out over the sea. Raper was really burned up about that when we got back. At 3:15, 2 hours after take-off, we passed out over the coast of England to the North Sea at 18,500 feet. I made a note that the temperature reading was –32° C.

Fifteen minutes out, the #3 engine started running rough and throwing out black smoke. My heart gave a jump because I immediately saw ourselves going all the way on three engines and attracting all the enemy fighters in the sky. It continued the way to target and then quit smoking after the bombs were dropped. At 4:35, we had completed that long haul across the North Sea and entered Germany just below Denmark at 27,000 feet. At that point, we put on our flak suits. The thermometer at that altitude read –45° C. It was the coldest altitude I had ever experienced before, but I was absolutely warm as toast because the electrically heated suit was working splendidly.

At 4:45, 10 minutes inside Germany, I noted the first flak below the group ahead of us. It was so far off the formation that it didn't cause much concern. But only a couple minutes later, the bomb bay doors of all the planes were opened, and my heart came up in my mouth for the first time at the realization that "this is it" and that in a few minutes, we would be over the target and those 100+ flak guns. About 10 minutes before this, we had begun to see some of our own escorting P-51's, and by now, they were thick all around. We were glad to see them too, because we know that north Germany had the biggest concentration of jet planes. The bombing run was 8 minutes long, but it seemed like an eternity. I had my camera along and was all cocked and primed to snap a picture of "bombs away" of the ship on our right. But between watching the flak and a few other distracting factors, I snapped my picture a little late I think. One thing strange about taking that picture was that I had much difficulty seeing the numbers on the film to roll it up to the next number, and it was only after I moved it into the direct sunlight that I was able to see the numbers at all. The flak was moderately heavy around the group ahead of us, but for the most part it was below and inaccurate. None got to our altitude of 27,000 feet—but I'm not complaining. Upon return, not a single plane in our group reported battle damage. The target was completely obscured by cloud, and we didn't know if we hit the large oil depot which was our target.

After leaving the target, we turned north and came back across the peninsula just south of the border of Denmark. At that location there was only about 5/10 clouds. One of the gunners remarked over the interphone, "We were lucky that the target was completely covered." I thought that was a remarkable statement, though not at all surprising. He was simply expressing the attitude of 90% of the flyers in being more concerned about getting 35 missions done safely than in being able to see the target and stand a better chance of hitting it. That's the whole American attitude about this war—but even at that, we don't seem to be doing so badly these days in the air and on the ground.

At 5:34, we left the coast of Germany without my having seen any of the Fatherland except a few patches through the cloud. I was rather sorry, but not really too disappointed—besides, I too felt a lot safer since the Krauts were unable to see us. The descent was gradual, and the trip back was long. Fortunately, I had prepared for the trip back by taking along A Tree Grows in Brooklyn. I had thought I might even read it on the way to the target while flying over the water, but it was much too exciting for that. At 7:30, I was gratified to see the English coast again. It was 8:55, however, and just after sundown before we were able to land. That made about 7 hours 40 minutes actual flying time. The trip was called a "milk run" by all concerned. About 800 planes also went along.[11]

Just before landing, it dawned upon me with a flash why I had difficulty seeing the numbers on my film over the target. Because of the excitement of the situation and the altitude, I had gotten relatively anoxic. That was true even though I know all my oxygen equipment was working properly. For months our radar operators have been complaining about their scopes working perfectly until they get to the target, then a lot of them seem to get fuzzy over the target. I am convinced that those radar operators have exactly the same trouble I had over the target. Col. Cobler from the 3rd Division has thought for two or three months that relative anoxia has been to blame, but I didn't pay too much attention to it. Now I know he is right, and it can be easily corrected by turning up the oxygen supply a little for the radar operators. If that corrects the difficulty, then the observation which I accidentally made on a cheap box camera today will add tremendously to the blind bombing accuracy of 1st Div. aircraft. It's too bad I didn't demonstrate that to myself months ago. I went on this mission just for the hell of it, and it may turn out to be most worthwhile and beneficial. If so, it refutes my old argument that flight surgeons have no place on operational missions. I shall go into this problem with our radar navigators tomorrow.

April 4 - Went to Cambridge tonight on the liberty run to see a play which turned out to be very poor. I went a couple weeks ago to a ballet which was also poor. It looks like I have a run of bad luck there because they usually have good plays in Cambridge, so they say. I have spent very little time in that town, although it is very interesting and only 20 miles away. We, back in the States, used to speak of Cambridge with a tone of reverence, sort of like talking about the Bible. To a lot of officers and enlisted men at this headquarters, Cambridge will be, henceforth, "that town the liberty run went to."

April 9 - Went with Maj. Coppage to Podington today to have a look at the sick quarters. Yesterday morning an alcohol burner exploded and burned out the entire office section, the treatment rooms, pharmacy, dental offices and kitchen. Maj. Henry, the station surgeon was much more calm about it than usual. The air ministry is trying to say the war is too near over to worry about rebuilding it. We say, however, that the sick quarters is the one place which will continue to function after V-E day. I think we will get our way.

April 11 - The bombing the last 2–3 days has been superior. Mostly the targets have been airdromes and the destruction has been tremendous. It is impossible to permanently knock out an airfield, but if you can put out enough of them simultaneously, Jerry has no place to land his planes. The logic of that was evident yesterday when the fighter planes went down to strafe airdromes and destroyed almost 300 enemy planes on the ground. They caught them concentrated on unbombed areas of a few airdromes and even parked along road sides. The 8th A.F. lost 25 bombers yesterday, but the Luftwaffe took a much worse beating. Their fighters were up yesterday in strength again, which shows they are not completely licked even at this late date.

I am getting to be disgustingly athletic here of late. Day before yesterday I played 2 games of volleyball before supper and then played 9 holes of golf after supper on the course over at St. Ives. Last night after supper, it was several games of badminton. Now I shall rest a week to recover.

Today I spoke briefly to the meeting of the P.F.F. [radar] navigators here at this headquarters regarding the possible inefficiency at altitude due to relative anoxia and told them what to look for and what we are doing about it. In a week we expect to have all the radar navigator oxygen regulators changed to give a greater oxygen flow. I'm anxious to see the results.

April 12 - Tonight I entertained Lt. Col. McEwen, Lt. Col. Fortune and Lt. Col. Kane from the hospital at Diddington. We fortunately had steak and ice cream, and they really enjoyed it. Longworth and some of the brass around here joined in to make it a good little party.

The one very sour note of the evening was the notification that Major [John C.] Walker, the group surgeon of the 91st Bomb Gp., was killed in a plane crash this afternoon. He was in a B-17 which was accidentally struck by a friendly P-51 which was making passes at it. It's such a terrible shame, and it has certainly ruined the medical organization at that station. He is the only one who was worth much there, and I shall have to try to sell the Group Commander on the idea of importing an outside man. Walker is one of the old originals who arrived here in Sept. 1942, and one of our most likeable medical officers. Only two days ago he spent the entire morning showing five of us, including some high powered visitors from Diddington, around his station, and we had lunch with him. He showed the visitors a lot of crashed planes that day. He is the one officer in the whole division who has begged most to try to fix up some way for him to get home for just a few days, and he has been doing this for the last six months. It's just as if he had a premonition that something was going to happen. Others want to go home too, of course, but he seemed to me to display an abnormal anxiety about getting home for a man who is single—to the point where I almost got annoyed at him. It makes one wonder about some psychic medium.[12]

April 13 - The news on the radio this morning that President Roosevelt died suddenly last night came as a tremendous shock to everybody. Even Roosevelt's opponents all concede that this is a most inopportune time for this tragedy to happen, though most everybody expected it sooner or later. Though Truman deserves the benefit of the doubt, since he is certainly an unknown as far as great responsibility is concerned, everybody is justifiably jittery about his leadership at a time like this. In fact, it seems to me there is a bit of chagrin on the face of most, and fewer people are today bragging about having voted the Democratic ticket last fall. The English are certainly taking it hard—and they should.

April 15 - Went to memorial services for President Roosevelt this afternoon. The little chapel was filled to overflowing, even Gen. Beaman was there. Thank goodness we are not going to have to wear black arm bands for a month as is customary in peacetime. It was a nice service.

Gen. Turner's promotion to Major General was announced today. The reaction to it was pathetic. There was no comment, no particular feeling about it at the headquarters. When Gen. Williams got his promotion to Maj. Gen., there was not a single officer at the headquarters who was not proud of him and happy for him, and few failed to express it in one way or another. Today I particularly observed for the reaction, and over a period of 16 hours I have heard only 2 different people make a comment. The coolness toward him is getting to be too obvious, and there are those who openly criticize and are antagonistic toward him. That is a most unhealthy sign. Unless he commands the respect and leadership of his staff, officers, he is lost. It is only natural for a staff to be proud of its headquarters and its commander, and if it is worth its salt, it will think it is the best headquarters in existence. This staff feels it has a good headquarters in spite of the Commanding General. It is difficult to know exactly what is the matter entirely. As far as I am concerned, he has made it difficult for me to see him. Others have the same difficulty. I fear for our organization under these circumstances.

Yesterday the bombers went to the French coast near Bordeaux, and they went back there today. They spent their time bombing gun emplacements, which is a job for fighter bombers. We are definitely running out of targets. For the first time, we have come to the realization that the mission of the 8th Air Force has already come to an end! It has been several days since we have had a target that could not just as well be bombed by a tactical Air Force. In fact, there are very few targets left in Germany to bomb—only in the Munich-Regensburg area. The Russians have even excluded Berlin from available targets. A couple days ago this division sent about 250 heavy bombers to knock out a little marshalling yard so small that only a small percentage of the bombs could possibly hit it, and which could have been knocked out just as well with a dozen fighter bombers. It is the belief of some that we are now keeping up our activity just to keep the name of the 8th A.F. in the limelight.

Thurleigh had a bad plane crash yesterday which killed 10 including Emily Rea, the girl formerly with the Officer's Red Cross Club in Bedford. They were on their way to north Ireland and crashed smack into the Isle of Mann. Capt. Butterfield, the squadron operations officer, and several other outstanding personnel were on the plane. These crashes on routine flights are getting entirely too frequent around here.[13]

April 19 - Yesterday was a most delightful day off, the first one I have had this month. Capt. Kent invited me to go with him and a couple of officers from Podington to attend a couple of plays at Stratford-on-Avon. We drove over in time for lunch, saw "Twelfth Night" in the afternoon, had supper, then saw "Othello" at night, and returned back to the station about midnight. "Twelfth Night" was well acted, but I didn't get much of a kick out of it, but "Othello" was the finest performance I have ever seen of any play on the stage, not that I am any authority on plays. I was completely unfamiliar with any part of Othello and really didn't know what to expect, exactly. But it held me practically on the edge of the seat most of the way through. By less gifted actors, it could be very dull, I'm sure. Though it is a terribly difficult play to do well, according to those who know, it was the top in dramatics the way it was done in the Shakespeare Memorial Theater at Stratford-on-Avon. Kent is quite a dramatic critic himself, and he insists it was just a shade below Paul Robeson,[14] who packed them in at New York last season. Never did I think I'd ever be so enthusiastic about anything Shakespeare.

They are still going out every day to rail targets in Germany, anywhere they can find one. We are having clear weather now such as we seldom see in England, but the targets are scarcely worth the trouble. Bombing accuracy during this clear weather has been for the most part, superior. The ground forces continue to take targets which have stricken terror into our Air Force time and again—Magdeburg, Leipzig, Nuremburg. Both Bremen and Emden are just about down and out too. Things are moving rapidly now.

April 22 - Last night I learned that Lt. Kahler, the pilot I rode with to Kiel on April 3, was shot down this last week. He was on his 33rd mission. I hated awfully bad to hear that. He was a very fine young chap and an excellent crew commander as well as a good pilot. The war still isn't over.[15]

April 25 - At long last I have made that first trip into Paris. I say first because I intend to go back there again. On Sunday afternoon, 22 April, Nowack and I went over to 3rd Division and spent the night with Col. [Eugene S.] Coler. On Monday morning we took off with Lt. Col. Young from 2nd Division and went to France in a 3rd Division fortress from Honington. We landed about 1030 hours at Villa Coublay and went on over to USSTAF Headquarters which is at St. Germaine, one of the suburbs of Paris. We were in conference with various individuals of the surgeon's office most of the rest of the day, and even had quite a long session with General [Malcolm C.] Grow himself. This was the purpose of our visit, to discuss medical problems associated with plans for re-deployment either directly to the Pacific or indirectly via the U.S.A. The meeting was worthwhile—I think. But having completed most of our business on Monday, we spent the entire of Tuesday in Paris.

Words just are not adequate to describe the beauty of Paris at this season. The others were more interested in doing a little shopping, but since there is nothing of value that can be bought there, I preferred to break away from the party and take the Red Cross conducted tour of the city. Purely by accident I ran squarely into Lt. Murphy, one of the original nurses formerly with the little hospital at Las Vegas, Nevada. She is with a hospital stationed in Paris. We had a most enjoyable time discussing some things in common during the tour.

We saw the usual points of interest which, are a "must" on any tourist list—the Arc de Triomphe and the tomb of the unknown soldier, the Eiffel Tower, the Trocadero, Napoleon's Tomb, Notre Dame, Sacre Coer, Place de la Concord, and a ride up the Champs d 'Elysees. I got a particularly big kick out of visiting Napoleon's tomb, partly because it is architecturally one of the finest buildings I have ever seen, but mainly because I was reminded of those publicity pictures of Hitler strutting around the tomb in 1940. Here we were walking around the same spot. There just isn't any other city in the world to my knowledge which will compare in beauty to Paris. It is a delightful mixture of the very old and historic with the ultramodern, with all periods in between represented by the best of the period. London just isn't to be mentioned in the same breath with Paris as far as beauty of the city is concerned. The streets are very wide and there is a profusion of trees which are now fully leafed. The Champs d' Elysees cannot be compared to any other street I know.

We had supper at the Casual Officers' Mess, and afterwards went to the night club called Bal Tabarin, one which was universally recommended to us as having the best show of its kind in Paris, even better than the Folies Begere. And it did turn out to be one of the most beautiful productions I have ever seen on a stage. The women were displayed in various stages of undress and before the show was over, we had seen quite an assortment of mammary glands, but the whole thing was presented without even any suggestion of vulgarity and in a true artistic fashion. The staging was something which might even give ideas to Cecil B. DeMille. The average French woman does not measure up to the reputation which has been given them, but some of them meet all the specifications.

My most peculiar experience at the Bal Tabarin was in going to the men's room during the evening. It was quite a strange thing for me to see a couple women standing not more than 8 feet away from the row of urinals and collecting 2 francs from each man after or while he was buttoning his pants. That is proper and customary in France. The street urinals with only a small screen around them are always a source of wonder and humor to every American on his first trip to Paris.

This morning we stayed out at headquarters for a conference again with the people at USSTAF, tying up any loose ends on our conference. We took off again by fortress this afternoon from Villa Coublay and fortunately, we had a pilot who was kind enough to deliver us right to our destinations. I landed at Kimbolton at 5 o'clock completing a most enjoyable and educational short trip to Gay Paree.

I forgot to mention a real thrill I had the first night over there. We had been inside the officers' club after supper for a couple of hours, and when we walked out on the terrace after dark, there was Paris only 10 miles or so away, brightly lighted (or so it seemed to me). I just couldn't believe my eyes—I have been so anxious to see that sight again. The last lighted city I saw was Springfield, Mass, on the night of 3 Sept. 1942. That was almost 32 months ago and seems such a long time. It was like stepping out into an entirely different world for a moment.

April 26 - This morning, the first thing back on duty, I learned that a couple days ago, we had another plane pile into the Isle of Mann on the way to North Ireland. That is getting to be too common. This one had the amazing number of 31 on it, four officers and 27 enlisted men, all instantly killed except 2 who died soon afterward. This plane was from the 381st Gp. at Ridgewell.[16]

This morning I was called into the office of Maj. Schapp, the security officer, and given a dressing down about a letter of mine which I had written to Manning back home and which had been intercepted because of some censorable material in it. I had written him a few details about my mission to Kiel 3 weeks ago. The censor took a very, very dim view of that. It is conceded that I did say a number of things which conflicted with existing regulations, but certainly nothing the Germans do not know in detail. This is the first time one of my letters has ever been intercepted.

Croix de Guerre with Palm, presented May 4, 1945. Left to right: Robison B. Patton, Jr., Thurman Shuller, Roberts P. Johnson Jr., Joseph F. Damidovic, Herbert M. Mason. Courtesy of the Thurman Shuller Family Collection.

April 29 - The above mentioned scrape with the security officer has resulted in a reprimand from Gen. Beaman. It won't have to be filed with my record, fortunately. Gen. Beaman said he hated to have to sign it, and I hated to have him do it, but justice must be had, so they say.

There has not been a mission since 25 April in which our division sent some 250 or so planes to Pilsen, Czechoslovakia and lost eight [aircraft], six to flak and two to a mid-air collision over the target. With German territory rapidly narrowing and targets becoming so scarce, the raid of 25 April 1945 may well be the last. It is ironic that there should have been so many planes lost on that one.

May 2, 1945 - The radio late tonight announces that Italy has been surrendered as well as Berlin itself. It can't be much longer now, surely.

Today I have named Maj. Wise to be flight surgeon on a 1st Bomb. Div. fortress crew which is to make a 30-day tour of the Pacific battle area for reporting to this headquarters. Why do I always have to be dishing out these juicy plums to others when I would much rather have such a trip myself?

May 4 - At last, I am a hero! I have a medal even if it is a foreign decoration. A French Lt. General was here today and presented some sixty of the awards of the Croix de Guerre to officers of this division, of which I received one. There were 12 officers at this headquarters to receive them, 10 present. I was given one simply because I happened to be a section head, not that I have contributed anything at all as far as the French are concerned. But in spite of the fact that the Croix de Guerre was given out in ridiculously large numbers after the last war, I am a little proud of the fact that the command here saw fit to nominate me for the award. It was quite a ceremony with a band and a reviewing stand. After playing the Marseillaise and the Star Spangled Banner, the presentation took place. The traditional kiss was given with the awards to the four generals, but we lesser fry had to be satisfied with a handshake. After shaking my hand he remarked, "Huh! A doctor."

The radio program was interrupted tonight with the news flash that all northwestern Germany, Holland and Denmark has been surrendered. That is wonderful news. Surely the end will be only a matter of two or three days.

May 6 - My 31st birthday was very routine except that in the late afternoon Lt. Col. Johnson came by and took me out to Sir Ernest Shepperoon's place for tea.

May 7 - This is what we have been fighting for. This morning about 9:30, I was in Col. [Fred C.] Slagle's office when a teletype message came in which said that Gen. Eisenhower announces that the German high command signed unconditional surrender terms to become effective one minute after midnight tomorrow night. We have waited so long for this, but the end has been so gradual that there appeared to be nothing dramatic about it. Col. Slagle remarked, "I have been at this headquarters over 3 years just waiting for this very same teletype message, and now that it is here, it doesn't mean much more to me than any other message." Gen. Beaman called us together at 10 o'clock and made the official announcement.

May 8 - This is a date to remember in years to come! This is officially V-E day. Mr. Churchill made his announcement at 3 p.m., and the King at 9 p.m.. The headquarters made some effort to maintain business as usual, but especially this afternoon there was little or no work anywhere. Mrs. Evans, across the street from the headquarters, opened up a case of gin she had bought and stored away in 1939 which she had been saving especially for V-day, and by the time she had invited over most of the officers, nobody was in much of a mood to work. At 1:30 p.m. we had a real formation with band and flags out on the softball field and had a Thanksgiving service, led by Gen. Beaman. He made such a nice tittle speech. The Catholic, Protestant and Jewish chaplains all had their say. The theme all, however, was caution about too enthusiastic celebration because of our brothers in arms in the Pacific. Tonight the ordnance section set off a tremendous lot of flares which had been left over. It made a remarkable display. This has been a day few of us will forget.

May 10 - Yesterday I went with 22 other officers over to Stratford-on-Avon for a double header of plays at the Shakespeare Memorial Theater which included Goldsmith's "She Stoops to Conquer" and Shakespeare's "Anthony and Cleopatra." They were much enjoyed by all. That is an awfully good company of players over there. I have seen four plays over there in the last 3 weeks, and a number of the players had leading parts in all four of them. I can't understand how they can remember their lines. We got lost on the way home, and it was 2:30 a.m. when we got home.

This morning I finished giving individual briefings to each group surgeon on the procedure for processing physical examinations and other medical records. This is going to mean a lot of work for most groups for the next few days.

This afternoon, I have started out on what I hoped to be a nice adventure. Am beginning a 4-day period of temporary duty with the 811 Air Evacuation Squadron at Grove, which is just South of Oxford. McKim is with me. We were driven down by car. Near Aylesbury, we saw a bit of excitement on the side of the road and stopped to investigate. There were 5 small boys of about 8 years lying on the road who had their feet and legs in various stages of being blown off. They had found some small bombs about 2 lb. in weight in a nearby field and were carrying them and getting ready to get on a bus, when one of the boys evidentially dropped one. At the time we arrived, there was only a man and a woman with a first aid kit, and much confused. After about 15 minutes ambulances and medical personnel began to arrive from nearby camps. One child had one leg so nearly off that we just snipped it the rest of the way off. One other had both feet so nearly off that I'm sure they were amputated at the hospital. All the others had broken legs too. The remarkable thing was that there was a sum total of no more than a dozen whines out of all 5 of them, and not a single one cried. One tittle rascal, after I had splinted his two broken legs and placed him on a litter, looked up and sheepishly asked, "Got any gum?" Those were the only words the child spoke all during the time. They reminded me of that year at the Children's Hospital in Little Rock. I have always maintained that small boys are the best patients in the world—provided their mothers are not around. These were as bad war casualties as I have seen all during the war, and these only 2 days after V-E day.

We have arrived at Grove tonight and are all set to get an early start in the morning.

At 2:30 this afternoon just before leaving my home station, I attended a presentation of awards meeting at the conference room and was flabbergasted to hear my own name called for the award of the Air Medal. The citation said the usual thing about meritorious achievement while participating in aerial combat heavy bomber missions over enemy territory. Gen. Turner said it was for my observations on anoxia at altitude in connection with vision. It was certainly a surprise and undeserved honor. The medal is usually given after 6 operational missions, and I have done only two.

May 11 - Today we flew in a C-47 piloted by a Lt. Merritt over to an airdrome several miles northeast of Nuremburg to pick up some patients to bring back to England. It was an eight o'clock take off. There were no flight nurses because all of them had been given the day off to attend the wedding of one of them, so we went along with one of the medical enlisted men. Nor was there any freight to be hauled in that direction as there sometimes is. The pilot was most friendly and anxious to show us all the sights. We went in over Aachen, Duren and Cologne and others. Such destruction I have never seen before. It does no good to see pictures of it. One has to see the entire expanse to appreciate it. Duren was the flattest of all, with several blocks in the center of town with not even a piece of a wall siding anywhere. We had hoped to pick up a few souvenirs, but we were on the ground only an hour or so, so we couldn't leave the station. Those beautiful hangars were all intact except the windows, but the inside and the furnishings certainly gave evidence that our G.I.'s don't tread lightly when they go through a place.

Air evacuation has about played out as far as really sick patients. In fact our load on return consisted of 27 hungry British ex-prisoners. The sightseeing was much more profitable than the observation of air evacuation.

May 14 - The interval since last writing was mainly spent in Paris. Two days ago we took off in a C-46 which was hauling some troops to Paris, since there was no interesting air evac flight that day either. We picked up our troops (about 35 of them) at Stanstead. When we landed there, we saw the most amazing collection of aircraft any of us had ever seen. There were supposed to be 700 aircraft there, of which 500 were B-17's. Imagine that—as many as our whole division ever put up on a maximum effort, and not one of them had ever seen combat. And I'm wondering if any of them will ever be used. What a waste! But 2 ½ years ago there were weeks after weeks when we couldn't get even one new plane.

We caught the bus into Paris for lunch, then we spent the entire afternoon looking for a place to stay. Since we didn't really have any authorization to be in Paris, we couldn't get any authorized billets. The unrequisitioned hotels will not accept Americans by agreement with the Army. An American Red Cross girl at an Officers' Red Cross Club finally found us a room at a Salvation Army Leave home for British soldiers. It was a real nice room with bath. We just had time to get our supper and get to the Folies Bergere. The Folies were quite disappointing—the scenery and lighting were excellent, but the routines very poor. The Bal Tabarin which I visited last time was much superior.

Yesterday morning McKim took the conducted rubber-neck tour of Paris while I went out to the Central Records Bureau to try to find where Henderson is. Found he had been in a hospital in Verdun so that didn't help any. In the afternoon, we walked, walked and then some more. We should surely know our way about Paris now. Last night we struck out after supper to see a little of the notorious Parisian night life—and we saw in no uncertain terms.

We had planned to spend this morning shopping, but to our sorrow, we discovered this was a holiday and none of the shops were open. After lunch we returned to Villa Coublay and caught a ride on a Fort coming to within 5 miles of our home base. That terminated our temporary duty with the Air Evacuation Squadron. Oh well, it wasn't intended that we devote much of our attentions to air evacuation anyway.

I arrive back here to learn that Longworth, my assistant, has been transferred into another headquarters. Even though I have been expecting this, it came as a sudden shock, and I'm suddenly faced with the necessity of getting a new helper. I shall worry about that tomorrow.

May 15 - The dam broke today. An order came down last night which stated what every bomb group (except one) would do, and every change is to be completed in about 3 weeks. Two groups are being transferred to Marseilles, two to Casablanca, and two to the 9th Air Force. The others are going home. The fighter wing is unsettled yet. It is anticipated that our headquarters will eventually be transferred to the 9th Air Force and move to the continent. That relieves all tension of uncertainty certainly, but what a blow. The great 1st Air Division of which we have been so justly proud is suddenly disintegrating like a soap bubble. In spite of all I had hoped, it looks like I am certain to be banished to the occupational air force.

May 16 - Today I made a "command" flight with Gen. Turner and Gen. Beaman over Holland, the Ruhr and up the Rhine River. As badly as I needed to work, I couldn't very well refuse. There just isn't anything left in those Ruhr cities. But they have at least cleaned enough rubble out of the streets to remove the road blocks, and there were a few people in wagons, on bicycles and on foot to be seen. There was no living thing to be seen anywhere in the more central sections of Germany.

May 17 - My new assistant, Capt. Lusk, reported for duty this afternoon. I'm expecting him to be an excellent man.

I have really been making enemies thick and fast the last two or three days. Am pulling some of the fellows with least overseas experience out of the groups which are going home and replacing them with some of the older fellows who are in groups which are staying. Is there screaming!

May 23 - Capt. T.R Stepman, the officer who was with me at Las Vegas, Nevada, has just come overseas and has joined this command. I'm assigning him to the 92nd Bomb Gp. It sure is good to see him and talk over old times when we were new in the Army together. I like Stepman very, very much. He has married a Gentile girl.

The readjustment and reshuffling of doctors among the groups which are going home is working out better than I dared hope. Some of them got a little sore, but less sore than I expected. It was accomplished only because the command here at this headquarters stood squarely behind me and made the changes even though the groups objected. It isn't usual for this headquarters to force things on the group without their will, and I took this as a real vote of confidence.

The final chapter of my E.T.O. romance closed today. Received a letter confirming her marriage yesterday to her fiancé of 4 years who has been a British medical officer in Burma all these years, and is just back. For 1 ½ years, we saw each other at sometimes frequent, sometimes irregular intervals. It's an excellent ending for the both of us, because on more than one occasion, I have thought how nice it would be to have her as a wife, and I doubt that it would work. One can't put off such considerations forever, but I'm still hoping to be living in America again someday. She is a perfectly wonderful little girl, though. I hope she will be happy—and I suppose she will.[17]

The night of 19 May, I had as guests for supper, Lt. LaChasse and Lt. Wilkins and tonight, the great Capt. Bill Casey. All are just back from the German Prisoner of War camps and are awaiting transportation back to the States. LaChasse was with Capt. Olsen, who was shot down on the first raid the old 306th made in Oct 1942. Casey and Wilkins have been in prison since the spring of 1943. The excitement of seeing these lads is indescribable. We have been waiting for this a long time. Casey had to leave shortly after supper tonight, but LaChasse and Wilkins stayed the other night until 2 a.m., talking excitedly about their experiences, and we hung onto every word of it. They didn't seem to have had it so badly until they started moving as the Germans fell back. They are very appreciative of little kindnesses and are enjoying their new freedom to its fullest, particularly food. It's very gratifying to see them put away an enormous plate of food. Of all the interesting things they told, I think I was most impressed with their discovery that tooth powder was excellent for making cakes rise, and with their escape tunnel which was equipped with a trolley car during the process of digging, with electric fights and with an air conditioning system constructed of a rowing machine, a barracks bag for a bellows and a conducting pipe made of Klim (dried milk) cans. I wish we could see all of our P.O.W.s, but most of them will be evacuated through France. We are seeing only those who hitch-hiked directly to England by plane.

June 2, 1945 - Have found it a little difficult to get down to writing the last few days. I have been busy—but not that busy. It has been a peculiar feeling of let-down and lack of enthusiasm for anything. Have not figured out exactly what is behind it, but for the very first time, I notice that I am losing interest, or something. Perhaps that is inevitable with the end of hostilities and with so many of my army friends getting ready to take-off for the States. Maybe it's just homesickness. I don't like to feel this way. I hate to think that I am worn-out, even though I have been overseas for 33 months. Haven't had a day off since I came back from Paris, and am going to London for a couple days day after tomorrow.

Last night Lt. Col. [Nathan I.] Roberts, Lt. Col. [Roberts P.] Johnson, [Jr.], and I went to Deenethorpe to have supper with some of the staff. It was just a little social farewell call. Am going to miss Earl Mulmed up there. The night before we threw a real roaring party for Col. [Guy V.]

Whetstone who was leaving yesterday. It was the finest farewell tribute that any of our officers had had, and Whetstone was really flattered. Today I drove through the airdrome at Molesworth, and it was so lonesome and sad looking, it made one want to cry. There was one lone fortress on the field which was too lame to get off the ground. It is just impossible to realize that things are breaking up so rapidly. We went over to the 303rd Sta. Hospital to pick up some supplies that they were getting ready to throw away. They are closing down and have already gotten rid of their patients.

June 6 - Tonight a large number of the officers of this headquarters turned out for a "farewell" reception given by the Earl and Countess of Sandwich at the George Hotel in Huntingdon. They are a weather beaten old couple, but they are king bees in this country. It was too stuffy for me and I left at 9 o'clock.

June 8 - I have been fighting tooth and toe nail the last two days about a personnel change which has been ordered by higher headquarters against our wish, but I had to admit defeat this afternoon. The bosses here at this headquarters were behind me, but 8th A.F. headquarters couldn't be budged. I had Maj. Mozersky all set to go back to the States with a unit which is returning, when he decides he sees a 90-day job in Germany which he wants before he leaves and gets a friend of his in higher headquarters to direct that it be arranged. So this order comes down to assign him as an overage in a group which is remaining with the occupational air force and send him away on temporary duty for 90 days. We have hard enough time keeping our majors from piling up on us without directing us to keep some more. Although, I must admit this tactic was somewhat similar to some tricks I resorted to myself recently, I guess it just hurts my pride a little to have to submit to the same treatment.

June 9 - Today I went with 18 other officers from this headquarters on a flight in a C-53[18] to Kassel, Germany. It was a planned tour to demonstrate the effectivity of high altitude bombing, which we saw in abundance. It was my first tour through a bombed German town. It was about a four-hour tour through all the downtown district, and about four industrial plants which the 8th A.F. bombed with great accuracy. It is simply impossible to describe the destruction of that town. Except in the outskirts, no buildings are habitable. The downtown district is nothing at all but rubble which has been swept off the street as far as the curb. The real destruction of the town was done one night in Oct 1944 when the R.A.F. dropped 2,000 tons of bombs. It isn't known just how many were killed that night, but it's generally estimated between 40,000–60,000. Although it is 8 months later, it is estimated that there are still tens of thousands of bodies still buried under the rubble, and it still smells badly on a warm day. When one realizes this is just one city in Germany and that dozens [of] others are just like it or even worse, one can only then begin to see just how badly that country has been destroyed. The reactions of the German civilians to us were 100% the same. As we drove down the street, each man, woman or child stopped where he was and just stared with a uniformly expressionless face. They all looked exactly the same way. No smile, no scowl, but just a cold blank expression of defeat and of hate. Our troops are in for [it] and are already experiencing a miserable time in Germany. The German people will never really be conquered.

June 10 - We learned today that one of the 351st Bomb Gp. planes from Polebrook crashed yesterday on the way over to Valley to take off for home. It ran into a hill in Wales and all 20 passengers were killed. That is such a tragedy. Those lads had been sweating this war out over here for 2 years and get knocked off on the way home. Military aircraft just aren't too safe.

This reminds me that I forgot to mention one week ago today that I had lunch with Maj. Fay Bounds, navigator, at Polebrook. It was good to see one of the old hometown fellows again. He came over recently on an ordinary crew as a major and in 2 ½ months ran off 16 missions before the war was over. They all said at Polebrook, he was a swell fellow and a splendid navigator. He has already gone back to the States with the flight echelon.

June 11 - Received the first letter from Mother since they learned I was not coming home yet. I am certainly thankful she recognizes Army authority, and that there is nothing we can do about it. I have read several letters fellows here have received from their folks at home which beg them to come home as if they had it in their power to pick up and go when they got ready. Some have actually accused the men of not wanting to come home—men whom I know are just eating their hearts out to go home. That is such a thoughtless thing to do and only makes things worse. How fortunate I am to have parents who are so grand and brave about it.

June 13 - Made out a new will today and mailed it to Dad. I hope it will never be opened for cause.

June 14 - Had a most delightful trip today. Lt. Col. Roberts invited various officers to go to London with him to meet some of the big-shots of the city of London whom he met on some of his Masonic functions. There were seven of us in the party. We arrived in time for lunch with Sir

Frederick Roland, one of the chief aldermen and several other city dignitaries. Sir Frederick then took us at 1 o'clock to the Guildhall of London (the city courthouse) where we attended the meeting of the Common Council of the city of London, presided over by the Lord Mayor of London. The Lord mayor entered with much pomp and ceremony with all his robes and jewels. At the close of the session, he stopped, and we were presented to him and he chatted with us for a while. His name is Sir Frank Alexander and he seems like a nice old duck. We were then shown over the Guildhall, including all the bombed-out portions and at the end, were each presented with a rare copy of the history of the Guildhall, autographed by Sir Frederick and the chief commoner.

We were then taken to the Old Bailey, which is the most famous London court and prison. I have wanted very much to see the Old Bailey because it figures so much in English stories. Lord Haw-Haw[19] is expected there tomorrow and will probably be tried there. We sat for a few minutes in court and saw all the white wigs and other things peculiar to English courts. We met the Lord High Sheriff as well as others, and went all through the building including the jail (and the bombed-out portion also). Nearly all the public buildings are damaged because they are located in the vicinity of St. Paul's cathedral, which is the worst bombed section of the city.

It was only 2 days ago that Gen. Eisenhower was presented the freedom of the city by these same people. They were profuse in their praise of Gen. Eisenhower and were struck by his simplicity and genuine friendliness. I think they were sincere too. He seems to have completely overwhelmed them. For that to be true, when they have tried so hard to build up Montgomery as their hero, is a major American triumph. Eisenhower will surely be known in years to come as not only a great soldier, but one of the most accomplished statesmen of our time.

This little trip was a rare and exclusive privilege which came about for me only because some Americans were invited, and I happened to be around when the invitations were handed out. As far as I know, it's the only thing I have gotten out of the Masons, but I really enjoyed it and will not soon forget.

One interesting bit of history I picked up is that the city of London was never actually captured by William the Conqueror, but instead he granted them a charter in the 11th century without taking them. Therefore, still holding to tradition, the Lord Major is technically the "king" of London, and the King of England doesn't dare enter the square mile which constitutes the governmental center of the Borough of London without first asking the permission of the Mayor.

England is so steeped in tradition they can never change. That's why there will always be an England.

June 16 - Early this morning I got up and went to Grafton-Underwood to catch a plane to Istres, France (near Marseilles) where the 40th Wing is setting up to operate their two groups. It was a 3¾ hour flight which would make it about 650–700 miles south. It is only about 7 miles from the Mediterranean, but we didn't see it. They are setting up in the awfulest barren spot you ever saw. It is hot and dry, no vegetation, and the formation reminds one of Arizona or the desert of California. They are going to live in tents under real field conditions, which is quite a fall from the relative convenience they have had in England. Longworth took me all over the camp and to the spot where they are setting up the wing head-quarters. I hadn't realized there was actually desert in France. The last 75 miles across the Rhone Valley on either side is very, very rough and moun-tainous—such a contrast to the France we have been seeing in the north. The purpose of the flight for the ship in which I rode was to haul chairs for the officers' club—rather an expensive freight rate. After 3 hours, I had finished my business, and we returned to England in time for supper, fly-ing on instruments through rain much of the way. The 7½ hours flying time really tired me out.

There are a large number of German P.W.'s down there working on the airdrome. Most of them are young and most unimpressive looking fellows. They are fed on rather short rations I understand. Hope they're doing the same back in the States now. At the camp there everybody refers to them as "the supermen." They look anything else but.

In my humble opinion, it is cause for distress that our Armies are in-structed to withdraw 150 miles to allow the Russians to take up occupa-tion to a "pre-arranged zone of occupation." It is a mistake to expect the cooperation from Russia that most people generally do. Nothing will be accomplished except to give her just that much more land to Communize. It is realized it will take a lot of men to police Germany, but it must be done, and strongly—no more to control Germany than to impress Russia that we are still on the continent in force. Russia has never been given to cooperation yet, and there is no reason to suspect she will soon learn how. I hate to have to be a member of that occupation force because I know we are going to be perfectly miserable, but I am willing to do it for a while so I can be in a position to demand the same sacrifice of others. Patton is to be criticized for telling a class of youngsters they'll be fighting the next war, because it implies that this one is fought in vain even before it is finished. But he spoke what he felt, no doubt, and I agree. There will be no real peace in our time. Like Germany, Russia will also be impressed only by force. The day we come to blows will be a tragedy for the world. (Note: This paragraph was written in 1945.)

June 18 - Today I made that command performance I have intended for many months—went flying with Gen. Beaman in his AT-6. He is 53 and quite a nervous individual, but he hasn't killed himself yet. As a matter of fact, he did a very good job of flying the ship; a little rough on the controls but O.K. It was a very pleasant 1½ hour ride. I am ashamed that I have been here for 22 months without ever riding with him before.

June 19 - Drove down to Pinetree today for a short conference with [Colonel John M.] Talbot who is now the 8th A.F. surgeon since Col. Armstrong left. Took Hicks and McNeil with me. After leaving Pinetree, we went on over to the home of some of Hick's relatives and bought a lot of cherries for the mess—and ourselves.

I never cease to be intrigued by all the varieties of names which English pubs have, and always notice them every time I'm out driving. The English pub is truly a great national institution. But the names all run toward a certain type and all bear evidence of their being named for objects common to the public centuries ago when most of them were named—The "head" series is a common type such as The Queen's Head, The King's Head, The Duke's Head, The Nag's Head. The most common ones have to do with farm animals or implements such as The Wheat Sheaf, The Barley Sheaf, The White Horse, The Wagon & Horses, The Black Cat, The Plow, The Plow and Team, The Sow and Pigs. Then there are such familiar things such as The Bell, The Three Bells—The Anchor, The Crown, The Three Horseshoes. These could go on indefinitely. But two I've seen strike me as being particularly funny—The Snort and Whistle and The Wait for the Wagon. If I could get the film I'd start a collection of photographs of pub signs. That would be a most interesting collection.

June 21 - Squadron Leader Bumpass, R.A.F. officer who has worked in this headquarters as a British liaison flying control officer, has been "posted" to another assignment incidental to his job being finished here. Today he bought a barrel of beer and placed it on the bar for all with a caption over it which read "Sq./Ldr. Bumpass. Thanks, Yanks, for a wizard [fabulous] 2 years." He has been a swell fellow, and so have a couple other of the half dozen R.A.F. officers we have had about.

June 24 - Capt. Lusk and I drove up to 3rd Div. today for a short conference with Col. [Eugene S.] Coler about the personnel he is leaving in the three groups which will be transferred to us. It looks like everything is under control. We had a nice lunch too.

June 26 - Thus was another day devoted entirely to "education." I was almost afraid after these 3 years (almost), I might actually leave England without having witnessed their national sport, but today was it. Lt. Col. Errol Holmes, who is our British liaison flak officer and has been with us all along, also happens to be the Babe Ruth of English cricket, having played on the English championship team all over the world prior to the war. He had invited some of the officers from this headquarters to go up to Sheffield to see the match between England and Australia. Although he is well past his prime, he is still playing on the English team.

We arrived at 12:45 and the game had started at 11:30, or rather I should say the playing had started at 11.30 because the game had started on Saturday, and this was the third day they had been playing on that game. It was the first game of cricket any of us had seen (Maj. McNeil, Maj. Cargill or myself) so we sat in a complete confusion until they took time out for lunch. Then Errol took us under his wing and turned us over to his wife who explained it to us as it went along.

The most amazing thing is that a batter might bat all day long. In fact one who was batting when we arrived had started out at 11:30 and was not put out until the middle of the afternoon, a total of about four hours.

At 1:30 they all took off for lunch. After 45 minutes, the same batters got back up and started in again. At 4:15 they called time for tea and after 30 minutes, they resumed the bitter but gentlemanly conflict.

One of the customs of the game involved cheering (orderly clapping of the hands) at specified times. For instance, a couple of the players during the afternoon scored more than 60 runs each. On their 50th run, they were given a very special round of applause because they had passed the 50 mark. I asked what happened when they passed 100 and was told he would be entitled to a bit more applause. In the same way when the Australian team passed the 200 mark (total) they were offered a round of cheering in the typical English reserved manner.

I was disappointed not to see Errol Hohnes[20] at bat, but he was playing in the field all day, having batted on the two previous days. The game was over about 5:30. They all agreed that it was a very exciting match, and being Americans, we were in no position to disagree. The English had won by about 50 runs. As a matter of fact, we had, under able assistance and constant prompting, caught on to all the main points of the game by the end and were beginning to see some virtue in it, but if I had hold of the rule book, I think I could change a few rules and liven it up a bit. I thoroughly enjoyed the experience, to my surprise, but I wouldn't care to see another cricket game soon.

July 2, 1945 - Have already gotten in my required flying time for the month. Last night I went over to Alconbury and made a night flight with the 36th [Bomb] Squadron. The main reason for the flight was that I wished to make a flight in a B-24. It would be disgraceful to say I have been a heavy bomber man all these years without ever so much as being inside a B-24. Furthermore, I have never made a real night celestial navigation flight since coming to England. I hate night flying and just wouldn't do it before the end of the war when proper lights could not be used, but felt it was about time I refreshed myself with some of the problems, so conveniently, I killed two birds with one stone. I flew the ship for 15–20 minutes. Being so fond of the old battle wagon, I could hardly be expected to give an unprejudiced opinion on the B-24, but did find the flight interesting, though it was 5 hours long, and we did not land until almost 3 a.m.

July 4 - It seems strange to actually be celebrating this as a holiday. The celebration consisted of nobody reporting for work except a skeleton staff of one officer and one enlisted man in each section. I let Lusk do the honors today while I went into Bedford and conducted a little business and flubbed around with Tommie in the C-45 this afternoon. He gets a big kick out of letting me fly it. I'm a stinker of a pilot. But it was wonderful weather and lots of fun.

Beginning last Sunday, we no longer have staff meetings on Sundays, and we operate with a skeleton staff on those days. This is for the first time since 7 Dec. 1941 that I have seen Sunday observed otherwise than as a regular duty day, I took the first duty day myself. This is our very first step toward reconversion to peacetime status.

Tonight the ordnance boys are shooting off some aerial flares—some [of] which were left over from operations. This is our 4th of July celebration. They do make a pretty display. Xander, who is doing most of the firing, is looped to the gills.

July 5 - This morning at 9:15 Lt. Col. Ashcraft took off from Alconbury

Thurman Shuller (right) and General Beaman at Villacoublay airdrome. Courtesy of the Thurman Shuller Family Collection.

in the C-45 to take Brig. Gen. Beaman to Germany to look at some possible sites for location of our headquarters. I was fortunate enough to get on this trip. McNeil also flew over with us. We landed after a 3 hour flight at Bad Kissengen, near Schweinfurt, the location of the 9th A.F. headquarters. We had lunch there and drove about 80 miles south through Surzburg to Bad Mergentheim, a possible location. It is a bath resort center and has several resort hotels which could be perfectly adapted for our use. The 63rd Infantry division is occupying it at the moment, but they expect to leave in a couple months or so. The commanding general was not there, but we had supper with one of his lieutenants, and a very good one at that. Gen. Beaman felt without looking further that this is our place, if we can get it. Upon return, we stopped at the airdrome where one of our Bomb Groups is to locate. It is a pitiful mess. There is absolutely nothing there. The buildings are flat and they are even rebuilding the runway. We are spending the night at 9th A.F. They sure aren't standing short. They have all the resort hotels sewed up and are really living in comfort.

Tonight I met Col. Hall, the new 9th A.F. surgeon who will be my boss, and had a long talk with Lt. Col. Geo. Richardson, an assistant who is returning to the States in a couple of days. We interned together at Charity. Medically speaking, I have accomplished nothing on this trip except to meet the fellows, but that's all I expected to do.

July 6 - About 11 o'clock we took off from Bad Kissengen for Munich via Nuremburg in the most stinking weather. But we got there safely, had lunch with Lt. Col. [William R.] Laidlaw, who is in Munich on a special press project, and then started out by car in the afternoon for Garmish, where there is another possible site. It was a wonderful drive through the most fertile and beautiful country I have ever seen. Garmish is in the shadow of the Bavarian Alps and surrounded on three sides by 6,000 foot peaks still covered by snow. It is also a resort with innumerable small hotels, but a little more scattered. It is less adapted for our use, but if we were more interested in a comfortable and lovely spot for living than in commanding some Bomb Groups, this would certainly be the place.

The primitive hand methods of cutting and stacking hay interested me. And I don't believe it is the result of the war either. There is something most characteristic about the Bavarian peasants and their houses. The war has certainly affected their transportation. A few still have teams of horses, some have teams of oxen, some have one horse and an ox, some have one ox, and some even hitch milk cows to wagons. It was of interest to me that Bavarian oxen are hitched to a wagon by running the trace chain around the forehead and attached to the horns of the animals so that they pushed with their heads.

It was an odd feeling to be riding about the streets of Munich and in front of Hitler's beer hall as well as other hallowed places of Hitler. We saw Dr. Ley's[21] home. The beautiful city of Munich is lying in complete destruction. They have cleaned the rubble back off the main streets as far as the fronts of the buildings, but they haven't started to tackle the inside of them. They have actually run a narrow gauge railroad down the side of several streets to carry away the rubble. In spite of all this, the streets seemed to be relatively crowded. It is the first time I have seen German crowds.

We took off after supper and flew back as far as Paris tonight, but I didn't get settled in our rooms until after 11 o'clock, so there is little to do but go to bed. It is practically unheard of to come to Paris just to sleep.

July 7 - We got up early this morning (8:30) to be on our way back. Gen.

Major General Howard M. Turner, commanding the First Air Division, receives the keys to the city of Bedford. Courtesy of the East Anglia Air War Collection.

Beaman's rank got us a Cadillac to take us back to Villa Coublay to the plane, and we did a little detouring on the way for sightseeing purposes. It is the first time Gen. Beaman has seen Paris since the last war, and he seemed to enjoy it as much as the rest of us. We drove through Versailles on the way back. We took off just after 11:00 and got back here in time for late lunch. This was the end of the most interesting short trip I have taken overseas, and most enjoyable, although it was in the conduct of business. Gen. Beaman is one of the finest men I know and was lots of fun.

July 8 - Tonight the boys are raising Cain down the hall. It is a farewell party for Tom Morrow. One by one, our old-timers are leaving. Tom is supposed to get out of the service.

July 12 - This afternoon I took my first golf lesson at Bedford. It was quite an experience and was certainly worthwhile provided I really get interested in the game. Mr. Moore charged only 5 shillings for a 45 minute lesson, which is ridiculously cheap by U.S. standards.

July 19 - Today was quite a "do" in Bedford. The mayor and town council presented the freedom of the city to Gen. Turner. It was quite an impressive ceremony with the major and aldermen in their red robes trimmed with mink. They all came in with much pomp and ceremony, made a couple of long speeches about how happy they have been to have the 1st Air Division stations in their midst and how much they appreciated its contribution to England, thus to their town, Bedford. Then Gen. Turner was presented the scroll in a beautiful silver cask, amidst much flashing of camera bulbs, of course, followed by a speech of thanks on behalf of his command. Gen. Turner made a very nice speech and rather did himself proud.

Although the "freedom of the city" bears no privileges, the city considers it the highest honor it can bestow upon one, and it is only the fourth time it has been given in 40 years. It is the first time it has been given to anyone other than a British citizen. So it was quite a gesture on their part.

Afterwards there was tea at the Town Hall. It is now the standing saying that this means another cluster to our "tea" ribbon.

July 24 - Today I have committed myself. They circulated blanks to all requesting statement as to desires concerning remaining in the service until the defeat of Japan. Since I know perfectly well a doctor my age has no possible chance of getting out, anyway, I elected to sign as preferring to remain for the duration of the emergency. Am hoping that those who signed will be given first choice on any possible leave in the future. At any rate, I know I won't be in the service longer by having signed.

Still we have no place definitely assigned us for our headquarters. Nobody in higher headquarters seems to be particularly interested, and in fact, there has been no outward demonstration of great concern on the part of our Commanding General. I'm personally getting worried about it, because I sure don't care to sleep in tents this winter. Naturally the ground armies are not going to evacuate anything voluntarily, and USSTAF and ETO headquarters are both so confused with personnel changes now, they don't know if they are coming or going.

July 28 - Lusk and I went over to 3rd Div. today and visited the three groups which are soon to be transferred to this command for the O.A.F. The doctors with the groups seem to be in a relatively good frame of mind about staying in the O.A.F. for a while. About 1/3 of the personnel have over 85 points. It was a nice trip.

Last night Gen. Turner came back from USSTAF with the news that it is now likely that this headquarters will not be under the 9th A.F. at all, but may be on a par with that Hqs., and we are to have command of only the heavy bombers. If that is true it will certainly throw much greater responsibility upon my office. We shall see what happens. The plans no doubt will be changed tomorrow.

The last couple days have been interesting to observe from a political standpoint. It was a shock, even to the Englishmen, to see how badly Churchill was let down, but no one seems to doubt that there will be no change in England's progress of the war. I'm sure old "Winnie" must feel awfully badly about this, but even as they voted against his party, he is still as popular as he ever was, if not more so, with the English public.[22]

July 31 - Yesterday and today I sat on my first court-martial. It lasted for about 15 hours and was quite a difficult case. It was a Captain who was being accused of embezzling $3,200.00 in soldiers' deposits and safe keeping money, etc. We found him guilty and gave him a dismissal from the service and 2 years confinement. Though it was long and drawn out, I was rather fascinated by the proceedings which were well conducted. I don't know why in all these four years, I have never been called on before, but am afraid it will be a too frequent occurrence, now that it has started. It does give one a peculiar feeling to be a party to a decision on "justice," and a very uncomfortable feeling.

Aug 4, 1945 - Today, I have just returned from 3 of the most pleasurable days in many, many months. The Camdens are on a 30-day holiday at Cadgwith, in Cornwall, and they invited me down for a few days. It had been so long since I have had an official pass that I had more than saved up for a 3-day pass.[23]

First of all, three days ago immediately after early supper, Lt. Col. Ashcraft flew me down to Predannack in the droop-snoop P-38. He had promised me a ride in that plane [for] a long time, so it served a multiple purpose this time. It was a thrilling ride and my friends were most impressed when I arrived at Predaimack exactly on schedule at 7:30 p.m., 250 miles away in exactly one hour from takeoff.

The three days were the fullest I have ever had in the way of relaxation. Cadgwith is a small fishing village just a couple miles or so east of Lizzard Point, the southernmost point in England. They still use methods in that village which their fathers used 300 years ago and are thoroughly Cornish to the core. At this village, only a couple hundred yards from the house where I stayed, there is a sort of double cove. On one side is where the fishing boats are pulled up on the beach on runners which slide over small poles which are laid on the ground in front of the boat as it is pulled up.

Lt. Col. Hugh G. Ashcraft, First Air Division, and his special P-38 aircraft (below). Ashcraft piloted Shuller on a number of flights during the war. Courtesy of Ashcraft Family Photographs, East Anglia Air War Collection.

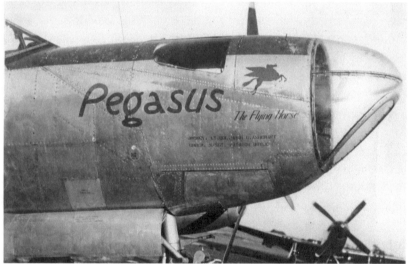

On the other side of the cove is where bathers swim in the delightfully cool channel water from the Gulf Stream, or just bask in the sun completely unmolested.

I hardly know where all the time went. It was spent eating, bathing twice a day on two different beaches, talking with other friends of the Camdens' (the Clarence Raybolds) or walking the narrow paths along the high, rugged cliffs of the coast for miles around. Fortunately, I had three absolutely cloudless days and the channel was as smooth as glass. Yesterday, I went out in a motor boat fishing for four hours. We went out a couple miles or so from the coast (another man and I), and the boatman set out four trawl lines (two each) for us. For the first three hours there was little excitement.

At Cadgwith, a small fishing village on the coast of Cornwall. Shuller is pictured on the beach with "Barbara, Joyce, Mr. and Mrs. Raybold, and son, Anthony." Courtesy of the Thurman Shuller Family Collection.

I had caught a couple pollock weighing about three pounds each plus a couple mackerel, and the other fellow had caught three mackerel. But during the last hour, the mackerel began to bite, and we really pulled them in. It is the first time in my experience that I just didn't have enough hands to operate two lines. Several times we ran through a school and had a fish on all four lines, and as soon as you threw the hook back in another fish was on it. That was real sport, and my hands were actually cut by the fishing cord from pulling it in so much. We got about 60 altogether.

Maj. Thomas flew down in the fort to pick me up. He and the navigator had lunch with us and enjoyed the beach during the early afternoon. So I was again spared that terrible 15 hour train ride during the holiday rush and made it back in 1 1/2 hours. That's a service which will probably never be mine after leaving the Army. We arrived back in camp in time for supper. In three days, I have acquired a sun tan which is immediately the envy of the fellows back here, and I feel completely rested and at peace with the world. Tomorrow I shall start worrying about our newly acquired responsibilities in the Occupational Air Force.

Aug 7 - The whole world was electrified by the news of the atomic bomb today. I'm having just as much difficulty as anybody else trying to understand the working of it. This day may mark the beginning of a new era.

As of today I have a better idea how a man might feel who missed his own wedding. I came back to my quarters a half hour early at noon in order to get a haircut. This happened to be the morning Gen. Turner decided to present some awards upon short notice. The public speaking system here at the quarters also happened to be out of order for the moment, and it was after lunch that I learned they had been desperately looking for me to give me the Legion of Merit. Is my face red! Guess I'll get it at a later date.

Aug 8 - The radio gave us the news (in between all the day-long chatter about the atom bomb) tonight that Russia has declared war on Japan effective tomorrow. It is generally considered as a good thing, and it adds to the beginning talk about the rapidly proceeding progress of the Jap war. Personally, I can't forget my profound fear and distrust of Russia. I can't see where it's going to be at all to our advantage for Russia to take Manchuria, even if it does shorten the war some. I don't see how we can ever have a real understanding with Russia.

Aug 10 - 8:00 a.m. I was entertained more sumptuously last night than ever before in England. Went with Lt. Col. Poinsett Johnson, Lt. Col [Nathan L.] Roberts and Maj. Wilfred Johnson to the home of Mr. and Mrs. Nathan Boch in Northampton for dinner last night. The lavishness with which they entertained is out of all proportion to the war.

Mr. and Mrs. Boch are Jews who came to England from Warsaw 35 years ago, have become English citizens long ago and have grown very rich in the shoe manufacturing business. But ever since the Americans came to Northampton from some of our 1st Division stations, they have been entertaining Americans in huge numbers. Several nights a week, they took them in for dinner, 12–15-20–30 [number of invitees] and even lawn parties of 90–100, and they have done that every week. Last May, Gen. Beaman presented them with a silver plaque for their contribution to the well-being of our soldiers. Their entertainment has run mainly to the Jewish men, of course, but they have taken in many, many others. Where they get all the food, I have no idea. He has an enormous stock of the very finest pre-war liquors. Their house is furnished lavishly, and never have I seen such enormous amounts of fine silver. They have seven children, three of whom are at home. They are lively youngsters and such filial respect and courtesy, I have never seen. Mrs. Boch had some sisters who lived in

Paris, but who were destroyed at Lublin[24] by the Nazis. They are much to be admired and respected for their "share the wealth" policy. I know of no Englishman who would do the same, and not many Americans.

Aug 10, 1945 - 8 p.m. - This afternoon we were electrified by the sudden announcement that the Japs have offered to surrender. We were casually sitting in the lounge after lunch reading the papers and waiting for the usual 1 o'clock radio news. Today was the semiannual officers' club election day, and somebody was running a line of chatter on the loud speaker about some candidate when the radio came on. At the first words "Japan has broadcast her willingness to accept the allied surrender terms," everything else stopped dead, and there was a mighty surge in the direction of the radio. As of tonight, there is no additional information, but everybody is waiting with much anticipation. It is almost too good to be true. All afternoon we have been postulating upon what this will mean to us personally. The consensus of opinion is that it will not affect our immediate movement to Germany, but that it may certainly speed up our replacement.

The officers who live out in the huts really organized and elected their ticket this time over the usual Colonels or Lt. Colonels who live in the big house. They are throwing a real victory celebration tonight and have a big bonfire going out in the backyard. There has certainly been a lot of excitement for one day.

Aug 12 - Our grandchildren will probably read about this past great week in history.

1. Russia declares war on Japan
2. First atomic bomb dropped on Japan
3. Japan offers surrender

That is a pretty big order for one single week.

Today we gave up control of the 67th Fighter Wing and inherited the three OAF bomb groups from 3rd Division. This is the first real step in our reorganization.

Yesterday Kent, Weinstein and I went over to Stratford-on-Avon to see a couple more of the Shakespeare plays they are presenting this year. We saw "Henry VIII," which is not one of his better plays, in the afternoon. It was beautiful pageantry, but little else. But at night they showed "Romeo and Juliet" in a superior manner. With my superficial knowledge of Shakespeare, I couldn't pass any expert opinion on it, but I did find their performance extremely entertaining and absorbing. That's a good enough criterion for me. Kent had seen Katherine Cornell and Lynn Fontanne each do Juliet, but he said they neither played nor looked the part like this one. All the parts were very splendidly cast, and all in all, it was a most entertaining evening.

Aug 15 - Last night I went to bed quietly at 11:45 and was wakened at 12:45 by Maj. Schapp who was running madly up and down the hall yelling that the war is over. It had been announced over the radio a few minutes before. It just wasn't any use trying to sleep with a party already starting down in the bar. Those officers, who had a private bottle of their own, brought them out and things really got underway in short order. About 2 o'clock Capt. Smith, the PRO officer, under stimulus of a certain amount of liquid fire, called up Gen. Turner and told him the war is over and that the officers were all coming over to help him celebrate. To this he replied in a sleepy and disgruntled manner, "Don't bother me!" But the General had a change of heart, I suppose, because he and Gen. Beaman showed up about an hour later. Things began to quiet down a bit about 4:00 after the WAC's and G.I.'s got through clamoring for the General at the front of the officers' quarters, after all the flares had been shot off, and after a bonfire had burned down and the air raid sirens shut up—so I again turned in. My only interruption was a half hour later when my roommate, Lt. Col. Her began making his rounds of everybody's bed with a stirrup pump and a pail of water trying to give everybody an enema.

Aug 16 - This celebrating of victory is more difficult in some respects than the pursuit of the war, and I'm getting disgusted with it. I came in just before midnight last night, having taken the liberty run to Cambridge to attend a show, and found things in various states of inebriation. The G.I.'s and WAC's had a bonfire out back of the camp, and someone took out some punch which was well spiked. Some drunk started running a jeep round and round the fire and ran over a G.I. and a WAC who were sitting on the ground. Fortunately their injuries were not severe. I was on call for the dispensary and about 2:00 a.m., I was gotten out of bed to sew up a man's forehead after he had gotten into a fight at the E.M. club. Before I was through with him, a second had been brought in with two stab wounds of the back, and before finishing that one a third one came in with his finger nearly off. Then we had two WAC's who were vomiting all over everything at the same time, one because of morphine we had given her for a terrific set of menstrual cramps, and the other one who had her vomiting center stimulated by an overdose of some "beverage." As Andy says, "I's requested!"

One of the more pleasant phases of this V-J holiday, however, was my golf game this afternoon over at Cambridge with Maj. Harry Hance. As golfers, we stink, but we did have an awful lot of fun at it. And too, we got lots of exercise because we got to take lots of swings while making the usual round. I haven't been playing enough lately to really make any progress.

Aug 17 - The theater commander extended the holiday to three days so it was another idle day, though I did go to the office a while this afternoon.

This morning we had a formation for Thanksgiving similar to the one we had after V-E day. We fell in behind the band and marched out to the baseball field where we listened to the chaplain give his speech and also Gen. Beaman. Gen. Beaman's opening remark was to express Gen. Turner's deep regret that he was unable to personally attend himself, but each of us stifled a snicker because we all knew the General and three other officers left at 7:30 this morning for a golf course. Otherwise it was a very well conducted service. We could all join in with genuine Thanksgiving that it is apparently all over, and I'm anxious to start forgetting about the many unpleasantnesses and heartaches which paid for this victory.

Gen. Beaman announced this morning that Bad Mergentheim has definitely been selected as location for our headquarters. That's the place I visited with Gen. Beaman and Lt. Col. Ashcraft over a month ago. We are all tremendously relieved that it is now definitely settled. It will be comfortable and as pleasant as anything we could find anywhere in that section of Germany. Air movement will get cracking in short order now. Five officers and some enlisted men will leave in a couple days, and we should all be out within a month.

Aug 24 - Returned this afternoon from a 2-day temporary duty at US-AFE, Paris. Went with about five other officers. The purpose of my visit was to clarify our position and discuss certain problems incident to the transfer of this headquarters directly under that headquarters which is supposed to take place tomorrow. Needless to say, that headquarters is in a terrific turmoil because of the rapid progress of world events, and with the pressure getting strong from home to cut down the size of the occupation Army in Germany, so they really don't know who is going to be occupational and who isn't, nor who is going to command whom. At least, if it is known, the department heads down there haven't been told. Therefore, in portions of three days at the Surgeon's office there, I accomplished very little. About the most which was accomplished was extra-curricular activities. I fell in with the Ordnance people and went into Paris for dinner and a night spot afterwards on both nights. We visited the Monseigneur Club the first night for a considerable price, but it was probably worth it to see a really nice typically European night club once. The second night we saw the Casino de Paris, a burlesque. I've seen all the burlesque I care to see in Paris now. In fact I don't much care to see any more of Paris!

Aug 26 - Rumors are running wild. There is now a rumor that our headquarters and 5 of the heavy bomb groups are not going to Germany at all, but may be returned to the States instead. And it looks like there might be some foundation for the rumor. Nevertheless, I have been scheduled to go with another contingent of the advanced party to Bad Mergentheim tomorrow, and I will go as planned. I don't care to believe anything anymore until I see it in writing, and even then it will probably be changed. However, if the Air Force is going to release so many people on points, they're going to have to cut down some of the organizations over here or else send us some replacements—and fast.

Aug 27 - It was a little less than a three-hour flight from Alconbury to Giebelstadt this morning but with the 1 hour time change, we were late for lunch at Bad Mergentheim. However, the sergeant fixed some cheese sandwiches for us. It was about the smoothest flight I have ever had in a B-17. There were six officers and six enlisted men in this contingent, and we found the officers who had come over here previously madly making preparations and taking over real estate even though there is actually some question about our coming over here now. The orders to the advanced party are to continue with the preparations just as though we knew we were coming.

The area here looks even better this time than I saw it the first time. This is definitely a super spot for a headquarters. It is noteworthy that every single person who has seen this place (even the most homesick ones) seems to have a desire to spend a few weeks here before going home.

Aug 29 - Everybody is pretty busy here accomplishing tasks relative to his own section. Most of yesterday I spent meeting the surgeon of the 63rd Infantry Division and his staff, and I also went up to introduce myself to the staff at the 105th Evacuation Hospital which services this town. Then I looked over a building which had been picked out for a dispensary. It has its virtues but some faults too, and I shall make up my mind about it definitely later. The greatest problem to which I have more or less assigned myself is the question of water supply. Drinking water is hauled in to the mess halls in 5 gal. cans from a water control point several miles

Thurman Shuller at the old castle at Weikersheim, Germany. Courtesy of the Thurman Shuller Family Collection.

away where there is a potable Army chlorinating plant. It is forbidden to drink the tap water here, although the civilians do and have all along. The municipal plant was not damaged by the war. Today I inspected the water supply from its source right on through, and I must say I've never before seen such pure appearing water and such modern efficient equipment in a big water plant. It seems obvious to me that this water was condemned for Army use along with all German water during hostilities, and that nobody has ever bothered to investigate it after the cessation of hostilities, even though it is now almost 4 months later. The town mayor, the water plant engineer, and the public health doctor whom I consulted today all seemed extremely helpful and familiar with all aspects of the problem concerned.

But we haven't spent all of our waking hours at work. Every night after supper, we have driven out some different road to see the sights. This is all agricultural land here. The farmers are not prosperous this year, but they are all working hard this year, and they are sure not going to starve in this section of Germany. The Germans certainly have a lot of admirable qualities along those lines—such a contrast from the contemptible French. If only they knew how to govern themselves. The scenery in this vicinity is superb. Hills rise up several hundred feet on several sides, and from one of those hill tops the scene is particularly pretty at sundown. Last night we drove up to an old moat surrounded medieval castle overlooking the town. This place has so many, many possibilities for making something pleasant out of it. The only thing which will always be missing is a friendly American townspeople and friends. And such food as this infantry outfit has here. Tonight we had fried chicken, French rolls, and ice cream with bananas. The bananas were very small Spanish ones, but they were bananas—the first in over three years.

Aug 31 - Yesterday I saw a wine cellar such as I never expected to see. Not that I'm an authority on wine cellars, because I had never seen one before. This is at a little village about 10 miles from here called Weikersheim. The cellar is about 20 feet under an old castle down about 30 stone steps. They still roll those heavy wine barrels up those stairs on a couple of logs as they did centuries ago. Down there were hundreds of thousands of wine bottles besides hundreds of barrels of all sizes up to casks holding almost 1000 gallons. This particular company had a huge cellar in Bremen during the war but removed their remaining stock to this place after a particular bombing which hit a storage area of 1,000,000 liters (about 250,000 gallons). This deluge of wine is said to have flowed into a bomb shelter and drowned several hundred people. What a business.

The Infantry Division is sure kept in hot water all the time. The movement schedule is changed on them almost every day or two or three times a day. The latest information is that they'll be cleared out of here in six more days. But they're no more unsettled than we, because we are more or less spinning our wheels until some higher headquarters decides what is to become of us.

The Infantry fellows are very friendly to us and our relations with them have been most pleasant. For some weeks our people have been very solicitous of the personnel of their outfit because we knew we had to get along with them. Several of their officers have been flown to England by our planes. Their General has seen London and the Riviera in one of our planes. All this is really paying big dividends now because they are turning over all their good contacts to us. That's further proof of the old saying

that you can catch more flies with honey than with vinegar. But if the profit angle didn't enter into it at all, the relationship here would still be ideal. Of course the Infantry considers the Air Corps a bunch of slouches when it comes to dress and military bearing—and they are right. But on the other side of the ledger we of the Air Corps in England (officers) have been required to dress in blouse or jacket for dinner every night for the last three years. However, we don't point that out to the Infantry because that might not fit into their idea of soldiering either. Continued garrison life in the Air Corps during wartime is something we mention as little as possible to the Infantry. The eight or 10 officers here, I have noticed, are most restrained in our dress. Not one is wearing any sort of decoration, though no mention has ever been made of it. I'm not sure what the others are thinking, but I rather suspect they feel as I—a little humble in the presence of the Infantry. But there is a healthy respect for the other as far as both sides are concerned.

Sept 2, 1945 – Lt Col. Johnson, Lt Col. Ashcraft, Maj. Faulkner and I attended the 63rd Infantry church services this morning at 9 o'clock. It was held in the Evangelical Church which is part of the old medieval castle here in town. It is not a big church, but inside I thought it was one of the most beautiful churches I have ever seen. The pulpit is trimmed in rose marble and the front of the altar is done in sky blue marble. It was built 200–300 years ago by the war lords of the day who occupied the castle. The beautiful painted murals on the walls and ceiling were representations of religious characters, but nearly all of them were armed and carried spears, which proves their warlike characteristics even in those early days. On one side was a plaque containing about 25–30 names of Mergentheim's sons who fell on the western front in the last war, and on the other side was a plaque of a similar number who fell on the eastern front. At the front of the building were two big boards which bore over 100 names of sons of Mergentheim who gave their life for the Fatherland in this war, though it is a town of only 7,000.

But the service itself was well planned and interesting—the most like a regular church service I've ever attended in the Army. They had a corporal tenor who sang three different numbers who is, I believe, the finest church soloist I have ever heard. The organist was good also. The sermon was by a North Georgia Methodist preacher and was interesting. I thoroughly enjoyed it, though it did give one a queer feeling to be worshiping in the church of an enemy people. As we came out at 10:00, the German civilians

Advanced Headquarters officers and enlisted personnel employ a German photographer at the Officer's Club. Thurman Shuller is fifth from left in the first row standing. Courtesy of the Thurman Shuller Family Collection.

were going in and waiting outside for their service. Quite a few old ladies came in before we were actually finished. All the people were dressed in their Sunday best and looked exactly like a congregation of similar size anywhere in the USA—only when they speak are they different.

For 1½ hours tonight, five of us officers rode the horses from the stables which we took over the other day. It's the first time in four years, I had even been on a horse. Guess I'll feel it tomorrow.

Sept 4 - Today I start wearing my sixth overseas stripe. May I never wear another. That 4 Sept morning three years ago when we hopped off from Westover Field, Mass, seems like an awful long time ago.

Almost my entire day was spent in making an automobile trip to Darmstadt to the 1st Medical Laboratory to take up some water samples. Ate lunch on the way at 7th Army Hq. at Heidelberg. My water survey had hit a snag when the lab had previously said they didn't do water analysis unless ordered by 7th Army, but upon personal contact I find that the Bacteriologist there is an officer I knew at Wendover Field, Utah. So after we remembered a lot of old times together, he decided the tests could be run without any difficulty at all. On the way back from Dannstadt to Heidelberg, we drove a little out of the way to ride on one of Hitler's Reich's autobahns. One will rarely see a finer, straighter road than that. In spite of regular signs forbidding speed above 40 miles per hour, the driver opened it up to 65 and let her roll. Since it was the first time since leaving the States that I had seen a road, one could risk that speed, I figured it would be worth it if we got fined for speeding. Was sorry I didn't get to wander around Heidelberg a little more. It is probably the largest city in Germany which was not bombed.

Sept 6 - This place is now ours completely. The main part of the 63rd Infantry Hq. left by convoy yesterday morning, and the Commanding General and his staff left this afternoon for LeHavre via one of our airplanes. That cleaned out the very last of them, and there is now nobody in this whole section of town except our advance party. Gen. Turner and Gen. Beaman were here last night, and they added somewhat to the tenseness of the situation, but as of 1:30 this afternoon, we are back to normal.

For the last week and until yesterday afternoon, it has been fun seeing and talking to Jimmie Bratton, a fellow with whom I went to Ark. Tech and who is now living in McAlester. He is a major in the Inspector General's Dept.

Since the exodus of the 63rd Div. Brass, we have taken over their rooms and have moved out of the basement tonight. The one I have chosen has two rooms, one for a bedroom and the other a sitting room, also a private bath. There's a wash basin in the sitting room, two in the bedroom and one in the bathroom. There is a big clothes closet in both rooms. The bathtub sits in a little recess in the wall, the room is completely lined with white tile, and it is complete even to the douche bowl seen in all good European hotels. The bed is soft, the wall paintings (original) are good, the window drapes are heavy, and the lighting is good. Never before have I occupied such sumptuous quarters. It is almost worth the $125.00 allotment for rooms which I never get as a single man. It gives one a sort of satisfaction to exploit all this at the expense of the Germans, just as I derived a certain pleasure from driving 200 miles, day before yesterday, through Hitler's Reich.

Sept 9 - Still no more word about the movement of our headquarters to Germany. But regardless, the headquarters has to get out of Brampton Grange by Sept 15, so this week they are getting ready to move to Alconbury, our nearest airdrome, about four miles from Brampton. For that reason, I flew with Lt. Col. Ashcraft back to England in his P-38 day before yesterday and returned at noon today. I packed my things for movement, and what a job it was! I have at least twice as much junk as when I came overseas. Since I have made only one movement in three years, and that only a few miles, I have had no occasion to do any elimination, but the day isn't long off.

We made the trip there [to England], about 575 miles, in exactly 2 hours, but with a headwind on return [to Germany], it took two hours and 10 minutes. That's some traveling. Since there is little else for the officers back in England to do, they are deeply engrossed in a squabble over quarters at their new base. They are actually getting bitter at each other about it. That's what comes of having too little to do.

Capt. Lusk had become a major in my absence. He and Hicks have all plans made for our office at Alconbury so I'm not needed there. When there is so little to do anywhere, one might as well be as comfortable as possible while he is doing it. Therefore I elect to stay with the advanced party in Germany.

While in England this time (7 Sept), I was finally presented the Legion of Merit Medal for which I have been on orders for several weeks and missed some time ago. Though I'm perfectly aware that I, personally, am most unworthy of the award, I do feel that my section has done a superior job and has contributed more than somewhat to the success of the 1st Division. For that award, I'm indebted most to the able assistance of Maj. Longworth, Capt. Hicks and Maj. McNeil. No section head ever had more able support. I got the medal because I happen to be the ranking member of the department. Nevertheless, I am genuinely proud of that award. To receive the very highest award a non-combat officer below the rank of general is likely to get is considerable and far beyond my wildest dreams. Though I received it at the hands of Gen. Turner, it was Gen. Williams and Gen. Beaman who recommended it.

Sept 11 - Yesterday a plane came over from England bearing several officers and some enlisted people who had just come along for the ride. When they got ready to go at noon today, Col. Johnson noticed something among the baggage of one of the WAC's which looked suspiciously like a picture frame. A shakedown inspection was held, and the picture and frame along with other articles were found. The WAC's are the worst collectors of all. That sort of thing has been considered more or less legitimate for a long time now, but Col. Johnson has taken the position (and rightly) that it is high time we considered the war over, and that looting of personal property is a thing of the past and no longer to be tolerated. If

Legion of Merit presented to Lt. Colonel Shuller by Major General Turner, September 1945. Courtesy of the Thurman Shuller Family Collection.

that sort of thing is allowed to continue, we're certainly in no position as a nation to criticize Germany for her looting of her conquered countries, not that Germany will particularly appreciate that fact. France and Russia are certainly exacting their pound of flesh. And there is still the possibility that Germany will consider such action on our part as further evidence of our "softness and decadence."

Sept 16 - We received word from back at home base in England today that it has been directed from higher headquarters, that there is no such thing as being declared essential any more, regardless of the situation, and that all officers and enlisted men with more than the critical score, who do not volunteer for further overseas service, will be returned to the States within 60 days. That is the very first encouraging word we have had. Sixty days! That means that not later than Nov 15, I shall be on my way. Oh! Happy day! There is still no definite word about the eventual fate of our headquarters, but the fact that all promotions in this organization have been frozen as of today indicates that the whole organization has been slated for return to the States. Let us hope so. I have no desire to return to the Z.I. as a casual officer if it can be helped.

This afternoon Lt. Col. Johnson, Maj. Johnston and I drove over to Rothenburg, about 30 miles away. It is an old walled medieval city which has been preserved in its natural state for the purpose of attracting tourists. It was on the "must" list of all peace time European sightseers. Unfortunately, it is about ½ destroyed by incendiary bombing, the most unfortunate part being that it was unscratched all during the war until it was attacked only 2–3 weeks before the final capitulation on 10 May this year. The most remarkable thing about the city is its similarity to the old walled cities of England such as York and Lincoln. It was a most pleasant trip, in spite of two flat tires, and very interesting, but I think we failed to be duly impressed, most likely because we have seen so much of this sort of thing before. We took several pictures and bought some.

Sept 17 - Lt. Col. Johnson, Lt. Barta and I drove down to Garmund today where Johnson had some business concerning taking over the property here. After that was finished, we drove on to Goppingen where a factory which makes toy electric trains has been put back into operation. We had hoped to make arrangements for some for Christmas use, but it seems the 36th Division has them pretty well sewed up since they are guarding the place. We returned by Stuttgart and saw a great deal of the damage our bombers did to them on their many trips to that target. We didn't get back until well after dark. Every time I get out on the road, I never cease to marvel at the beauty of the German countryside. German peasants are the neatest farmers one can possibly imagine. There isn't a foot of wasted ground anywhere and the pastures and roadsides are heavily coated with grass with not a weed anywhere. I just don't know how it's done. The peasants are poor as far as any luxuries and conveniences are concerned, but by hard work, they have a bountiful supply of the necessities. However, their practice of building the barn right against the house and throwing the manure out in the front yard would hardly be accepted as proper practice in America.

Sept 18 - About 10 o'clock last night, several of us officers paid a courtesy call to the ground forces officers who were having a house warming in the new club they have just opened a half mile down the road. They are from an Engineer Battalion and an Artillery Battalion. There was some degree of conflict when we arrived because the Engineers had brought nurses to the dance, and the Artillery had brought German women, whereupon the nurses refused to associate with the German women or the other officers. The ticklish situation was solved by putting the two factions in each of two rooms. We all thought the nurses' point was extremely well taken and were happy to see them stick by their guns. We couldn't help noting, however, that the German women were much the prettier.

Ever since we have been here, a six-piece German orchestra has been engaged to play through the dinner hour from six to seven. Every officers' mess in Germany, almost, does the same, but ours is really professional caliber. In fact, they are six of the best artists from their local symphony, including the conductor who is a violinist. I love that European custom of music at dinner, particularly when it is good. They were unusually good tonight. They will play anything upon request on the following night, after they can get the music.

Sept 20 - While walking down the streets of Bad Mergentheim this morning, I saw a blacksmith nailing a shoe on the front hoof of an ox which interested me no end. It's funny, it never occurred to me before that oxen required shoes. There are more oxen and cows pulling wagons than there are horses. I had thought at first that this may have been a wartime measure, but one of the natives the other day told me it isn't. He also told me the cows which are used are primarily beasts of burden, but that they do give a small amount of milk in addition. That's real double duty.

Sept 27 - The latest rumor is that 1st Air Division will come to Bad Mergentheim after all, to command only 5 heavy bomb groups until such time as the super forts arrive next year. But personally I don't care one whoop, because I won't be here. It will not affect in any way the present plans to transfer us into units going home. I am scheduled to be among the last to leave the Hq. about Nov. 1. The first bunch are joining the 435th Service Group which is alerted to be ready for movement by Oct. 1. About 35 of our officers have been transferred to that outfit, which includes Capt. Hicks. This is the first mass disintegration. In view of this, four or five of our party over here went back to England today to join that outfit. Those of us who are to leave England later, will return to England next Sunday. The WAC's left here today also. All WAC's will probably leave the head-quarters entirely in the next few days.

Another development is the transfer of Gen. Turner to 8th Fighter Command, which leaves Gen. Beaman in command of the 1st Division. It is an odd coincidence that Gen. Beaman (then Lt. Col.) was in charge of the small detachment which came over here 3 ½ years ago to later form the 1st Bomb Wing which grew into the 1st Air Division. During all this time, he has remained here as Chief of Staff under 7 different commanders (that must be some sort of record), and now he is to command the disintegration of this most proud and once powerful command. He must feel an intense pride to be in a position to do this. He is truly a wonderful person and a great Army officer.

Sept 30 - The last of the high pointers from Bad Mergentheim all came back to England today. So we have said goodbye to Germany (possibly). I sort of hated to leave that comfortable spot in Germany, but this is our first step toward getting in a position to be started on the way home. It seems funny though to be coming to Alconbury rather than Brampton.

For the first time in my life, I got up at 6 o'clock this morning and went deer hunting with five other officers. Three of us branched off and struck out through a woods and some fields. I saw only one deer but cracked down on him from 50 yards with a carbine and killed him. He was a very small buck but was grown at that. They are a very small species. My performance stood the other boys on their ear, because I bagged the only deer of the morning the first time I had ever fired a gun at deer on my first deer hunt and expended only one bullet during the entire morning, and it was the first shot I had ever fired with a carbine. All the others got several shots at deer and missed, some of them experienced deer hunters, too. Frankly, though, nobody was more surprised than I. Wait until I tell Albert this one. There seems to be hundreds of deer around Bad Mergentheim.

Oct 3, 1945 - The latest rumor about disposition of the 1st Air Div. is that it will be disbanded here at Alconbury and all personnel transferred out within the next few days. The rumor factory grinds copiously lately.

Since our senior officers' billet is so far from headquarters, Gen. Beaman is permitting certain officers to drive. I obtained my drivers' permit today after demonstrating my driving proficiency by starting and stopping a jeep. I'll probably get knocked off the road for forgetting to drive on the left side of the road. In Germany, I did a little unauthorized driving, but they drive on the right there. Driving came back quite naturally, even though I hadn't sat behind a wheel in over 3 years. I detest this business of providing officers with so many servants. It makes us entirely too lazy and is certainly a luxury most of us will never afford again.

Oct 5 - This morning I flew with Maj. Johnson to Prestwick, Scotland to take Maj. Provan up there to school. As we approached the airdrome, it was inevitable that I reflect a bit upon an approach upon that airdrome 37 months ago tomorrow. It was about 9 o'clock in the morning, and we had just completed about a 10-hour flight from Newfoundland. Boy, how good that land did look! What we lacked in knowledge of what this war is all about, we made up for in enthusiasm and eagerness. After eating in the terminal mess, I went up to the desk to pay for my lunch and when the girl said, "2 shillings please," it reminded me that 37 months ago at the same desk, a girl asked for 2 shillings, and I hadn't the slightest idea how much 2 shillings would be. We have been here so long now, I almost have to think twice about the value if one were to say 40 instead. Some pretty big events have transpired between these two landings 37 months apart. Those landings weren't very important as far as the course of war and peace is concerned, but they meant a lot to me.

Oct 9 - Tonight we listened to the thrilling sixth game of the World Series. It seems just like peacetime when one sees fellows getting so excited over the Series. That's a good sign. Always before there were so many other things going on which seemed so much more important. It was hard to get really excited about such things when so many people were dying around us. But this year it's just like the folks back home. There are quite a few bets floating around.

The latest rumor is that this week we will all be transferred to the 652nd Bomb Sq. which has a readiness date of 6 Nov. If so, I will go home as a squadron surgeon. We shall see how closely this rumor comes to the actual fact.

Oct 10 - Maj. Lusk has just returned this afternoon from a trip to Tangiers, Spanish Morocco, via Istres, France, and he brings back great stories of things to see and bargains to buy. He brought back a lot of watches and leather goods at ridiculously low prices. Since I've had my heart set on taking a trip to North Africa for some time, I got immediately in high and procured orders this afternoon for a leave beginning tomorrow. Capt. Cleary, Capt. Cannon and Capt. Black are going with me. We hope to catch a plane for Istres from Thurleigh tomorrow. It is strictly illegal for troops in England to take leave outside England, but with some slightly forged permits, we hope to swing it.

Oct 11 - We are quartered in the dispensary at Istres, France (Near Marseilles) tonight, thanks to the hospitality of Capt. Beamer, the Group Surgeon 92nd B.G. We left Alconbury by car at 10:30 and took off by plane from Thurleigh at 1:30 and were here after about 3 ¼ hours, in time for late supper. But we are disappointed to learn that the squadron at Port Leyote in French Morocco, from where they jump off to Tangiers, is already pulling back here, and the last plane will arrive back from there tomorrow. And furthermore, the last plane expected to go to Tangiers left this field this morning. So our prospects for getting to Africa are rapidly diminishing. But fortunately, we find that Lt. Col. Chapman, one of the squadron commanders, is going to Rome tomorrow afternoon and will return Sunday afternoon. Capt. Beamer is looking after all the details of getting us on that flight, and at the moment, the prospects look good.

Oct 12 - The Rome trip actually did materialize, and we have taken up lodging at the Excelsior Hotel here in Rome, one of the largest and finest in the city, after an uneventful, but interesting 2-hour and 10 minute flight. We passed along the Riviera coast over Cannes and Nice, then down across the upper Mediterranean over the northern tip of Corsica, over the island of Elba and down the west coast of Italy to Rome. It's easy to see why Corsica did not have too much military importance when one sees how barren and mountainous the terrain is. It is even rougher than Scotland. Elba is little better, but it did have a little city out on a small peninsula, and it looks as though Napoleon may not have had it so bad after all. Italy from the air is a sorry looking sight. The city of Rome, however, even from the air, is most impressive and looks strictly modern. The only points I could recognize from the air were the colosseum and St. Peter's Cathedral. By the time we had landed, caught the A.T.C. bus into the city, gotten our rooms, and eaten supper, it was too late to make arrangements to go out. Besides, it was not necessary. We looked in for a while at the dance at the Red Cross Club, then returned to the Excelsior. They had a magnificent ballroom and good orchestra with an hour-long floor show. The accommodations here are really sumptuous. All rooms have baths, and the whole thing is constructed of marble throughout and is quite a massive building. The hotel had retained all of its civilian staff, including a whole herd of "white tie and tails" waiters. The food ration is G.I., but the preparation is by Italian cooks and is not recognizable as Army chow. Such service must cost a pretty penny in peacetime, but to us it is available at the rate of $1.00 a day—everything included.

Oct 13 - We were up bright and early this a.m. to prepare to take the conducted Red Cross tour through the Vatican museum and the Sistine Chapel. The tour lasted 3 hours, during which we walked several miles, but the time passed quickly. Never have I seen such treasures in art and other things. The museum contains many of the most priceless original sculpture and paintings from B.C. onwards. Never before have I been much impressed by cold marble statues or by classical painting, but I now discover that's because I had never seen it in the original before. Pictures of them just don't capture their beauty. There were dozens of the statues we have all seen in history books, but I was most impressed by the "Group of Laocoon" a Greek statue of B.C. which shows a Priest and his two sons being killed by two large serpents. The perfect anatomic features and facial expressions in the death struggle even down to the veins in the legs and tendons in the feet cannot be adequately photographed or described. The same is true of many others. In spite of the fact that Michelangelo and Raphael did their paintings in the Vatican over 400 years ago, the colors are still very vivid on most of the ceiling of the Sistine Chapel (where the Popes are elected) shows the most beautiful depth that one will ever see. They don't look at all like they were painted on a flat surface. He lay on his back for 4 years painting those pictures. Raphael's paintings and tapestries are more numerous in spite of the fact that he died at the age of 30. One can't comprehend how one man can turn out such magnificent things in such large quantity. There is no use trying to describe all these things. There is not enough space, and besides I don't know enough adjectives.

The Vatican Library contains about 2 million volumes of books from B.C. to the present. An awful lot of work went into the production of some of those handwritten and painted parchments. And such rich gifts as have been presented [to] the Popes through the ages! There are religious equipment and figures made of all sorts of precious stones and metals. The one which made me blink was the 24-pound statue of a shepherd and his flock made of gold, presented by the Emperor of Austria. Russia, the Middle East, all Europe, and America have made similar fabulous contributions of one thing or another. Three days rather than 3 hours would be a much better schedule for that museum.

The afternoon was devoted mainly to shopping. Prices are terrific— absolutely fantastic; but by the proper application of certain trading materials in a manner which seems to be accepted (at least overlooked), we were able to get a few souvenirs. Most of the stuff in the shops is just plain junk, and there is little of any value to buy. They are really trying to cash in on the "wealthy" Americans. There are not as many American soldiers in evidence as one would imagine. Street hawkers and beggars are a terrible nuisance and require some firm handling. Some of us wanted very badly to go to the Royal Opera House tonight, but upon checking, we found they were showing a ballet which none of us cared to see. Besides, we all discovered we were so tired from a long day, we didn't leave the hotel very far.

Oct 14 - This a.m. we got up early to take another Red Cross conducted tour. This included the Circus Maximus, where Ben Hur stood them on their ear in the good old days; the square where Mussolini used to hold forth from his balcony; the magnificent old colosseum where the gladiators used to perform and where Nero gave some of his countrymen a bad time; and many others I can't name. But the real joy of the trip was saved for the last—St. Peter's Cathedral in the Vatican. I had not been too enthusiastic about visiting St. Peter's because I had always been a little disappointed or at least not completely impressed by other famous old church-

Thurman Shuller in front of the entrance to St. Peter's in Rome. Courtesy of the Thurman Shuller Family Collection.

Touring party at the Vatican. Shuller is standing directly behind the officer seated fifth from the left. Courtesy of the Thurman Shuller Family Collection.

Shuller, Nowack, and Coler at the Arc de Triomphe in Paris. Courtesy of the Thurman Shuller Family Collection.

Thurman Shuller in front of the Eiffel Tower in Paris. Courtesy of the Thurman Shuller Family Collection.

Advanced Headquarters at Bad Mergentheim, Germany, August-September 1945. Courtesy of the Thurman Shuller Family Collection.

es, which for the most part are very cold in atmosphere. Therefore, I was not prepared for the dazzling beauty and richness which we saw at St. Peter's. It, even more than the Vatican museum, defies adequate description. To begin with, it is the largest church in Christendom, being more than twice as long as a football field, and undoubtedly it must be the most richly adorned—not even King Solomon's temple excepted. Having seen that, anything else in the way of churches will be small pickings. There isn't a square foot of floor, wall or ceiling which isn't ornamented in one way or other with inlay marble work, mosaic pictures, statues, columns, bronze work or gold leaf trimming. Yet, it does not give the impression of over decoration. It is all in extremely good taste. There was a funeral, a wedding, some communion services and others—at least a half dozen—all going on simultaneously on the same floor, none interfering with the other, not to mention the two or more parties of rubber-neckers on tour. It still looked empty. There is a column on display which was taken from King Solomon's temple, and the four huge columns of the bronze altar are exact replicas of it. When one considers that the entire roof is heavily decorated with gold leaf, it can be appreciated that the gold alone costs a pretty penny.

Finally, we moved on into the Vatican treasury where the richest Vatican riches are stored. There were solid gold crucifixes and other statues 4 or 5 feet high. There were robes trimmed with real gold wire and huge precious stones. There were diamonds, rubies, and pearls by the bushel on various ceremonial pieces, jewelry, or other ornaments. Never in my wildest childhood dream did I ever imagine such a collection existed in one spot. The reader won't believe it anyway, so I shall say no more. It's fortunate for the Pope that he has to pay no taxes. It's difficult to see just how all of this fits in with the worship of God, but at least it is awe inspiring and shows what can be accomplished in 2,000 years of collecting.

We rushed through the very last of the tour to dash madly out to the airport to catch the plane back to Istres, which brought to an end one of the richest 48 hours in my life. This was just an introduction to Rome, but perhaps, it was better to leave before we got tired of it and were still filled with enthusiasm. England had seemed very old to us, but when one stands in the presence of things so much, much older and so much more magnificent, England seems dull by comparison. Even Paris must take a back seat.

We are now setting about to see what we can cook up for the rest of our leave period.

Oct 15 - This morning we made all necessary arrangements (we thought) for Cleary and me to go to Tangiers, Spanish Morocco, tomorrow and were enthusiastic about it no end because that is the place we were aiming for when we left England. However, when we returned to the field tonight, we found that Lt. Col. Smyrl, the new C.O. here, had found out about our arrangements and vetoed it most emphatically. We couldn't criticize his action in taking our names off the loading list and substituting some of his own officers, but we sure are sorely disappointed. We had expected to do most of our Christmas shopping there since prices are cheaper there than anywhere else in the world at the present time—besides it is said to be an interesting and lovely spot.

But we did have a very fine day, anyway. We flew over to the Air Force rest center at Cannes, France, on the Riviera to pick up Captain Stepman. It was a nice flight for 1 hour in spite of the fact we were in a Norseman C64, a plane in which I have very little confidence. The Air Force officers occupy the Martinez Hotel, which is about 50 yards from the sandy Mediterranean beach. It is one more beautiful spot. The weather was fair and warm and the water was crystal clear. Such luxury as those fellows down there do have. Those rooms in peacetime went for $30.00 to $60.00 per day. Maj. McGregor and Maj. Joe Henry took care of us and showed us around. At lunch each table had 4 or 5 waiters to do things up in real French fashion. Capt. Black and Capt. Cannon elected to stay the rest of their leave there, which Cleary and I would have done also if we knew then what we know now. Maybe I can wangle a "legal" trip down there if we have to stay around England long. It looks like our shipping may be delayed with the sudden withdrawal of the *Queen Elizabeth* and the *Aquitania*.

Oct 16 - Capt. Beamer took Cleary and me up to Avignon today, by jeep, about 60 miles north of here. I was surprised to learn that Avignon was the site for the Vatican for a period of 105 years in the 14th and 15th centuries and had a reign of nine Popes. This, apparently, was because France seemed to be running things in those days and figured Rome was beneath the dignity of the French as a Vatican. It is little more than an empty shell now and is nothing at all compared to the Vatican in Rome, but the trip was worthwhile mainly because it was the first time I had had an opportunity to drive a considerable distance through the French countryside. We had lunch at a good French hotel and shopped for a while but bought little because of the prices. Upon return toward Istres, we were flagged down by about 5 Frenchmen and a woman waving huge rolls of money at us and wanting to buy cigarettes or anything else. We stopped to "investigate" the situation and made ourselves vulnerable to a little trading. Capt. Beamer ended up even selling his old worn out G.I. shoes for 800 francs ($16.00). He came on home in his sock feet so that we had to drive the jeep right up to his barracks door for him to get some more shoes to wear to supper. Best we all get out of France before we lose what little self-respect we do have. We are scheduled to return to England tomorrow. Our leave is not up, but there is little else to do under the circumstances, and besides I'm anxious to see how my transfer is progressing.

Oct 17 - Our flight back to England was cancelled today because of weather (in England, of course), so we stayed around the post during the morning. In the afternoon, Beamer and Crawford took Cleary and me by jeep to Marseilles. Crawford had been there before and acted as guide. Marseilles looks good from a distance, but upon driving into it, one discovers that it is just another dirty, dingy, ragged, and smelly port town, only more so. We did very much enjoy the view from Notre Dame church on the high hill overlooking the city and the Mediterranean. It was splattered with a few bullets since the Germans held that point as a lookout for a few days. After getting our supper, we returned to camp.

Oct 18 - Had an uneventful trip back to England today via B-17. As usual, we knew when we crossed the English coast by looking straight ahead instead of down, because that's where the clouds began, and inland it became quite foggy. We landed at Bury St. Edmunds, and drove by car about 50 miles back to Alconbury.

Upon arrival back at camp, we immediately learned that all of us remaining high pointers had been transferred to the 96th Bomb Group for the purpose of return to the States. However, for the time being, we are going to continue to live here at Alconbury since the accommodations are better. We are all pleased about that. This is the first real step in getting us home. Tomorrow I shall ring the death knell on my office by completing the destruction of whatever records we have left after other disposition. After that, I expect all my duties and responsibilities as a staff officer to have come to an end. After 26 months in that office, it is a little sad to see all our work come to a complete and deadly stop, but I am glad to be the one to close it.

Oct 20 - This was an historic day for the 1st Air Division, and one we'll all remember. To begin with, at 9 o'clock the final staff meeting was held.

Gen. Beaman made a final statement of appreciation, and that was it. After he left the room, Lt. Col. Johnson announced that the War Dept. had awarded Gen. Beaman the Distinguished Service Medal. That award has every officer's approval. Never was there a man in a position of great responsibility who was more beloved and respected by his subordinate officers. He has an incredible record, and he has just reason to be proud of it, and we of him. He opened up the headquarters in June 1942, remained as Chief of Staff under a succession of seven commanding generals, and closed up the headquarters in Oct 1945. Never has his efficiency faltered or his popularity suffered. What a phenomenal record!!

Then at 11 o'clock, the 435th Service Group carrying about 60 or 70 of our 1st Division high point officers and a proportional number of our enlisted men boarded the train at Huntingdon to go to Southampton and board the aircraft carrier Lake Champlain which sails tomorrow. This is the only mass movement that our headquarters had had or will have, therefore, it called for an all-out celebration. Those of us who remained went to the station to see them off and the band played continuously as their last official act for the division. There were a lot of English women (some with babies) at the station to see their husbands and sweethearts off. It was a most touching sight to see the train pull out amid all the good-byes, shouts, and tears.

It was a fortunate coincidence the final staff meeting and the leaving of the 435th Service Group fell on the same day. This was such a fitting finale for the 1st Air Division. It has left us with a mixed feeling of joy, sadness and intense pride in an outfit which has been mighty in battle and glorious in victory.

Chapter 6

Farewell to England

October 21, 1945–December 9, 1945

When Shuller opened a new notebook to begin his last volume for his war-time diary, he had only a few weeks left in England. On October 21, 1945, he wrote that no one had any duties, and that he and everyone else were "to amuse themselves" while waiting for orders to board ship for the journey home. A few of his friends joined Shuller in a motor tour through the lake country of England, and through Scotland and Ireland. It proved to be an apt end to his military service in World War II England.

Shuller's last weeks in Britain saw a continuation of rumors, confusion, and disorder within the First Air Division as leadership in the Eighth Air Force and the air divisions across East Anglia consolidated with departures, transfers, and downsizing. The time came for the voyage home, but not on the Europa, as early scuttlebutt had indicated, but on the Queen Mary from Southampton.

Shuller's descriptive narrative and assessment details the voyage home and the processing at Camp Kilmer and Jefferson Barracks in St. Louis. He chronicles the Queen Mary's arrival in New York and the impact the Statue of Liberty had on him and the others who crowded on the decks as the Queen Mary sailed past the iconic symbol; he was surprised at the emotion the sight evoked in him. It was a fitting conclusion for a journey begun just three years before, as he sat in the nose of a B-17 departing the United States, flying into the unknown.

*

Oct 21, 1945 - This final short volume will be more or less an anticlimax since none of us now have any duties except to amuse ourselves while we are waiting for a shipping date.

This morning Lt. Col. Johnson and I went to the church in Huntingdon which Cromwell used to attend. As before in English churches, I found the service cold, uninspiring and unattended. I do not intend to attend any more English church services.

Oct 22 - Rumor has it that our Bomb Gp. is scheduled to leave on 24 Nov. That is still strictly rumor, but it is the first time anybody has gotten around to setting a date of any kind and naturally we are very excited about it.

I have started giving all our fellows the necessary vaccinations preparatory to the boat trip.

Oct 23 - In accordance with our resolution and expressed policy of getting away from camp as much as possible and seeing as much of Europe as we can while over here, I have been invited tomorrow to accompany Lt. Col. Johnson, Lt. Col. Her, and Maj. Crucius on a motor trip. Since all our subordinate commands have turned in their cars, there are plenty of cars and gasoline. Gen. Beaman has given permission to use one of the sedans. On this proposed trip tomorrow, we have only one plan—that is, to have no plans. All my life I have wanted to make such a trip. We shall call the home station every day or two to see that we are not getting left in any possible change of situation, and we are starting out in the morning, not knowing where we will go, how long we will stay there, or when we will come back. I'm going to like this. This is going to be a trip for the books.

Oct 24 - At almost 9 o'clock, after returning for Crucius' toilet articles, which he forgot, we started off up the Great North Road toward the general direction of Scotland in a hard, un-English type of rain. We didn't stay with the Great North Road long, however, but bore left at Stamford and went up through Nottingham. We stopped for lunch at a hotel in Macclesfield, and there Crucius expended a guinea for one of those famous Macclesfield all-silk ties.

By the middle of the afternoon, we had arrived at Liverpool, and after having a look at the enormous docks, going through the huge new cathedral and driving about the city for a while, it was getting dark, and we have put up for the night at the Adelphi Hotel. The Adelphi is excellent, but the city of Liverpool is an awful city—dirty, ragged, smoky and ugly, and it seems to have thousands of dirty kids in the street. Much more of Liverpool has been destroyed by bombs than any of us realized.

Oct 25 - This morning we drove north through the lake country. The fact that we enjoyed and were tremendously impressed by the scenery, in spite of an almost constant downpour of rain, is evidence enough of its rare beauty. There are numerous small lakes, but the largest and best known is Lake Windermere. We drove along the entire length of Winder-mere, almost 12 miles, and it is easy to see why the English think so highly of it. The entire length of Windermere and several of the others is lined with hotels and summer cottages. The English have only the seacoast, the lake country, and Scotland for their summer holidays. The flood rains had swollen the streams completely out of their beds, which exaggerated the numerous small waterfalls and made them even more beautiful. Some-thing which impressed all of us, and me in particular, was the fact that the flood waters were crystal clear and looked fit to drink. Even our most thickly forested lands back home seem to drain off water which is at least a little muddy.

We drove past Lake Thirlmere to Keswick (pronounced Kes-ick) on the back of Lake Derwentwater, and we had lunch at the Royal Oak hotel, which in the good old days, had such impressive guests as Robert Louis Stevenson, Shelley, Coleridge, Wordsworth, and John Ruskin. This coun-try should surely inspire most anybody to write. The dining room at the Royal Oak has stained glass windows such as a church, but commemorat-ing those above mentioned and other noted guests. But more important than this, the hotel had good food—broiled chicken, in fact.

The afternoon trip north was mountainous and very beautiful in spots, when we could see for the rain. But after going north through Carlisle, there was nothing but ordinary country into Glasgow. We are staying at the Red Cross Club in Glasgow since there are no hotel accommodations to be had. Glasgow is one of the leave centers for American troops and is pretty crowded with soldiers. Glasgow, like Liverpool, is an awful damp, smoky, dirty, dismal city and all the people look anemic. We are here only as long as it takes to get out.

Oct 26 - During the night we cooked up a scheme to go to Ireland and take the car with us, if possible. Johnson wrote out our own travel warrants with which we obtained boat passage from Stranraer tomorrow morning without any difficulty. Since we didn't need to be in Stranraer before night, the entire day was devoted to sightseeing. As it turned out, we happened onto one of the most wonderful day's travel in our life. From Glasgow we took a circuit north, west, and then south to Stranraer. Our policy in the beginning of following only our whim of the moment is cer-tainly paying big dividends thus far.

The drive took us first about 20–25 miles southwest to the lower end of Lock Lomond. We drove almost the entire length of the lake and the road most of the way followed right along the water's edge of the west bank. The rugged mountains with autumn colored leaves, the clear blue water, the many small green islands, the low hanging clouds, and the spotty mixture of sunshine and mist made a picture which could not be reproduced. The bonnie banks of Loch Lomond are worth singing about.

At the top of Loch Lomond, we turned left down the east bank of Loch Long for about 30 miles. It is about the same length but not so wide. Its scenery is very similar to that of Loch Lomond except that it is filled with ocean going vessels, and at the lower end is lined with miles of ship building docks. We ferried across the lower end of the Clyde River on the way down in order to miss Glasgow. The ferryman, whom we tried to pay, recognized we were from England and said, "Yer in Scotland neow, ye rides free."

We continued on down the coastline of the Firth of Clyde past the tremendous docks and on down to Stranraer, a distance of about 100 miles from the river crossing. The entire Scottish coastline, in that area at least, is terrifically rugged, but the road hugs right along the water's edge most of the way. The wind was high enough to make white caps on the Firth, and the water pounded against the rocks with such fury that at times it almost seemed the water would spray up over the car. Nowhere do I know where one can find such a long and rugged seaside drive of such breath-taking beauty. We are so lucky to have had a car. It would have been utterly impossible to have seen so much in one day otherwise.

At Stranraer we got the car refueled at a British Army Camp, had our supper and then contacted the Marine super about taking our car across to Ireland. He balked at permitting it on our Army leave pass, but for the unusual freight fee of £4-9-0 ($17.00) we got it on. The British Army people were also a little stuffy about letting us on at all, since our leave ticket didn't have the approval of a General, but we argued them down and got on through.

So at this writing, the four of us are bedded down in berths in a stateroom about 5x6 feet, ready to set sail in the very early morning, and are at the moment trying to cook up some sort of scheme to get ourselves on into the Irish Free State. We shall see how that works out.

Oct 27 - The boat was considerably late sailing this a.m. for some reason unknown to us. They were still loading fish as well as passengers at least an hour after sailing time. Upon arising, we were relieved to see our car actually in the hold of the ship. The two-hour trip to Larne, Ireland on the

2,000-ton Princess Maud was smooth and uneventful, but cold. The car, much to our relief, again, was unloaded without mishap and got us into Belfast in time for a good steak dinner with cold fresh milk. In Belfast, our party of four has been joined by Maj. Provan and Lt. Kaufman, who are here taking some special courses. We are fortunate to have them show us some of the spots about town. The afternoon trip included my first introduction to a soccer match and also a rugby match, then a visit to the beautiful and modern State Government House of Ulster known as Stormont. The evening gave us a wonderful steak and mushroom dinner at the Carlton Restaurant and a visit to the Allied Officers' Club and the Embassy Club to round out a full day.

Oct 28 - Today being Sunday we couldn't do any of the shopping we hope to do while here in Ireland, so the entire day was spent on a 220-mile trip along the northern coastline to Londonderry and back by an inland route. Part of the coast road was really rugged and steep and made the drive more interesting, if not quite so beautiful as the Scottish drive day before yesterday. The point of greatest interest was the "Giant's Causeway" on the coast near Portrush. It is a natural geological deposit of closely fitting hexagonal stone pillars about 12–15 inches thick which is a true wonder of nature. It is impossible to imagine how nature has fitted them together so accurately and perfectly.

The old walled city of Londonderry, after stopping at Portrush for lunch, looked like an interesting place, but we didn't have time to do anything but drive through it. Throughout the whole trip, we were all fascinated by the process of digging and drying peat. Most of it was just barely under the surface of all those wet soggy heather-covered hills (instead of in swamps as I had imagined) and was in layers of 3–5 feet thick. We saw hundreds of thousands of tons of it, and it looks like they have enough left for a few more hundred years.

The food here in Ireland is excellent and in no way compares with England. There seems to be an abundance of meat, eggs and milk. The Irish people are most genuinely friendly, particularly the girls. We find a lot of the girls are widows of American soldiers killed in North Africa when the soldiers stationed in Ireland joined the invasion there. They like Americans, and the tradition of smiling Irish eyes is not fiction—they have it even up to the old grandmothers. I find Belfast much more attractive than on my first visit 2 ½ years ago.

Oct 30 - Yesterday we spent most of the morning shopping in Belfast.

Most of us spent rather extravagantly on Irish linen and lace, but we felt it was worth it to have something from Ireland.

The consular authorities turned us down on allowing passage of our car into Eire (the first failure we have encountered on this trip), but we drove south as far as we could yesterday afternoon and spent the night at Rostrevor so as to be in position for the early train this morning to Dublin. Again we wrote our own letters of permission to visit relatives in the vicinity of Dublin, and they got us over the border without question. At the border, I had my first experience with customs officials on both sides of the border, but this presented no difficulty since none of us was carrying luggage. We arrived in Dublin about 1 p.m. and went immediately to the Gresham Hotel for lunch, but it turned out to be a feast. We asked the waiter how their steaks were, and he said they had the best in Dublin. We said we wanted the best he had with all the necessary trimmings. He started with a most delicious lobster cocktail. Then he brought out the most enormous porterhouse steaks any of us had ever seen—three for the six of us. Each steak was approximately 15 inches long, by 10 inches wide by about 1 ½ inches thick and was so tender and juicy, it fairly melted in one's mouth. I personally had never seen nor imagined such steaks ever existed. Her and Crucius, each of whom considers himself quite a connoisseur of New York steaks, say they have never seen anything like it in New York, ever. Then there was a poached egg on the top, with fried onions and French fried potatoes, followed by Peach Melba for dessert. Needless to say, the bill at the end gave our pocketbook quite a jolt, but we all felt it was well worth the splurge.

During what was left of the afternoon, we caught a street car and rode out of town a way, visited the civic center of Dublin, returned for a short shopping tour but very little buying, and then walked around the side streets some. Not two blocks away from the hotel where we had that luxurious meal, we found some of the worst slums and more poverty and misery than I have ever seen before. There seemed like millions of dirty, ragged, hungry looking kids out in the street, all tagging along and begging, "Any gum, chum?" That seems to be the universal greeting to a Yank in any country. Southern Ireland is a very poor country, but one thing they can raise plenty of is kids. By night we had all had enough of Dublin and are happy enough to be back across the border at Rostrevor again tonight. It would have been a much better trip if we could have had the car.

Oct 31 - We drove back to Belfast this a.m. where we dropped off

Kaufman, but Provan is returning to England with us. So early tonight, we boarded the steamer at Larne and had a rather rough crossing back to Scotland, and are put up for the night in the George Hotel in Stranraer. They were making big plans for Halloween on the Irish side tonight, but we see no evidence of it here. We all have enjoyed our trip to Ireland very much.

Nov 1, 1945 - We had to bring Provan back to Glasgow for him to finish off some details concerning his school in Ireland, but fortunately, it didn't take long. This afternoon we started out north on a trip which we expected to take us to Aberdeen, and drove through the extraordinarily beautiful mountain country to the Trossachs Hotel where I visited last year. The autumn colors of the trees made the scenery even more beautiful than I remembered it last year. We had no difficulty getting rooms for the one night since it is now "off-season."

Before dark we had time to take that lovely stroll over to the gorgeous shores of Loch Katrine. When we arrived Miss Larrimer, the hotel manageress, recalled she had seen me before, but I decided not to remind her of my association with the Eisenhower son—Queen Marie of Yugoslavia incident of last year when she got so furious. She'd throw us out if she connected me with that.

But alas! All good things have to end sometime, and ours is impending. Johnson called our home station tonight and received strict orders to have the car back at the earliest possible moment. They didn't seem to care two hoots about us, but somebody wants the car. How inconsiderate of them! Why, we have only been gone eight days!!!!

Nov 3 - We left the Trossachs early yesterday a.m., as instructed, to return home. We went via Stirling to Edinburgh, where we took time out to tour the Castle and the Palace of Mary, Queen of Scots, then shopped a little and had lunch. After that we drove very hard, and even after dark to get as far south as possible, and spent the night at Darlington, England. For about an hour we drove through some wonderful mountains covered with clouds, but for the most part our entire return trip was just ordinary English countryside.

This morning we got another early start and only deviated from our course to take Her and Crucius via the old walled city of York. We arrived back at Alconbury about 2:30 p.m. to find Gen. Emil C. Kiel from Fighter Command here and hopping mad because we had the car away, though we have had our trip now, and he doesn't intend to do anything about it.

In the 10 days, we drove almost 1,600 miles and had not the slightest bit of trouble—didn't even have to put any air in the tires at all, we used 2 pints of oil, and had plenty of gasoline for the asking, simply by driving into any British Army post and signing a paper for it. Of course, the government has to pay for it, but if we traveled by train, the government would pay for that too—lend-lease. It was a very enjoyable and most interesting trip throughout, and the fact that we had our own car makes it a rare feat for the US Army. The Army certainly does offer some opportunities for an officer when one learns how to take advantage of them.

But upon arrival back here I find myself confronted by two other sets of orders. First, the bunch here at Alconbury is ordered to move on over to Snetterton Heath day after tomorrow. Secondly, the request I made some weeks ago for two weeks temporary duty on the Riviera has been approved, and I find I am already three days late in reporting for duty. Furthermore, there is a very late, hot rumor that our shipping date has been advanced, and that we might leave by 15 Nov. If so, I wouldn't have time to finish my duty in France. So that officially puts me on the spot. Things are now moving too fast for me, so I think I'll just sit down, and wait to see what happens. I can't do anything until we move to Snetterton Heath, anyway. I have wanted that Riviera job a long time, and it is unfortunate it has come so late, but getting on that boat is my primary interest now—besides, I'm about to get my fill of running around for a while.

The Trossachs Hotel in Callander, Scotland. Courtesy of the Thurman Shuller Family Collection.

On a final motor trip of the English Lake Country, Scotland, and Ireland, Provan, Shuller, Kaufman, Her, and Crusius watched a soccer match in Belfast, Ireland. Courtesy of the Thurman Shuller Family Collection.

Sailing on the Firth of Moray at Inverness, Scotland, with Wing Commander Jamaison and his girlfriend Mrs. Green. Courtesy of the Thurman Shuller Family Collection.

On Lough Neigh, North Ireland. Shuller is sitting third from left. Courtesy of the Thurman Shuller Family Collection.

The staff car being loaded onto the *Princess Maud* for Ireland. Courtesy of the Thurman Shuller Family Collection.

Nov 5 - We completed our move to Snetterton Heath this afternoon. The accommodations are adequate, but not nearly so comfortable as at Alconbury. My first duty upon arrival here was to collect my pay for last month which I had been unable to do up to now. And believe me, I felt a little bad about collecting it considering I have done nothing but have a good time at the expense of the government.

Since the sailing date still is not definitely known, I have received permission to go ahead with the trip to France, even though I am late, and have made arrangements for them to call me in case an early sailing date is set. I shall go to London tomorrow to arrange a flight by A.T.C.

Nov 7 - My trip to Cannes did not get very far. I came to London yesterday morning as planned and went immediately to A.T.C. to get passage to Paris, but since the weather has been bad recently, the flying has been limited, and there has been created such a back log of passengers for Paris, I could not get passage for today and maybe not tomorrow. In the meantime I called Johnson back at Snetterton Heath this a.m., and he stated that our outfit would almost certainly sail on the *Europa* on the 17th, so after seeing the transportation difficulty getting there and anticipating similar difficulty returning, we have decided against our carrying out this assignment, and Johnson has ordered me back to base within the next couple days. That suits me O.K., because I can complete some of my Christmas shopping.

I spent last night with the Camdens, who have moved from Great Barford back to their home in London. I left them a lot of my clothing and other supplies which I do not intend to carry back home with me, and they were overwhelmed. There must have been at least 50 pounds of it.

Nov 9 - I bade London goodbye again this morning and have returned to base to find things in about the same state as when I left—still planning to sail in about a week. Had a miserably cold ride from London in an open command car with Maj. Krannawitter.

But there is one thing which could throw a monkey wrench into my plans at the last minute. Just learned this afternoon that Gen. Kiel still hasn't forgiven our trip to Scotland in the car, in spite of Gen. Beaman's approval. He actually has his Trial Judge Advocate investigating the possibility of disciplinary action. I am not much afraid of his actually going through with it, and wouldn't mind too much if he did, but he could have as a motive simply dragging out an investigation long enough for us to miss the boat. That would be simple enough for him, and I don't believe he is above doing it.

Nov 11 - The trouble with Gen. Kiel over using the car on our trip is all blown over now and everybody's happy—especially us. That just goes to show what one can get by with in the Army, if he uses proper discretion and chooses his right time. If only I could have known four years ago all the angles and ways and means and loop holes I know now, I could have really cashed in - but then I wouldn't have done a very good job, so it's probably well I didn't.

Yesterday afternoon and this morning, I went flying with a Lt. Eakin and others in a C-64 to get in my flying time. Part of the time there were some hectic and anxious moments. Eakin had not flown a C-64 before, but he has 1,500 hours, and I didn't consider him unsafe, or rather no more unsafe than with anyone else in a C-64. But when he allowed the co-pilot to try to land it, we did the first ground-loop I have ever experienced in all the flying I have done. Fortunately, the runway was wet and slippery, so no damage was done to the plane. This may be the last flying for pay I'll ever do.

Nov 14 - Still no definite dope when we leave. I have been assigned the exciting job of baggage inspector for the senior officers. We're to see no unauthorized govt. equipment or restricted items are taken back to the States. By tonight, it is said all administrative preparation will have been completed and then we'll have nothing to do but await the call.

Nov 18 - At last, at last, definite dope! We sail on the Queen Mary, rather than the Europa, on 23 Nov. Only 5 more days of waiting. Waiting is getting on the nerves of all of us. We all had our heart set on sailing on the Europa, but now any of us would be almost willing to sail in a rubber dingy. Our heavy baggage was taken to the port yesterday, so we feel there is no doubt about it now.

Nov 19 - How fast things move when they do start happening. Here I was minding my own business and twiddling my thumbs this morning, when I received notice I was to leave with a small advanced party for the port this afternoon. So I dashed madly about and washed what dirty clothes I had, turned in a few items of equipment, got 46 pounds 10 shillings changed into American money (good old American greenback) and was packed and ready to go by 4 p.m. The others will come by troop train tomorrow night. The date for sailing has been set up again and will leave

Lt. Colonel E. R. T. Holmes (British Army) and his wife and daughter see the officers of the 435th Air Service Group off as they leave Huntingdon Station for Southampton, where they boarded the *Queen Mary* to return to the United States, October 20, 1945. Courtesy of the Thurman Shuller Family Collection.

in the very early morning of the 22nd. We got as far as London tonight and will go on to Southampton in the morning.

Nov 20 - We caught a taxi to go to Waterloo station for the 9:30 train, and our farewell to London was just about as we first saw it—foggy. In fact, there was heavy fog all the 2 ½ hour ride to Southampton. We went immediately to the docks and carried our heavy baggage up the gangplank and up four decks to our staterooms.

Boarding the ship was not as exciting as I had been anticipating, because we got on two days ahead of sailing and in a party of seven, rather than our complete organization. But the *Queen Mary* herself is awe inspiring. At close range and on board, she is far more impressive than I remember her from a distance in the New York harbor.

I am bunking in a stateroom for 10 officers, but I hope some of them don't show up. It's comfortable enough and actually better than I expected. We had a K-ration for lunch, but the evening meal was quite good. At 3 p.m., I tried to report to the transport surgeon to see what my duty assignment is to be. I found the right deck O.K., but it took at least 15 minutes walking and hunting to find the office after I got on the right deck. It is impossible to comprehend the immensity of this ship from the outside. My duty assignment is the unglamorous role of medical inspector. It won't be bad though, and it will get me into most of the ship before the voyage is over.

Nov 21 - The day dragged very slowly. All day long, troops came on board in one almost endless chain, from trains one after the other. At 10:30 tonight, we had an officers' meeting at which it was announced that all troops are finally on board. There are 12,000 passengers, of whom less than 1,000 are officers. That is a little less than the usual complement of officers, but it is still plenty. The food is extraordinarily good, but the worst part of it is we are served only 2 meals a day. It is American food for the most part, but cooked and served in proper courses by the British staff. The G.I.'s say their food is excellent too, but they have to eat out of mess gear. There are three sittings for officers, mine is the third at 9 a.m. and 7 p.m. It sure is a long time between meals.

Nov 22 - Thanksgiving 1945 at sea on the *Queen Mary*. We were pulled away from the dock by two tugs at 12:30 p.m., 1/2 hour late. We are now actually on our way home—so difficult to realize. It was foggy again today, so our very last glimpse of England was [not] what one might call "normal conditions." The sailing was without fanfare, but a few moments before the gangplank went ashore, an R.A.F. Commodore came aboard and made a very nice little speech of "thank you for everything, goodbye, good luck and come back to see us under more normal times" over the public address system. There were a number of British on the dock to wish us off. Everybody tried to get to the rail or a port hole for the farewell to England, but there were far too many for all to see. One gets the impression there must be hundreds of thousands aboard. This morning at breakfast time, I walked down one of the corridors on a deck, and it seemed I had never seen such a busy "street."There were hundreds of G.I.'s dashing about with their mess gear—and that was only one corridor on only one of the eight decks which carries military personnel.

The Thanksgiving dinner tonight was excellent. The menu said we were being served Vermont turkey, but whether it was from Vermont or Texas, it was still good. It was served in 5 courses with all the usual trimmings plus a few others, including fresh salmon steak.

And don't we have plenty to be thankful for this year. One year ago, it was just before the Ardennes bulge, one of the most anxious moments of the European war, and since that date a lot of men have been written off. I recall the striking Hubert cartoon on the front of the last Thanksgiving Stars and Stripes which showed Hubert sitting shivering in the snow trying to warm his coffee over a miserable little fire and looking very tired, thoroughly worn out, saying, "I'm thankful I'm alive—I think." How different this year. Nearly all our soldiers are well situated and most, including me, already home or on the way. Next year, I hope we can be thankful for a just peace.

Nov 24 - Yesterday we sailed along very uneventfully, hoping we might run into a storm so we could have a little excitement. This morning we awoke to find the boat pitching quite a bit into a moderately rough sea. In fact, this huge hulk rolls and pitches much more than any of us imagined, and this morning there was vomitus everywhere. At eleven o'clock, just at inspection time, I even lost my pride, along with my breakfast, but was immediately afterwards able to continue with the inspection and wasn't even troubled with nausea afterwards. Seasickness is a strange and unpredictable thing. It was a thrilling experience this afternoon to walk out on the forward deck. The wind was so strong, one had extreme difficulty standing up and with the bow plunging deeply occasionally, the spray came up as high as the bridge and would have drenched us if we didn't duck at the right time. But it was fun and most invigorating.

We are now slightly more than half way home. Nothing can happen to make us turn back now. This is the 129th Atlantic crossing of the Queen Mary.

Nov 26 - Our sea journey is about over—we dock at noon tomorrow. Today has been very smooth sailing, but yesterday was rough. It is said this has been an unusually rough crossing, but at that, it hasn't been so bad. When the boat is rolling, one gets the most peculiar sensation while riding one of the elevators on the boat. It is literally possible to be going in three directions at once. It was amusing day before yesterday at the movie to see the officers trying to stand at attention to the "Star Spangled Banner." The unsteady floor caused the whole audience to sway in unison in all positions except straight up.

I accidentally fell into a bit of luck today. As we were going into our inspection, one of the permanent staff said the Captain of the ship wanted to invite six of the officers up to the bridge at noon today. By being at the right place at the right time, I was one of those six. We sat in his office for a while and accepted his offer of sandwiches and punch. Then he took us onto the bridge and showed us all the controls and radar equipment. The pilot wheel is only about 2 ½ feet across but is hydraulically operated. A lad about 20 years old was at the controls while we were there. I was surprised to learn they had exactly the same navigation aids our bombers carry. I wouldn't have missed that chance for anything. The only other more interesting place might be the engine room. The Captain is a nice old gent named Captain [Ernest M.] Fall who started out as an artillery man in the Boer War. Until recently, he commanded the Queen Elizabeth.

Nov 27 - Camp Kilmer, New Jersey. We have just eaten that huge steak dinner, 6 p.m., with milk and ice cream, etc. which the War Dept. has decreed as the first meal for all troops returning from overseas—and it was delicious. I enjoyed it particularly because it was my first meal today. And that was because I was too excited to worry about eating breakfast. Since I could not eat until 9, and we were scheduled to pass the Statue of Liberty shortly afterwards, I couldn't afford to lose a chance of getting a good spot to see the sights.

Outside the New York harbor, a boat with a band aboard came out to meet us. All the boat traffic saluted us as we passed, and several of the harbor fire boats came out to meet us with all hoses spurting up spray like a gigantic fountain. But the Statue of Liberty herself was the thing which gave all of us the thrill we expected. She was glistening white, and she seemed almost to smile as she looked down upon us when we passed. It seems strange that this statue should so gladden the heart of every returning American when it is actually a gift from the French, whom most American soldiers now hold in a certain degree of contempt. But it still means home to us, and all the things we like about America. As we passed the tip of Manhattan, great quantities of paper were dumped from all the windows of the tall buildings in the Wall Street district. As we approached the pier, another lively band struck up, and there was a lot of good natured remarks exchanged with the civilians on the docks.

By the time we tied up, the boat was leaning sharply toward the dock because of the excess thousands of soldiers trying to get to that one side. Ours was the first whole unit off. On the dock, while we were waiting for the ferry, Red Cross women served each of us doughnuts and coffee or a whole pint of milk. New York does seem to try to give the fellows a good reception, especially since they have so many. An official on the pier said that in the last 24 hours, New York harbor had handled 27,000 troops in one way or another. The half-hour ferry trip to the Jersey side, and the

A quiet moment on the stern aboard the *Queen Mary* with the Ninety-Sixth Bomb Group, November 22–29, 1945. Courtesy of the Thurman Shuller Family Collection.

A view of the bow, aboard the *Queen Mary* with the Ninety-Sixth Bomb Group, November 22-29, 1945. Courtesy of the Thurman Shuller Family Collection.

The *Queen Mary* in New York harbor on one of its many trips bringing American troops home in 1945. Courtesy of the East Anglia Air War Collection.

hour train ride to [Camp] Kilmer completed our trip thus far. We'll be here a couple days. We are restricted to the post while here, so we won't be seeing New York on this trip. Thus far we don't see too much evidence that we are in the good old USA, except from the train we saw so many, many nice long shiny cars, such as we have seen used only by generals for the last 3 years. Kilmer itself might easily be Snetterton Heath, except that is consolidated rather than dispersed construction.

Nov 29 - 4 p.m. Have orders to entrain at 8 p.m. for Jefferson Barracks. It will be a troop train of 11 coaches, and since I am the senior officer, I will be the troop commander for the trip. It's not going to be a pleasant trip, but it is getting us nearer home. The weather here has been miserable these two days—a hard driving rain constantly. Kilmer runs things reasonably efficiently, considering the volume of work. Approximately 12,000 –15,000 troops have entrained at this camp in the last 9 hours. The boys are sure getting home in a hurry now.

Dec 1, 1945 - Arrived at Jefferson Barracks station about 10:30 this morning, an hour late on one of the most miserable train rides I have ever had. 38 hours sitting up in one of those old World War I coaches is no fun, particularly when it includes two nights. But there was no hitch anywhere, and was one of the most orderly bunch of soldiers I have ever seen. They were most orderly on the Queen Mary, for that matter. Most of them are much, much older and more settled than when they went away from home, two or three years ago. However, quite recently, Kilmer did have much trouble with the 71st Infantry Division which went on a mass destruction and raping spree while there.

The only thing accomplished this afternoon was to visit the Air Force counselor, who was a young captain bombardier who knew about as much about counseling as a 10 year old, but he had two forms to sign, one of which said you wanted to be relieved from active duty, and the other said you wanted to stay in the service until June 30, 1947 and waive all chances of getting out. I hesitated maybe as much as three seconds before signing the first one. We start through the processing line early in the morning.

At Kilmer, the last of the old bunch separated and went our respective ways. As we left the station, I discovered that of the 549 who were going to board the train to come to Jefferson Barracks, there was not one single officer or enlisted man whom I had known more than a week. That has been one of the most unfortunate features of my Army experience to have been associated almost entirely with people from other sections of the country—by that I mean as far as forming enduring friendships. There are quite a number I'd love to continue to know in years to come, people I've worked closely with and like and respect, but there is not a single one from the whole state of Arkansas, either officer or enlisted man, with whom I have been really closely associated in my entire Army experience. There are advantages to meeting other people, of course, but at the same time, it is such a terrible waste to lose entirely in one stroke of redeployment, practically all the friendships it has taken years to make. I don't suppose I'll see more than a half dozen of them ever again—maybe a few more than that. We were all a little more sad at the final breaking up than we really expected to be, I think. Certainly, it did somewhat dull the enthusiasm for going home and getting out of the service, which we have all anticipated so long.

Dec 2 - I joined the production line, or rather the demobilization line early this a.m., and it ran smoothly and efficiently for me until I learned I could not start my terminal leave, and then turn into a hospital after Christmas for excision of my pilonidal sinus on Army time. That has thrown a complete block into my getting out now. But the real problem is to get it done on Army time (which it should be) and still be in position to be home Christmas. The Air Force liaison officers here are most sympathetic with my wishes, and we should be able to work something out. It's going to involve a lot of sitting around, however. I'm hoping to get home at least for a couple days immediately. I'm most disappointed about that, and I know that Mother and Dad will be.

Dec 7 - The 4th Anniversary of Pearl Harbor. Four years ago today, I was the O.D. at the hospital at Las Vegas, Nev. Lt. Shuller in those days had very little foresight of things to come. Nobody could have been more surprised to be told he'd still be wearing the uniform 4 years later, and even more so if he'd been told he would be wearing silver leaves on his shoulders. It has now been so long that it is actually difficult to remember quite what being a civilian is like. But one thing I'm sure, I'd like to find out again. But it isn't without some regrets that I propose to take off the uniform in the not too distant future. There has been a lot of bitterness, a certain number of heartaches, a lot of stuff to put up with which has been hard to take. But there have been lots of pleasures and worlds of new and interesting experiences. The good in these four years outweighs the bad. In that, I have been fortunate because hundreds of thousands of other soldiers, perhaps millions, have had it much the opposite.

This business of waiting is getting awfully monotonous. Surely, it won't be long now. I can't get interested in doing anything except getting home. Going into St. Louis or to a show doesn't help much. Went flying for a while out at Scott Field a couple days ago. Had a real treat tonight, however. Heard Paul Robeson at the Keil Auditorium in St. Louis. He certainly has one of the richest and most beautiful male voices I have ever heard.

I didn't care too much for his printed program, but his unusually large number of encores were beautiful. He ended his program with a bit of his interpretation of Othello, which he did on Broadway some months before, and with considerable feeling. I sat right next to a colored couple. It is said he will not sing to a segregated audience. I thoroughly enjoyed his singing and am glad I heard him.

Dec 9, 1945 — "Goin' Home."

Epilogue

Thurman Shuller wrote this concluding essay on May 1, 2012, five days before his ninety-eighth birthday, and just a little over six months before he died. He looks back over his military service and offers glimpses of his postwar experience. Although he had not written the piece to be a part of his diary, it is a fitting conclusion to his World War II story. Shuller revisits his military journey with the insight and reflection that only comes with the perspective and wisdom gained from more than a half century of living since the war. It is clear that at age ninety-eight Thurman Shuller's memory was sharp and precise, and his discernment was clear and steady. It is fitting that the final words in this book of World War II history are his words, looking back in assessment and contemplation.

My Military Service Before Pediatrics[1]
By Thurman Shuller, Col., Medical Corps, US Army Air Force (Ret)
Presented to the Pittsburg County, OK Genealogy Society
In honor of Armed Forces Day, May 1, 2012

It was July 1941. I was twenty-seven years old, having finished medical school and a two-year hospital internship, but undecided where and what type of medical practice I wanted to begin. I had previously joined the Army Medical Corps Reserve upon graduation from medical school in 1939. With war raging in Europe, it seemed that the practical thing to do was to spend one year of service in the army, which was being offered at the time. I accepted a commission and was assigned as a first lieutenant to the Air Corps Gunnery School at Las Vegas as a general physician. That was a new post just organized, and I served there for five months. The only other doctor there at the time was an experienced but kindly major who took me under his wing and gave me two pieces of advice which served me well. He advised me that the future in the military was with the Army Air Force, and that I should apply for admission to the School of Aviation Medicine. Secondly, as a young officer, I should pay special attention to the promptness, accuracy, and appearance of all my reports. Five months later Pearl Harbor extended my one-year active duty assignment to nearly five years.

I did take the major's advice and enrolled in the School of Aviation Medicine with the goal of becoming a flight surgeon, a three-month course of study at Randolph Field, San Antonio. Among other things, we were required to take three one-hour segments of flight instruction. I had never before set foot in a plane. We were immediately warned that if we became air sick and contaminated the cockpit, the penalty was to buy a carton of cigarettes for some private to clean up. I had to pay off. Another special activity was to sit in a decompression chamber where we were taken to a simulated height of thirty thousand feet to experience symptoms of rarified air, such as altered speech and vision and the requirement of oxygen.

Upon graduation I was assigned to Wendover Field, Utah. This airfield was just starting from scratch at a desert village of about twelve houses and a very small hotel which straddled the Utah-Nevada state line. A small cadre headed by two senior officers, Col. Overacker and Lt. Col. LeMay, received the three of us newly graduated first lieutenants, and each was assigned as a physician to a newly developed squadron of the 306th Bombardment Group. The next day a couple of B-17 planes were flown in along with two experienced B-17 pilots and a half-dozen young pilots who had never before flown anything larger than a two-engine plane. My first ride in a B-17 was with one of the experienced pilots who was giving a first lesson to three of the inexperienced pilots. I was impressed with the flight.

Expansion of the group was rapid, and the duty slots began to fill up rapidly. Nearly everybody was inexperienced and was forced to learn on the job. There had never before been an air force organization like this one and the three others also being similarly newly organized. Our medical enlisted men came in with little or no training and had to be taught. I and three of my medics got some practical training one day when a pilot, who had slept in the bed adjacent to mine in the barracks, crashed on a training flight, killing himself and four others. We got the gory experience of picking up the pieces.

Two months into our training, the group surgeon was transferred out, and I was selected to take his place on the basis of having been in grade longer than the other physicians by three weeks. That made me head doctor in the group and scared to death of the responsibility. I was promoted to captain on my twenty-eighth birthday, May 1942.

After four months training at Wendover, we began to move eastward in two echelons, air and ground. Each of the four squadrons had nine planes, each with a crew of four officers and six enlisted gunners, a total of thirty-five planes in the group—one short. The ground echelon went by train to the east coast and eventually sailed on the *Queen Mary* to England. The air echelon flew to Westover Field, Massachusetts, where they were refitted with thirty-five new B-17s. After a month of practicing formation flying, in early September 1942, we flew on to England with an overnight stopover on the island of Newfoundland. Each plane carried one extra passenger. I, as group surgeon, flew as an extra. That overnight flight was not without tragedy. One plane did not arrive. A couple of the crews saw a bright flash in the sky which was presumed to have been an airplane explosion. Another plane ran out of fuel in sight of land near Ireland. The plane sank, but all the crew were rescued.

Our assigned station in Thurleigh, England, was far better than expected. It was an operating RAF station which was turned over to us for the duration, needing only to lengthen the runways. There was a dispensary with twenty beds and full equipment for our needs. Unfortunately, the nearest US Army hospital was ninety miles away.

The group's first activity in England was practicing high altitude formation flying, which resulted in tragedy. One of the crews had an inexperienced gunner who misused his oxygen mask and passed out from anoxia. The pilot put the plane into a very steep dive at high speed. When he pulled out of the dive the tail section broke off completely. The tail gunner remained inside the tumbling tail section and survived. All the others died in the crash. Thus, the group had lost three planes and two crews before we ever got into combat.

Shortly after arrival in England, all officers were issued bicycles. At age twenty-eight, I had never ridden a bicycle in my life. After a few spills I gradually began to ride quite capably, though never as gracefully as those who grew up on that vehicle as kids.

The theory of high-altitude pinpoint bombing had been developed in the desert where there was perpetual visibility, and bombardiers bragged that they could drop a bomb into a pickle barrel from twenty thousand feet. Not so in England. In Europe the almost constant shifting clouds often obscured the target.

The US Air Force began combat from England in October 1942, with four heavy bombardment groups, namely the 306th, 305th, 303rd, and 91st.

Their missions were coordinated through Bomber Command. Their first strike was the railroads at Lille, France, where the 306th lost one out of twenty-four planes. Only one crewman bailed out of the stricken plane and was taken prisoner. Another plane was lost on the second mission.

Preparations for combat missions were time consuming: wake up at 3:30 or 4:00, breakfast at 4:30, dress for mission at 5:00, and then briefing. I almost always attended the briefing where the officers learned the details of the mission for the day.

The third mission was to St. Nazaire, France, a submarine base. This was an experimental one at eight thousand feet instead of twenty thousand feet. It was a vicious battle in which we lost four planes, plus one man brought back killed. The returning planes landed on an RAF base near the English coast, as planned. The low-flying mission was a failure and never tried again. Several weeks of bad weather followed the St. Nazaire disaster, resulting in multiple cancellations of missions after they had been briefed and also responsible for sinking morale and sloppy discipline.

Poor discipline of an organization, regardless of cause, is usually blamed on the commanding officer. General Eaker of Bomber Command, with three or four associates, called on the 306th to investigate. As the general's car approached the gate, the sentry sloppily motioned the car on through without even looking up. The general got out and gave the sentry a lesson on military courtesy. Therefore, the general was in a very poor mood to face Col. Overacker, commander of the 306th. With a minimum of comment, the general told Col. Overacker he was relieved of his command and to get his things and go back with him to division headquarters. Then he turned to Col. Armstrong, who accompanied him, and ordered that he would now assume command, and he would send his things to him. Thus, the change in command of the 306th was as depicted in the movie *Twelve O'Clock High*.

It was very shortly after this event that I was notified that I had been promoted to major, as provided in the Table of Organization. I had been a captain for only six months.

The group shaped up under Col. Armstrong's leadership and was ready for the next mission. On January 27, 1943, Col. Armstrong led it himself in the first plane over Germany to Wilhelmshoven. That qualified the 306th to adopt the slogan, "First Over Germany." It was a successful mission with no casualties and the morale of the combat crews soared.

In the performance of our duties in the medical section, we were most fortunate to have a compatible group with five doctors, besides myself, and were able to work as a team. I turned most of the duties of sick call and care of patients in our dispensary over to the others. The squadron doctors and aid personnel went with the ambulances to the various squadron areas to meet returning planes. My duties were concerned primarily with the combat crewmen personally and their fitness for flying. I regularly attended the pre-mission briefings and was at the control tower on their return. I made it a practice to spend time in the evenings at the officers' club with a single drink in my hand making myself available in case one of the officers felt the need to talk. That procedure evolved early on after one of the pilots, whom I already sensed to be a little insecure, approached me and admitted he had become afraid to fly. Being new to the situation, I just fluffed it off and didn't respond to that confession sufficiently. The very next day on a high-altitude mission, he ran into another plane in the formation, manned by one of the leaders of the group, both planes going down out of control and twenty crewmen killed. To this day I still grieve over the mistake I made by not responding as I should have to what that young pilot was trying to communicate to me. That was an expensive lesson for me. That taught me that one needs to really listen to what a combat man is saying to interpret what he really means. Sometimes a sympathetic flight surgeon is the only one he feels comfortable talking to confidentially. He may only need someone who will really listen. I did thereafter make a sincere effort to determine what was best for the man and for the service.

Bad cloudy weather continued on into spring 1943. Mission after mission was fully prepared for and cancelled at the last minute. On occasion they were recalled after they were actually over enemy territory and had to return with their bombs. Other times they couldn't see the target but were instructed to bomb anything they could see. They suffered unbearable casualties in personnel and planes, yet at the same time realizing their effort hadn't done one thing to further the war effort. Then one day they got a clear day and bombed the target, but at unbearable cost. The 306th put up fifteen planes and lost ten. The 305th had put up fifteen and lost thirteen. Crews coming back to base that night slept in barracks half-full of empty beds. A state of general depression among the combat crews set in. Only occasionally were they able to run a successful mission where they were able to hit the target solidly while sustaining few losses. One of the finest pilots who had flown nineteen missions came in and announced that he was quitting. All the few remaining original crews had completed twenty missions and saw no hope of surviving, except for the rare possibility of bailing out and being taken prisoner.

The doctors in the 306th were constantly discussing the depression problem. A meeting of flight surgeons was held at the division level and even at the Bomber Command level about the necessity of setting a maximum number of missions expected of combat crews. Talk, talk, talk, but nobody was doing anything about it. I consulted with Col. Putnam, my group commander, who was sympathetic to my concern and promised to back me up on an official protest. In March 1943, I wrote a letter to General Eaker describing the deteriorating morale and hopelessness of the combat crews, and the necessity of his establishing term limits to give them some hope of survival. The letter was sent up through channels. It caused considerable heated discussion at Bomber Command headquarters. Three weeks after my letter was mailed, an order was written setting twenty-five as the number of missions required before relief from combat duty. The crews were jubilant because they now had hope that they had a chance of survival. About this time, Col. Putnam was pulled out of command of our group and sent up to division headquarters for another assignment.

Along with those changes, another disturbing situation arose. Air force headquarters in Washington got into the act of pressuring Bomber headquarters to order "maximum effort" missions against critical targets in Germany. That was interpreted to mean cancellation of any and all leaves of combat personnel. That even meant crews on medical leave for two days in London for recuperation from a particularly harrowing experience. In one instance such a crew had just gotten to London and was recalled. The mission was canceled because of weather, so they went back to London. They were recalled again and went back to the base. That mission was again cancelled because of weather, and the crew still had no leave and were worse off for the effort. In May 1943, I fired off another letter, this time directed to the surgeon of Bomber Command, and asked for his direct intervention with the general. It was later before I got action on that.

In June 1943, there was another major shakeup involving me directly. Lt. Col. Streeter, division surgeon, had been removed from office, and I was warned that I was being considered as his replacement. I vigorously protested because it would remove me from a job where the action was and into a desk job, even though the change would mean another promotion. I wrote a letter to my former commander, Col. Putnam, asking for his help on stopping the transfer. That turned out to be not a good action on

General Robert B. Williams with his staff at First Air Division headquarters at Brampton. Courtesy of the East Anglia Air War Collection.

my part, because I later discovered that he was pushing my appointment to that new job. I had no choice but to comply. I had been jumped over three regular army majors and a couple other reserve majors with longer service. I received the order at noon to report to my new post by 4:00 that afternoon, not giving me a chance to say goodbye to the folks at the 306th, whom I would miss terribly. After supper that evening, I stood out on the lawn of my quarters with tears in my eyes as I watched a formation of planes overhead returning from a mission with me not there to greet them.

The next day, as is military custom, I called on the commander, General Williams, to introduce myself. I said, "Major Thurman Shuller reporting for duty as your flight surgeon, Sir." He motioned for me to have a seat as he said, "I hear you didn't want this job." I said, "Yes, Sir." What else could I say? He then said, "I don't care if you know how to put a bandage on an injured finger. What I want from you is to keep me advised as to how the combat crews are holding up physically and mentally at the various stations." I sat there thinking that he had just removed me from the position where I could tell him that and into a supervisory job where I would have to take somebody else's word for it. I could only say, "I'll do my best, Sir." As I got up to leave, with my hand on the door knob, General Williams said, "By the way, there won't be any more maximum effort missions." Bingo! I had the answer to my second letter.

The first unpleasant job as division surgeon which was given to me was to fire Major Schnabel, one of the other group surgeons. I had never before been in a position of having to fire somebody. He was intensely disliked by the other doctors in his group and the combat crews did not like him. It was just a personality misfit. If a flight surgeon is disliked by the combat men, he is useless. I had a sleepless night before that encounter, but he didn't seem to mind too much. I think he probably was glad to be relieved of the job, but it was a learning experience for me as a new "executive."

A division surgeon's duties were primarily supervisory and required a lot of traveling, checking on the medical operation of the various groups in the division, and attending conferences at Bomber Command. Schedules were much more flexible, allowing more leisure and opportunity to accept invitations. Promotion to Lt. Col. came in an unbelievable short time in December 1943, making the advancement to that rank from entrance into active duty as a first lieutenant to Lt. Col. in only two years and three months.

During the last year of the war, there had been an explosive expansion of groups. Whereas in the beginning of combat there were only four heavy Bombardment Groups, at the ending there were thirty-seven groups. The number of planes in each squadron was expanded from originally nine to more than twice that number at the end. The German air force became largely decimated, but flak from German antiaircraft guns remained deadly until the very end.

Col. Tracy, Bomber Command surgeon, had from the beginning actively promoted the policy of flight surgeons going on at least one combat mission to be familiar with the stress the flight crews were going through. I strongly opposed this policy because it was putting our flight surgeons under hazardous conditions for no apparent benefit. The crews also opposed it because they preferred having their docs waiting for them back on the ground. However, I finally did go on a couple of missions. As I approached the end of my service, I began to feel that my war experience would be incomplete without having done so. The first one was made with my old 306th Bomb Group to Reims, France, at twenty thousand feet, turning out to be completely uneventful. The second was with the 303rd Bomb Group to Kiel, Germany, which almost touches Denmark. That mission was to bomb a shipyard at twenty-seven thousand feet, an eight and a half-hour trip almost totally over the water of the North Sea. No enemy aircraft were seen, but there was a heavy blanket of flak under us all the way on the approach to the target. There were numerous puncture wounds to the skin of the aircraft from flak, but no personal injuries.

I was able to make one contribution as a result of the flight. Navigators had complained that at very high-altitude blips on their radar screen often seemed to fade or disappear. I had taken with me a little Kodak box camera to snap a picture of "Bombs Away." After I snapped the picture and started to roll the film, I couldn't see the numbers on the film. My mind took me back to that decompression chamber at flight surgeon school, and I realized the problem was insufficient oxygen, simply solved by turning up the oxygen regulator. That observation came too late in the war to be of much help. Incidentally, I learned that the plane on which I made the second trip was later shot down, possibly the last one in the air war.

After the war ended, the 306th Bomb Group, being one of the first to begin combat, was the last to leave. I had remained behind to help dismantle the air force in England, then in December 1945 I sailed home on the *Queen Mary* along with twelve thousand others.

On my pre-release physical examination in St. Louis, a condition was found which would delay my final release. However, I was allowed leave time to visit family after more than three years overseas. Surgery was contemplated, requiring extended convalescent leave before I was given permanent release from active duty.

I had voluntarily gone on active duty in the first place because I hadn't made up my mind at that time what direction I wanted my medical career to take. Now, five years later, I still hadn't made up my mind. The delay in my release from the military actually turned out to be a most fortunate turn of events for me. During that time, within a ten-day period, I made three important decisions which defined the rest of my life.

1. I accepted the offer of a position at the McAlester Clinic in the specialty of pediatrics, if I'd prepare myself for that position.

2. I applied for and was accepted for a two-year residency in pediatrics at the Tulane Medical School.

3. I proposed marriage to a young woman named Joanna Carter, and she had accepted.

Dr. Thurman Shuller after the war with premature infant, taken during his pediatric residency at Charity Hospital, New Orleans, circa 1946-48. Courtesy of the Thurman Shuller Family Collection.

I received my discharge from active duty in May 1946 along with a terminal promotion to full colonel.

Fast forward forty years:

Even before final release from the service, I had made up my mind that I would put all things military behind me and commit my life to the practice of medicine as originally planned, except only what was required to keep my membership in the army reserve active. Therefore, I did not participate in the activities of the local veterans' groups.

Then thirty-seven years after the war ended, the veterans of the old Eighth Air Force decided to organize a veterans' reunion. It was so successful that they decided to meet annually. At the third one there were so many veterans from the old 306th Bomb Group which was originally organized at Wendover, Utah, we decided we should organize our own reunion.

The first annual reunion of the 306th Bomb Group veterans was held in Omaha, Nebraska, in October 1983. I was asked to be the after-dinner speaker at the Saturday night banquet. In preparation, I combed my diary for any amusing incidents I could recall to try to make it entertaining as well as factual, and I was able to hold the attention of the four hundred veterans and wives for a full hour. Upon closing, I was given a standing ovation that wouldn't quit. As I got off the stage and started to sit, they were still clapping, so I got back on the stage and gave them a salute. It troubled me for years afterwards as to why that demonstration. I thought I had given a good speech—but not that good. The answer came much later.

By this time in my life I had begun to cut back some in my medical practice and began enjoying attending most of the 306th reunions which were rotated all over the country. However, I never participated to the extent of becoming an officer in the organization because it would have required some traveling, which I didn't want to do. I have never forgotten one incident at a reunion at least fifty years after the war. I was standing alone in the lobby of the host hotel when a man approached me, grabbed my hand, and said only six words: "Thanks, Doc, for saving my life." He walked away without giving me a chance to respond.

Fast Forward to October 2011:

I was fortunate to have been chosen, at age ninety-seven, to participate in an Honor Flight, a one-day round trip of WWII Veterans from Oklahoma City to Washington, DC, to see the WWII Memorial in our honor. There were 103 of us veterans, several of us in wheelchairs, and we were truly honored and recognized in every possible way. My son, Henry, was my escort and granddaughter, Jennifer, and her family came up from Virginia Beach, VA., to meet me, which added much to my trip. But the crowning joy of the occasion developed after I got back home. The secretary of the 306th Bomb Group Association had notified the membership by email that I was to be on this flight and gave the Oklahoma Honor Flight address where they could contact me if they wished. Upon return, I was handed a manila envelope containing twenty-five personal letters from fellow veterans, widows, and children of 306th veterans, from California, Florida, Detroit, Georgia, New York, all over. All were addressed to me personally, thanking me for my help in getting their man home. The one that really pierced my heart was from a woman in her upper sixties who thanked me for life itself. If her father had not got back, he never could have planted the seed that resulted in her conception and become one of the earliest baby boomers. That letter brings tears to my eyes every time I think about it.

One morning lying in bed contemplating the events in my past, it suddenly came to me the answer to that demonstration after my speech at Omaha twenty-eight years earlier. That audience was almost entirely composed of combat crew veterans and their wives and former sweethearts who had personally benefited from the twenty-five mission limit which I helped establish. I didn't realize at the time, that they were actually expressing their gratitude to me in such a very positive way forty years after the fact.

As for my total military experience, there was a lot of stress and sadness, but for me personally, those were far exceeded by the joys and pleasure experienced. It was a period of maturing, growth, and development in so many ways that have served me well throughout my lifetime. I thank

God every day that I was so lucky to have been granted the opportunity to serve.

*

Colonel Thurman Shuller's service extended beyond the routine duties that he performed as a squadron surgeon, group surgeon, and the chief surgeon for the First Air Division. When he took the risk of sending letters arguing for a maximum mission tour up the chain of command to General Ira Eaker, he helped save countless air crews throughout the rest of the war. Without the new policies, how many officers and enlisted crewmen wouldn't have survived their tours, lived full lives, and had families after the war? What did the impact of the elimination of maximum effort missions have on the well-being of aircrews and their survival? Whatever the net result of these emerging new policies, Shuller's contribution in bringing about change was consequential and compelling. His diary and the supporting documents reveal his role in those events and give history an additional perspective on the air war in the ETO.

Endnotes

Introduction

1. In 2002, Dr. Vernon L. Williams established the East Anglia Air War Project (EAAWP) with the goal to preserve the memory and history of community in wartime England, in particular the community established between the American airman who came in large numbers beginning in 1942, and the British families who lived in rural England near and around the American bomber and fighter bases. The project focuses on the agricultural areas north of London where large numbers of American air bases were established among the farming villages and towns that stretch from Norwich on the east to Kettering to the west of Cambridge. The target oral history interview audience has been American aircrews and ground personnel stationed in the Eighth and Ninth Air Forces, and British family members who were children or young adults during World War II. The underlying oral history methodology continues to rely heavily on an archival research design and a literature review of a growing historiography of government records and documents, memoirs, diaries such as Thurman Schuller's, regimental histories, and the growing secondary materials on the air war in the European Theater of Operations (ETO).

2. The First Air Division underwent several reorganizational and name changes during the time Shuller served in England. Initially the 306th Bomb Group became a part of the First Bomb Wing, but the command was reorganized as the First Bomb Division in August 1943, and the Wing was renamed First Combat Bomb Wing. Later the First Bomb Division became the First Air Division as the command expanded to include bombers, fighters, and a host of support units as the Eighth Air Force organization became more efficient in its design and development. Vernon L. Williams, "The Built Environment: Military Architecture, Design, and Place in Support of the Air War in World War II England" (paper presented at the Southwestern Historical Association annual meeting, San Diego, California, April 6, 2012).

3. Thurman Shuller, "My Military Service Before Pediatrics" (paper presented to the Pittsburg County, Oklahoma Genealogy Society, May 1, 2012), copy in the Thurman Shuller Historical Collection, East Anglia Air War Archives (hereinafter EAAWA).

4. Shuller, "My Military Service Before Pediatrics."

5. Shuller, "My Military Service Before Pediatrics"; Special Order 23, 306th Bomb Group (H), April 16, 1942, EAAWA.

6. Special Order 67, 306th Bomb Group (H), July 1, 1942, EAAWA; Russell Strong, 306th Bomb Group Personnel Card File, Teall and Shuller entries (unpublished manuscripts), 306th Bomb Group Historical Collection, EAAWA.

Chapter 1

1. Timothy N. Parish, "A Brief History of Nellis Medical Activity (1941–2000)," Office of History, Headquarters Air Warfare Center, Nellis Air Force Base, Nevada, 7. Copy in the Thurman Shuller Historical Collection, EAAWA; "Las Vegas Army Air Base," Online Nevada Encyclopedia, accessed June 26, 2020, http://www.onlinenevada.org/articles/las-vegas-army-air-base.

2. Parish, "Nellis History," 7.

3. Parish, "Nellis History," 7–8; Thurman Shuller, "My Military Service Before Pediatrics" (paper presented to the Pittsburg County, Oklahoma Genealogy Society, May 1, 2012), copy in the Thurman Shuller Historical Collection, EAAWA.

4. Parish, "Nellis History," 7–8; William Houlihan, interview by Vernon L. Williams, October 22, 2005, San Antonio, Texas, EAAWA; Thurman Shuller, interview by Vernon L. Williams, October 25, 2005, San Antonio, Texas, EAAWA.

5. Thurman Shuller, "Diaries" (unpublished manuscripts, 1941–1945), scanned copies of the original diary books in EAAWA; Parish, "Nellis History," 7–8; Russell Strong, 306th Bomb Group Personnel Card File, (unpublished manuscripts), 306th Bomb Group Historical Collection, EAAWA; Houlihan, interview; Shuller, interview.

6. Mary T. Sarnecky, *A History of the U.S. Army Nurse Corps* (Philadelphia, Pennsylvania: University of Pennsylvania Press, 1999), 265–69; Army Nurse Corps, Rank, Pay, and Allowances, 77th Cong., 2d Sess. (December 22, 1942); *Public Law 828 in United States Statutes at Large* 56, part 1 (Washington DC: Government Printing Office, 1943) 1072–74; Parish, "Nellis History," 9; Army Nurse Corps, 78th Cong., 2d Sess. (June 22, 1944) Public Law 350 in *United States Statutes at Large* 58, part 1 (Washington DC: Government Printing Office, 1945), 324–26.

7. Charleston Mountain, located about thirty-five miles from Las Vegas, was a popular recreation area. Summer activities included hiking, camping, and picnicking. The area was first designated a forest reserve in 1906 as part of President Theodore Roosevelt's national parks program. More information about the recreation area that Shuller and his friends encountered can be found at this current website: https://travelnevada.com/discover/31447/spring-mountains-national-recreation-area-and-mt-charleston-wilderness-area, (accessed August 15, 2020).

8. None of the people that Shuller listed in this entry were relatives. Daughter Mary Beth Carney suggested that these could be former classmates in college, medical school, or from his two year-internship at Charity Hospital in New Orleans. Mary Beth Carney, telephone interview by Vernon L. Williams, August 11, 2020, EAAWA.

9. The Meadows Club in Las Vegas had once been a popular casino and hotel, but by the time that Shuller's group visited the establishment, it was on its way out. It closed for good in 1942, as the city began to improve conditions for the rapidly growing military presence in the city during World War II. "Meadows Club," Online Nevada Encyclopedia, accessed August 15, 2020, http://www.onlinenevada.org/articles/meadows-club#:~:text=The%20Meadows%20Club%20was%20one%20of%20the%20first,the%20modern%20casinos%20that%20followed%20in%20the%201940s.

10. The term "64s" refers to the medical examination form used for elgibility to serve in army aviation. The Form 64 and the various uses and applications of the data changed

over the course of the war. For more information on the development and the uses of the Form 64 examination, see Link and Coleman, *Medical Support*, 311, 326, 374, 380, 452, 548, 677, 678, 752, 797, 852.

11. Mae Mills Link and Hubert A. Coleman, *Medical Support of the Army Air Forces in World War II* (Washington, DC: US Government Printing Office, 1955), 144–59.

12. James W. Headstream was a close friend and classmate in medical school and both Headstream and Shuller graduated in the class of 1939 and served their internships together at Charity Hospital in New Orleans. Headstream entered the Army Air Corps in 1940, serving in the Medical Corps for five years. He left the army at the end of the war as a lieutenant colonel. Obituary of James W. Headstream, copy in Thurman Shuller Historical Collection, EAAWA; "Report of the Charity Hospital of Louisiana at New Orleans, July 1st, 1940 to June 30th, 1941," privately printed, copy in the Shuller Historical Collection, EAAWA.

13. Wayne King was a longtime big band leader, singer, and composer whose band was popular from the 1920s onward. His appearance in San Antonio was one of the last performances he booked before disbanding his orchestra and joining the army in 1942. He ended the war as a major, and after the close of hostilities, he reorganized his orchestra and continued to perform throughout the 1950s and early 1960s. He died in 1985. Wayne King Obituary, accessed August 15, 2020, https://www.findagrave.com/memorial/154539460/wayne-king.

14. Psychasthenia is "a neurotic state characterized especially by phobias, obsessions, or compulsions that one knows are irrational." "Psychasthenia," *Merriam-Webster Dictionary*, accessed July 4, 2020, https://www.merriam-webster.com/dictionary/psychasthenia.

15. Shuller met Harold Deane Munal at the School of Aviation Medicine while they were students there. Munal received his MD degree from Baylor Medical School in 1940 and immediately joined the Army Air Corps. At the conclusion of the course at Randolph Field, both Shuller and Munal received orders for Geiger Field in Spokane, Washington. Following a short leave, Munal drove to Oklahoma City and picked up Shuller for the drive to Seattle. The journey proved to be the beginning of a long association for the two young army doctors, who both ended up with the 306th Bomb Group at Thurleigh, England. Obituary of Harold D. Munal, Jr., *Monitor* (McAllen, Texas), June 26, 1988; Strong, Card File, Munal entry, EAAWA.

16. Albert Theodore Shuller, an older brother who taught school, served as a school principal, and later had a career as superintendent of schools at Berryville, Arkansas. Other brothers included: (1) Frank Shuller, who served in France during WWI and had a career in Civil Service in the Veterans Administration; (2) Edgar Shuller, who served as a minister in the North Carolina Conference of the Methodist Church for thirty-seven years; (3) Elbert Shuller, a medical doctor who was one of four founders of the McAlester Clinic in Oklahoma and practiced medicine for fifty years (Thurman joined Elbert in the McAlester Clinic after the war); (4) Herbert Shuller served as a teacher, businessman, and administrator for the Methodist Church in Palestine, Texas, and was executive director of Lakeview Methodist Assembly there. Mary Beth Carney, "Shuller Family History Notes," Mary Beth Carney to Vernon L. Williams, July 29, 2020, Correspondence File, Thurman Shuller Historical Collection, EAAWA.

17. Headquarters, 306th Bomb Group, Special Orders Number 9, Wendover Field, Utah, April 15, 1942, 306th Bomb Group Collection, EAAWA; Strong, Card File, Teall, Manning, Munal, and Shuller entries, 306th Bomb Group Collection, EAAWA.

18. Strong, Card File, Teall, Manning, Munal, Shuller, and McKim entries, 306th Bomb Group Collection, EAAWA.

19. Colonel Charles P. Overacker, Jr. was the second group commander selected for the new Eighth Force about to move into the European Theater of Operations. Overacker reported to the 306th Bomb Group at Wendover on March 1, 1943. He commanded the group through training, overseas movement, and the first months of combat. He was relieved of his command on January 4, 1943, and transferred to Headquarters, Eighth Air Force Bomber Command at High Wycombe, codenamed Pinetree.

Overacker's relief was the basis for the motion picture *Twelve O'Clock High*. Although it was highly fictionalized, Bernie Lay, who cowrote the book and the screenplay, was present at Thurleigh when Overacker was relieved. After the war he wrote the story based on his wartime experiences as General Ira Eaker's aide. More about this story will appear in Chapter 2. The group surgeon in the film is based, loosely, on Thurman Shuller. Strong, Card File, Overacker entry, 306th Bomb Group Collection, EAAWA; 306th Bomb Group, Special Orders No. 1, March 18, 1942, 306th Bomb Group Collection, EAAWA; Luke Truxal, "Twelve O'Clock High: A Comparative Look at the Film and the 306th Bomb Group in World War II," *Echoes* 33, no. 2, April 2008. Abilene, Texas: 306th Bomb Group Association Editorial Offices, pp. 1, 3, 306th Bomb Group Collection, EAAWA.

Chapter 2

1. Annex Number 1, Operations Order Number 5, 306th Bomb Group (H), July 31, 1942, Special Orders, EAAWA; 306th Bomb Group Combat Diary, July–August 1942 entries, EAAWA; 367th Combat Diary, July–August 1942 entries, EAAWA; 368th Combat Diary, July–August 1942 entries, EAAWA; 369th Combat Diary, July–August 1942, EAAWA; and 423rd Combat Diary, July–August 1942 entries, EAAWA; Russell Strong, *First Over Germany: A History of the 306th Bombardment Group* (Charlotte, North Carolina, privately printed, 2002), 22–23.

2. Special Order 116, 306th Bomb Group (H), July 31, 1942, EAAWA.

3. 423rd Bomb Squadron Diary, August 1–14, EAAWA; Special Order 116, July 31, 1942; Shuller diary, Book 2, August 2, 1942.

4. Colonel Albert H. Schwichtenberg, later a brigadier general, had a long and distinguished career as a medical officer in the army and later in the Army Air Force. In 1934 he attended the School of Aviation Medicine at Randolph Field. At the time of Shuller's arrival, Schwichtenberg served as post surgeon at Westover and assisted Shuller with his preparations for organizing a first aid program and continuing medical and dental support of the group. Schwichtenberg biographical and obituary files, Schwichtenberg Historical Collection, EAAWA.

5. Workers in New York were working to convert the French luxury liner into a troop ship when a welder accidentally ignited some burlap-wrapped life preservers. The fire spread quickly, and the workers and first responders were not able to put the fire out. The Normandie capsized and lay in the mud until after the war. Visitors to New York routine-

ly viewed the wreckage lying in the mud at Pier 88 until 1946, when the vessel was broken up and sold for scrap. Docents of the NJ Maritime Museum, "The S.S. Normandie burns at Pier 88," *Beach Haven Times*, Asbury Park, New Jersey, December 1, 2016, 10A.

6. Thurman Shuller, interview by Vernon L. Williams, October 25, 2005, EAAWA; Strong, *First Over Germany*, 23–25; Headquarters, 306th Bomb Group, Operations Orders Number 6, Westover Field, Mass., August 28, 1942, 306th Bomb Group Collection, EAAWA.

7. As late as the first half of the twentieth century, neurasthenia was a common diagnosis for a variety of maladies associated with nerves, where in some cases during wartime, certain psychiatric conditions rendered a soldier unable to continue in his duties. In more recent times, physicians tend to consider other factors in similar circumstances "such as clinical depression, fibromyalgia, post-traumatic stress disorder, postpartum depression, and perhaps chronic fatigue syndrome and mononucleosis," where earlier physicians labeled the condition neurasthenia. "Neurasthenia & the Culture of Nervous Exhaustion," a historical exhibit by the University of Virginia Claude Moore Health Sciences Library, accessed July 9, 2020, http://exhibits.hsl.virginia.edu/nerves/.

8. Sgt. John M. Loftus broke his leg at Westover and did not go overseas with the 306th Bomb Group. Russell Strong, 306th Bomb Group Personnel Card File, unpublished manuscripts, EAAWA.

9. Meanwhile the ground echelon prepared for the next stage of their journey across the Atlantic by ship. Since leaving Wendover by train on August 1, the ground echelon spent about nine days at Richmond Field "receiving passes and leaves, the rest of the time being spent in drilling and receiving equipment." On August 14 the men boarded trains, bound for their "staging area at Fort Dix, New Jersey." At Fort Dix Shuller made a quick trip to check on the squadron doctors and medics and preparations for the ground echelon's departure. Strong, *First Over Germany*, 23; 306th Bomb Group Combat Diary, August 1–15, 1942, EAAWA; 423rd Bomb Squadron Combat Diary, August 1–31,1942 EAAWA; 368th Bomb Squadron Combat Diary, August 8–16, 1942 EAAWA; 367th Bomb Squadron Combat Diary, August 1–13, 1942, EAAWA; 369th Bomb Group Combat Diary, August 1–14, EAAWA.

10. "Toward the end of the month [August 1942] an epidemic of mumps broke out in the 423rd Bomb Squadron and all men were confined to the barracks area for the last three weeks of our stay in the U.S." While the rest of the ground echelon departed New York harbor aboard the *Queen Elizabeth* on August 31, the 423rd was delayed by the quarantine. On September 4, "the trip from Dix to Hoboken, NJ, and then by ferry to the Queen Mary was tough, but once again the men proved themselves good soldiers and all went well." 423rd Combat Diary, August 15–31, September 4, 1942, EAAWA.

11. Major Watts S. Humphrey, Jr. was the group intelligence officer in the 306th until October 22, 1942, when he was promoted to the First Combat Wing, and later he moved up to headquarters, Eighth Air Force. Humphrey was a World War I pilot, graduated from MIT in 1921, and was an engineer during the interwar years. He left the service in 1947 as a colonel. Strong, Card File, EAAWA; Watts S. Humphrey, III, interview by Grady Booch, Part I transcript, February 22, 2010, accessed July 10, 2020, https://www.informit.com/articles/article.aspx?p=1567322.

12. John F. Kieran was a well-known sportswriter who, after many years of writing a bylined column, Sports of the Times, went into radio in 1938. He broadcasted on NBC's "Information Please," a popular sports information program. At the time that Shuller saw him at Wiggins Tavern in Northampton, Kieran was nationally known for his radio show. Jack Zerby, "John F. Kieran," Society for American Baseball Research, accessed July 10, 2020, https://sabr.org/bioproj/person/john-f-kieran/.

13. Lt. Ralph J. Gaston was shot down on a mission to LaPallice on November 18, 1942. His plane was "hit by flak after bombing target. Could not feather No. 3 engine, turned in direction of Brest Peninsula." Gaston was captured and held as a POW until the end of the war when he returned to the United States. Group Combat Diary, November 18, 1942, EAAWA; Strong, Card File, EAAWA.

14. Strong, *First Over Germany*, 24–27; Joe Albertson, interview by Vernon L. Williams, August 29, 2003, Ely, England, EAAWA; 306th Bomb Group Combat Diary, August 30–September 11, 1942, EAAWA; 423rd Combat Diary, August 30–September 12, 1942 EAAWA; 368th Combat Diary, August 30, 1942 [no copy of the September 1942 entries for the 368th BS has survived], EAAWA; 367th Combat Diary, August 30–September 12, 1942, EAAWA; 369th Combat Diary, August 30–September 6, EAAWA.

15. RAF Cardington was located just to the southeast of Bedford and about twelve miles from Thurleigh. Shuller used Cardington for occasional support needs during the early days before Thurleigh became fully equipped and other American medical facilities were built nearby. RAF Cardington Camp History, accessed August 16, 2020, http://rafcardingtoncamp.co.uk/#.

16. The Key Club was a small bar owned and managed by Norman and Stella Knowlton in downtown Bedford at 84a High Street. Every member had a key to the front door on the ground level, with stairs leading up to the next floor where they signed in. The bar area had a tropical theme and often the owners would squeeze in a small band for entertainment. Stuart Antrobus, email message to Vernon L. Williams, December 17–18, 2019, in author's files, Abilene, Texas; Key.AERO Aviation News Forum, April 21, 2017 and February 24, 26, 2020, accessed July 10, 2020, https://www.key.aero/comment/1915519#comment-1915519.

17. Each of the four engines on the B-17 bomber had a supercharger attached to permit a greater flow of air and fuel and allow aircraft to fly higher, faster, and travel longer distances. For more information on superchargers and the B-17, see https://airpages.ru/eng/mn/b17_18.shtml.

18. William J. Gise, the navigator on Olson's crew, bailed out and successfully evaded capture, eventually making his way back to Allied control. Gise served in World War II and the Korean War, retiring from the air force as a colonel. He died in 2015 at the age of ninety-four. Strong, Card File, EAAWA; Gise obituary, March 23, 2015, Tres Hewell Mortuary, Obituary Files, EAAWA.

19. Albert W. La Chasse bailed out and was captured by the Germans. La Chasse was held at Stalag Luft III until the end of the war when he returned to the United States. Strong, Card File, EAAWA.

20. Timothy N. Parish, "A Brief History of Nellis Medical Activity (1941–2000)," Office of History, Headquarters Air Warfare Center, Nellis Air Force Base, Nevada, 7–8;

Shuller, interview, EAAWA; William Houlihan, interview by Vernon L. Williams, October 22, 2005, EAAWA.

21. Delmar E. Wilson to Russell A. Strong, June 1986, 306th Bomb Group Correspondence Files, EAAWA.

22. Wilson to Strong, June 1986, EAAWA.

23. A special USO show came to Thurleigh just as morale had sunk to a low ebb as losses continued to mount. "Four actresses, who attracted much attention wherever they went, included Carole Landis, Mitzi Mayfair, Kay Francis and Martha Raye." After the show the four joined many of the officers at the Officers' Club where they spent considerable time with the grieving men. Carole Landis wrote a book about the tour, and a movie called *Four Jills in a Jeep* made the rounds of movie houses everywhere. "Seven of the 306th flyers are mentioned in the Landis book." Strong, *First Over Germany*, 50.

24. An article in the *Stars and Stripes* newspaper reported on Lt. William J. Casey's crew that shot down seven German fighters and Casey breaking formation to escort another bomber in distress, flown by Captain Robert C. Williams. "'Casey at Bat' Means Certain Grief to Nazis: Port Which Got Seven FWs in 12 Minutes Helps Flaming Bomber," *Stars and Stripes*, December 1942, copy pasted in Shuller diary, book 1, Shuller Historical Collection, EAAWA.

25. On December 7, 1942, the 2nd Evacuation Hospital traveled to Diddington in Huntingdonshire to occupy a "750-bed Station Hospital of Nisen Huts," then under final construction. The hospital was located about twelve miles from Thurleigh. The hospital staff struggled as they endeavored to make the hospital operational, in light of unfinished water and sewage systems that were "undergoing extensions to the Hospital's necessities." Other problems included "supplies, both general and medical, were still incomplete."

"Beginning January 15, 1943, weekly professional meetings were held which were well attended by Medical Officers from surrounding airfields." Shuller's diary entries included numerous mentions of these lectures, which he found rarely useful, but he enjoyed spending time with the medical staff at Diddington. 2nd Evacuation Hospital database entry, WW2 US Medical Research Centre, accessed July 14, 2020, https://www.med-dept.com/unit-histories/2d-evacuation-hospital/.

26. In 2005 Dr. Shuller spoke about Overacker's relief: "I was not on base. I was attending a postgraduate course of study for four or five days in London on the day that he was relieved. So I was not there so I cannot testify from personal knowledge of what took place." But he added that he was "perfectly agreeable with the idea that he let his personal feeling for the combat crews affect his judgement. He took it personally, and I don't think there is any question that led to his downfall." Shuller never saw Overacker again. "He just disappeared, and I didn't know what happened to him. I learned later that he was taken up to headquarters and later was sent back to the States."

27. Delmar Wilson had more to say on Overacker's relief: "Chip used to fraternize with crews too much, in my opinion. Frequent trips to the pub in Thurleigh," and to the Key Club in Bedford, "and participating in drinking sessions with crew members would not be my pattern as a commander." Wilson summed up the reasons for Overacker's relief: "liquor, repeated and heated confrontations with higher headquarters, too much

fraternization, excessive losses, failure to identify the cause for the high losses and to devise corrective action, and the episode at Land's End." Shuller, interview, EAAWA; Wilson to Strong, June 1986, EAAWA.

28. Gene Raymond, a major motion picture star in the 1930s, underwent pilot training before Pearl Harbor and received a commission in the Army Air Corps soon after war was declared. Eventually, Raymond served in the Ninety-Seventh Bomb Group in England and soon was promoted to assistant operations officer for the Eighth Air Force. His visit to Thurleigh on January 27, 1943, as part of the preparations for the first American raid into Germany, made quite an impression on Shuller and the men of the 306th Bomb Group. Gene Raymond obituary, May 28, 1998, *Independent*, Obituary Files, EAAWA; American Museum in Britain entry for Gene Raymond, accessed July 12, 2020, http://www.americanairmuseum.com/media/53.

29. "No Thriller Stuff—Just Blasts Target," *Stars and Stripes*, March 10, 1943.

Donald Bevan was a waist gunner on the Warren George, Jr. crew. On a mission to Bremen on April 17, 1943, Bevan's aircraft was one of ten lost by the 306th Bomb Group. Bevan successfully bailed out and was captured on the ground. He spent the remainder of the war at Stalag Luft 17B in Austria. While in the POW camp, Bevan and Edmund Trzcinski collaborated on entertainment sketches and programs that they staged in a makeshift theater that they built in the camp. After the war, Bevan and Trzscinski cowrote "Stalag 17" that became a successful Broadway play and later was adapted into an Academy Award film. Bevan became a successful playwright and artist. Donald Bevan obituary, May 29, 2013, Obituary Files, EAAWA.

30. When the 306th Bomb Group arrived at Thurleigh in September 1942, there were then only four heavy bomber groups in England—the 92nd, 97th, 301st, and the 306th. These bomb groups struggled on operations with aircraft hampered by limitations as they flew into target areas without the armament they needed or the fighter escorts that would bring a measure of safety to the missions. B-17Es and B-17Fs needed more armament and protection from the open gun positions in the sub-zero winds at altitude. The days of thousand plane raids and sleek model "G" B-17s lay far ahead for the first four heavy groups. But as Shuller noted, help was arriving. Wesley Frank Craven and James Lea Cate, *The Army Air Forces in World War II: Plans and Early Operations, January 1939–August 1942, Volume 1* (Washington, DC: Office of Air Force History, 1983), 647–68.

31. Lewis P. Johnson, Jr. received the Silver Star for his actions on the May 1 mission, his last mission. In the debriefing after landing at Thurleigh, Johnson simply told the debriefing officer that "this is a hell of a way to finish." Strong, Card File, EAAWA; Strong, *First Over Germany*, 107.

Chapter 3

1. Vernon L. Williams, "A Survey of Heavy Bomber Groups Arrival Patterns in the ETO, 1942–1944," EAAWA; John H. Woolnough, ed., *The First Five Years of the 8th AF News, 1975–1979* (Hollywood, Florida: The 8th Air Force News, 1981), 18–97; Roger A. Freeman, *The Mighty Eighth: A History of the U.S. 8th Army Air Force* (London: Macdonald and Company, 1970), 20–32, 46–54.

2. John F. Guilmartin and the Editors of Encyclopaedia Britannica, "P-51 Aircraft,"

Encyclopaedia Britannica online, accessed on July 20, 2020, https://www.britannica.com/technology/P-51; Roger A. Freeman, *Mustang at War* (New York: Doubleday and Company, 1975), 66–77.

3. "P-51 Mustang Fighter," Boeing Aircraft Historical Snapshots, accessed July 20, 2020, https://www.boeing.com/history/products/p-51-mustang.page.

4. The history of the 306th Bomb Group published at the end of the war explained how the 367th Bomb Squadron got the name "Clay Pigeons." "Dubbed the Clay Pigeons by a *Saturday Evening Post* correspondent, because as one of the members said, 'They went down just like clay pigeons, losses were so heavy,' the name the 367th had acquired stuck, and by the end of the year 1942, the squadron, in truth, appeared to be living up to it. It seemed for a time that no one could possibly stay in combat in that squadron and survive. Losses were heavy, heavier than those of any other squadron in the ETO at that time, but the caliber of the work of the men behind the planes was evident in the comparatively few turn backs due to mechanical failure." Arthur P. Bove, *First Over Germany: A Story of the 306th Bombardment Group* (San Angelo, Texas: Newsfoto Publishing Company, 1946), 9, EAAWA; Jack Alexander, "The Clay-Pigeon Squadron," *Saturday Evening Post*, April 23, 1943, 14–15, 70–75, EAAWA.

5. *Flare Path*, written by Terence Rattigan, while on an RAF mission to West Africa during World War II. The play opened at the Apollo Theater on Shaftesbury Avenue in London. Shuller attended the play about halfway through the play's run of 679 performances. The play is "set in the lounge of a hotel close to an R.A.F. bomber airfield." As Shuller mentioned in his diary entry, the play centered on many things that were familiar to Shuller's wartime experiences. "The plot follows the emotions and interactions of a group of airmen, their wives and loved ones during the night and following morning of a night bombing mission over Germany." John Russell Taylor, *The Rise and Fall of the Well-Made Play* (New York: Hill and Wang, 1967), 149–50; Terence Rattigan biographical sketch, Biographical files, EAAWA.

6. Mrs. Archie Camden was a "professional pianist, cellist, composer and songwriter who operated under the stage name of 'Jan Kerrison.'" During the early days of the war, the BBC Symphony Orchestra moved to Bedford to escape the dangers of the German bombing during the Blitz. Mrs. Camden's husband was Archie Camden, the "principal bassoonist of the orchestra." During the Bedford years, "Mrs. Camden had an interest in the St. John Ambulance Brigade Cadet movement and worked with Barbara Cartland on welfare and fund-raising issues." Her interests also included "the welfare of servicemen," and during that time she became "friendly with the American officers at Thurleigh." It appears that during the war, Dr. Shuller was a frequent invitee to events hosted by Mrs. Camden. Trevor Stewart and Linda Ayres, "Notes on Camden and Kerrison," July 20, 2020, copy in Correspondence File, EAAWA.

7. Mrs. Hugh McCorquodale, who wrote under her maiden name, Barbara Cartland, died in 2000 at the age of ninety-eight. At the time of her death, she had written 723 books and left behind numerous manuscripts that would be published later by her grandsons. Shuller and McCorquodale joined forces, often reluctantly on Shuller's part, in support of local causes and society events in Bedford.

After her London home in Grosvenor Square was bombed and following a brief trip to Canada, McCorquodale spent most of the Second World War living at River Cottage, near the River Ouse, in Great Barford, a village located just a few miles northeast of Bedford. In a recent communication to Vernon L. Williams, Stuart Antrobus and Trevor Stewart, British historians based in Bedford, added some additional detail concerning McCorquodale's activities. "During the war she joined the Women's Voluntary Service (WVS), as Chief Lady Welfare Officer for Bedfordshire (1941–1945), with responsibility for looking after servicewomen." McCorquodale expanded her wartime work to other related areas, and "she also worked as a volunteer organizer for the St John Ambulance Cadets in Bedfordshire, which is why Colonel Shuller would have come across her." Barbara Cartland obituary, May 22, 2000, *Washington Post*, Obituary Files, EAAWA; Thurman Shuller, interview by Vernon L. Williams, October 25, 2005, EAAWA; Stuart Antrobus and Trevor Stewart notes on McCorquodale, Stuart Antrobus to Vernon L. Williams, July 18–19, 2020, Correspondence File, EAAWA.

8. Simpson was transferred to the United States on June 18, 1943. Russell Strong, 306th Bomb Group Personnel Card File, unpublished manuscripts, Simpson entry, EAAWA.

9. The reports that reached Dr. Shuller that the Smiley crew were safe in a prison camp was in error. All ten crewmen were killed when their plane, B-17F, Serial No. 42-5251, crashed into the sea, just north of the target, Bremen. All ten crew were declared dead, although no remains were recovered. Missing Air Crew Report, April 17, 1943, 306th Bomb Group Historical Collection, EAAWA; Mission Report, April 17, 1943, EAAWA.

10. Eighth Air Force planners considered this raid on Heroy, Norway, a very successful mission, but not so by the Norwegian government exiled in London. They were worried that the infrastructure damaged in raids in Norway would hurt reconstruction efforts after the war. The allied planners did not consult the Norwegians, and the July raid went forward without any advance notice to the Norwegians in London.

In the raid that Shuller mentions in his diary, "167 Flying Fortresses dropped more than fifteen hundred 500-pound bombs on a large fertilizer factory complex at Heroy, near Oslo, causing heavy casualties among the population." The Norwegians filed diplomatic protests in London and Washington, DC, but it was clear that the Allies were focused on destroying the German industrial network, and considerations of reconstruction would have to wait until after the war. Richard Petrow, *The Bitter Years: The Invasion and Occupation of Denmark and Norway, April 1940–May 1945* (New York: William Morrow and Company, 1974), 233–34; a good overview and detail of the 306th Bomb Group's experience on the raid can be found in the mission report for the July 24, 1943 mission. Mission Reports, 306th Bomb Group Historical Collection, EAAWA.

11. Colonel Conway Hall, 381st Bomb Group, led the task force to Schweinfurt, remembered how the mission went wrong from the beginning: "There were two briefings on Schweinfurt. One was briefed and the weather was a little bad and we didn't go. We were briefed again and we were delayed again. And so by this time, obviously, the Germans knew we were coming." When the bomb group finally took off and the bomber stream crossed the English Channel, Hall later described what happened to his formation. "When we crossed the [French] coast, there they were. The ME109s, I didn't see any 190s, the ME109s, they were all over us." Hall began losing planes in the gun battle across the continent. "The first plane to go down in my group was my deputy, who was flying

on the right wing. Well, you always have another one move up, and when he did, he went down. Jack Painter, the pilot, and he didn't survive. And number 3 moved up and he went down and I said, no more—leave the position open." When the formation finally reached the target and "we went in, we came out, we had fighters on us constantly, except over the target, where we had anti-aircraft fire. And we lost, think it was, 12 airplanes that day." When the survivors landed at Ridgewell, "there was several generals in there, and one of them asked me, of course, about it. And I said, the SOB that planned this one should have been on it. Well, it was General Eaker, and he was the one that planned it. He said, I agree with you. But it was a sad day at Ridgewell, but not only for our group, but for the other groups." Conway Hall, interview by Vernon L. Williams, January 7, 2003, tape 1, North Little Rock, Arkansas, EAAWA.

12. Special Orders 211, paragraphs 4–5, HQ VIII Bomber Command, September 2, 1943. Copy in 242nd Medical Detachment, Station #167, accessed July 16, 2020, https://web.archive.org/web/20170824155433/http://www.381st.org/Unit-History/War-Diaries/242nd-MD-War-Diary. Nothing is known about Schnabel's next assignments. He was discharged from military service in March 1946, then moved to Arizona where he was born and where he graduated from high school. Schnabel settled in Tucson, Arizona, where he practiced medicine until his death in 1991. Schnabel Historical Collection, documents drawn from digital searches for Garfield P. Schnabel at ancestry.com, accessed and downloaded on July 18, 2020.

13. Radar navigation was a relatively new tool for the air crews in 1943. With the frequency of overcast skies over target areas and cancelled missions due to weather, radar was incorporated into the heavy bomber campaign. By the spring and summer 1944, more and more B-17s were equipped with radar. George Spenser, a radar navigator, who arrived in England in April 1944, remembered the struggles still experienced in trying to make the radar equipment work on missions where bombs could not be dropped visually.

"After a few weeks in England, I was soon transferred to Chelveston because they had more radar planes than anyone else. We would take a plane the night before [a mission]" and fly to some base who were leading the mission the next day. The radar crew "would lead the thirty-six ships the next day on a mission over Germany." Soon more and more radar aircraft were positioned in the other bomb group inventories. "On the first of August, I was transferred to Thurleigh, the 306th Bomb Group and remained there for the rest of the war in Europe."

"They called the radar navigator, 'mickey.' The first mission that I dropped on [with the radar navigation equipment], we went up the North Sea and in the Elbe River. The river went into south Germany and made a left hand turn. Right at the turn, there was a factory that they wanted destroyed." Spencer followed the river down to the turn. "Of course, the factory was loud and clear on the radar with that water/land contrast. I had it all figured out, and I reached up and pushed the toggle switch and the bombs went away." The formation turned for a course back to England, not knowing where the bombs had actually landed.

A week later, photographs from a photo recon mission arrived at Thurleigh with a bomb damage assessment of the factory target. "We had two bombs through the roof of the factory. We had totally annihilated the shed where the employees parked their bicycles. Across the river on the other side, in the fields where they grew cabbage, we had over three hundred bomb craters. I felt that we had seriously damaged the sauerkraut production for that year."

Such results caused the crews to do some serious thinking about how to improve the use of radar. Spencer remembered that "that mission led some of the bombadiers and radar navigators to the conclusion that we needed something a little better. And we developed a system where the radar would give the bombardier slant ranges from the plane to the target—fifteen miles, ten miles, five miles. And they would set up a rate on the Norden Bombsight. They couldn't see anything because it was cloudy underneath us, but the bombsight is tracking across the ground that you can't see. And then the bombsight dropped the bombs."

Many of the crews did not have much confidence in the radar navigation and Spencer remembered that "there was a lot of controversy. I remember one captain, and I was still a first lieutenant so I didn't dare hit him, but he said 'You are just killing women and children.' I certainly wasn't trying to kill any women and children. I was trying to attack military targets, but we didn't always make it."

Eventually, the slant range system worked, and bomb assessment corroborated that success. That achievement led to a more sustained attack on targets with a dramatic drop in mission cancellations. Shuller was on hand to watch the early stages of radar bombing and remark on the new technique occasionally in his diary. George Spenser, interview by Vernon L. Williams, June 19, 2004, San Antonio, Texas, EAAWA.

14. Billy Gilbert was a successful star in short and feature comedy films beginning in 1926 and through the war years. He married Ella McKenzie, whose family was from Northern Ireland. The couple arrived in Ireland to entertain American troops and spent time with Ella's family while there. They later continued their USO shows in England, arriving in the First Bomb Division area where Shuller attended their show. Leonard Maltin, "Billy Gilbert," in *The Real Stars: Profiles and Interviews of Hollywood's Unsung Featured Players*, eBook edition (Great Britain: CreateSpace Independent, 2015), 103–21.

15. See note 11 for additional details on the first Schweinfurt raid. The first Schweinfurt raid occurred on August 26, 1943, and the second raid targeted Schweinfurt and Regensburg on October 14, 1943. Both missions sought to destroy the ball bearing plants at Schweinfurt and incurred very high losses for the American air crews. Wilbur "Bud" Klint, interview by Vernon L. Williams, July 10, 2006, Fort Worth, Texas, Oral History Historical Collection, EAAWA.

On August 17, 1943, the Eighth Air Force sent 315 B-17s in a "two-pronged attack into Germany, marking deepest penetration of German territory" up to that time. The two targets "are the Messerschmitt complex at Regensburg" and the ball bearing "factories at Schweinfurt." The bombers meet an intense fighter defense, but both attacking forces drop their bombs on the two targets. Bombing is more successful at Regensburg, but the "Schweinfurt raid had been a failure." Losses included sixty bombers and five fighters lost, 7 KIA, 21 WIA, 557 MIA or POW.

On October 14, 1943, "229 of 291 B-17s hit the city area and ball bearing plants at Schweinfurt, Germany in 2 groups; the first group bombs at 1439–1445 hours, [and] the second group at 1451–1457 hours." The cost is heavy for the attacking force: "60 B-17's are lost, 7 damaged beyond repair and 138 damaged" with high casualties: "5 KIA, 40 WIA and 594 MIA." Although the raid caused "great damage and interference with [ball bearing] production" and led to disruption and restructuring of the German ball bearing industry, American losses were unsustainable. "Fierce opposition of great numbers of [German] fighters, many of them firing rockets, accounts for the 60 US aircraft shot down." Eighth Air Force officials suspended "daylight bombing against strategic targets deep in Germany" until early in 1944 when the new, high-powered P-51 fighters arrived to escort the bomber stream into Germany. Kit C. Carter and Robert Mueller, compilers, *U.S. Army Air Forces in World War II: Combat Chronology, 1941–1945* (Washington, DC: Center for Air Force History, 1991) 203, 231; Russell Strong, *First Over Germany*, 140–73; Donald L. Miller, *Masters of the Air: America's Bomber Boys Who Fought the Air War Against Nazi Germany* (New York: Simon & Schuster, 2006), 200–02, 208–13; Klint, interview, EAAWA; Thurman Shuller, interviews by Vernon L. Williams, October 25, 2005 and November 1, 2008, Oral History Collection, EAAWA; Conway Hall, interview, EAAWA.

16. "Coombe House was built in 1886 on a 50-acre site, a mile to the east of Shaftesbury in Dorsetshire." The estate later opened as the "Coombe House Hotel and as the war approached, the hotel was "ideally equipped and located to become a USAAF Rest Home."

Shuller and other surgeons used rest homes, also known as "flak houses," for escape from the horrors the missions over Europe. Shuller sent crews who endured a series of difficult and costly missions or crews who suffered from the "jitters," to a rest home for a week of relief, "using the tranquility, comfort and freedom from military routine achievable at English country houses or hotels."

"At the rest home, they were provided with civilian clothes, and American Red Cross girls acted as hostesses, supervising the recreation and dining. The American Red Cross also employed and managed the civilian staff needed to run the house and maintain the grounds.

"Coombe House joined the programme on 20th September 1943. It was set up to accommodate 50 officers and was allocated to the 2nd Bomb Division.

"Soon after the war, Coombe House was sold and became St Mary's, an independent, Roman Catholic School for girls." "Coombe House," American Air Museum in Britain website, accessed July 6, 2020, http://www.americanairmuseum.com/place/135081.

17. Gerald had no more problems with excessive abortions of missions. He completed his tour of twenty-five missions on March 14, 1944. He arrived at the 368th Bomb Squadron on November 11, 1943, and was assigned as a copilot and finished up with his own crew as first pilot. Strong, Card File, Gerald entry, EAAWA.

18. The commanding officer of the Ninety-First Bomb Group, Clemens L. Wurzbach, did not last much longer than his two pilots who were removed for excessive abortions on missions. On December 12, 1943, Wurzbach was relieved of command and replaced by Shuller's former commanding officer at the 306th, Claude E. Putnam.

19. Colonel Claude Putnam's dressing down or whatever Colonel Kermit Stevens had to say to him had no impact on the young pilot. Lt. Winston Cavaneau flew only one mission with the 360th Bomb Squadron in the 303rd Bomb Group. On that mission, Cavaneau aborted due to "losing the formation" and returned to Molesworth. After that

mission, Cavaneau disappears from the records of the 303rd Bomb Group. It appears that he used up whatever grace Shuller delivered up for him. Gary Moncur, historian, 303rd Bomb Group Historical Collection, accessed July 16, 2020, www.303rdbg.com.

20. Lt. Clyde W. Cosper's Silver Star citation explains what happened on November 13, 1943, in Cosper's B-17 after reaching English air space: "Due to turbulent cloud conditions, his aircraft went out of control and into a spin. Working skillfully he returned his plane to level flight and ordered the crew to bail out.

"After five crewmen had taken to their parachutes, the airplane again went into a spin, dropping to an altitude of 1000 feet, before he regained control. Though his plane was almost unmanageable, he managed to keep it stable long enough for the balance of the crew to bail out safely.

"Probably knowing that his chance of surviving was very small, he gallantly decided to crash-land his bomb-laden aircraft where he would not endanger the lives of civilians. He found a small clearing away from the town over which he was flying [Princes Risborough, Buckinghamshire, England] and brought his plane down. The aircraft immediately burst into flames and exploded a few seconds later, killing Lt. Cosper. His gallantry, flying skill and devotion to duty saved the lives of his crew and undoubtedly those of many civilians."

21. Two B-17s from the 364th Bomb Squadron, 305th Bomb Group had just taken off for a practice mission, just after noon on November 15, 1943. The two aircraft were Daisy Mae, 42-30666, and Wolfess, 42-29953, both planes carrying their full crews plus Captain Varney D. Cline. Both planes were "flying near Newton Bromswold, two fields away south of the end of the main runway at Chelveston at 1500 feet at 12.36pm." Everything appeared routine, but "Wolfess's pilot, 2nd Lt. Wetzel F Mayes was blinded by the sun and rose up and struck Daisy Mae, piloted by Denzel M. Smith." Other aircrews in nearby planes reported what happened next. "Fire was seen to break out on contact with both B17's, each cut in half by propellers." The two planes "plunged down together, each plane carrying 1,700 gallons of fuel, causing terrific explosions, strewing wreckage over several hundred yards." No parachutes were reported, there "was no time," and all twenty-one men on board the two planes were killed on impact. Details regarding the collision drawn from Peter Hill, 305th Bomb Group, Facebook, November 15, 2012, https://www.facebook.com/groups/54028564457/.

22. The term refers to the amount of ground area obscured by clouds and is expressed in "tenths." Thus 1/10 coverage means only one-tenth of the ground area is obscured by clouds, while 10/10 coverage means a solid layer of cloud completely obscuring the ground.

23. General Malcolm C. Grow entered the Army Medical Corps in 1917 and had a long and distinguished career in the Army Air Corps leading up to World War II. "In July 1943, General Grow received the Legion of Merit for developing body armor to protect combat crews." Drawing on a study looking at the causes and types of wounds for air crew casualties, Grow recognized that "nearly 70 percent [of the wounds] were caused by missiles of relatively low velocity. He led the way in developing a light body armor and steel helmet that saved many lives and materially improved combat crew morale."

Just before the invasion of Normandy, Grow received the Distinguished Service

Medal "for developing a device to protect gunners from windblast" and a host of other innovative air crew equipment items that made a difference for combat crews. Grow was instrumental in developing and bringing into common use "electrically heated clothing, gloves, boots, hand-warmers, and casualty bags for wounded, wind and fire resistant face and neck protectors." The result of these innovations, "frostbite cases decreased and flight efficiency increased." Grow was involved in many other developments that addressed problems on long range missions, "psychiatric failures, rest homes, a new special pass system, and special training for medical officers in tactical units." Major General Malcom C. Grow biography, U.S. Air Force, no date, copy in Obituary Files, EAAWA, accessed July 17, 2020, https://www.af.mil/About-Us/Biographies/Display/Article/106898/major-general-malcolm-c-grow/.

24. Colonel Claude E. Putnam served as commanding officer of the Ninety-First Bomb Group from December 12, 1943, until May 16, 1944. Colonel Henry W. Terry succeeded Putnam on May 17, 1944, and remained in command until the end of the war in Europe. Both were old 306th hands, and Shuller had a long history with both officers. Strong, Card File, Putnam and Terry entries, EAAWA; https://91stbombardmentgroup.com/WEBPROTECT-historyofthe91st.htm (accessed July 17, 2020).

25. Major James H. Howard did receive the Medal of Honor and retired from the air force as a brigadier general. "Brig. Gen. James H. Howard: Medal of Honor Recipient," *Los Angeles Times*, March 25, 1994, 424. Copy in obituary files, EAAWA.

Chapter 4

1. The B-29 was used primarily in the Pacific Theater of Operations during World War II. The B-29 that Shuller saw at Bassingbourne on March 10, 1944, was the YB-29-BW, serial number 41-36393, a service test model that was sent to England and flew to several airfields. Nicknamed the Hobo Queen, the aircraft was in England as part of a disinformation campaign to convince the Germans that the B-29 would be deployed to Europe. Peter M. Bowers, *Boeing Aircraft since 1916*, 3rd ed. (Annapolis, Maryland: Naval Institute Press, 1989), 323; "Sternenbanner Leaflet," February 29, 1944, page 1, copy in EAAWA.

2. The evolution of mission limits in the Army Air Force emerged as a tangled web of confusion, policies that were at odds to organized practice in the various theaters of operation, and included inconsistent tour and sortie plans that never reached combat commands and were never put into practice as official guidelines. In England at the beginning in 1942, aircrews had no limits, but Shuller's memo in March 1943, arguing for a twenty-mission limit, led to an official mission tour limit of twenty-five missions. Over the next two years, under General Ira Eaker and his successor General Jimmy Doolittle, the mission limits were fixed at twenty-five, then thirty, and finally thirty-five missions. As the Luftwaffe's opposition gradually declined, the mission tour limits gradually changed. Shuller recognized that things had changed for the better since 1943, and "frankly, I have been expecting" the change to a thirty-mission tour "for a long time now." Thurman Shuller to Claude Putnam [sent to Putnam to be forwarded with his endorsement], Memo, March 12, 1943, Shuller Historical Collection, EAAWA. For more details on how the question of mission or tour limits developed army wide, see Historical Studies Branch, USAF Historical Division, "Combat Crew Rotation: World War II and

Korean War" (Maxwell Air Force Base, Alabama: Aerospace Studies Institute, Air University, 1968), 1–34.

3. *The Memphis Belle: A Story of a Flying Fortress,* filmed in 1944, was intended to be shown in movie theaters in the United States to illustrate the rigors of combat missions and serve as a morale-building film for the home front. In May 1943, Pilot Robert Morgan and the crew of the Memphis Belle was the third heavy bomber aircrew to finish twenty-five missions in the Eighth Air Force and the first to return to the United States. Major William Wyler, heading up the First Motion Picture Unit project, chose the Morgan crew and their plane for the film.

Wyler had 35mm cameras and equipment shipped over to England, but the ship was sunk by German U-boats. The entire film used footage shot from handheld 16mm cameras, specially equipped with electrically heated pads to keep the cameras from freezing in the −40 degree temperatures at high altitude.

The film crew flew on thirteen combat missions and filmed over sixteen thousand feet of footage. One cameraman, Lt. Harold Tannenbaum, was killed when his bomber was shot down over France. The other two cinematographers, Major William Wyler and Captain William C. Clothier, flew five missions while working on the film in England.

The documentary film was a resounding success and in 1990 Wyler's daughter, Catherine Wyler, produced a fictional version of the story. Gabriel Miller, *William Wyler: The Life and Films of Hollywood's Most Celebrated Director* (Lexington, Kentucky: University Press of Kentucky, 2013), 209–32; William Wyler, "Flying over Germany," *News Digest* 2, no. 13 (August 15, 1943): 25–26; Bosley Crowther, "Vivid Film of Daylight Bomb Raid Depicts Daring of Our Air Forces; Bomb Film Shows Our Fliers' Daring," *New York Times,* April 14, 1944, 1; "Memphis Belle (1944)," AFI Catalog of Feature Films: The First 100 Years, 1893–1993, American Film Institute Catalog, accessed July 28, 2020, https://catalog. afi.com/Catalog/moviedetails/24069.

4. In his court-martial proceeding, Captain Pervis E. Youree "maintained that the incident was an accident." The Braniff Airways pilot reported that the army plane was flying close formation with the airliner. Youree explained that "he and a student were flying a direct course from Wichita Falls, Texas to Ardmore and were concentrating on instrument drill." Youree testified that "he discovered the airliner almost underneath his ship and [he] hesitated to veer away until making a gradual climb to obtain room for maneuvering his plane." The court did not buy his explanation and "recommended a dishonorable discharge for Youree."

Governor Robert S. Kerr of Oklahoma and Youree's Congressman, Jed Johnson, appealed to President Roosevelt. "Protest Against Flyer Discharge," *Sapulpa Herald,* May 19, 1944, 6; "Reprieve Granted Oklahoma Pilot," *Daily Oklahoman,* November 1, 1944, 1.

5. *While the Sun Shines* was another comedy by the British playwright Terence Rattigan. Rattigan's work was popular during the wartime years, and his humor, directed at both the British and the Americans, found favor in the mixed audiences of the day. Shuller enjoyed Rattigan's work and his diary is filled with complimentary comments about the plays that he saw at various theaters along Shaftesbury Avenue in the West End. The first performance of *While the Sun Shines* opened to the public in 1943 at the Globe Theater in West London, and the play proved to be Rattigan's longest running West End

play, 1,154 performances. John Russell Taylor, *The Rise and Fall of the Well-Made Play*, 150.

6. Alfred Lunt and his wife, British-born Lynn Fontanne, were a successful acting couple in the American theatre. During World War II, the couple appeared in a number of London productions and made many appearances in New York. For more details about the two actors, see the Ten Chimneys Foundation story and the quest to honor the Lunts at their home and estate at Genesee Depot, Wisconsin. http://www.tenchimneys.org/about/about-lynn-alfred.

7. Peg Haapa, interview by Vernon L. Williams, October 22, 2005, San Antonio, Texas, EAAWA.

8. On many missions, bomber crews suffered heavy losses after bombing the target, when the formation turned back to England for the return flight. The Germans were waiting for them. A plan was devised for the formation to bomb the target, but instead of returning to England, the bomber stream flew on to Poltava and other fields in Russia. These missions were dubbed "shuttle" missions.

The Eighth Air Force flew a shuttle mission deep into Germany to bomb targets in the Ruhrland on June 21. The raid was successful, but when the bombers flew on to Poltava, a German reconnaissance plane followed the formation and reported the information to Luftwaffe Control. Later that night, while the crews were resting and their planes were lined up on the airfield, the Germans bombed Poltava and the fleet of B-17s on the ground. "The Luftwaffe destroyed 43 of the B-17s on the ramp and damaged another 26. Fifteen P-51s and assorted Russian aircraft were destroyed as well." The two-hour attack destroyed "450,000 gallons of high-octane fuel, which had been brought to Poltava and most of the munitions in the bomb dump were also lost." The photographs that Shuller saw in the intelligence office revealed the massive loss and destruction on the ground at Poltava the next morning. "Poltava," a segment in the documentary film *Fortress for Freedom: The 388th Bomb Group and the Air War in Wartime Suffolk, 1943–1945*, directed and written by Vernon L. Williams (Abilene, Texas: Old Segundo Productions, 2016); John T. Correll, "The Poltava Debacle," *Air Force Magazine* 94, no. 3 (March 1, 2011): 64–68.

9. As soon as war was declared after the invasion of Poland by Germany, Britain expected an air assault of the British Isles. It was not long in coming. On September 1, 1939, the British government began evacuating children and others from cities and other areas considered at risk to German air attack. During the war other waves of evacuation took place to move people into rural and other isolated areas. Many children made the journey without their parents, but some mothers joined in the evacuation.

Once the Blitz began in London and other British cities, evacuations began to increase as German attacks brought heavy casualties into areas such as the docks and shipping locations in East London. For the duration of the war, evacuees were a part of many rural areas where they were housed in private homes. In other cases, entire schools and faculties were evacuated to safer places. The Americans and their experiences with British children included evacuees and the neighboring children near American bases and installations scattered across East Anglia and other rural parts of England.

Shuller's description of the party held for London children who had been evacuated to Brampton was typical of the hospitality and nurturing care taken with British children everywhere. Published and unpublished histories and oral history interviews of both the

Yanks and the British children are filled with the stories of Christmas and Easter parties and other special memories during the war. Often army trucks were sent out to nearby villages to bring the children to the base for a party, a special meal, and perhaps a movie. Chris Mackie, interview by Vernon L. Williams, June 12, 2005, Norfolk, England, Oral History Collection, EAAWA; Ray Aggett, interview by Vernon L. Williams, June 6, 2005, Bedford, England, Oral History Collection, EAAWA; Ethel Collins, interview by Vernon L. Williams, August 20, 2003 and June 15, 2005, Great Ellingham, England, Oral History Collection, EAAWA; Martin Mitchell and David Bernstein, eds., *Well Remembered Fields: The Story of One School's Evacuation, 1939–1945* (Chippenham, Witshire, England: Antony Rowe Ltd, 2004) 248–331.

10. In addition to the evacuees in the various villages in rural England, children who lived close to American bases or in villages nearby had extensive relationships and memories of the Yanks during the war. Shuller's brief comment about "chewing gum has been a mighty weapon in promoting future Anglo-American friendship" reflected his long-term experience in watching the officers and men at Thurleigh and at other First Air Division stations and their close relationships with British children. Ralph Franklin and Sammie Lammie lived on the edge of Thurleigh, and in oral history interviews with the author, provided many stories and memories of the 306th Bomb Group during the time that the group surgeon served at the base. Many others have had similar experiences with the Americans.

Percy Prentice often disappeared from home and school to live among the Yanks in the 388th Bomb Group at Knettishall. The Yanks provided him with a bunk area in one of the huts and had a uniform made for him. Despite worries from his parents, he spent many of his childhood days and nights living among the Yanks, doing odd jobs for them, and experiencing the air war up close and personal. Other children had less intense experiences, but the Yanks became a vibrant part of their growing up during the war. For more examples of their experiences with the Yanks, see examples of oral history interviews of children who lived in the Eighth Air Force areas during World War II. Percy James Prentice, interview by Vernon L. Williams, September 4, 2003, Hillside Farm, Market Weston, England, Oral History Collection, EAAWA; Clement Squires, interview by Vernon L. Williams, June 10, 2005, Great Ellingham, England, Oral History Collection, EAAWA; Ralph Franklin, interview by Vernon L. Williams, September 3, 2003, Keysoe, England, Oral History Collection, EAAWA; Gordon Dye, interview by Vernon L. Williams, June 10, 2005, Great Ellingham, England, Oral History Collection, EAAWA; Gerry Darnell, interview by Vernon L. Williams, September 3, 2003, Rushton, England, Oral History Collection, EAAWA; Arthur Farey, interview by Vernon L. Williams, August 28, 2003, Higham Ferrers, England, Oral History Collection, EAAWA; Anthony Jeckels, interview by Vernon L. Williams, April 25, 2006, Seething, England, Oral History Collection, EAAWA; Gerald J. Turner, interview by Vernon L. Williams, April 25, 2006, Seething, England, Oral History Collection, EAAWA; Patricia Steggles, interview by Vernon L. Williams, August 26, 2003, Great Ellingham, England, Oral History Collection, EAAWA; Alexander Sammie Lammie, interview by Vernon L. Williams, June 7, 2005, Keysoe, England, Oral History Collection, EAAWA; Margaret Beales Cracknell, interview by Vernon L. Williams, June 15, 2005, Wymondham, England, Oral History Collection, EAAWA.

11. "Four Jills in a Jeep," Subject Files, East Anglia Air War Historical Collections, EAAWA; Russell Strong, *First Over Germany: A History of the 306ᵗʰ Bombardment Group* (Charlotte, North Carolina, privately printed, 2002), 50.

12. Furzedown House was a large property used as a rest home for First Air Division air crews coming off intense mission schedules. The house opened on June 26, 1944, not long after D-day, and was located north of Southampton in the south of England. The American Red Cross girls supervised all the activities and staff at the house. Imperial War Museum, "Furzedown House." For more details, see: http://www.americanairmuseum. com/place/135295 (accessed July 29, 2020).

13. During the war, Walcot Hall was the headquarters for the Sixty-Seventh Fighter Wing of the Eighth Air Force. Much of the operational planning for fighters escorting the bomber stream and for tactical air operations leading up to D-day and beyond was housed in the Operations area at Walcot Hall. USAF Historical Division, Air University, Tactical "Operations of the Eighth Air Force, 6 June 1944–8 May 1945" (Maxwell Air Force Base, Alabama, 1952), 19–24.

14. Faye Compton was a stage and film actress who began her career on stage during the WWI years in Britain. At the time that Shuller saw her appearance in *No Medals* in October 1944, she was one of Britain's most well-known actresses. Americans knew her from her work in many American theaters and in film, although she was better known for her stage productions than for her seventy films and television credits. Faye Compton biographical sketch, Biography files, EAAWA.

15. The rumors that Shuller mentioned regarding the 801st Bomb Group at Harrington were probably due to the heavy losses that the 492nd Bomb Group suffered before disbanding and merging with the 801st. The 492nd Bomb Group flew sixty-seven missions and lost fifty-five B-24 Liberators. On August 7, 1944, the 492nd flew their last mission and "was chosen to be disbanded due to their high casualties. All personnel and aircraft were scheduled for transfer to other units." Three days later, the 492nd unit was disbanded, and all "designations and identity" were assigned to the 801st Provisional Group, flying top secret "covert Carpetbagger missions" at night, dropping agents and equipment and supplies behind enemy lines for the underground. Shuller and most other officers would have not known the details about the Carpetbagger missions or the success that the Group achieved in supporting the underground throughout the war. The reputation of the 492nd Bomb Group, however, was well known. George Bledsoe [pilot, 801st/492nd BG], interview by Vernon L. Williams, February 26, 2004, San Antonio, Texas, Oral History Collection, EAAWA; Robert W. Fish [commanding officer, 801st/492nd BG], interview by Vernon L. Williams, August 20, 2005, San Antonio, Texas, Oral History Collection, EAAWA; Robert W. Fish, "Memories of the 801st/492nd Bombardment Group," privately printed by the 801st/492nd Bombardment Group Association, 1990, copy in EAAWP; "The 801st/492nd Bomb Group," Carpetbagger Aviation Museum at Harrington, accessed July 28, 2020, https://harringtonmuseum.org.uk/the-801st-492nd-bomb-group/.

Chapter 5

1. Robert R. Palmer, Bell I. Wiley, and William R. Keast, *The Army Ground Forces: The Procurement and Training of Ground Combat Troops* (Washington, DC: Center of

Military History, United States Army, 1991), 219–20; for additional material on Eisenhower and his efforts to select soldiers for infantry retraining, see Chapter 3 in Vernon L. Williams, "Crucible of War: The Anglo/American Cultural Exchange in World War II England, 1942–1945," a book manuscript to be submitted to Texas A&M Press, copy in the editor's files, Vernon L. Williams Historical Collection, EAAWA.

2. Palmer, Wiley, and Keast, *The Army Ground Forces*, 220.

3. Thurman Shuller, April 1945 entries, Shuller original handwritten diary Book 4, copy in EAAWA.

4. Shuller diary, May–October 1945 entries, EAAWA.

5. Shuller diary, January 1945 entry, EAAWA.

6. These nine officers were Medical Administrative Corps officers who were not medical doctors, but men who went through MAC training centers trained to take the administrative load off of medical doctors in Army units. "The MAC was created in 1920 after World War I demonstrated the need for medical administrators." During that war, physicians and surgeons "had spent much of their time carrying out administrative duties as medical supply officers, registrars, adjutants, and so forth, instead of tending to patients." During the years leading up to World War II, "the MAC provided medical administrators to do paperwork and other duties so the Medical Corps (MC) doctors and surgeons could focus on patients."

During Shuller's time in England, he was involved in the practice of taking the best administrative sergeants in the medical units and submitting them before a commissioning board to commission them as MAC officers. Shuller was afraid that the arrival of so many MAC officers from the United States might jeopardize the chances for commissions for some of his best noncommissioned sergeants.

Camp Barkeley was the largest medical replacement depot and medical OCS training base in the US during World War II. Camp Barkeley was the source of many of the enlisted medics and MAC officers assigned to the Eighth Air Force during the war. Grant Harward, "Camp Barkeley," *Handbook of Texas*, Texas State Historical Association, accessed July 30, 2020, https://tshaonline.org/handbook/online/articles/qbc02; Tracy Shilcutt, *Infantry Combat Medics in Europe, 1944–1945* (Basingstoke, England: Palgrave Macmillan, 2013), 10–28.

7. During 1942 and 1943, high altitude frostbite casualties became an increasing problem as the Eighth Air Force added bomb groups in England and numbers of missions increased dramatically. "The largest single cause of high-altitude frostbite was wind blast, which was responsible for 39 percent of all cases in the 14-month period ending in December 1943 and for almost 55 percent of all cases in 1944." Even when the B-17 Model G arrived in large numbers and gun positions were closed in, wind blast from combat damage from fighters and flak remained a real threat to air crews.

There were other contributing causes that originated with problems with equipment available or not available to air crews the early years of high altitude missions over occupied Europe. The "lack of equipment, failure of equipment, and removal of equipment which should have continued in use" were determined to be the chief contributing factors to the high rate of "cold injury." "The first few months of aerial warfare in Europe clearly revealed that Air Force personnel, including medical personnel, had not been adequately trained in the prevention of cold injury." The air crews "had been fully alerted to such dangers as flak and air collisions, but most of them did not know how to protect themselves against the dangers of cold." Other deficiencies included poorly engineered equipment such as electric suits, boots, and gloves that failed frequently at high altitude. Another serious problem rested with the supply system that was inadequate and unable to guarantee that the crew equipment was in good working order or that sufficient supplies of that equipment was on board every departing heavy bomber.

Eventually the Air Surgeon's Office and Air Force leadership solved these problems of training and the need for an equipment officer in each bomb squadron, and more effective personal gear designed for high altitude combat.

Equipment officers were trained in a new two-week course at Pinetree and assigned every combat unit. These equipment officers "worked in close cooperation with medical officers" and were charged with a number of specific duties: "(1) To provide facilities for drying, testing, and storing all flying clothing; (2) to provide means for checking oxygen masks and systems; (3) to assist in all matters pertaining to procurement and alteration of protective flying equipment; and (4) to train airborne personnel in the correct use and maintenance of personal protective equipment."

Because of these innovations and changes, by the latter part of 1944, cold injury casualties were brought under control. Dr. Shuller's comments that the frostbite problem had been a concern until "ten months ago," reflected that he and the medical commands had instituted the needed reforms by the fall of 1944. Tom F. Whayne and Michael E. Debakey, *Cold Injury, Ground Type in World War II* (Washington, DC: Office of the Surgeon General, Department of the Army, 1958), 130–34.

8. Palmer, Wiley, and Keast, *The Army Ground Forces*, 219–20; for additional material on Eisenhower and his efforts to select soldiers for infantry retraining, see Chapter 3 in Vernon L. Williams, "Crucible of War: The Anglo/American Cultural Exchange in World War II England, 1942–1945," a book manuscript to be submitted to Texas A&M Press, copy in the editor's files, Vernon L. Williams Historical Collection, EAAWA.

9. Dakin's solution is a dilute solution of sodium hypochlorite, which is commonly known as household bleach. Dakin's solution, developed first in World War I, was used in the treatment of infected wounds. The treatment continued to be used in World War II and beyond. The benefit of Dakin's solution is that it has "minimal tissue toxicity" while sterilizing a wound. *Advances in Skin & Wound Care: The Journal for Prevention and Healing* 26, no. 9 (September 2013): 410–14.

10. During January and February 1945, Eisenhower and his generals executed his plan for "the first phase of the advance into Germany." The plan focused on the occupied areas west of the Rhine, with "the overall objective . . . to effect 'a massive double envelopment of the Ruhr to be followed by a great thrust to join up with the Russians.'" Eighth Air Force operations were in support of this broad front, leading to ground forces crossing the Rhine River and all that followed. During March and April, the Allies moved beyond the Rhine and brought to a conclusion the war in Europe. Michael Reynolds, "Patton's End Run," Warfare History Network, accessed August 13, 2020, https://warfarehistorynetwork.com/2016/07/21/pattons-end-run/.

11. For more information on this mission, see Mission Report 350, 303rd Bomb Group,

Gary Moncur to Vernon L. Williams, August 5, 2020, Correspondence File, EAAWA.

12. The B-17 "Peacemaker" had been "grounded for a few days while the mechanics changed and overhauled the engines." On April 12, 1945, the aircraft was scheduled to slow-time the engines, and Surgeon Walker took the opportunity to get some flight hours in for his monthly flight pay. The flight "had been air borne about 1 ½ hours on a local slow-time flight when it was reported crashed at 1545 hrs. by radio call from an unknown A/C." The plane came down "at Weston, Herts., 3 miles south of Baldock, Herts., killing all personnel and totally wrecking the A/C." At the time the report indicated that the "cause for accident was A/C flying at too low altitude with reason undetermined. Responsibility was undetermined." History of the 91st Bomb Group (H) AAF for the Month of April 1945, Microfilm B0174 (pages 1831–2461), Air Force Historical Research Agency at Maxwell Air Force Base, AL, 36112.

13. The B-17 took off from Thurleigh on April 14, 1945, for Langford Lodge in Ireland with eleven crew and passengers on board. They were bound for an "R&R" trip. The aircraft was 42-37840, named Combined Operations and piloted by Lt. Robert A. Vieille, from the 367th Bomb Squadron. Those who were lost in the crash included: Lt. Robert A. Vieille, Lt. Collins E. Liersch, Red Cross Director Emily Rea, Capt. George E. Cubberly, Capt. Wilbur B. Butterfield, Lt. Collin E. Liersch, Lt. Austin J. Parrish, F.O. Chester Smalczewski, M/Sgt. Derrell Jones, Sgt. Ernest E. Gallion, and Sgt. William C. Starbuck.

Shuller wrote about Emily Rea, who was killed in the crash. Rea had served at the Officers Red Cross Club in Bedford before being assigned to a new club in France later in the war. She had a special relationship with the medics and surgeons in the 306th Bomb Group. In a letter from Paris, just weeks before her death, Rea wrote to Bill Houlihan and the group of 367th medics. Her letter is filled with endearments for the medics, calling them her "darlings." Many years later, Houlihan wrote about Emily, "she was madly in love with one of our medics, Bill Chapman, who was in charge of the first aid station we set up in the Red Cross Club in Bedford." Houlihan minced no words about Chapman, "he was a womanizer and an [expletive] who eventually broke Emily's heart." According to Houlihan, during and after her relationship with Chapman, "she was adored by all of the Thurleigh medics—officers and enlisted men. We were very fond of her, and were devastated by her death." Russell Strong, *First Over Germany: A History of the 306th Bombardment Group* (Charlotte, North Carolina, privately printed, 2002), 313; Emily Rea to Bill Houlihan, March or April 1945, Bill Houlihan Correspondence File, EAAWA; Bill Houlihan to Russell Strong, April 23, 1992, Bill Houlihan Correspondence File, EAAWA.

14. Paul Robeson was an acclaimed twentieth-century performer in stage productions, such as *The Emperor Jones* and *Othello*. Robeson worked for civil rights, using his fame and talent to force integration of his audiences and other venues. https://www.biography.com/musician/paul-robeson (accessed August 22, 2020).

15. On April 17, 1945, just about two weeks after Shuller had flown with Kahler and his crew, the Kahler crew suffered "direct hit from anti-aircraft fire in the gas tank, setting the right wing on fire." Observers in other aircraft saw that "flames streamed back over the top of the B-17 and all around the bomb bay." Soon after the flak hit the wing, "there was a large puff of smoke, flames and debris as the B-17 exploded in the air. It went down in the vicinity of Brux, Czechoslovakia."

There was some confusion from eyewitnesses, in the air and on the ground, regarding what happened to the crew. Official German accounts report that "Lt. Kahler's body was in the wrecked B-17 and that he died from head wounds sustained in the air." The report added that the tail gunner, Sgt. Theodore R. Smith, "died from a broken neck, leg, and arm when he hit the ground in a partially opened parachute."

Another report, however, stated that both Kahler and Smith were "murdered by German SS and civilians and their bodies were hung in a tree near Libkovice, Czechoslovokia." These two conflicting reports have not been reconciled, and no conclusive findings have since been reached by any government agency. The rest of the crew were captured and held as POWs until the end of the war. Mission Report 362, 303rd Bomb Group; Moncur to Williams, August 5, 2020, EAAWA; Missing Aircrew Report 14169, Record Group 92, National Archives, College Park, Maryland, copy in EAAWA.

16. Colonel Conway Hall, commanding the 381st Bomb Group at Ridgewell in Essex, notified that no missions were scheduled, decided to select a number of ground crew for an R&R trip to Northern Island. Hall selected Captain Charles E. Ackerman to pilot the flight and thirty-one crew and passengers departed Ridgewell on April 23, 1945. The aircraft never reached Nutts Corner. The B-17 crossed the coast of the Isle of Man in low clouds and flew over Glen Mona and Corrany as the aircraft approached the slopes of North Barrule. The plane with thirty-one men on board flew into the steep southern slope of North Barrule, just two hundred feet below the summit of the hill. All were killed.

When notified of the disaster, Colonel Hall requested permission from British authorities to fly a plane to the site and bring the bodies back to Ridgewell. Permission was refused, but Hall flew to Ireland anyway and recovered all the bodies for burial at the American Military Cemetery at Madingley near Cambridge. Conway Hall, interview by Vernon L. Williams, January 7, 2003, North Little Rock, Arkansas, Oral History Collection, EAAWA; William L. Palmer, interview by Vernon L. Williams, August 14, 2010, Nashville, Tennessee, Oral History Collection, EAAWA.

17. Shuller never mentions this relationship in earlier diary entries. He admits that he may have considered the idea of marrying the British woman but was never serious about the possibility. Shuller never talked about her later in life, nor does his family even know her name. The only clue to her existence is this single diary entry written on May 23, 1945. Mary Beth Carney, telephone interview by Vernon L. Williams, August 11, 2020, EAAWA.

18. The C-53 aircraft, known as the *Skytrooper*, is a version of the C-47 Skytrain or Goony Bird. The C-53 was designed primarily for passenger service and not for cargo work. The C-53 was delivered without the C-47's heavy reinforced floor, larger cargo door, or other cargo handling equipment. http://www.historyofwar.org/articles/weapons_douglas_C-53_skytrooper.html (accessed August 22, 2020).

19. William Joyce, known as Lord Haw Haw, did arrive at the Old Bailey soon after Shuller's visit there. Joyce was tried for treason, found guilty, and executed.

Born in the United States to an Irish father and an English mother, Joyce grew up in Ireland. His wartime broadcasts from Germany made him famous in Britain and a marked man after Germany's surrender. William Joyce's background drawn from his appeal transcript, Document A.C. 347, House of Lords, copy in EAAWA.

20. Errol Holmes was a well-known cricket player from the 1920s through the postwar era. During World War II, Holmes served as a British flak liaison officer with the First Air Division from 1942 to the end of the war.

21. Robert Ley was a high-ranking Nazi leader who committed suicide at Nuremburg prior to going on trial for crimes against humanity. Ronald Smelser, *Robert Ley: Hitler's Labor Front Leader* (New York: Berg Publishers Limited, 1988), 1–6, 296–308.

22. For an explanation of Churchill and the conservative loss in the election of July 1945, see the BBC website for an analysis of the political environment surrounding the event. http://www.bbc.co.uk/history/worldwars/wwtwo/election_01.shtml (accessed August 20, 2020).

23. Cadgwith is a village and fishing port located in Cornwall on the extreme southwestern tip of England.

24. Mrs. Boch's sisters and possibly more family members lived in Paris, but the family was from Warsaw, Poland. It is not known how the sisters ended up at the Lublin Ghetto, but they were part of the large number of Jewish families who were transported and liquidated from there in November 1942. Shuller's diary entry dated April 10, 1945, long after Germany's surrender indicates that the Boch family had learned of the fate of the sisters at Lublin.

The Lublin Ghetto was established in March 1941 by Nazi Germany in the city of Lublin in occupied Poland. The Lublin Ghetto included primarily Polish Jews and some Roma (Gypsies) families and were among the first ghettos to be liquidated. Between March 1941 and November 1942 about thirty thousand inmates were delivered to their deaths in cattle trucks at the Bełec extermination camp and about four thousand at Majdanek. "Of the some 40,000 Lublin Jews, no more than 300 are thought to have survived the horrors of Nazi occupation." "The Holocaust: Ghettos in Nazi-Occupied Poland," Jewish Virtual Library, accessed August 9, 2020, https://www.jewishvirtuallibrary. org/holocaust-ghettos-in-nazi-occupied-poland; Kerry McDermott, "Inside a Doomed Ghetto: Chilling Images of the Jews of Lublin Captured on Film by German Soldiers," *Daily Mail*, November 13, 2012, 1.

Epilogue

1. Thurman Shuller, "My Military Service Before Pediatrics," (paper presented to the Pittsburg County, Oklahoma Genealogy Society, May 1, 2012), copy in the Thurman Shuller Historical Collection, EAAWA.

Appendix A:

Thurman Shuller Chronology

May 6, 1914, Thurman Shuller, born on the family farm, five miles north of Ozark, Arkansas

1920–1928, attended New Hope School. The school was named after his grandfather's New Hope Church in Georgia, before the family immigrated to Arkansas.

1928–1932, attended Ozark High School

1932–1934, attended Arkansas Polytechnic College, Russellville, Arkansas (2 years)

1932–1935, served in the Arkansas National Guard as a private

1934–1935, attended Hendrix College, Conway, Arkansas (1 year)

1935–1939, attended University of Arkansas School of Medicine, Little Rock, Arkansas

1939–1941, internship at Charity Hospital, New Orleans, Louisiana

June 6, 1939, commissioned First Lt., Medical Corps Reserves, upon graduation from the School of Medicine, University of Arkansas

July 17, 1941, active duty with assignment at Station Hospital, Army Air Force Gunnery School, Las Vegas, Nevada, as general duty medical officer

Jan – Mar, 1942, attended the 12-week School of Aviation Medicine, Randolph Field, San Antonio, Texas for qualification as Flight Surgeon

April 15, 1942, assigned as 369th Bomb Squadron Surgeon, 306th Bomb Group, which was being organized at Wendover Field, Utah

May 6, 1942, promoted to Captain

July 1, 1942, advanced to Group Surgeon, 306th Bomb Group

August 1, 1942, departed Wendover, Utah for Westover Field, in transit for movement overseas

September 1, 1942, departed with air echelon from Westover Field to Thurleigh, England

Sept 17, 1942, 306th Bomb Group arrived in England as one of the early bomb groups in the Eighth Air Force

Sept 21, 1942, promoted to Major

Aug 16, 1943, advanced to Wing Surgeon, First Bomb Wing. This headquarters became the First Bomb Division and finally the First Air Division.

Remained Surgeon of the First Air Division until deactivation in Nov, 1945, a total of twenty-seven months.

Dec 1, 1943, promoted to Lieutenant Colonel

Dec 7, 1945, returned to US and assigned to Army Air Force Regional & Convalescent Hospital at Lackland Field, San Antonio (during this time he received corrective surgery and recuperated before discharge)

May 7, 1946, promoted to Colonel (Shuller was notified of this promotion on August 25, 1961, backdated to May 7, 1946)

May 7, 1946–Sep 3, 1946, terminal leave

Sept 3, 1946, discharged from active duty

June 19, 1946, married Joanna Carter

Aug 14, 1947, birth of daughter, Mary Elizabeth Shuller

1946–1948, Pediatric Residency at Charity Hospital on the Tulane Service, New Orleans

July 1948, joined the McAlester Clinic in the practice of Pediatrics, McAlester, Oklahoma. His brother, Dr. Elbert H. Shuller, was a founder and in practice at the clinic at the time he joined the firm.

Aug 14, 1949, birth of son, Henry Allan Shuller

Sept 24, 1951, death of mother, Sarah Elizabeth McWhorter

Oct 22, 1950, birth of daughter, Margaret Helen Shuller

Nov 9, 1952, birth of son, Frank Carter Shuller

Apr 27, 1958, death of father, Edgar Wallace Shuller

Sept 1, 1961, received notice of promotion to Colonel, backdated to May 7, 1946

1986, death of brother, Edgar Ralph Shuller

1987, death of brother, Benjamin "Frank" Franklin Shuller

May 5, 1989, retired from medical practice after forty-one years at the McAlester Clinic and a total of fifty years in the practice of medicine.

1992, death of brother, Albert Theodore Shuller

1995, death of brother, Walter Herbert Shuller

1996, death of brother, Elbert Henderson Shuller

Jun 22, 2010, death of wife, Joanna Carter Shuller

Nov 24, 2012, Thurman Shuller died at McAlester, Pittsburg County, Oklahoma

Appendix B:

Thurman Shuller's Pleas to Limit Missions

OFFICE OF THE GROUP SURGEON
306TH BOMBARDMENT GROUP (H)
A.P.O. 634

12 March, 1943.

SUBJECT : Combat Expectancy of Fliers.

TO : THE COMMANDING OFFICER, 306th Bombardment Group (H), APO 634.

1. The following statement is quoted from an Eighth Bomber Command letter dated 18th September, 1942, Subject : "Enclosed Correspondence—Guide for Care of Fliers" to the Commanding Officers of 1st, 2nd, 3rd, and 4th Bombardment Wings and signed by Major General EAKER: "Of this I am certain, and you can count upon it, that as long as I retain command of this organization, a combat crew must be told what their combat expectancy is, and further they must be told that when they have completed that period they will never again be required to man a combat crew station in an airplane on operations against the enemy."

2. It should be called to the attention of the Commanding General that although Groups have been operating in this theatre for seven months, this maximum combat expectancy still has not been fixed. As a result of this indefinite state of affairs and in view of our high rate of losses the Group and Squadron Surgeons all feel that the crews in this Group are on the verge of a complete psychological breakdown.

3. In this Group we have lost 20 of our original 35 combat crews in addition to several replacement crews, yet very few have seen as many as 15 missions. This would seem to indicate that the chance of surviving even 20 missions over German territory is very small. Such a figure, though difficult to attain, would offer a far greater incentive to keep fighting than they now have.

4. The fliers are now actually saying among themselves that the only apparent hope of survival in this theatre of war is either to become a prisoner of war or to get "the jitters" and be removed from combat. This has brought about a state of morale that can soon become disastrous. One of our officers who has now been on 19 missions has already said that he is turning in his wings, if need be, after completing his 20th mission. And I dare say no Board composed of non-combatant officers could have the nerve to suggest this officer is a coward or that he has not already served his country well.

5. It has been recently rumored that relief from flying in this theatre will be impossible because of lack of replacements. However, it is the consensus of opinion of all our medical officers, that the number of personnel lost through completion of the maximum number of missions would actually be fewer than the number brought before the Central Medical

Board for reclassification, if a definite policy is not established very soon.

6. It is suggested that 20 operational missions should be a very maximum expected of any man, and according to all our present data 15 would be nearer the ideal. But even a limit of 20, which relatively few can actually reach, would be an invaluable morale factor in giving these men at least a small hope for the future and a goal toward which to strive.

7. It is the opinion of the Medical Department of this Group that this is a matter of paramount importance and worthy of immediate consideration and action.

> THURMAN SHULLER,
> Major, Medical Corps,
> Group Surgeon.

21 April, 1943.

SUBJECT : Combat Crew Expectancy.

TO : COMMANDING OFFICER, 306th Bombardment Group (H), APO 634.

1. Your attention is invited to enclosure, subject "Combat Crew Expectancy" addressed to The Surgeon, 8th A.F. at his request, dated March 14, 1943. It will be noted in paragraph 2. of that letter that 20 raids was predicted a maximum for the original fliers of this group. The following table, which has been brought up to date is presented for your information.

Original Officers Assigned to 306th Bomb Group	- Squadron -			
	367th	368th	369th	423rd
Total fliers entering combat	34	41	34	38
Total M.I.A., K.I.A., and W.I.A.	26	25	23	16
Percentage M.I.A., K.I.A., and W.I.A.	76%	61%	67%	42%
Total fliers remaining on combat status	6	9	11	16
Percentage fliers remaining	18%	22%	33%	42%
Average No. missions of remaining fliers	16.6	15.3	15.8	17.1

2. Of the original officers, 28.7% are remaining at this date with an average of 16.3 raids each. This rate would indicate that the original officers would become extinct after an average of 22.8 missions for the remaining officers. This compared closely with expectancy of 20 missions estimated in par. 2 of the enclosure, in spite of the fact that 7 missions have been run since then, 5 of which were without loss.

3. On the last mission run by this Group we lost 8 officers who were on their twentieth or more mission and 5 who were on their fifteenth to nineteenth mission. This definitely refutes the theory that it is not the older men who suffer the high rate of losses.

4. At this time there is one officer who has completed his 25th mission, 2 officers with 24 missions, 6 officers with 21 missions and 5 officers have 20. In other words, 9% of the original officers have reached 20 missions at this time. It should be safe to estimate that no more than 5 to 10% of the officers of this Group can ever hope to reach 25.

5. These figures are submitted in further support of our contention that 20 missions should be the maximum expected of combat personnel in this theatre of war.

> THURMAN SHULLER, Major, M.C.
> Group Surgeon.

Appendix C:

Thurman Shuller's Arguments against Maximum Effort Policy

OFFICE OF THE GROUP SURGEON
306TH BOMBARDMENT GROUP (H)
A.P.O. 634

12 May, 1943.

SUBJECT : Cancellation of Leaves for Maximum Effort Operations.

TO   : THE SURGEON, VIII Bomber Command, A.P.O. 634.

1. It is requested that strong protest be immediately registered with the C.G., VIII Bomber Command, against the calling of combat crews back to the home station from regular passes in order to participate in a so-called "maximum effort."

2. The first such mission was run on 4th April when several of our crews were called back from a two-day pass in London. One of these crews was on its first pass in over four weeks at that time. Although they were a little vexed at having their well-earned pass broken up, they returned willingly because they felt that it must surely be a most unusual circumstance and that it would not be a frequent occurrence. However, a few days later a maximum effort was called again. It was finally scrubbed, but not until crews had been called back from London again. On 4th May such a mission was called for a third time and a pilot, who had gone into London with his crew the evening before for his first two-day pass in weeks, was re-called to the base. The mission was later cancelled and this pilot and crew returned to London to resume their pass. The next day, 5th May, a maximum effort was again called and this same crew was re-called to the base a second time in 24 hours. This mission was likewise scrubbed and they still had no leave after two attempts, neither was the mission run.

3. It should not be necessary to point out just how disastrous this practice can be to the morale of the fighting men if this policy is continued. It completely nullifies the real purpose of a pass, that of complete relaxation in the knowledge that one will not be called on for duty for a definite period of time. As a result, our crews can no longer go into London with any more assurance that they will not be called upon than if they were not on leave at all.

4. It has long been recognized that regular and frequent leave is one of the essentials in the prevention of flying fatigue. Therefore, it would seem that it should be an extraordinary case indeed which would interfere with that policy, and especially should the cancellation of leaves after they are already in effect be most vehemently condemned. It would seem that such an effort can be justified only by a target vastly more important than any thus far assigned. It is difficult to see how the advantages the few extra planes operated by such means can possibly, at this time, outweigh the

- 1 -

inevitable increase in flying fatigue and the tremendously decreased morale that most certainly will become apparent shortly.

5. It is requested that operations of "maximum effort" not be interpreted to include crews whose regular two-day passes are already in effect.

THURMAN SHULLER,
Major, Medical Corps,
Group Surgeon.

22 May 1943.

210.712

MEMO)
      :
TO   ) Major Shuller, Group Surgeon 306th Bomb Group, APO 634.

1. Reference your recent letter concerning cancellation of leave or passes of combat crew members, I have taken this matter up with General Longfellow with little or no satisfaction insofar as getting results are concerned. Pressure from higher headquarters necessitates getting every possible plane in the air on "Maximum efforts" and now that we have been getting additional forces over here instances such as you described probably will not be frequent. General Eaker has had a very difficult time convincing the arm-chair-strategists back home that raids by American bombers from British bases was really worthwhile. The past year has been not only a trying one for the few original groups that had to bear the brunt of carrying out the convictions of our Commanding General but for General Eaker as well. He fully realized the tremendous load these crews were being asked to carry and certainly is aware that certain measures and means that were used to make the best showing with a small force operating under difficult personnel and supply conditions, were not the best from a standpoint of morale. However he has won his fight for a large force of bombers over here and our original groups have had to win it for him.

2. I am heartily in accord with the opinions you have expressed concerning leaves and passes for combat crews and am taking the matter up with Colonel Grow to see if we cannot get a policy established that will exclude the possibility of personnel on pass, leave or DS being recalled for any reason except a dire emergency.

E. J. TRACY,
Colonel, M.C.,
Surgeon.

CONFIDENTIAL.

Selected Bibliography

These primary and secondary sources were used by the editor to produce the annotation and commentary that provided explanation and additional historical context for the diary entries.

GOVERNMENT DOCUMENTS AND PUBLICATIONS

Army Nurse Corps. Rank, Pay, and Allowances. 77th Cong., 2d Sess. (December 22, 1942). *Public Law 828 in United States Statutes at Large,* Volume 56, Part 1. Washington DC: Government Printing Office, 1943.

Army Nurse Corps. 78th Cong., 2d Sess. (June 22, 1944). Public Law 350 in United States Statutes at Large, Volume 58, Part 1. Washington DC: Government Printing Office, 1945.

Link, Mae Mills and Hubert A. Coleman. *Medical Support of the Army Air Forces in World War II.* Washington, DC: US Government Printing Office, 1955.

Parish, Timothy N. "A Brief History of Nellis Medical Activity (1941–2000)." Unpublished manuscript, 2000. Office of History, Headquarters Air Warfare Center, Nellis Air Force Base, Nevada.

Whayne, Tom F. and Michael E. Debakey. *Cold Injury, Ground Type in World War II.* Washington, DC: Office of the Surgeon General, Department of the Army, 1958.

MANUSCRIPTS AND ARCHIVAL MATERIALS

306th Bomb Group Historical Collection. East Anglia Air War Archives (hereinafter cited as EAAWA), Abilene, Texas.

Antrobus, Stuart and Trevor Stewart. "Notes on McCorquodale," July 18–19, 2020, EAAWA.

Correspondence Files. Thurman Shuller Historical Collection, EAAWA.

Obituary and Biographical Collection. EAAWA.

Biographical Collection. EAAWA.

Historical Studies Branch. USAF Historical Division, "Combat Crew Rotation: World War II and Korean War." Unpublished manuscript, 1968. Maxwell Air Force Base, Alabama: Aerospace Studies Institute, Air University.

History of the 91st Bomb Group (H) AAF for the Month of April 1945,

Microfilm B0174. Air Force Historical Research Agency, Maxwell Air Force Base, Alabama.

Missing Aircrew Reports. Record Group 92, National Archives, College Park, Maryland.

Shuller, Thurman. "Flight Surgeon: A War Diary, 1941–1945." Unpublished typescript and a series of digital scans of the original diary notebooks, EAAWA.

Shuller, Thurman. "My Military Service before Pediatrics." Unpublished manuscript, May 1, 2012. Thurman Shuller Historical Collection, EAAWA.

Stewart, Trevor and Linda Ayres. "Notes on Camden and Kerrison." July 20, 2020, EAAWA.

USAF Historical Division, Air University. "Tactical Operations of the Eighth Air Force, 6 June 1944–8 May 1945." Maxwell Air Force Base, Alabama, 1952.

Williams, Vernon L. "A Survey of Heavy Bomber Groups Arrival Patterns in the ETO, 1942–1944." Unpublished manuscript. EAAWA.

Williams, Vernon L. "Crucible of War: The Anglo/American Cultural Exchange in World War II England, 1942–1945." Unpublished manuscript, forthcoming.

INTERVIEWS

Aggett, Ray. Interview by Vernon L. Williams, June 6, 2005, Bedford, England. Oral History Collection, EAAWA.

Albertson, Joe. Interview by Vernon L. Williams, August 29, 2003, Ely, England. Oral History Collection, EAAWA.

Bledsoe, George. Interview by Vernon L. Williams, February 26, 2004, San Antonio, Texas. Oral History Collection, EAAWA.

Carney, Mary Beth. Telephone interview by Vernon L. Williams, August 11, 2020. EAAWA.

Collins, Ethel. Interview by Vernon L. Williams, August 20, 2003 and June 15, 2005, Great Ellingham, England. Oral History Collection, EAAWA.

Cracknell, Margaret Beales. Interview by Vernon L. Williams, June 15, 2005, Wymondham, England. Oral History Collection, EAAWA.

Darnell, Gerry. Interview by Vernon L. Williams, September 3, 2003, Rushton, England. Oral History Collection, EAAWA.

Dye, Gordon. Interview by Vernon L. Williams, June 10, 2005, Great Ellingham, England. Oral History Collection, EAAWA.

Farey, Arthur. Interview by Vernon L. Williams, August 28, 2003, Higham Ferrers, England. Oral History Collection, EAAWA.

Fish, Robert W. Interview by Vernon L. Williams, August 20, 2005, San Antonio, Texas. Oral History Collection, EAAWA.

Franklin, Ralph. Interview by Vernon L. Williams, September 3, 2003, Keysoe,

England. Oral History Collection, EAAWA.

Haapa, Peg. Interview by Vernon L. Williams, October 22, 2005, San Antonio, Texas. Oral History Collection, EAAWA.

Hall, Conway. Interview by Vernon L. Williams, January 7, 2003, North Little Rock, Arkansas. Oral History Collection, EAAWA.

Houlihan, William. Interview by Vernon L. Williams, October 22, 2005, San Antonio, Texas. Oral History Collection, EAAWA.

Humphrey III, Watt S. Interview by Grady Booch, Part I transcript, February 22, 2010. Accessed July 10, 2020. https://www.informit.com/articles/article.aspx?p=1567322.

Jeckels, Anthony. Interview by Vernon L. Williams, April 25, 2006, Seething, England. Oral History Collection, EAAWA.

Klint, Wilbur. Interview by Vernon L. Williams, July 10, 2006, Fort Worth, Texas. Oral History Collection, EAAWA.

Lammie, Alexander Sammie. Interview by Vernon L. Williams, June 7, 2005, Keysoe, England. Oral History Collection, EAAWA.

Mackie, Chris. Interview by Vernon L. Williams, June 12, 2005, Norfolk, England. Oral History Collection, EAAWA.

Palmer, William L. Interview by Vernon L. Williams, August 14, 2010, Nashville, Tennessee. Oral History Collection, EAAWA.

Prentice, Percy James. Interview by Vernon L. Williams, September 4, 2003, Hillside Farm, Market Weston, England. Oral History Collection, EAAWA.

Shuller, Thurman. Interview by Vernon L. Williams, October 25, 2005, San Antonio, Texas. Oral History Collection, EAAWA.

Spenser, George. Interview by Vernon L. Williams, June 19, 2004, San Antonio, Texas. Oral History Collection, EAAWA.

Squires, Clement. Interview by Vernon L. Williams, June 10, 2005, Great Ellingham, England. Oral History Collection, EAAWA.

Steggles, Patricia. Interview by Vernon L. Williams, August 26, 2003, Great Ellingham, England. Oral History Collection, EAAWA.

Turner, Gerald J. Interview by Vernon L. Williams, April 25, 2006, Seething, England. Oral History Collection, EAAWA.

BOOKS

Bove, Arthur P. *First Over Germany: A Story of the 306th Bombardment Group.* San Angelo, Texas: Newsfoto Publishing Company, 1946.

Bowers, Peter M. *Boeing Aircraft since 1916.* 3rd ed. Annapolis, Maryland: Naval Institute Press, 1989.

Carter, Kit C. and Robert Mueller, compilers. *U.S. Army Air Forces in World War II: Combat Chronology, 1941–1945.* Washington, DC: Center for Air Force History, 1991.

Craven, Wesley Frank and James Lea Cate. *The Army Air Forces in World War II: Plans and Early Operations, January 1939–August 1942, Volume 1.* Washington, DC: Office of Air Force History, 1983.

Freeman, Roger A. *Mustang at War.* New York: Doubleday and Company, 1975.

Freeman, Roger A. *The Mighty Eighth: A History of the U.S. 8th Army Air Force.* London: Macdonald and Company, 1970.

Maltin, Leonard. "Billy Gilbert" in *The Real Stars: Profiles and Interviews of Hollywood's Unsung Featured Players,* eBook edition. Great Britain: CreateSpace Independent, 2015.

Miller, Donald L. *Masters of the Air: America's Bomber Boys Who Fought the Air War Against Nazi Germany.* New York: Simon & Schuster, 2006.

Miller, Gabriel. *William Wyler: The Life and Films of Hollywood's Most Celebrated Director.* Lexington, Kentucky: University Press of Kentucky, 2013.

Mitchell, Martin and David Bernstein, eds. *Well Remembered Fields: The Story of One School's Evacuation, 1939–1945.* Chippenham, Witshire, England: Antony Rowe Ltd, 2004.

Palmer, Robert R., Bell I. Wiley, and William R. Keast. *The Army Ground Forces: The Procurement and Training of Ground Combat Troops.* Washington, DC: Center of Military History, United States Army, 1991.

Petrow, Richard. *The Bitter Years: The Invasion and Occupation of Denmark and Norway, April 1940–May 1945.* New York: William Morrow and Company, 1974.

Board of Administrators. Report of the Charity Hospital of Louisiana at New Orleans, July 1st, 1939 to June 30th, 1940. New Orleans: privately printed, 1940.

Board of Administrators. Report of the Charity Hospital of Louisiana at New Orleans, July 1st, 1940 to June 30th, 1941. New Orleans: privately printed, 1941.

Sarnecky, Mary T. *A History of the U.S. Army Nurse Corps.* Philadelphia: University of Pennsylvania Press, 1999.

Shilcutt, Tracy. *Infantry Combat Medics in Europe, 1944–1945.* Basingstoke, England: Palgrave Macmillan, 2013.

Smelser, Ronald. *Robert Ley: Hitler's Labor Front Leader.* New York: Berg Publishers Limited, 1988.

Taylor, John Russell. *The Rise and Fall of the Well-Made Play.* New York: Hill and Wang, 1967.

Strong, Russell. *Biographical Directory of the Eighth Air Force, 1942–1945.* Manhattan, Kansas: Aerospace Historian, 1985.

Strong, Russell. *First Over Germany: A History of the 306th Bombardment Group.* Charlotte, North Carolina: privately printed, 2002.

Articles and Conference Papers

Alexander, Jack. "The Clay-Pigeon Squadron." *Saturday Evening Post*, April 23, 1943.

Correll, John T. "The Poltava Debacle," *Air Force Magazine* 94, no. 3 (March 1, 2011).

Levine, Jeffrey M. "Dakin's Solution: Past, Present, and Future." *Advances in Skin & Wound Care: The Journal for Prevention and Healing* 26, no. 9 (September 2013).

Truxal, Luke. "Twelve O'Clock High: A Comparative Look at the Film and the 306th Bomb Group in World War II." *Echoes* 33, no. 2 (April 2008). Abilene, Texas: 306th Bomb Group Association Editorial Offices.

Williams, Vernon L. "Innovation and Emerging Medical Realities in High Altitude Daylight Bombing: Group Surgeon Thurman Shuller and Military Medicine in the Eighth Air Force in World War II." Paper presented at the Medical History of World War 2 Conference, San Antonio, Texas, February 2014.

Williams, Vernon L. "The Air War and Military Medicine in the Eighth Air Force: Developing Technology and the Impact of the High Altitude Daylight Bombing Campaign on American Forces in East Anglia in World War II." Paper presented at the Southwestern Historical Association annual meeting, Denver, Colorado, March 2009.

Williams, Vernon L. "The Built Environment: Military Architecture, Design, and Place in Support of the Air War in World War II England." Paper presented at the Southwestern Historical Association annual meeting, San Diego, California, April 6, 2012.

Wyler, William. "Flying over Germany." *News Digest* 2, no. 13 (August 15, 1943).

Documentary Films

Williams, Vernon L. *Fortress for Freedom: The 388th Bomb Group and the Air War in Wartime Suffolk, 1943–1945*. Abilene, Texas: Old Segundo Productions, 2016.

Williams, Vernon L. *Thurleigh at War: Bedfordshire and the Anglo-American Struggle for Victory in World War II*. Abilene, Texas: Old Segundo Productions, 2010.

Williams, Vernon L. *Thurleigh Memories: The 306th Bomb Group (H) in WWII*. Abilene, Texas: Old Segundo Productions, 2005.

Websites

303rd Bomb Group Historical Collection. Gary Moncur (historian). Accessed July 16, 2020. www.303rdbg.com.

381st Bombardment Group. "242nd Medical Detachment War Diary, Station #167." Accessed July 16, 2020. https://web.archive.org/web/20170824155433/http://www.381st.org/Unit-History/War-Diaries/242nd-MD-War-Diary.

Addison, Paul. "Why Churchill Lost in 1945." BBC. Last Updated February 17, 2011. Accessed August 20, 2020. http://www.bbc.co.uk/history/worldwars/wwtwo/election_01.shtml.

AFI Catalog. "Memphis Belle (1944)." American Film Institute Catalog of Feature Films: The First 100 Years, 1893–1993. Accessed July 28, 2020. https://catalog.afi.com/Catalog/moviedetails/24069.

American Air Museum in Britain. "Coombe House." Accessed July 6, 2020. http://www.americanairmuseum.com/place/135081.

American Air Museum in Britain. "Gene Raymond." Accessed July 12, 2020. http://www.americanairmuseum.com/media/53.

Aviation News Forum. April 21, 2017 and February 24, 26, 2020. Accessed July 10, 2020. https://www.key.aero/comment/1915519#comment-1915519.

Biography.com. "Paul Robeson Biography." Last Updated August 18, 2020. Accessed August 22, 2020. https://www.biography.com/musician/paul-robeson.

Boeing Aircraft Historical Snapshots. "P-51 Mustang Fighter." Accessed July 20, 2020. https://www.boeing.com/history/products/p-51-mustang.page.

Carpetbagger Aviation Museum at Harrington. "History of the 801st/492nd Bomb Group." Accessed July 28, 2020. https://harringtonmuseum.org.uk/the-801st-492nd-bomb-group/.

Guilmartin, John F. "P-51 Aircraft." Accessed July 20, 2020. https://www.britannica.com/technology/P-51.

Harward, Grant. "Camp Barkeley." Handbook of Texas. Texas State Historical Association. Accessed July 30, 2020. https://tshaonline.org/handbook/online/articles/qbc02.

Hill, Peter. "Mid-Air Collision." 305th Bomb Group. Facebook, November 15, 2012. Accessed July 24, 2020. https://www.facebook.com/groups/54028564457/.

Jewish Virtual Library. "The Holocaust: Ghettos in Nazi-Occupied Poland." Accessed August 9, 2020. https://www.jewishvirtuallibrary.org/holocaust-ghettos-in-nazi-occupied-poland.

Online Nevada Encyclopedia. "Las Vegas Army Air Base." Accessed June 26, 2020. http://www.onlinenevada.org/ar.ticles/las-vegas-army-air-base.

RAF Cardington Camp. "RAF Cardington Camp History." Accessed August 16, 2020. http://rafcardingtoncamp.co.uk/#.

Reynolds, Michael. "Patton's End Run." Warfare History Network. Accessed August 13, 2020. https://warfarehistorynetwork.com/2016/07/21/pattons-end-run/.

Richard, J. "Douglas C-53 Skytrooper." Accessed August 22, 2020. http://www.historyofwar.org/articles/weapons_douglas_C-53_skytrooper.html.

Ten Chimneys Foundation. Genesee Depot, Wisconsin. Accessed July 11, 2020. http://www.tenchimneys.org/about/about-lynn-alfred.

University of Virginia Claude Moore Health Sciences Library. "Neurasthenia & the Culture of Nervous Exhaustion." Historical exhibit. Accessed July 9, 2020. http://exhibits.hsl.virginia.edu/nerves/.

WW2 US Medical Research Centre. "2nd Evacuation Hospital database entry." Accessed July 14, 2020. https://www.med-dept.com/unit-histories/2d-evacuation-hospital/.

Zerby, Jack. "John F. Kieran." Society for American Baseball Research. Accessed July 10, 2020. https://sabr.org/bioproj/person/john-f-kieran/.

NEWSPAPERS

Beach Haven Times (Asbury Park, New Jersey)

Daily Mail (London)

New York Times

Sapulpa Herald (Oklahoma)

Stars and Stripes (London edition)

8th Air Force News (Hollywood, Florida)

Daily Oklahoman (Oklahoma City)

Index

About the Author

Growing up on a modest farm in rural Arkansas, there was little indication that THURMAN SHULLER would one day become a flight surgeon who would make a difference in the lives of air crews in World War II England. The group surgeon character in the motion picture *Twelve O'Clock High* was based on Shuller during his time as Group Surgeon of the famed 306th Bomb Group at Thurleigh, England.

About the Editor

DR. VERNON L. WILLIAMS is a military historian and director of the East Anglia Air War Project. Williams's writings and documentary films record the stories of ordinary people who did extraordinary things in American military history. Williams edited the Shuller War Diary, bringing the surgeon's journey to life as part of a much larger story of war.